Syndicating Web Sites with RSS Feeds For Dummies®

Using an RSS reader

Button	Function	Action
RSS	Capture the RSS feed's URL	Right-click the button and choose Copy Shortcut or Copy Link Location.
Add	Subscribe to an RSS feed	Click the Add Feed button or choose File⇨New Feed. In NewsGator, choose Subscriptions⇨Add⇨Add Feed.
	Configure an RSS reader	Choose Tools⇨Options.
Update	Get the latest feeds	Click the Update, Refresh, or Get button.
Mark read	Mark as read	Click the Mark Read or Mark as Read button.
Delete	Unsubscribe to a feed	Click the Delete button or right-click and choose Delete.

Creating an RSS feed

Button	Function	Action
	Create a new feed	Click the Add Feed button or choose File⇨New Feed.
	Add a new topic (item)	Click the Add Topic (or New Item) button.
	Publish a feed	Click the Publish or Upload button.
Validate	Validate a feed	Go to feedvalidator.org, enter your RSS feed's URL, and click the Validate button.
...	Add an enclosure	Click the Enclosure (Ellipsis) button to add the URL, length, and type of enclosure.

Minimum RSS feed (0.91)

```
<rss version="0.91">
  <channel>
    <title>The Name of Your Feed </title>
    <link>http://www.put_website_url_here.com/</link>
    <description>Feed description</description>
    <language>en-us [or other language]</language>
    <item>
      <title>Title of First Item</title>
      <link>http://www.put_website_url_here.com</link>
      <description>The item 1 content.</description>
    </item>
  </channel>
</rss>
```

For Dummies: Bestselling Book Series for Beginners

BESTSELLING BOOK SERIES

Syndicating Web Sites with RSS Feeds For Dummies®

Typical RSS 2.0 feed with enclosure

```
<rss version="2.0" encoding="iso-8859-1"?>
<channel>
  <title>The Name of the Feed</title>
  <link> http://www.put_website_url_here.com</link>
  <description>Feed Description.</description>
  <language>en-us</language>
  <copyright>Copyright 2005 by You</copyright>
  <pubDate>Day, dd Mon yyyy hh:mm:ss CST</pubDate>
  <lastBuildDate>Day, dd Mon yyyy hh:mm:ss CST</lastBuildDate>
  <managingEditor>you@put_website_url_here.com</managingEditor>
  <webMaster>webmaster@put_website_url_here.com</webMaster>
  <item>
    <title>Title of First Item</title>
    <link>http://www.put_website_url_here.com</link>
    <description>The item 1 content.</description>
    <author>You@put_website_url_here.com</author>
    <pubDate>Day, dd Mon yyyy hh:mm:ss CST</pubDate>
    <enclosure url="http://www.put_website_url_here.com/sounds/filename.mp3"
length="3125097" type="audio/mpeg"/>
    <guid isPermaLink="false">2005-04-12-01</guid>
  </item>
  <item>
    <title>Title of Second Item</title>
    <link> http://www.put_website_url_here.com </link>
    <description>The item 2 content.</description>
    <author>You@put_website_url_here.com</author>
    <pubDate>Day, dd Mon yyyy hh:mm:ss CST</pubDate>
    <enclosure url="http://www.put_website_url_here.com
/sounds/filename.mp3" length="4275349" type="audio/mpeg"/>
    <guid isPermaLink="false">2005-04-12-01</guid>
  </item>
</channel>
</rss>
```

Syndicating Web Sites with RSS Feeds FOR DUMMIES®

15, 33, 40

Syndicating Web Sites with RSS Feeds FOR DUMMIES®

by Ellen Finkelstein

Foreword by Chris Pirillo

Wiley Publishing, Inc.

Syndicating Web Sites with RSS Feeds For Dummies®

Published by
Wiley Publishing, Inc.
111 River Street
Hoboken, NJ 07030-5774

Published by Wiley Publishing, Inc., Indianapolis, Indiana

Published simultaneously in Canada

For general information on our other products and services, please contact our Customer Care Department within the U.S. at 800-762-2974, outside the U.S. at 317-572-3993, or fax 317-572-4002.

Wiley also publishes its books in a variety of electronic formats. Some content that appears in print may not be available in electronic books.

Library of Congress Control Number: 2005923220

ISBN-13: 978-0-7645-8848-8

ISBN-10: 0-7645-8848-6

Manufactured in the United States of America

10 9 8 7 6 5 4 3 2 1

1O/SR/QT/QV/IN

About the Author

Ellen Finkelstein has written numerous best-selling computer books on AutoCAD, PowerPoint, Flash, and other topics. She writes articles on AutoCAD and PowerPoint for Web sites, ezines, and magazines. As an Adjunct Instructor of Management at Maharishi University of Management, she has taught courses on Human Resources and eBusiness. Her Web site, `www.ellenfinkelstein.com`, offers tips and downloads for AutoCAD and PowerPoint and that's where you'll find her RSS feeds. She writes at home so she can take the casserole out of the oven on time.

Dedication

To MMY, for teaching that communication is the process of bringing out what's inside me; and that inside and outside are really the same.

Author's Acknowledgments

This book was quite a new venture for me in terms of the topic and I was assisted by many people who are as energized about RSS as I am. But first, I'd like to thank Melody Layne, my Acquisitions Editor, who fought for this book for months, because RSS wasn't quite big enough on the radar yet. Her support made this book possible.

While I was writing this book I received able advice and help from my project editors, Becky Huehls at the beginning and then Nancy Stevenson. Nancy's developmental editing helped make the book clearer and more logical. She also kept track of numerous production details that brought this book through to completion. John Edwards (no, not the Senator) was my copy editor. Not only did he do a great job of correcting my grammar and punctuation, but he made some excellent suggestions that added to the book.

I came across Jeff Barr, the owner of the well-known RSS site, Syndic8.com, when I was preparing my proposal. He was cheerfully helpful in answering my questions and I was grateful when he agreed to do the technical editing. Jeff is an RSS expert and has been involved with RSS for years, before most of us even knew it existed. His comments and corrections have immeasurably improved this book. He even wrote me little stories of RSS lore, some of which were very funny. Thanks, Jeff!

Chris Pirillo, the owner of the well-known Lockergnome Web site kindly wrote an excellent foreword for the book. Chris is passionate about RSS and maintains one of the best RSS feeds on the subject. Chris' excitement about RSS shines through as he makes the case for RSS, so be sure to read the foreword.

Nita Travis was my researcher. Because I was writing on such a tight deadline, she was there to find me numerous Web resources related to RSS, including RSS and blogging histories, great articles, and more. How this engineer, turned mother of three, turned researcher (and that's not all she does) does it all, I don't know, but I'm very thankful. And she does it all very well.

I became interested in RSS through the evangelism of two people: Amy Gahran (blog.contentious.com) and Robin Good (`www.masternewmedia.com`). Their infectious enthusiasm shone through and made me decide that RSS would make a great topic for a *For Dummies* book. Along the way, many other people supported me, mostly by answering my questions. Some of these people, in no special order, were Dale Janssen (NewsletterByRSS), Rok Hrastnik (author of the ebook *Unleash the Marketing and Publishing Power of RSS*), Renee Blodgett (Blodgett Communications), Rodney Rumford (The Info Guru, LLC), Dan Connolly (W3C), Campbell Mander (NewzAlert Composer), and Anne Hennegar (TimeAtlas.com). I'm sure there are more, so please excuse me if I omitted your name. The point is that there's a great community out there, willing to support people who want to learn about RSS. Thanks to all of you.

Finally, I want to thank my family who put up with my constant writing. They are always supportive.

Publisher's Acknowledgments

We're proud of this book; please send us your comments through our online registration form located at www.dummies.com/register/.

Some of the people who helped bring this book to market include the following:

Acquisitions, Editorial, and Media Development

Project Editor: Nancy Stevenson

Acquisitions Editor: Melody Layne

Copy Editor: John Edwards

Technical Editor: Jeff Barr

Editorial Manager: Carol Sheehan

Editorial Assistant: Amanda Foxworth

Cartoons: Rich Tennant, www.the5thwave.com

Composition Services

Project Coordinator: Maridee Ennis

Layout and Graphics: Carl Byers, Andrea Dahl, Stephanie D. Jumper

Proofreaders: Leeann Harney, Jessica Kramer, Joe Niesen, Carl William Pierce, TECHBOOKS Composition Services

Indexer: TECHBOOKS Composition Services

Publishing and Editorial for Technology Dummies

Richard Swadley, Vice President and Executive Group Publisher

Andy Cummings, Vice President and Publisher

Mary Bednarek, Executive Acquisitions Director

Mary C. Corder, Editorial Director

Publishing for Consumer Dummies

Diane Graves Steele, Vice President and Publisher

Joyce Pepple, Acquisitions Director

Composition Services

Gerry Fahey, Vice President of Production Services

Debbie Stailey, Director of Composition Services

Contents at a Glance

Table of Contents

Foreword

RSS stands for Really Simple Syndication, but for many, it's not really simple. Even many seasoned geeks are still wrapping their minds around the power that RSS provides. *Syndicating Web Sites with RSS Feeds For Dummies* is a perfect first step for everybody, including those who may already have an Atom or RSS feed on their site or blog.

You don't have an RSS feed? You don't know what RSS is? Don't waste another minute. It's essential that syndication become a part of your Web efforts. Expecting a visitor to add your site to their Bookmarks or Favorites is a hopeless cause. Think about your own habits for a moment; how many Bookmarks/Favorites do you have? How many of them do you visit on a regular basis? How often do you remember to visit the sites you've stored for future perusal? If it's any more than five, I'd be surprised.

So, why not rely on the tried and true e-mail newsletter? From your visitor's point of view, RSS is really (pun intended) a much better option. Need further proof?

How many rules have you set up for your incoming e-mail messages? How long did it take before your inbox was completely organized? How many times have you tried to unsubscribe from an e-mail newsletter, only to be caught in an endless loop of "sorry, your e-mail address isn't in our database" responses? RSS solves every one of the aforementioned problems, inherently.

When I preach the wisdom of jumping on the RSS bandwagon, you should know that I practice what I preach. I wrote one of the first books on e-mail publishing, illustrating how creative people could cultivate viable relationships with their subscribers. In 1998, the toughest e-mail distribution hurdle to overcome was mastering the nuances of your mailing list engine. My team and I grew my resource, Lockergnome.com, from a single title to over a dozen in a few short years, continually refining our brand. We've invested a lot of time, energy, education, and money in the "e-mail" business model, but it was suddenly becoming cost and career prohibitive to continue down that path.

The inbox used to be my playground, the avenue through which I could deliver my thoughts to hundreds of thousands of people all over the world. That was then, this is now. We started looking for a solution that enabled us to get back on track with our audience.

I'm not a guy who watches and listens to numbers and statistics; I watch trends, the same type of trends that inspired me to start my e-mail newsletter back in September 1996. Distributing information through a pull channel that users access several times a day is simple to facilitate. Too simple. Now e-mail is overused as a publishing medium, and the people who are abusing it show no signs of stopping. "They" say that end results are all that matter. "We" say that this trend has gone far past the point of forgiveness. Instead of being proud to say that we distribute content through e-mail, we now have to append our business model with "No, it's a confirmed opt-in process." Why should we have to say that? We have to come out and tell people that we're not guilty even though we were never charged with a crime.

If the world were a perfect place, e-mail publishing would still be a viable model for getting the word out. But marketers and morons (two groups that are far from mutually exclusive) have flooded the space with noise. So now, instead of spending our time on crafting quality content, we waste it with endless bickering. We now have to fight with ISPs, begging them to let our messages pass through without being filtered or flagged. We have to go out of our way to educate anti-spam solutions on our product to make sure we don't get blacklisted. We have to explain to our subscribers how someone between here and there is possibly blocking the transmission, possibly troubleshooting their software, trying to figure out if there's a utility that's keeping them from receiving the stuff they asked for. Ugh!

Enter RSS.

It was already out there, and it's always been free for anybody to use. Nobody owns it, nobody controls it. You've probably already seen it, but without knowing what you were looking at, it appeared useless for your purposes.

I'm used to being met with blank stares whenever I present the idea of RSS to either technical or non-technical groups. For people to understand RSS, they may need to see it in action. You may fall into this category, but that's where *Syndicating Web Sites with RSS Feeds For Dummies* comes in. During the course of reading this book, should you find yourself tilting your head to the side (much like my dogs do when I speak to them), take a break and play with what you've discovered about RSS to that point. RSS should be fun!

Imagine a world where search results come to you automatically on a residual basis when you ask for them. Imagine a world where you no longer have to give up your e-mail address and other private, personal data just to make your Internet lifestyle more convenient. Imagine a world where the publisher always controls the content and the subscriber always controls the subscription.

Okay, now stop imagining and start reading this book, because that's just what RSS can start doing for you and your site's patrons.

Chris Pirillo (chris@pirillo.com)

Podcaster, TheChrisPirilloShow.com

Publisher, Lockergnome.com

Coordinator, Gnomedex.com

Blogger, Chris.Pirillo.com

Introduction

Syndicating Web Sites with RSS Feeds For Dummies is your friendly guide to all things RSS. RSS stands for Really Simple Syndication (among other possible things), so you hold in your hands a "really simple book" that anyone can use to create news feeds quickly and easily. I start with lots of information about RSS readers so that you can get started reading feeds first, and then I move on to give you the information you need to create feeds yourself.

About This Book

After I had maintained my own Web site for several years, I had the opportunity to teach several courses on creating Web sites. Being a writer, I naturally emphasized the importance of content and organization. Then I started an e-mail newsletter and saw firsthand some of the problems that entails. When I first heard about RSS, I was immediately excited about the possibilities and thought it was a great idea. (My publisher took longer to come around!) And I was impressed with how quickly it seemed to be catching on.

Having written books on several other computer topics, I decided that I wanted to write a book on RSS. The only book available on the subject was directed toward programmers. I thought that people who weren't programmers also needed a tool to help them get started with RSS. After all, most people who have Web sites are not programmers; they are people who want to sell a product or service, or communicate news and ideas. These people need RSS, too.

Because RSS is fairly new, many people who want to create RSS feeds have never even subscribed to one. So I cover the topic from the beginning, assuming that you aren't already subscribed to dozens of feeds. The rest of the book provides you with the tools you need to create your own RSS feeds. I also ruminate on best practices and ways to promote your feed — and your Web site.

RSS is a rapidly expanding field, and it seems as if each day brings a new twist. I explain some of the more interesting uses for RSS, such as podcasting and republishing RSS feeds on your site.

How to Use This Book

You can use this book to find just the information you need and hop around from chapter to chapter as you see fit. If you know a little about RSS, you can skim through Part I and just read what interests you. Whenever you need to know more, you can come back, and this book will be there for you. If you later decide that you want to create your feed from scratch or market it more effectively, you can find that information when you're ready for it.

Keep *Syndicating Web Sites with RSS Feeds For Dummies* handy; it can be a loyal assistant whenever you need some RSS help.

Foolish Assumptions

I assume that you are computer literate and that you know some basics about Web sites. If you want more information about creating a Web site, try *Creating Web Pages For Dummies,* by Bud E. Smith (whom I know from the days when he was writing books on AutoCAD and whose too-busy schedule was what started me on my writing career — thanks Bud!) and Arthur Bebak.

I also expect you to know your operating system. RSS is remarkably platform independent, which means that you can read and create RSS feeds in Windows, Mac OS, or Linux (or any other operating system you're using). However, I work in Windows, so I wrote this book using Windows in all the examples. I provide a list of some RSS readers for Mac OS, Linux, and others. For the rest of the book, if you're not using Windows, you need to make some minor adjustments here and there.

If you're interested in creating a news feed for your blog, I assume that you know something about blogging.

Chapter 4 specifically discusses blogging, but for a great deal more, read *Buzz Marketing with Blogs For Dummies* by Susannah Gardner.

Conventions Used in This Book

Understanding typographical conventions helps you understand what I'm talking about. A typographic convention is *not* a convention of typographers. As you can see in the previous sentence (for the word *not*), I sometimes use italics for emphasis. I also use italics when I introduce a new term that you may not know. Look nearby for the definition.

Later in the book, when I discuss how to create an RSS feed from scratch, I show you some XML code and then I use a special typeface, `like this`.

If I give you an instruction to type something into a dialog box or Web form, I put it in boldface type, **like this**.

I often provide URLs (addresses) of Web sites (or RSS feeds). The convention `www.xxx.com` means `http://www.xxx.com`. Most browsers automatically insert the `http://`, so you can enter the URL without it. Other Web-site addresses do not begin with `www`; they begin with `http://` only. In these cases, I give you the address as `xxx.com`.

When I say "Choose File➪Save As" or something similar, it means to click the File menu at the top of the program you're in and choose Save As from the menu that opens. When you need to use a toolbar or dialog box button, I tell you to click it. On the other hand, if I tell you to select some text, it means to highlight it by clicking next to it and dragging across it with your mouse.

How This Book Is Organized

I've organized this book in the order that I think will help you understand RSS from scratch, and then I develop your understanding and skills to a more sophisticated level. I don't know exactly how much you already know or want to know, so I've tried to include all the important stuff in the order most people need to know it.

More specifically, I've divided the book into five parts plus an appendix. Each part has two or more chapters that relate to the topic of that part. In the next few sections, I explain what each part contains.

Part I: Controlling the Information Explosion

Part I provides you with an overview of RSS, including its context in the communication revolution and how RSS started. Chapter 1 explains why RSS is so useful for subscribers and why publishers like RSS so much. I also talk about how companies can use RSS.

Chapter 2 gets right down to choosing an RSS reader. I cover the two types of readers and the advantages and disadvantages of each. Chapter 3 goes on to explain how to find the best news feeds and get them into your reader so that you can start reading. I end up with a short section on getting RSS on your PDA or mobile phone.

Part II: Developing Great RSS Content

Before you create your RSS feed, you should consider what you want to write about and why. Chapter 4 is about blogging and how to use RSS to spread and publicize your blog. Chapter 5 is a more general chapter about writing to get the results you want. I talk about choosing an audience, deciding on a topic, and finding resources for content. Because many people use RSS feeds to bring traffic to their Web site, I also discuss how to optimize a Web site for best search engine ranking and how to use RSS to market your site.

Part III: Launching Your RSS Feed

In this part, I explain the ways to create an RSS feed. Chapter 6 discusses the various RSS formats so that you can choose the one you want. I start by showing you the easiest way to create an RSS feed from Web-site content in Chapter 6. I also explain how to structure a Web site for the easiest translation to an RSS feed.

Chapter 7 gets into the nitty-gritty of the XML files that are the basis of RSS and shows you how to create a feed from scratch. It isn't hard — I promise — and you don't have to understand XML to do it. But you see some of the advanced options that are available. I also show you how to make sure that your feed works perfectly, using a simple Web-based validation service. Then I explain some options for automating the creation of an RSS feed in Chapter 8.

Chapter 9 explains how to create the newest kind of RSS feed, a podcast. A podcast includes a multimedia file, usually an MP3 file. People use podcasts to create independent talk shows and music broadcasts.

Part IV: Getting the Most Out of RSS Feeds

Here I give you the information you need to continue to develop your feeds and increase their value. Chapter 10 discusses best practices, including validation, filename extensions, timeliness, and the choice of headlines.

Chapter 11 covers some ways to promote your feed, including registration with directories, links to your feed, your RSS or XML button, promotion of RSS, an e-zine, and more. Chapter 12 explains how to resyndicate RSS feeds by placing them on your Web site so that you can pull together and incorporate the most appropriate news for your visitors.

Part V: The Part of Tens

The *For Dummies* series is well known for the Part of Tens, where you get great lists that describe the best of the best. In this part, Chapter 13 includes my list of the ten best RSS readers. Chapter 14 covers ten ways to market your Web site, and Chapter 15 collects all the best RSS resources that I could find — in ten categories, of course!

In case you don't already have a Web site, I've added an appendix that explains the basics of how to set up a Web site, from registering your own URL and finding a Web host to choosing an HTML editor, organizing your menus, and adding your content. I briefly explain how to sell from your site, upload content, and test your site until it works just the way you want it to.

About the Companion Web Site

I've included so many useful URLs throughout this book that I wanted you to have an easy way to get to them. These days, Web sites have such convoluted URLs that they're often impossible to type. So, the companion Web site, at `www.dummies.com/go/syndicatingwsfd`, has all the URLs in this book as clickable links.

I've also provided downloads of templates for the four main versions of feeds so that you can start creating your own without having to type out the structure from scratch. Using one of these templates, just add some URLs and type a few descriptions — and you're done!

Icons Used in This Book

Those little pictures that you sometimes see in the margin are called *icons.* They let you know that the text is special in some way and help you quickly decide whether you should pay special attention.

This icon alerts you to information that you should keep in mind to avoid wasting time or messing up.

Sometimes I explain the technical details for those of you who care. This icon lets you know when I get overly geeky.

Tips offer techniques to help you save time or accomplish a task more easily.

When you see this icon, watch out! It tells you to tread carefully here.

Where to Go from Here

To the next page, of course. Enjoy!

Part I
Controlling the Information Explosion

"Amy surfs the Web a lot, so for protection we installed several filtering programs that allow only approved sites through. Which of those nine sites are you looking at now, Amy?"

In this part . . .

Part I introduces you to RSS — what it is and how it fits into the world of the Internet. Here you discover that RSS is a great new way to keep up with all the information that constantly pours out of the World Wide Web. If you're new to RSS, be sure to read this part to get an overview and understand why RSS is growing so rapidly. Even if you're already reading news feeds, you may want to skim through these pages. I guarantee that you'll learn something.

Chapter 1

RSS in the Communication Revolution

In This Chapter

- Dealing with an overload of information
- Blogging and RSS
- Taking a look at the state of RSS today
- Exploring advantages of RSS
- Running down the advantages for readers
- Assessing advantages for publishers
- Positioning RSS for companies

Just when you think that . . .

- Your e-mail inbox is going to explode
- You're going to have to add two hours to your day just to gather all the information you need from a dozen Web sites
- Your e-mail newsletter is doomed to go into recipients' Junk folders

. . . RSS comes riding into your life to save the day.

What is RSS and how can it help you with all these challenges? This chapter explains it all.

Everywhere an Information

It's true. Just as Old MacDonald's farm had oinks and neighs and moos everywhere, in today's world, we have information everywhere. It's hard to keep up, but competition in business and the fast pace of change in our lives demand it.

As a consumer, you need to collect information from many sources daily, digest the information, correlate it, and put the knowledge that you've gained into action as quickly as possible.

As a producer of information, you need to develop channels that connect with colleagues, clients, prospects, the media, and executives on a daily basis. (In your business, it's probably on an hourly basis, right?) Therefore, you need a way to update — and then deliver — that content immediately.

RSS comes to the rescue. What is RSS? (I'm not even going to tell you what RSS stands for until later in this chapter, because that's a whole story in itself.) RSS is:

- If you are a provider of information, a technology that feeds news information (usually from a Web page) to subscribers. That's why people call an RSS feed a news feed. Readers subscribe to your feed and then use an *RSS reader* to see your content.
- If you are a subscriber, a technology to receive updates of content, usually from a Web site. You use an RSS reader that is usually in the form of software on your computer, but can also be Web based to display the RSS feed. This software is sometimes called an RSS *aggregator,* because it aggregates many sources of data in one place for you.

You can compare RSS to an old fashioned news-clipping service that scours all the print publications for mention of your company or product and ships you an envelope of clippings every month. RSS feeds similarly gather online information and deposit it in your RSS reader.

Amy Gahran of `www.contentious.com` has championed the term Webfeed as an alternative name for RSS news feed.

If you are a publisher of an RSS feed, you are *syndicating* the information, because you are making it available to multiple sources (your subscribers) at once and because these subscribers can republish your content (if you allow it) on their Web sites. You do want the whole world to read what you publish on your Web site, right?

Just as a newspaper column or comic may be syndicated in many newspapers, the information that you publish in your RSS feed can find its way around the globe, via your subscribers, and at no cost to you.

Your RSS feed usually provides just a title, a short description of the content, and a link. Your subscribers click the link to go to your Web site and discover the full story. Therefore, RSS is a way to bring people to your Web site. Of course, that's exactly what you want — more traffic going to your site.

Figure 1-1 shows RssReader, one of the many programs available for reading RSS feeds. On the left, you see my subscribed feeds. In the middle at the top, you see the headlines of the selected RSS feed. At the bottom is the content of the specific headline that I've chosen.

Figure 1-1: An RSS feed in RssReader, a program for reading RSS feeds.

As you can see in Figure 1-1, the content of this feed is really a short teaser. The tip itself has a little more to it, so RssReader provides a link to read the rest of the feed either within the reader (Read More) or within the user's Web browser (Open in Browser). The feed provides enough information for readers to quickly see whether they want to read this tip.

News on every conceivable subject

RSS is all about publishing and subscribing to content. The content can be news of the kind that you may read in a newspaper or hear on TV or the radio. But many other kinds of content exist, as described in the following list:

- Product specifications
- Opinions on every conceivable subject
- Software or business tips
- Press releases
- Personal journals (common in *web logs,* referred to as *blogs*)

- Price lists
- Policies and procedures manuals
- Employee manuals

Whatever the content is (and I'm sure you can think of many other kinds), as a recipient you get most of this information in two basic ways: from Web sites and via e-mail. (You probably get paper information too: Okay, the Postal Service hasn't gone away yet.) The problem is that these two systems are not well coordinated. Some information is available via e-mail (perhaps in e-mail newsletters), while other information requires that you go to a Web site to get it.

The problem of delivery

If you're a publisher of information and you have a Web site, you know that getting people to come back to your site for new information is always a challenge. You may have started an e-mail newsletter but found that it has some of the following disadvantages:

- Creating the newsletter is time consuming. You can't automatically turn content on a Web page into a newsletter.
- Sending out the newsletter is time consuming.
- Some people don't sign up for the newsletter because they're fed up with all the e-mail that they already get.
- Some of your e-mail is considered junk e-mail (spam) and goes directly to the recipient's Junk folder, or is deleted. In any event, the recipient never sees it.
- People don't have an easy way to find information from old newsletter issues.

Aggregating news

As people become accustomed to getting information on the Web, they have become information junkies. They are also very choosy. So they go to the sites that offer the best information for their needs. For this reason, the quality of the content that a Web site provides is crucial to the success of the site because viewers can go elsewhere with the click of a button.

When customers go into a brick-and-mortar store to find a product, it's time consuming to travel to half a dozen stores to compare features and prices. Therefore, people often do what's easiest — buy at the first store and just take the best of the options available there. On the Web, comparison shopping for products, services, and information is effortless. In fact, some Web sites even

The Internet and content: A history

Why was the Internet such an important innovation for content? The Internet, as originally conceived, was a way to connect research centers at top universities in the United States. By storing data on networked computers that were widely distributed, original users of the Internet securely shared their content through the connections between computers. Security and sharing were therefore two great benefits of the Internet.

The following three innovations greatly enhanced the value of this content.

- The concept of *hypertext* was popularized by Ted Nelson in the 1960s and developed by Douglas Engelbart. Hypertext made it possible for researchers to link different documents that contained information about related concepts. Every time you click a link on a Web site to follow it to some other content, you are using the principle of hypertext.
- E-mail allowed personal communication among the researchers. With e-mail, people realized they could not only share documents, but they could also discuss them. And we haven't stopped discussing everything under the sun since then!
- When Tim Berners-Lee and Robert Cailliau developed the Web in the 1980s, and when the early Web browsers — Mosaic and Netscape — came on board in the 1990s, our modern Internet system was born. These browsers made accessing the content much easier than before.

When the Internet switched from being an educational and governmental body to a commercial enterprise, its growth became exponential. From 1990 to 2004, the number of Web sites has grown from 1 site to 46 million sites, originating in countries around the world.

Publishing was once a cumbersome and expensive process that involved typing and printing multiple copies. Distribution involved real trucks traveling down real roads. Readers had to travel to newsstands or bookstores to find those publications. If someone wanted to follow up on a reference in a newspaper or a book, he or she had to go to the library or find the referenced publication in a bookstore.

In contrast, publishing on the Web requires no costly paper, and distribution is at the speed of light (give or take a second or two). Readers can access content at their computer in their homes, from the mall or airport, or at work, and they can click from hyperlink to hyperlink to follow up on references. Low cost, high speed, easy access, and the connectivity of information are the reasons that the Web, as it has evolved today, is so important for content.

Those lonely researchers in academic ivory towers didn't know it, but apparently the world was full of people and companies just itching to publish their ideas, products, services, and wildest thoughts. So the Web exploded with content.

do the comparing for you, complete with reviews by actual users of a product or service.

However, even though flitting from place to place online is easy, collecting information from the Web on a regular basis becomes an endless process because the sources are so numerous. Whether you want the information for your personal use or you need to republish information from multiple sources, you can easily get overwhelmed as you click from site to site. Furthermore, even with a broadband connection, you need to wait for each site to load.

People have a real need for content. But wouldn't it be nice to have one location for all your content? In such a scenario, you wouldn't want all the information jumbled up indiscriminately; rather, you would want one window, containing all the content you need, organized by source. This would be a great timesaver (maybe even a hairsaver, if you're constantly pulling out your hair trying to find the information you need on a tight deadline). That's what RSS is all about — aggregating information in one place.

As Anne Hennegar, publisher of Targeted Technology Tips (`www.timeatlas.com`) notes in her RSS explanation page, "Using one of these newsreaders, I can easily monitor 200 sites. That's 200 websites where I don't have to type a URL or subscribe to an e-mail newsletter."

Keeping up with endless changes

Part of the reason for our information overload is the pace at which information changes. You may start with three pieces of information, but if that information changes three times a day, you now have nine pieces of information — all of which you need to keep track of.

Moreover, you need to understand the relationships among all this information. Does version 2 of information 1 change how you need to think of version 1 of information 2? Do you now need to change version 2 of information 3 because of the change in information 2? Are you confused yet?

The fact is, information doesn't exist in a vacuum — it's all related, and we need to know both the parts and the whole. RSS helps with this coordination process because it delivers information that is based on a Web site. The Web site contains the source of the information, and the RSS news feed describes the new content with a link for the full, coordinated story. You can now easily connect the parts with each other and with their entire context.

RSS is ideally suited to communication in an age where the amount of information is huge and constantly changing, and we need to understand it all — at least all of it that interests us.

Getting an Overview of RSS

To get a quick idea of what RSS is and why it's so popular, I need to provide you with a little background. In the sections that follow I think you'll see that the concept of RSS is really quite simple.

Examining the RSS infrastructure

The basic structure of a Web site is a collection of HTML documents on a Web server; viewers use their browsers to view the content of the site. Similarly, an RSS feed stores information and makes it available for subscribers to view.

Perhaps you have a Web site and you want to add an RSS news feed. Here are the (very) basic steps involved in creating and receiving an RSS feed:

1. **Identify content on your Web site that you update regularly and that you want people to be able to subscribe to.**
2. **Create an RSS document that describes and links to that content.**

   Most RSS documents contain several items, each linking to a different location on a Web site. The RSS document is in XML format. Figure 1-2 shows an RSS news feed. Part III of this book is all about creating the RSS document.

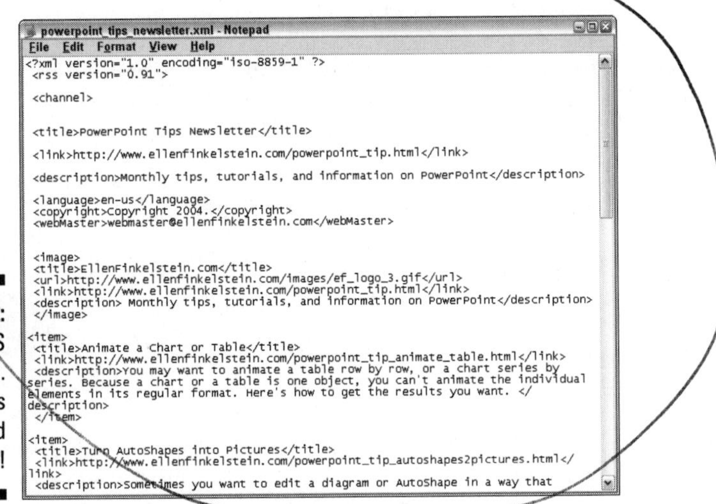


```
<?xml version="1.0" encoding="iso-8859-1" ?>
 <rss version="0.91">

 <channel>


 <title>PowerPoint Tips Newsletter</title>

 <link>http://www.ellenfinkelstein.com/powerpoint_tip.html</link>

 <description>Monthly tips, tutorials, and information on PowerPoint</description>

 <language>en-us</language>
 <copyright>Copyright 2004.</copyright>
 <webMaster>webmaster@ellenfinkelstein.com</webMaster>


 <image>
 <title>EllenFinkelstein.com</title>
 <url>http://www.ellenfinkelstein.com/images/ef_logo_3.gif</url>
 <link>http://www.ellenfinkelstein.com/powerpoint_tip.html</link>
 <description> Monthly tips, tutorials, and information on PowerPoint</description>
 </image>

<item>
 <title>Animate a Chart or Table</title>
 <link>http://www.ellenfinkelstein.com/powerpoint_tip_animate_table.html</link>
 <description>You may want to animate a table row by row, or a chart series by
series. Because a chart or a table is one object, you can't animate the individual
elements in its regular format. Here's how to get the results you want. </
description>
 </item>

<item>
 <title>Turn AutoShapes into Pictures</title>
 <link>http://www.ellenfinkelstein.com/powerpoint_tip_autoshapes2pictures.html</
link>
 <description>Sometimes you want to edit a diagram or AutoShape in a way that
```

Figure 1-2: An RSS news feed. It's not as complicated as it looks!

3. **A viewer subscribes to your RSS news feed by adding the location (URL) of the feed to his or her RSS reader.**

   The viewer gets the URL by clicking the RSS or XML button on your Web site, which is a link to the RSS document. Figure 1-3 shows a typical RSS and XML button. I explain the details of the simple subscription process in Chapter 3.

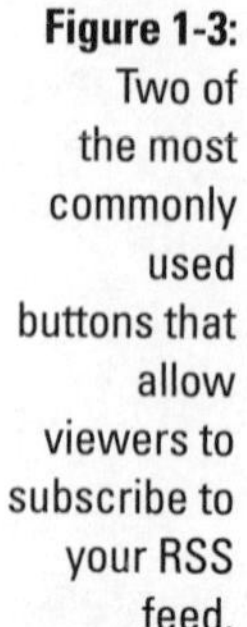

Figure 1-3: Two of the most commonly used buttons that allow viewers to subscribe to your RSS feed.

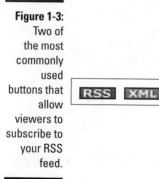

4. **The viewer opens the RSS reader and reads your feed.**

Don't let the format of a feed scare you! I explain more about XML in the "What is XML?" section of Chapter 7. For now, you just need to know that this is a specially-formatted, plain text document. You generally save the RSS document to your Web server, perhaps in the same location as your Web page.

Figure 1-4 shows the infrastructure of an RSS feed.

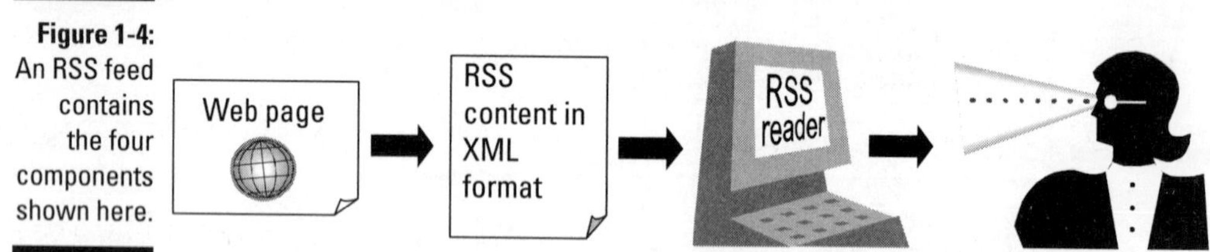

Figure 1-4: An RSS feed contains the four components shown here.

Figure 1-4 shows how one feed gets from a Web site to a viewer, but in practice, many Web sites have more than one feed and most viewers subscribe to several from a single site. In fact, subscribing to lots of RSS feeds is the whole point!

Who is using RSS?

Everybody! Well, almost everybody. Of course, you have two players in this game to consider — those creating news feeds and those subscribing to them.

While RSS has been around for several years (see the sidebar "How RSS started" for details), its use has recently exploded. News sites, such as the BBC, The New York Times, Reuters, USA Today, Slate, and many others have been especially quick to offer RSS feeds. After all, they're often called *news* feeds, so the news sites apparently felt they should jump on the bandwagon.

Naturally, technology sites have also been early adopters. Slashdot, CNET, eWeek, and ZDNet all have RSS feeds. Yahoo! has now created its own RSS reader on MyYahoo!.

To get an idea of how many feeds are available, go to the RSS directories. These directories list feeds so that you can subscribe to them. Some sites let you read the feeds right there. Others are simply a kind of telephone book, and you use your own reader to open and read the feeds. I discuss RSS directories in more detail in Chapter 3 (in the section "Using RSS directories") and in Chapter 10 (in the section "Registering Your Feed with Directories").

Of course no one directory contains all the feeds, and directories don't even use the same methods to count the number of feeds they include, but here are a few statistics:

- `www.Syndic8.com`: As of this writing you can find over 85,000 active feeds and over 277,000 total feeds at this site (some are inactive or are in the process of being approved).
- `www.Feedster.com`: Currently, this site tracks over 3,380,000 feeds.
- `www.LiveJournal.com`: This site lists over 2,467,000 active feeds out of a total of over 5,731,000 feeds.
- `www.PubSub.com`: This site is tracking over 7,944,000 total feeds, over 4,544,000 of which are active.

Syndic8.com has maintained statistics since 2001 (probably longer than any other site) and provides a great statistics page at `www.syndic8.com/stats/feed_count`. Figure 1-5 shows the graph on that site (as of this writing), documenting the growth of RSS feeds since 2001. Is this technology going into the stratosphere or what?

Why do the RSS directory sites report such a wide variation in the number of RSS feeds among the directories? There are a few reasons, such as:

- Some directories may have simply done a better job attracting people to sign up.
- Directories have varying standards and rules for inclusion.
- Some directories also use *scraping,* the practice of converting HTML to RSS. Scraping uses software to automatically create an RSS feed from a Web page. I discuss scraping in Chapter 8 in the section "Scraping from HTML."

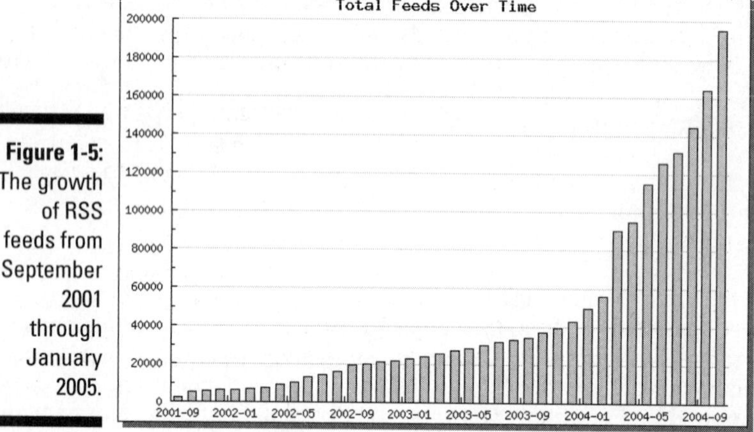

Figure 1-5: The growth of RSS feeds from September 2001 through January 2005.

- Web logs (blogs) usually create RSS feeds and directories may include all blogs that they can find which can make the count run into the millions. For example, Technorati (`www.technorati.com`) lists almost 6 million Web logs as of this writing. (I discuss blogs in more detail in Chapter 4.)

Regardless of the exact number — and, of course, that number changes daily — the number of RSS feeds is expanding rapidly. If you simply assume that an average of 100 people subscribe to each one, that's millions of users!

How RSS started

RSS started in 1997, when David Winer of UserLand (`www.userland.com`) developed the original format. He called the product scriptingNews, but it wasn't really RSS yet. Soon afterward, Dan Libby of Netscape designed the first version of RSS, based on Winer's work, to allow Netscape's Web site (`www.mynetscape.com`) to automatically add news from other sites to the Netscape site. The idea was to publish headlines so that viewers could click for further information and go directly to the original publishing Web site. This was the first version of RSS, numbered 0.90. (Why start with such an unusual number? The answer is lost in the annals of obscure Internet history.) However, visitors didn't have direct access to RSS; they only saw the results.

RSS stood for RDF Site Summary. Now we had an acronym inside an acronym, just to confuse people. RDF stands for Resource Description Framework. To understand RDF, a good starting point is HTML, which is more familiar to many. HTML has tags, such as `<b>`, that format text and tell your Web browser how to display the HTML file. However, you can only use tags that the developers of HTML designed into the format. XML is a format that looks like HTML, because it also has tags in angled brackets, but in XML, you can make up your own tags. You can use these tags to define objects or the structure of data. For example, if you are working with books, you could have a `<title>` tag and an `<author>` tag.

RDF is a type of XML language. RDF specifically represents information about data (resources) on the World Wide Web, such as the title, author, and modification date of a Web page. So, it's a framework that describes resources on the Web, hence the name Resource Description Framework.

At the urging of Winer and other users, in 1999, Libby updated RSS as version 0.91 to include more features and to make it simpler. One of the ways he made RSS simpler was to ditch the RDF format and make RSS a straight XML format. Therefore, he had to change its name. To keep the same acronym, he decided that RSS stood for Rich Site Summary. UserLand adopted this new variety of RSS, and Netscape then stopped developing RSS.

But people liked the idea, so late in 2000, a group of developers, led by Rael Dornfest, developed RSS version 1.0, which was again based on RDF. This version had modules that allowed developers to extend the functionality of RSS to meet their needs. For example, three standard modules were as follows:

- **Dublin Core module:** Specified data, such as the creator, title, creation time, publisher, and so on
- **Syndication module:** Gave hints for content syndication relating to the frequency of updates
- **Content module:** Allowed sending of the actual text of an item

This may sound complicated, and it is. The fact is you can create RSS feeds without knowing anything about RDF, as I explain in Chapters 6, 7, and 8. However, you will hear these terms so you may as well know what they mean.

Meanwhile, Dave Winer left UserLand but was still interested in RSS. So, in 2002, he came out with RSS 2.0 and decided that it would stand for Really Simple Syndication. Version 2.0 introduced the following major new features:

- A tag for a publication date — very important for blogging!
- A unique identifier, called a *guid* (Global Unique Identifier). A guid allows RSS readers to redisplay items if their name (or other information) changes.
- Support for namespaces (a *namespace* is a feature of XML that allows you to refer to a URL that specifies standards that you want to use) to allow you to add extended features to your RSS feeds, such as more formatting options.

Why all this information about RSS versions? (And I've left out some details!) Can't you just use the most recent one? Yes, you can, but all the versions still exist and are in use, especially 0.91, 1.0, and 2.0. Unfortunately, the versions are not always compatible with each other. Fortunately, most readers simply read all versions, so it rarely makes much difference which version you use. For example, if you write an RSS feed in 0.91, you can be sure that all readers can decipher it. Of course, if you are a developer and want to use the special features of one version over another, you should pick that version.

That might have been the end of all this version generation. But other developers, including Sam Ruby, were working in the field and came up with another format, called Atom. (Well, first it was called Echo, and then Pie, and finally Atom — oh, never mind.) Atom is also based on XML structure. These developers wanted to add new features to news feeds to improve control, add internationalization options, make the tag definitions more precise and standardized (including consolidating versions), and offer the ability to add features without changing the core structure. Some of the larger blog services use this method of creating news feeds, including LiveJournal, Blogger, and MovableType.

Atom is fairly new, and not all RSS readers can decipher Atom, but that is changing rapidly.

Even with all those people using RSS feeds, if you have a Web site, you can't assume that your visitors know what RSS is. RSS is a fairly new technology, and you still need to educate the public about it. I offer some specific ideas about how to do this in Chapter 10 in the section "Do Your Visitors Know What RSS Is?"

Like many Web technologies, RSS has an interesting and complex history. Even the initials, RSS, can stand for three — that's right, three — different phrases. See the sidebar "How RSS started" to find out about the origins of RSS.

Exploring the Friendship of Blogging and RSS

There's no question that the popularity of blogging has been a big factor in the rise of RSS. Although RSS existed first, blogging gave RSS a raison d'être — a reason for being.

Chapter 4 explains how to use RSS to spread your blog; the following sections just discuss why RSS and blogging go together so well.

Going from universal to personal

The World Wide Web brings together the world and is therefore very universal, but blogging has emphasized just how personal the Web can be. What a range!

Bloggers obviously have a lot to say, and typically they say it — that is, write it — almost every day. Makes you wonder if these people have anything else to do. Of course, you can find lots of mediocre blogs on the Internet, but the truth is that there's a lot of good stuff out there. The top blogs get millions of hits per month. Occasionally, they get millions of hits a *day*.

Anyone can be a publisher

Because publishing is so easy on the Web, any Tom, Dick, or Mary can whip up a few thoughts and instantly make them available to the world. Free blogging sites, such as Blogger and LiveJournal, have helped make blogging easy, even for people who don't have Web sites.

Blogging is also used in businesses. *The New York Times* has a blog, for example, and Microsoft has hundreds. Some are meant for external viewing, while others are internal.

Peeping in on millions of diaries with RSS

How do you get to all these diaries? Whether personal or professional — or both — they are everywhere. You can soon find yourself out of time, going from site to site.

That's where RSS comes in. RSS is a great boon to blogging because you can subscribe to all your favorite blogs right in your RSS reader. Open up your reader, and you'll immediately see all the latest entries in one place.

In fact, this friendship is so natural, that most blogging software now offers the ability to output an RSS feed. For more details, see Chapter 4.

Envisioning Where RSS Is Today . . . and Tomorrow

RSS has definitely come into the mainstream of Web publishing. In fact, the buzz is hitting the mainstream of print publishing. In June 2004, *Time* magazine had a four-page article on blogging. While it didn't mention RSS by name, the article gave links to several RSS directories to help people find blogs.

At about the same time, Bill Gates mentioned blogging and RSS at the annual CEO summit that Microsoft hosts. According to sources, Bill Gates said that blogs and RSS feeds make it easy to communicate with customers, suppliers, and employees.

Certainly if you publish an e-zine or you want visitors to come to your site daily, you need to think about your competition. If you don't start an RSS feed, you'll soon find that your competitors have already done so.

The landscape is variable right now. The basics of creating RSS news feeds are simple and the tools easy to use, as you'll see throughout this book. However, developers are coming up with new tools to enhance RSS feeds, and available features change every day.

And what about people who read feeds? While many people use stand-alone RSS readers now, this may change. In the future, some may prefer to go to one of the browser options. My Yahoo! is probably the best known, but several others offer great features. I discuss browser-based services in Chapter 2.

A couple of stand-alone readers integrate your feeds into your e-mail program. This is another possible future direction. As you can see from Figure 1-1, most readers look similar to e-mail programs. The three-pane layout is efficient for reading feeds. Perhaps e-mail programs will begin to include the ability to read RSS feeds.

With mixed feelings, I must report that people are trying to figure out how to include ads in RSS feeds. You're probably familiar with the ads that you see on the right when you do a Google or Yahoo! search. Advertisers pay Google or Yahoo! whenever you click on those ads. Yahoo! has recently indicated that it may start to include ads in RSS feeds. These ads would help the RSS feed's publisher to earn money from the feed.

A strong new trend is to enclose files with RSS feeds. When the enclosure is an MP3 audio file, the technique is called podcasting. Chapter 9 is entirely about this exciting new way to publish.

You can get RSS feeds on your Web-enabled cell phone or PDA. New software means that you are never far away from your RSS feeds, wherever you roam.

What's clear is that today, Web sites are sprouting those blue or orange buttons as if they've sprinkled RSS fertilizer on the pages. So you may as well sprinkle a little fertilizer on your Web site and see what grows.

Understanding the Advantages of RSS for Subscribers

Some new technologies take root over years — we're still waiting for videophones. Others seem to be everywhere after a few months — you're probably too young to remember the advent of fax machines, but trust me, one day it was "what's a fax?" and the next it was "where's my fax?"! Usually, the ideas that spread rapidly do so because they're useful to users, not because marketers push them. Users rule the marketplace.

So why is RSS taking off so quickly? Because people like it. It's easy to use, and most readers are free. What's not to like?

Here are some of the advantages of RSS feeds for subscribers, the people who read the feeds:

- **News all in one place:** You get your news consolidated all in one place, saving you lots of time.
- **News when you want it:** Rather than waiting for an e-mail, you go to your RSS reader when *you* want to. Furthermore, RSS feeds display more quickly than information on Web sites, and you can read them offline if you prefer.
- **Only the news you want:** Because RSS feeds come in the form of headlines and a brief description, you can easily scan the headlines and click only those stories that interest you.

- **Freedom from e-mail overload:** Wading through all your e-mail, whether legitimate or spam, is a chore. RSS avoids the e-mail trap. It is simply a different technology.
- **Easy republishing:** You may be both a subscriber and a publisher. For example, you may have a Web site that collects news from various other sites and then republishes it. RSS allows you to easily capture that news and display it on your site. (In Chapter 11, I delve into the methods for republishing RSS feeds.)

Exploring the Advantages of RSS for Publishers

As a publisher, RSS has many advantages for you, too. You want to get your message out easily and quickly. You want people to see what you publish, and you want your news to bring people back to your site. Here are some of the advantages of RSS if you publish on the Web:

- **Easier publishing:** RSS is really simple publishing. People subscribe (called opting-in), so you don't have to maintain a database of subscribers to send your information to. Publishing daily becomes a real possibility while also having a life.
- **A simpler writing process:** If you have the new content on your Web site, you need only write titles and short descriptions, and link back to your site.
- **An improved relationship with your subscribers:** Because people subscribe from their side, they don't feel as if you're pushing your content on them.
- **The assurance of reaching your subscribers:** RSS isn't subject to spam filters, so your subscribers get the feeds — and only the feeds — they subscribe to.
- **Links back to your site:** RSS feeds always include links back to a Web site. By carefully crafting your feed, you can increase traffic to your site.
- **Relevance and timeliness:** Your subscribers always have the latest news from your site and can act on it. You'll have the reputation for being cool and with it!

Don't forget that others can reuse your feed (if you allow it), thereby spreading your content far and wide. This is the fullest value of syndication. "Viral marketing at its best!" says Robin Good (a.k.a. Luigi Canali De Rossi) of MasterNewMedia (`www.masternewmedia.org`), an excellent resource on RSS.

BeTuitive Marketing, a specialty publisher of email newsletters and blogs, started blogging and offering the blog via RSS. On their Web site at `www.BeTuitive.com/blogresults.php`, they write about their findings, including:

- Because they are updated on a regular basis, search engines are in love with blogs. As a result, BeTuitive has appeared in the top ten Google search results under many terms and phrases, providing the equivalent of thousands of dollars in Web-based advertising for their site.
- Blogs are very non-threatening because 100 percent of the permission is in the recipient's control via the RSS subscription process.
- They are driving traffic to their Web site from their blog's RSS feed, which may turn into sales leads, newsletter signups, and online demo requests.

Using RSS at Your Company

While RSS may have started for news Web sites and become popular for blogging, as it hits mainstream, companies are starting to think about how RSS can help their businesses — both externally and internally.

How RSS facilitates online business

Companies that have Web sites, regardless of whether they sell products or services directly from the site, can use RSS to feed new information to customers, prospective customers, the media, investors, industry pundits, and so on. For example, many companies maintain a page of press releases. This page can easily be output as an RSS feed without any intervention using blogging or Web content–management software. All that is necessary is to put an RSS or XML button on the page, linking to the feed.

Some companies, such as clothing stores, depend on many small sales to the general public, and they may feel that they need to use e-mail to get to their customers. However, companies whose customers are more computer-savvy or who want to deliver updates more than once a week or once a month may find RSS to be an incredible boon to their online business.

For example, Amazon now has feeds on every conceivable topic. You pick a topic that interests you, and you can get a feed of all new books on the topic, as they come onto Amazon's site — or of any other type of product that Amazon sells. Pickajob (`www.pickajob.com`), a job-search Web site, offers a custom RSS feed based on your specifications. For example, you can create a feed for human resources jobs in Iowa and receive notification whenever a new job that meets those criteria appears on the site.

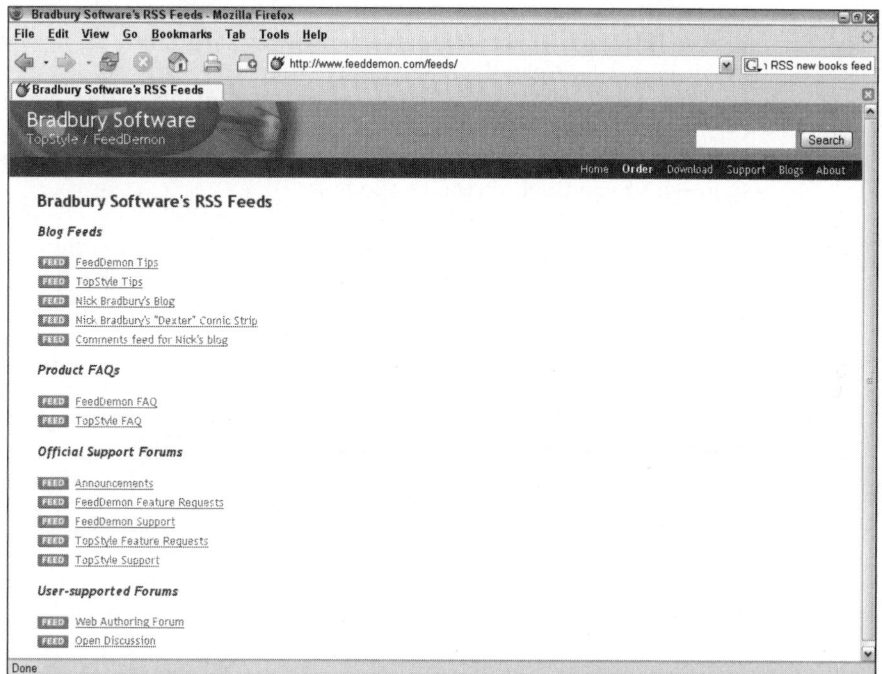

Figure 1-6: Bradbury Software's list of feeds on its site.

The site creates the URL for the feed instantly; you just transfer it to your RSS reader. These are excellent uses for RSS feeds.

Bradbury Software, a company that created the RSS reader FeedDemon, has its own feeds. Figure 1-6 shows the list of feeds. Note that this site uses an unusual Feed button, which makes the process seem less technical. You can see how one company can make use of a large number of feeds.

In Chapter 5, I talk more about using RSS to market your Web site.

Providing instant gratification on your Web site

As anyone with a Web site knows, there's a lot of competition out there. Visitors to a site can easily move from one site to another. If they come to a site via a search, the process is even easier — they just back up to the search and try another link on the search list. If a site doesn't quickly offer what they need, it's goodbye customer.

Of course, a well-designed site is the most important element to bring visitors to you. However, online companies are always searching for new ways to keep visitors interested and encourage them to return. In the attempt to find ways to make a site "sticky," sites have signed up visitors for e-mail newsletters to draw them back. However, visitors are getting shy of signing up. They have too much e-mail as it is. In addition, the e-mail may be rejected as spam before it's even read, so what's the point?

An RSS feed doesn't have the problems of e-mail and can bring users back to your site repeatedly. Whenever a user opens his RSS reader, he can see your newest sale items. You can get the most out of RSS by explaining it to your users. Chapter 10 is all about promoting your feed.

Being noticed amidst the buzz

You need to be noticed, but with so many sites, how can you rise above the rest? The same challenge applies to e-mail — how can readers find your e-mail amidst all the other e-mails?

RSS provides solutions from several different angles, as follows:

- An RSS reader generally provides a less cluttered environment than an e-mail inbox or the enormity of the Web. While some people have signed up for a couple of hundred feeds, most people have subscribed to only a few. Look at Figure 1-1 for an example of a software-based RSS reader. Figure 1-7 shows a browser-based RSS service, AmphetaDesk. Here, the feeds are listed down the page, and the user scrolls to get to the desired feed. In both cases, nothing interferes with the feeds. The RSS environment exists only for RSS feeds.
- Sites with RSS feeds are cool, new, different, and more helpful than sites without RSS feeds. Okay, the coolness factor may not make or break your business, but it can certainly help to make you stand out. Most RSS junkies learned about RSS from a particular site that offers one. They read about it on the site, tried it, and liked it.
- The many RSS directories can list your RSS feed. People who are looking for feeds can find yours by doing a search on these sites. These subscribers can then come to your site. These may be people who wouldn't otherwise visit your site.

Controlling information flow

More recently, companies have begun using RSS internally. After all, companies need to communicate with their employees, often over long distances. Think about using RSS to provide sales reps with the latest prices, for example, or to update employees with the latest procedures.

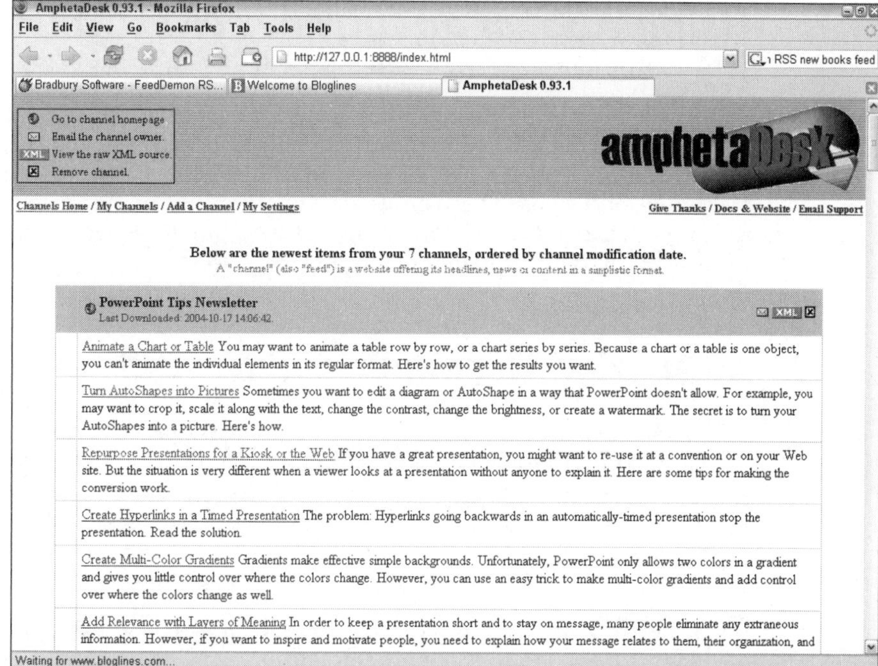

Figure 1-7: A news feed on Ampheta Desk, a browser-based RSS service.

E-mail may not be a good way to notify employees about important information. Important e-mail can get lost in the shuffle of many other e-mails. Although you can store e-mail for a long time, people can easily look up information in an older e-mail and not realize that newer information has arrived. With an RSS feed, you can easily delete old items so that the total feed always remains current and displays up-to-date information. The latest information is always at the top.

You could create a series of targeted RSS feeds with narrow topics, such as one with information for carpet salesmen (the latest carpet prices, colors, and shipping information) and another with information for floor tile salesmen (the hottest tile textures and grout colors). Another option is to organize feeds by the type of employee so that sales reps get one feed and division managers get another.

RSS gives you the option to control the information flow and target the people you need to reach.

Using RSS on an intranet or extranet

A company can use RSS on an intranet or extranet for security of internal data. Companies are starting to use blogs for several purposes — daily thoughts from the CEO (a must read for employees or else you're in trouble), the latest news from the Human Resources department, daily updates from Marketing, and so on. These blogs, or any other information, can be output in RSS format, making it easy for employees to get multiple feeds without going from location to location on the intranet or extranet.

Managing documents with RSS

All organizations need to keep a record of policies, procedures, current prices, and other important information. This information needs to be easily and quickly available for reference by employees, clients, or the public. In addition, companies need to advise these parties as changes are made. This combination of maintaining a permanent record and the need to inform everybody about updates can be time consuming and expensive.

When you store policies and procedures on paper, usually in binders, updating them is a real chore. Lately, companies have been using e-mail to advise people about changes, but e-mail is not a good way to store permanent information, and people often don't print that new page and insert it in the binder. As a result, records get out of date.

How can an organization keep a unified document up to date while notifying employees of changes instantly? With RSS, of course.

Companies are starting to realize the value of keeping records on the Web (or on an intranet), instead of on paper. The Web site is not only easy to update, but it is also well-organized and searchable, unlike a paper document. (If a paper document has a table of contents and index for easier searching, those need to be kept up to date, too!)

Because an RSS news feed is based on the content of a Web site, the RSS feed notifies subscribers of new items as they are changed and links to the original document on the Web. Finally, you have a system that combines a permanent, organized source of information with instant notification of changes, all in one process. Most RSS readers offer a pop-up notification feature so that readers know when a new item is available. Figure 1-8 shows an example of RssReader's pop-up window.

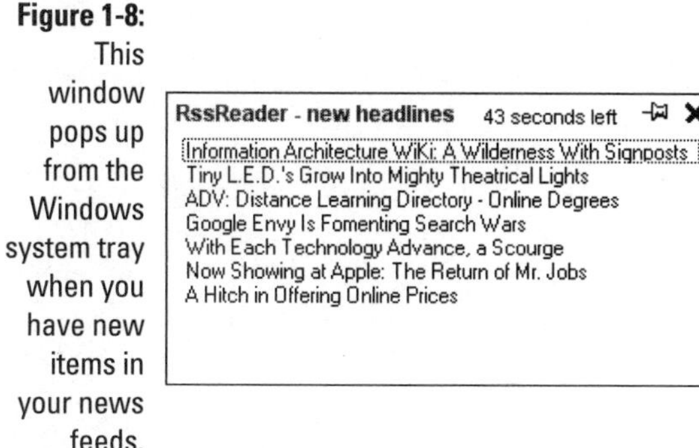

Figure 1-8: This window pops up from the Windows system tray when you have new items in your news feeds.

Put this system together and you have the best of all worlds: an organized, easily accessible, easily updated document and instant notification of changes.

Chapter 2

Choosing an RSS Feed Reader

In This Chapter

- Deciding on the type of reader
- Choosing a browser-based service
- Choosing software for your computer

You're ready to choose your first RSS reader, or aggregator. Getting a reader prepares you to open the world of thousands, or even millions, of RSS feeds. Choosing your reader is nothing compared to choosing from all those feeds!

Even if you are a publisher and want to create RSS feeds, the first step is to choose a reader and subscribe to some existing feeds. Reading other feeds helps you see how feeds are worded and formatted. You can figure out what works — and what doesn't.

When choosing a reader, you need to decide what features you want and whether you want to go with a browser-based service or to download software. Of course, you can always change your mind. Luckily, you can find many free options, so you may not be out a lot of bucks if you don't like your first choice. When you feel more comfortable with RSS, you can upgrade to a tool with more options.

Deciding on the Type of Reader

You can call it a reader or you can call it an aggregator; it doesn't make any difference. You still need one to read RSS feeds. You can choose from the following types of RSS (or Atom) readers:

- **Web-based (browser-based) service:** You open your browser, go to a Web site, log on (if the site doesn't recognize you immediately), and read your feeds there.
- **Software:** You download and install software. When you're online, you open the software (you may configure it to open when you start your computer) so it can download your feeds. You can read your feeds online or offline.

Which type of reader is best? It all depends on your needs, how you use the Internet, your situation at work (if you're at work), and so on. The following sections explain the advantages and disadvantages of each.

Web-based readers

Web-based RSS services are mostly free. (A few high-end Web-based services charge a fee. These are directed toward companies.) In most cases, you register with a username and password, and then you can add feeds. The site maintains your feeds in a database. When you log on, you see only your feeds.

Figure 2-1 shows Bloglines (`www.bloglines.com`), a free, popular Web-based RSS/Atom reader.

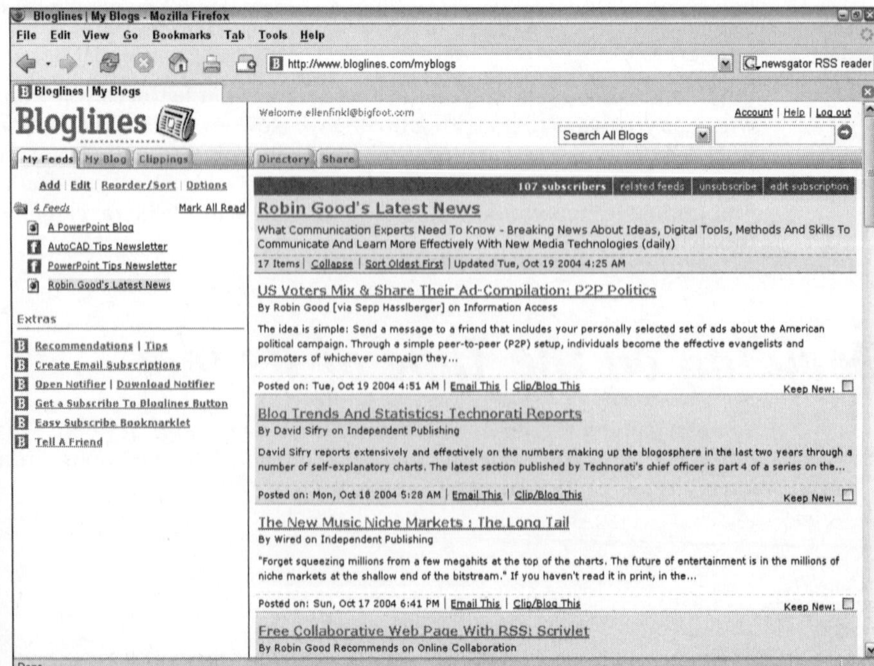

Figure 2-1: Bloglines lets you read RSS feeds in your browser.

Other Web-based readers are CompleteRSS (`www.completerss.com`), Feedster (`www.feedster.com`), and NewsIsFree (`www.newsisfree.com`). NewsIsFree sounds like the cry of a bunch of revolutionaries, and I give it my vote for the most appealing Web site name.

No list is complete without mentioning Yahoo!, which has embraced RSS in a big way. At its My Yahoo! site (`http://my.yahoo.com`), you can now subscribe to RSS feeds and put them front and center on your My Yahoo! site. Figure 2-2 shows my page at My Yahoo!.

If you click the Add Content link, you can add or delete feeds to your heart's content. Yahoo! also has two excellent pages of information on RSS. After clicking the Add Content link, click the Learn about RSS link for a general discussion of RSS. If you have RSS feeds of your own, then click the Learn How to Get Your Content on My Yahoo! link for a thorough overview for publishers.

Yahoo! is an important portal site, and My Yahoo! can contain news, weather, stock prices, and lots more. Many people use this page for the home page in their browser. By adding RSS feeds, Yahoo! allows you to quickly see what's of interest to you when you open your browser. Yahoo!'s adoption of RSS feeds is quickly educating many people about the trend.

Figure 2-2: RSS feeds at My Yahoo!.

Some Web-based services don't maintain a list of feeds for you. You simply enter a feed URL to view it or search their list (which is often exhaustive) and choose a feed. For example, Syndic8 (`www.syndic8.com`) was one of the first sites to offer RSS feeds. Syndic8 is a directory site because it maintains a list of feeds that you can subscribe to. (I explain more about RSS directories in Chapter 3.) If you have a feed, you can also register it here.

The Syndic8 site also offers a lot of information and statistics on RSS.

Figure 2-3 shows the results of a search on "PowerPoint." The buttons that say Atom are Atom feeds, while the buttons that say XML are the RSS feeds — even though both RSS and Atom use XML. When you click a link, you go directly to the content on the originating Web site of the feed.

The Firefox browser now detects most RSS feeds on a Web page and displays an orange icon in the lower-right corner. Click the logo to add the RSS feed's originating Web site to your bookmark (Firefox calls this a Smart Bookmark). Then you can go to the bookmark and see a list of feed updates.

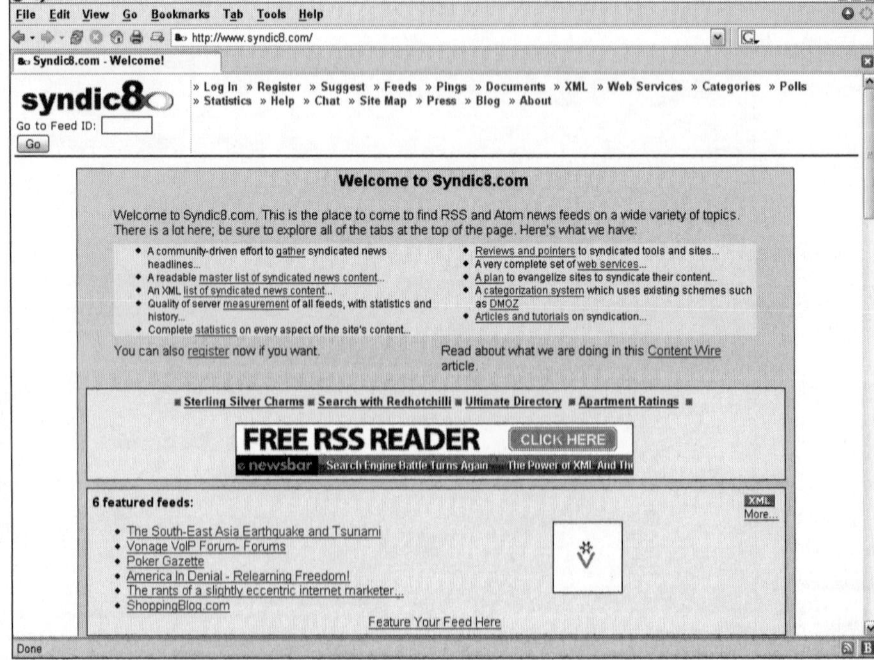

Figure 2-3: Syndic8's site enables you to search for feeds and then links you to them directly.

Advantages of Web-based RSS readers

Why would you want to read your feeds in a browser? You probably add most of your feeds while surfing the Internet in your browser. You go to a site and see one of those RSS or XML buttons. You copy the URL (I discuss this process in detail in the next chapter), and then it's pretty easy to open a new browser page, go to your Web-based RSS reader, and paste the URL. You never have to leave your browser, as shown in Figure 2-4.

If you like to use your browser a lot, a Web-based service can be a good place to consolidate your feeds. You're probably already very familiar with your browser, so you don't have to learn much, except how the service's Web site works. In most cases, the site is easy and intuitive to use.

Because the software is on the Web site's server, you don't need to worry about upgrades when the technology changes. Hopefully, the site will incorporate changes in RSS technology or add features when you want it to. For example, most sites now display the new Atom feeds.

Browser-based services are multiplatform, so you don't need to be using Windows to access them.

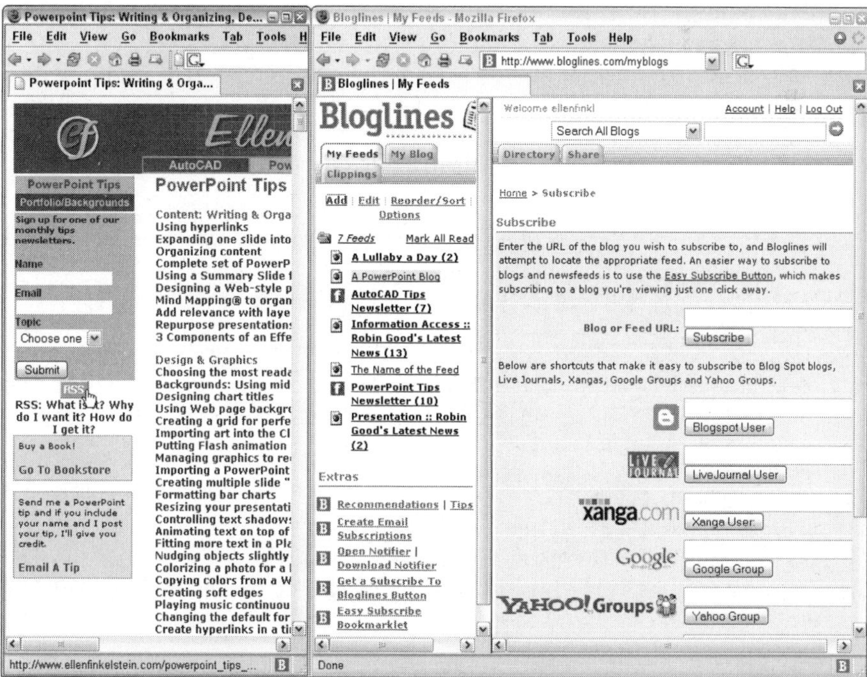

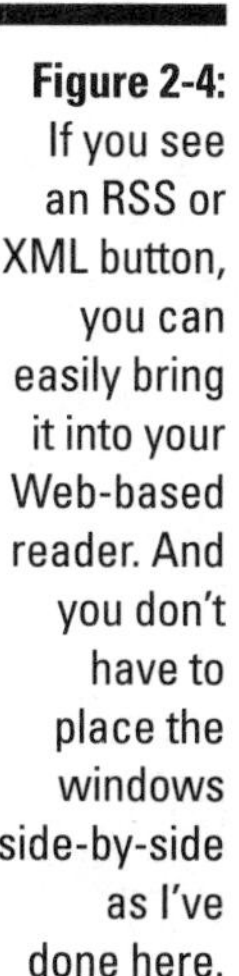

Figure 2-4: If you see an RSS or XML button, you can easily bring it into your Web-based reader. And you don't have to place the windows side-by-side as I've done here.

Disadvantages of Web-based RSS readers

Why wouldn't you want to read your feeds in your browser? One important factor is that browsers are much slower than readers. If you need to read many feeds each day, each feed that you click requires your browser to redisplay your screen. It's like displaying a regular Web site, and many sites take time to load.

Another reason to avoid the browser is when you want to read your feeds offline. Especially if you have a dialup connection, you may want to download your feeds and then go offline to read them. You can do that in a reader that is on your computer, but not with one that is in a browser.

In addition, Web site readers are less customizable than software. You can't change the layout or view as you can in some of the software that's available.

Software readers

Software readers are programs that you download. Some are free (some are even open source, meaning that you can get the base programming code and monkey around with it), and others charge a fee. Almost all have a free trial period. These programs run the gamut in functionality and have a wide range of features. Figure 2-5 shows FeedDemon (`www.feeddemon.com`), which costs $29.95. Usually, software that you pay for offers some additional features beyond those offered by the free software. For example, FeedDemon has a built-in browser, comes preconfigured with popular feeds, and can create "watches," which are custom feeds based on search keywords.

RSS readers for the Mac and Linux

Yes, Mac users, RSS readers are available for the Mac. The most notable is NetNewsWire (`http://ranchero.com/netnewswire`), because it was first and has received many accolades. It has a free Lite version. A new reader is PulpFiction (`http://freshlysqueezedsoftware.com/products/pulpfiction/`), which looks like Apple's Mail application. Another new reader for the Mac is called Shrook (`www.shrook.com`).

For Linux, check out Liferea (`http://liferea.sourceforge.net`). Liferea stands for Linux Feed Reader and works with the GTK/GNOME environment of Linux. Straw (`www.nongnu.org/straw/index.html`) also is another Linux option.

BottomFeeder (`www.cincomsmalltalk.com/BottomFeeder/`) runs on Linux and the Mac.

AmphetaDesk is available for the Mac and Linux, as well as Windows. HotSheet (`www.johnmunsch.com/projects/HotSheet/`) is written in Java 2, so it should run on your computer if you have a Java Virtual Machine that can run Java 2 applications. (You can download the Java part at the same Web site.)

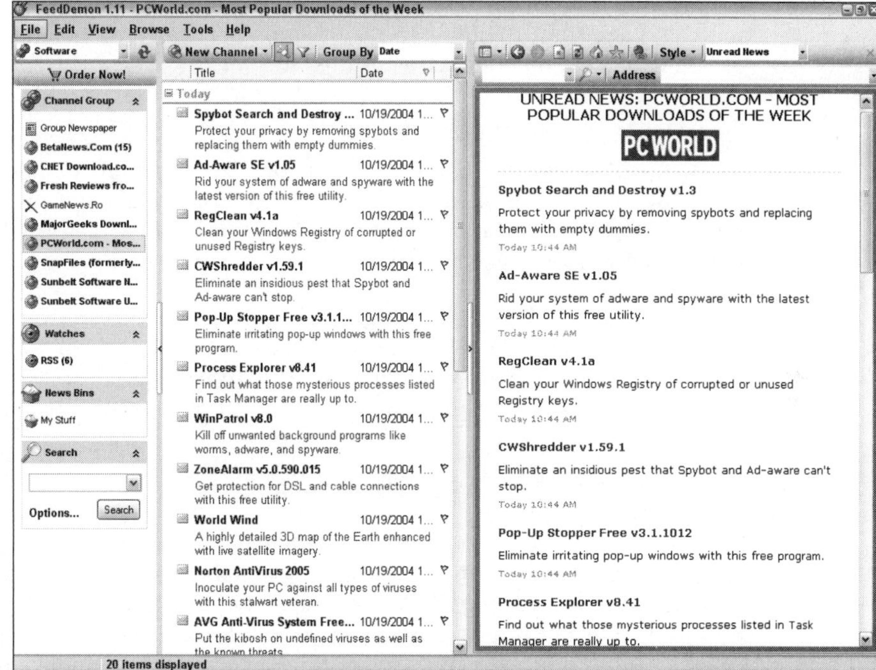

Figure 2-5: FeedDemon is a program that reads both RSS and Atom feeds.

Some other software readers that have been around for a while (which isn't long by RSS standards) are SharpReader (`www.sharpreader.net`), Active Refresh (`www.activerefresh.com`), Headline Viewer (www.headlineviewer.com), and NewzCrawler (`www.newzcrawler.com`). (You've probably made the connection between the name of the software and the URL by now.)

Advantages of software readers

Software readers are fast! They fetch your content as soon as you go online; after that, you can move from feed to feed instantly. For many people, especially those who want to look at many feeds a day, the whole point is to avoid the browser. Browsers constantly need to redisplay to show new content. If you've ever compared a discussion group using the NNTP Newsgroup protocol (which you read with a news reader, such as the one in Outlook Express) with one on a Web site, you know that browsers can be slow when you need to move from item to item.

Software usually offers more options and more customizability than Web-based services. For example, you can usually change the size of the columns or panes to meet your needs, just by clicking on the edges of the panes and dragging. I list some other common features in the section "Simple or full-featured?" later in this chapter.

With software, you can download your feeds (which usually happens automatically) and then go offline to read them. This is a great advantage to people with a dialup connection to the Internet.

Disadvantages of software readers

So what is the downside of a software reader? Some people just don't like to download and install software. Also, you may work in an environment where you need to get permission to install software. In that case, a Web-based reader may work better.

Because the RSS field is still young, it changes often. With software, you need to upgrade to get the latest features. A Web-based service can update the site and offer new services without any attention from you.

Simple or full-featured?

You may want a simple program that just lets you read your feeds and doesn't complicate your life. On the other hand, you may need password protection, a way to organize your hundreds of feeds, and more. Perhaps you would like to read your feeds in Outlook, as you can do with NewsGator, shown in Figure 2-6. NewsGator (`www.newsgator.com`, $29) integrates directly into Outlook so that your feeds appear as a new folder in the left pane. NewsGator is unique in that it also has a free Web-based service, which offers some additional services, for a fee.

Several programs and browser services have free basic options, with advanced features that you get for a price. This is a great way to start simply and then expand if you need to.

RSS is hot these days, and programmers are eagerly trying to get your business. The competition is fierce, so you can get an excellent reader at little or no cost. The only problem is choosing from all the possibilities, which change almost daily! Movers and shakers in the field are busy creating partnerships to make your reading easier. For example, several programs and browser services integrate with RSS directories to make it easy to sign up for feeds.

Some of the features offered are pretty interesting. Think about how you get information now, and you'll see that these features can help you do your job easier and faster. Some of the more common features allow you to do the following things:

- **Detect feeds:** Automatically detect news feeds on any Web site to make it easy to subscribe. This feature saves you from having to search an entire site for those XML buttons.
- **Drag a feed:** Drag from the RSS or XML button to your reader. You don't have to copy and paste.

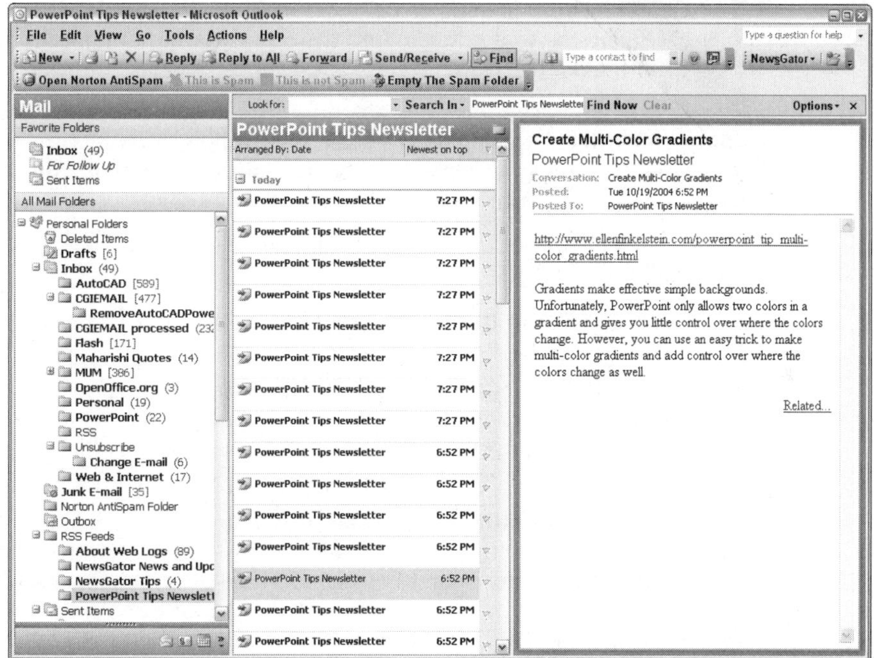

Figure 2-6: NewsGator in Outlook 2003.

- **Integrate with RSS directories:** Display lists of RSS feeds from top directories (I discuss directories in the next chapter.) Some readers integrate with several directories, so you have a choice of tens of thousands of feeds right from within the program.
- **Synchronize feeds:** Synchronize your list of feeds across more than one computer. This feature is great if you are a news junkie and need to get your info at work, at home, and on the road.
- **Read in multiple languages:** Get support for other languages.
- **Reduce bandwidth:** Reduce the bandwidth required to get the feeds (this helps the Web site more than you). Some software has a feature that allows you to download only changes instead of the entire feed. Another option is to choose how frequently the software checks for updates. Be kind to your feed provider, don't check every minute.
- **Import and export:** Save your lists of feeds, usually as an OPML file (or perhaps as an OCS file) so that you can change readers without losing your feeds, or send your feed list to your friends or colleagues.
- **Password-protect your feeds:** Keep your feeds secure from prying eyes. If you password-protect your e-mail, why not do the same for your feeds?
- **Configure the look:** Change fonts and colors of the reading area. Some programs offer several configurations for the panes.
- **Mark feeds:** Mark feeds as important, for follow-up, and so on.

- **Create custom groups or categories:** Organize your feeds into groups or categories so that you can find the one you want among the 1,000 that you've subscribed to.
- **Create a newspaper:** View all your feeds in one column so that you can easily browse through all of them by scrolling. This feature is helpful if you need to gather news from several sources, copy it, and then paste it into a report, your own feed, or an e-mail message.
- **Browse:** Browse the Internet using the included browser. Yes, some readers have their own browser.
- **Read your feeds from your PDA:** Don't miss your feeds, even when you're on the road.
- **Configure how much to show:** Decide whether to show just headlines, a description, or the entire feed. Note that not all feeds include the entire article; they just provide a short description with a link to the original Web site.
- **Get a pop-up notification:** Make sure that you are alerted to the latest news instantly with a pop-up balloon from the system tray (if you want). Many readers allow you to customize how often this balloon appears.

One of the more exciting features of readers is the ability to create feeds from searches. This option searches the Web and creates a feed from the results. Instead of reading existing feeds, the software or service is creating a feed that is customized to your interests. NewsGator's Web service (`www.newsgator.com`) can even create a feed based on the URL of your Web site so that you can find out whenever anyone mentions your URL on the Internet. NewsIsFree (`www.newsisfree.com`) has a premium service that creates an RSS feed from a keyword search. I discuss this further in Chapter 3.

See Chapter 14 for a list of services that create feeds from Web searches.

Some RSS readers also post blog entries. In other words, some readers can also create a blog and post it to your blogging service. Perhaps you often collect items from RSS feeds and then comment on them in your blog. Using this feature, you can write your blog entry in your RSS reader.

I discuss blogging in much more detail in Chapter 4.

Choosing a Web-Based Service

If you decide that a Web-based service is perfect for you, go to some of the service Web sites and look at their features. (Chapter 12 offers a list of most of these sites.) Look around each site and see all that they have to offer.

When you decide on the one that you want, you will probably have to register with a username and password. After you have registered and are logged on, you can start to add feeds. All the sites offer instructions and may have their own lists of suggested feeds or even a large directory of feeds. You can often do a search on a topic to get a list of the feeds you want. It's very easy, and once you begin assembling feeds, you're on your way to being an RSS insider!

Can't wait to get going subscribing to feeds? Chapter 3 explains how to subscribe to feeds, although I emphasize software over browser-based services in that chapter.

Choosing Software

If you've decided that software is the solution for you, you need to go to the Web sites of the companies that manufacture the software. See Chapter 12 for a list of some readers, including their cost. You may be able to find others that I don't list that have appeared by the time you read this book; new entries appear almost daily.

Read the list of the software features and decide which you need. Compare the cost and then choose one.

MediaThink (`www.mediathink.com`), a marketing agency, has a white paper called "RSS: The Next Big Thing On Line" that you can download. (Click the Articles link. You have to sign up for MediaThink's newsletter to get it.) The article compares a number of the major offerings and rates their capabilities and convenience, as shown in Figure 2-7. Free readers are indicated by small circles; readers that are not free sport large circles.

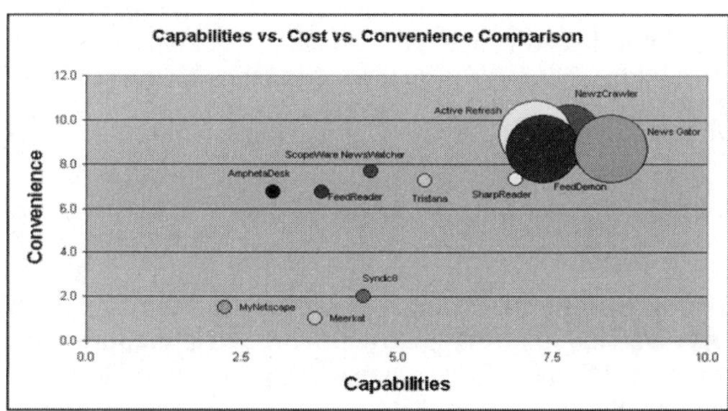

Figure 2-7: Media Think's chart compares some of the major RSS readers.

Going on trial

I recommend starting with the trial version of any software. The period generally varies from 14 to 30 days. I recommend this because, having tried several programs, I've noticed that programmers have different philosophies. Some want to provide you with lots of help all the time. This is wonderful, but sometimes it seems pretty intrusive. Others think you can figure it out mostly on your own, which is less "in your face" but may leave you wondering what to do. These are qualities that you can't find on the feature lists, so you really should try before you buy so that you can find a program that suits your way of working. Also, depending on your needs, sometimes you don't need all the bells and whistles, and you may find that a simpler program is easier to use and meets all your needs. Try out a program (or two or three) before you make your final decision.

A fairly new feature of readers is the ability to import and export lists of feeds. The feature list on any software site explains that this is great for sharing your feeds with your friends. That's true, but another value is that you can switch readers without losing your lists. (The Web sites don't advertise this advantage, of course.)

The most common format for importing and exporting feeds is called an OPML file, which is an XML file. Another format is called OCS. Some readers import but don't export feeds (they don't want you to leave).

Definitely choose a reader that exports your feed list in OPML format. Then, if you don't like the reader, you can export and save the file, try a new reader, and import the list. And, of course, you can always send your feed list to your friends.

When you've chosen the software you want, you generally download it or the trial version from the site. Some companies can send you a CD, but they generally charge a fee for this. (You're paying for the CD, postage, packaging materials, and so on.)

Targeted Technology Tips has a helpful tutorial in movie format on using RSS that includes details on using FeedDemon. You can find this tutorial at `www.timeatlas.com/tutorials/rss.htm`.

After you download the trial version, you may need to unzip the file, if it has been compressed in Zip format. Extract the file to a temporary folder. You then see an executable file, which is usually `setup.exe`. Double-click this file to start the installation process. The sites have installation instructions on their download page.

If you choose a program that you have to pay for, you must remit payment at the end of the trial period. The various trial programs have different procedures to follow to buy the full program. Sometimes a reminder pops up each time you start the program. You just click the Buy Now button and go to the Web site to pay. Other programs are less intrusive about this. After you pay, the company usually sends you a registration code that you can use to permanently register the software. Then all the annoying reminders go away!

Even Web sites offering free RSS readers sometimes ask for a donation. Other readers are shareware, which operates by the honor system. Either way, remember that someone worked hard to bring you this great software, and this work deserves a payday.

Chapter 3

Subscribing to RSS Feeds

In This Chapter

- Finding news feeds
- Getting the news feeds into your reader
- Using your RSS reader
- Reading RSS feeds on your PDA
- Unsubscribing to RSS feeds

The first step in subscribing to an RSS feed is to get a reader — the program or Web-based service that allows you to read your feeds. If you don't have one already, read Chapter 2 to find out about them. When you have chosen a reader and set it up, you are ready to get those feeds so that you can keep up on all the news from one place.

If you have a Web site and want to create an RSS feed, the first step to creating a great feed is to start reading other feeds. Reading other feeds gives you a good education in the types of feeds that already exist and how they are formatted. Also, you may want to create a feed using other feeds as a basis for your own creation. Many blogs take existing news and comment on it, for example. (Part III of this book is all about creating RSS feeds.)

Finding News Feeds

A long time ago (like two years ago) you had two options for finding news feeds. Either you clicked an RSS or XML button, or you went to an RSS directory site. RSS activity has picked up, and now you have several other possibilities that I discuss in this section.

Feeds are everywhere and are now hard to ignore. Figure 3-1 shows the Congress.org Issues and Action page at `http://congress.org/congress org/issuesaction/alert/`. The list goes all the way down the page. Is RSS taking over or what?

Figure 3-1: RSS feeds are all over the place.

Although the next few sections list the most common ways of getting news feeds, you may find one in an unusual way. For example, someone may send you a feed URL in an e-mail or even write it on a napkin. (How retro!) All feeders let you simply type in a URL, so consider that your fallback method!

Looking for the orange or blue button

The most common way to find a feed is to look for an orange or blue button that you see on many Web sites that usually says either RSS or XML. Figure 3-2 shows a number of RSS-type buttons, including some that are customized for specific readers. Some people who use the Atom variety of RSS use Atom buttons. Of course, you occasionally see other colors, but the blue and orange buttons are definitely the standard, with the orange the winner by far. The small size is also the rule, for no particular reason I can think of.

If you publish a feed, Yahoo! offers special code that you can attach to a button (it gives you the image, too) to allow visitors to your site to automatically subscribe to your feed and add it to their My Yahoo! page. You can find this information on Yahoo's RSS Syndication – Frequently Asked Questions for Publishers page at `http://my.yahoo.com/s/publishers.html`. Bloglines offers a similar feature at `http://www.bloglines.com/myblogs?mode=1`.

Why the XML button?

Pardon me while I rant a bit about the XML button. What is this book called? *Syndicating Web Sites with RSS Feeds For Dummies.* It's *not* called *Syndicating Web Sites with XML For Dummies.* And for good reason. XML is a format that developers use for many purposes; RSS is just one use. No one talks about XML news feeds or explains them in terms of XML, even though the filenames often have an `.xml` extension.

Meanwhile, Web sites still need to explain to their visitors what RSS is, because it's so new. Most viewers have no idea what that button is for. So why confuse them and ask them to sign up for an RSS feed by clicking a button that says XML? It makes no sense. Instead, it would be so intuitive to tell people to sign up for an RSS feed by clicking an RSS button. But no, we need to call it some completely different, obscure (to the viewer) acronym. Do you think that people who don't know what RSS is know what XML is? Actually, they don't know what either is, and they don't care. They just want to get their news quickly and easily.

Why is this rant useless? RSS was developed by programmers, of course. They wrote it using an XML format, and of course, they knew about XML. The first sites that offered RSS news feeds were run by technophiles (okay, I'm trying to avoid using the word *geeks*), and somehow they started using an XML button. It spread like wildfire and by now is a convention on the Web, regardless of whether it makes sense. Conventions are very sticky, so I don't have much hope that this convention will change. Nevertheless, thank you to those of you who use RSS buttons! End of rant.

Figure 3-2: Some common RSS buttons.

Although the buttons in Figure 3-2 are the most common, I've also seen text links that simply say "Subscribe to News Feed."

Regardless of what the button or link looks like they're pretty intuitive; when you see one, you know that you've found a news feed.

Do an image search on Google for RSS and you find lots of RSS buttons. You can do the same with Atom. Of course, you also get images of atoms.

Using RSS directories

What do you do if you don't know of a site that has the news or blog that you want? You may have a topic in mind and want to find all the feeds that cover that topic. In that case, you go to a directory.

RSS directories are Web sites that maintain lists of feeds. These directories collect the feeds by accepting registrations or by using programs to search for them. Chapter 14 contains a list of RSS directories.

If you have your own feed, you can go to these directory sites and register it. See Chapter 11, Promoting Your Feed, for more about this.

Robin Good maintains a list of the top RSS directories and resources. Go to `www.masternewmedia.org/rss/top55/`. He also has a premium list with many more sites on it that you can purchase for a reasonable cost.

Many of the Web-based RSS readers are also directories, because they want to make it easy for you to find feeds. You look for feeds that you want, subscribe, and then read them right away at the same site.

Figure 3-3 shows the search feature at Feedster (`www.feedster.com`), which is both a directory and a Web-based reader.

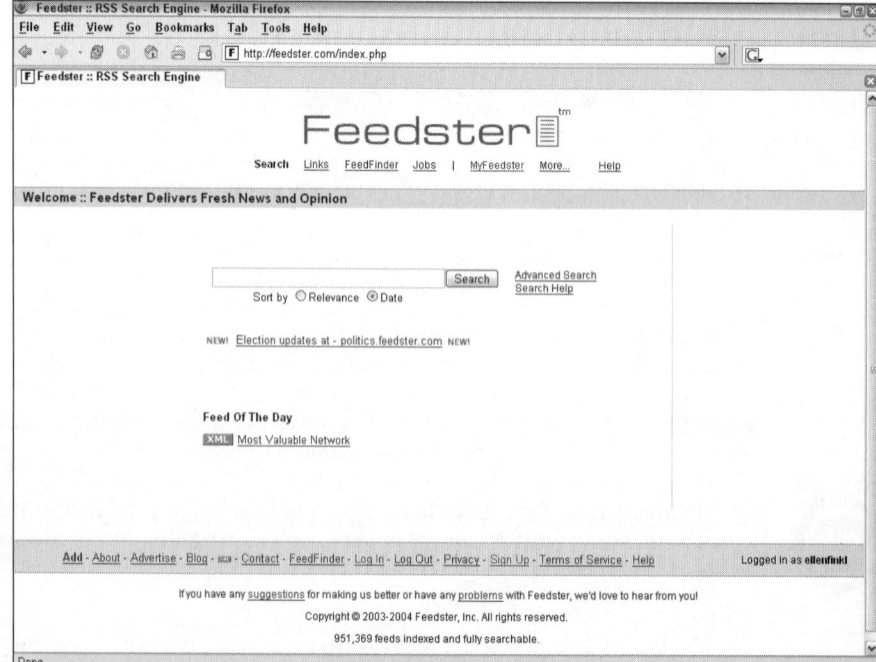

Figure 3-3: Feedster lets you search for the feeds you want.

If you want to find all the feeds on a specific topic, just go to a directory. Some directories, especially those that include blogs, include well over a million feeds!

Using the list in your reader

A number of readers come with preinstalled feeds. These usually include the most-read feeds and a variety of topics, such as news, technology, and so on. I must admit that I find this annoying, because I never want the ones they include, they clutter up the reader, making it hard to find the feeds I've subscribed to, and it's very time consuming to delete them all. Perhaps I just haven't found the secret "Delete them all" button.

I shouldn't complain — the purpose is to make it easy for you. If you're new to RSS feeds, you may like having some feeds available to read right away.

My first RSS reader, appropriately named RssReader (`www.rssreader.com`), is a simple, free reader with few extras. It's so easy to use that it has no Help feature. This reader includes its own small directory of feeds, but none of them are preinstalled; I like this approach.

Creating a new feed from a search

Some Web-based readers and Web sites let you create a custom feed from a search of news sources on the Web. I find this concept fascinating. It's like your own personal clipping service. Obviously, the uses for this are endless. Find out when a newspaper mentions your company — or you, for that matter. (Narcissists will love this!) You could enter a friend's name, the name of your school, your competitor, or anything else you can think of. This could get addictive!

You start by doing a search and then using a link or button to obtain an RSS URL. You don't have to use the original service to read your feed — you can copy the link's URL to your own feed reader.

One free option is PubSub at `www.pubsub.com`. First you choose what type of source you want to search. Most people choose Weblogs; however, you can also search SEC filings, press releases, and newsgroups. Then you enter your keywords using standard Web-search syntax. Figure 3-4 shows the PubSub site.

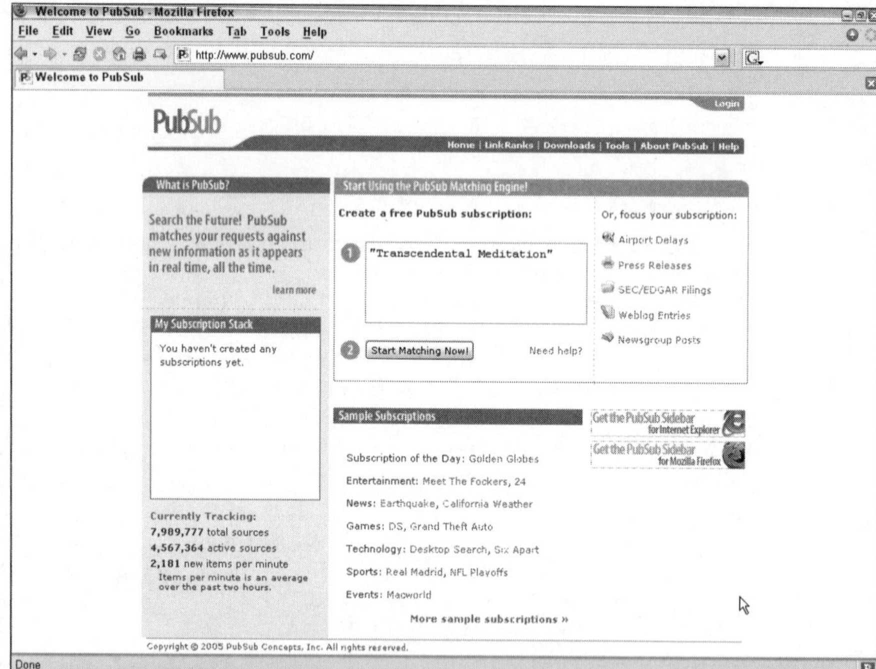

Figure 3-4: The PubSub site enables you to create an RSS feed from search keywords.

Moreover (www.moreover.com) is a premium RSS site; it offers free feeds and also offers custom RSS feeds, with a free 30-day trial version. The Moreover site specializes in news sources and has a more business-like approach than PubSub. Moreover even finds sources that don't have RSS feeds. Moreover was more successful than other sites in finding results for my search on "Maharishi."

Some other resources that search online sources and turn the results into RSS feeds are as follows:

- **Feedster:** Go to www.feedster.com.
- **FindArticles:** Go to www.findarticles.com.
- **Yahoo! News:** Go to news.search.yahoo, and then add the feed to MyYahoo!.
- **Justin Pfister.com:** Go to www.justinpfister.com/gnewsfeed.php.
- **NewsGator online:** Go to www.newsgator.com. Search feeds are part of their premium services, but are free with a registered copy of the Newsgator software RSS reader.
- **BlogDigger.com:** Go to www.blogdigger.com.
- **NewsTrove:** Go to newstrove.com/cgi-bin/CustomRSS.pl. They have basic, pro, and premium levels.

- **Daypop:** Go to www.daypop.com.
- **Gogglealert.com:** Go to www.googlealert.com. This service is not affiliated with Google but uses its search engine.
- **RocketNews:** Go to www.rocketnews.com. You can search news or weblogs.
- **Topix:** Go to www.topix.net.
- **NewsXS:** Go to www.newsxs.com. You can search in five languages.

See my list of my favorite search feed services in Chapter 15. In my opinion, if you aren't using search feeds, you're missing a lot of important information.

Importing an OPML file

An OPML (Outline Processor Markup Language) file is an XML file that contains a list of feeds. This file type has become the standard for sharing feed lists. Many readers let you export and import lists in this format. Another, less-often-used format is an OCS (Open Content Syndication) file, which performs the same function as an OPML file.

Some readers may let you import but not export an OPML file, so check the features carefully.

You use an OPML file for two purposes. One is to share your list with your friends and colleagues. If you have a great list of feeds, you can give your RSS newbie friends a head start by sending them your list so that they can start reading all that great stuff right away. After all, you spent a long time finding and choosing the best feeds out there.

The second reason is to move your feeds from one reader to another. Whether you decide to change readers or you have one reader at work and another at home, you can use this feature to get all your feeds. (Some readers offer a synchronization feature for reading feeds at more than one computer.)

Getting the Feed into Your Reader

You have some feeds that you want to subscribe to. How do you get them into your reader? Of course, each reader is slightly different, but they all have enough similarities that you can usually figure out the procedure if you know the basics.

Using the URL

If you see an RSS or XML button on a site, that button is a link to the RSS feed document. This document is on the Web site's server, so it has its own URL. For example, the URL of one of my feeds is `http://ellenfinkelstein.com/powerpoint_tips_newsletter.xml`.

Most RSS feeds use the `.xml` filename extension, but you may see feeds with an `.rss` or `.rdf` extension.

You need to get that URL into your RSS reader. But how do you capture the URL?

Copy and paste

This is the most obvious way to get the URL. Just follow these steps:

1. **Click the RSS or XML button for the feed.**

   After all, Web buttons are for clicking, right? You generally see something like Figure 3-5. XML files are not for reading! So repress your instinctive impulse to start reading the file. All you want is the URL at the top of the browser, in the address box, which in Figure 3-5 is `http://www.masternewmedia.org/robingoodlatestnews.xml`.

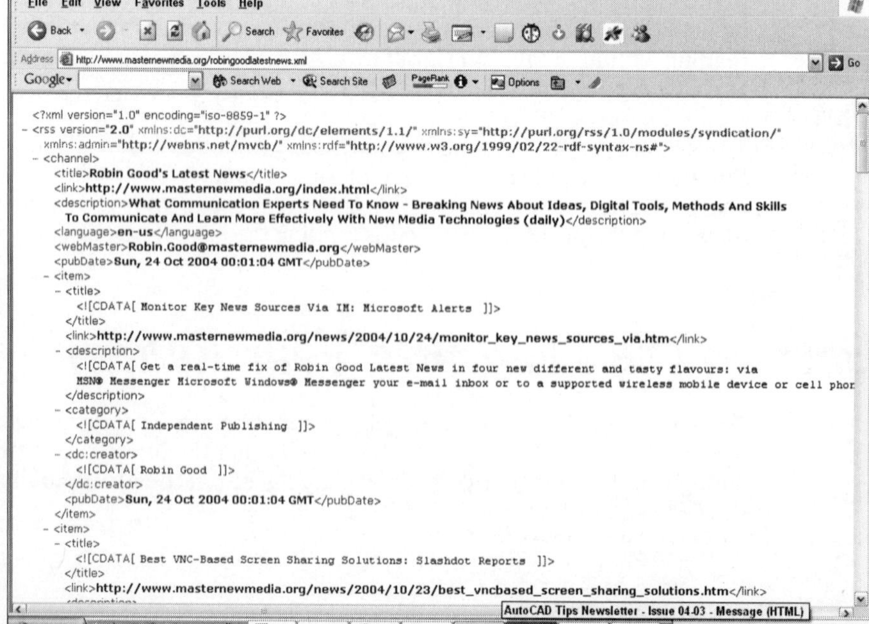

Figure 3-5: When you click an XML or RSS button, you see the original XML file in your browser, in this case Internet Explorer.

Occasionally, a clueless browser doesn't recognize the RSS feed's file type and presents you with a dialog box asking whether you want to open or save the feed. You don't want to save it, so select the Open option. If that doesn't work, try the technique in the next section, "Right-click."

2. **Select the URL with your mouse.**

   You often only need to click next to the URL to select the entire URL; however, if that doesn't work, drag across it with your mouse.

3. **Copy the URL to the Clipboard.**

   Pressing Ctrl+C is the easy way to copy anything that you select in your browser.

4. **Open your RSS reader.**

   Figure 3-6 shows RssReader's simple interface.

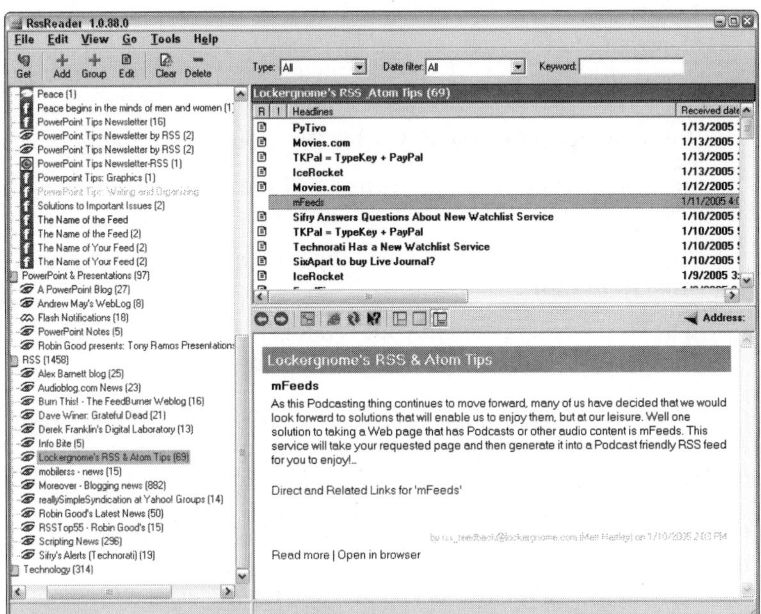

Figure 3-6: RssReader's main screen. You click the + (Add) button to add a feed.

5. **Use your RSS reader's command for adding a news feed.**

   For example, in RssReader, click the + (Add) button. The Add New Feed dialog box appears with your feed's URL already in the text box, as shown in Figure 3-7. The software readers that I've tried automatically pick up any URL that you've copied to the Clipboard. Of course, you can also type the URL into the text box. Most Web-based readers require you to paste the URL into an address box. At this point, in RssReader, you can also do one of the following:

- Click the Directory button to find a feed in the directory
- Click the Import button to import a list from an OPML file or any Web site

Most software readers, including RssReader, let you organize your feeds into categories. In RssReader, if you have already set up a category folder and want your new feed to go there, you can click the folder first and then click the + (Add) button.

Figure 3-7: The URL of the feed that you copied to the Clipboard is ready for you.

6. **Click the Next button and enter the feed title in the text box.**

   You may want to change the name of the feed to something that's shorter or means more to you, or just leave the title as is.

7. **Click the Next button, choose the feed group (or category), and click the OK button.**

   The feed now appears in your reader. Time to start reading! See the section "Using Your RSS Reader," later in this chapter, for some hints.

Of course, the procedure for your reader may be different. At this point, some readers ask you to make some choices, such as how often you want to check for new items and how you want to display the feed (titles only or entire feed).

Because RSS is a new technology, the terminology used in reader software is not yet completely established. For example, Newz Crawler's command for subscribing to a news feed is File⇨New⇨New Newsfeed Channel. The word *channel* has a technical meaning in an RSS feed's XML file, which I discuss in Chapter 7. For Newz Crawler, *channel* means a news feed. However, the term sometimes indicates a group or category of feeds.

Right-click

Although the natural temptation is to click the RSS or XML button, you can get the URL more quickly by right-clicking the URL and choosing a copy command, such as Copy Shortcut (Internet Explorer) or Copy Link Location (Firefox). All browsers have a similar option. This action copies the URL of the button's link to the Clipboard. You can then go straight to Step 4 of the previous procedure for subscribing to a news feed.

If you have a Web site and are considering adding an RSS feed to your site, you may want to include instructions for your visitors. I explain some factors to consider in Chapter 10 in the section "Explaining how to use RSS." Telling visitors to right-click helps them avoid seeing the confusing XML code, which is good. On the other hand, it's so natural to click that button!

Drag and drop

Some readers let you drag and drop from the button to the reader (see Figure 3-8). Arrange your windows so that you can see both the feed's button and your reader. You may need to drag to a particular location, such as an address bar.

If you start dragging and realize that your reader's window is minimized, drag to its button on the Windows taskbar. The reader then opens, and you can complete the operation.

Just type it

If someone gave you the URL for a news feed, you may just have to type it into the address text box. Sometimes, URLs are pretty long, so watch out for typos!

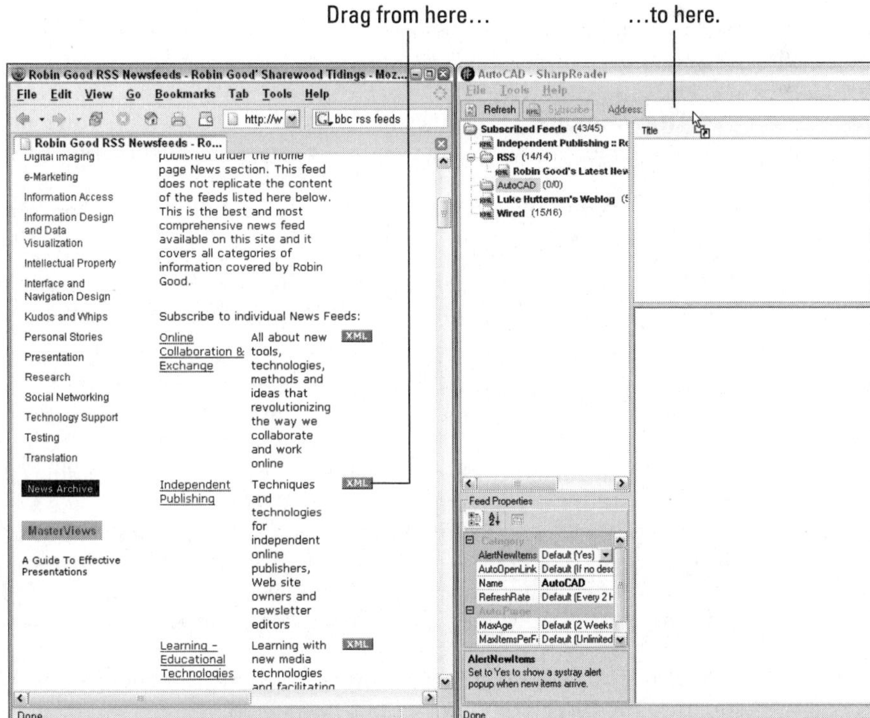

Figure 3-8: In some readers, you can drag from the RSS button to your reader.

Choosing from a list

Both software and Web-based readers often have a directory of feeds, so you can choose from a list and subscribe that way. Each reader is different in this regard, but look for a link or button that leads you to a directory of feeds.

Using Your RSS Reader

You subscribed to your feeds and now you want to read them. You may also want to configure your reader to fit your needs. This section explains how to get the most out of using and configuring your reader.

Choosing the feed

As soon as you subscribe to a feed, it appears in your reader, usually in the left pane, but perhaps all in a column, depending on your reader or service. Now you just need to choose the feed you want to read. Usually, the method for choosing your feed is obvious.

Understanding the components and structure of a feed helps you figure out what you're seeing. Feeds have the following three components:

- **Title or name:** Each news feed has a name by which you can easily identify the feed. This name does not change as the individual news items within the feed change. A title often includes the author as well as the topic, especially for blogs, such as Joe's Technology Blog. News sources always use their name, such as DesMoinesRegister.com: Home/Garden.
- **Item title or heading:** Feeds generally include several items and each item has a heading, which is like the heading of a newspaper article.
- **Description or body:** The main body of the feed can be a short description with a link to the rest of the feed or can contain the entire article or blog entry. Sometimes this component is absent, or not displayed.

Some of the terms for feed components have technical meanings, because they are part of the XML tags in the actual feed. Two examples are *item* and *description.* Don't worry! You don't really need to understand what these terms mean at this point — and perhaps you never do. (Is never good enough for you procrastinators out there?) If you want to read more, I explain these terms in Chapter 7, where I describe how to create an RSS feed from scratch.

Reading a news feed involves following these three simple steps, which correspond to the three components of a news feed:

1. **Click the feed title or name to select it.**

   If your feeds are organized into collapsible categories, you may need to expand the category you want first, usually by clicking the plus sign to the left of the category. Most readers organize feeds into categories that look like folders in Windows Explorer.

   You should now see a list of all the item headings in that feed.

2. **Click the title/heading of the individual news item that you want.**

   You should see the body of the feed, the actual text.

3. **Read the feed.**

Figure 3-9 shows this structure in RssReader.

Reading the headlines

When you choose the feed that you want, you can view all the new item headings to see which ones interest you. This method is an extremely quick way to scan the news that interests you every day — or even every hour. No other format provides you with news in such an efficient manner.

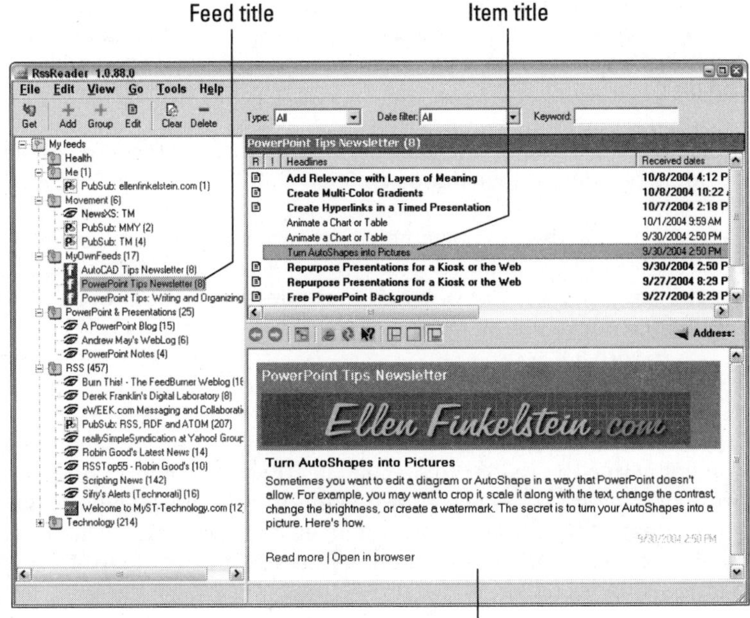

Description (body)

Figure 3-9: A news feed has three elements: a main title, an item title, and a description (or body).

When you start creating your own RSS feeds, as you read feeds, pay attention to the type of headings that grab your attention so that you can create headings that do the same. Also, you'll see that some headings simply don't provide enough information to be useful. Make sure that your headings are complete and meaningful, even out of context. I discuss more about how to write effective feed headings in Chapter 5.

Getting the rest of the story

In many cases, the body of the news feed is not the full article. Feed publishers can take the following three approaches:

- **Provide the entire article in the feed:** You get the story right away, without having to click a link to the Web site. Feeds are longer and therefore use more bandwidth.
- **Provide a short description and include a link to the Web site:** You have to click to read the full story, bringing you back to the Web site. Feeds are shorter and use less bandwidth.
- **Provide no description at all:** Sometimes you see only titles and no text. You need to click the title link to read the feed.

As a news feed subscriber, you may want the whole story up front, without having to click, but the publisher may have different considerations. The publisher's take on this issue depends on the type of site and the purpose of the feed.

In Chapter 5, I describe the issues that a publisher needs to consider when deciding how much to include in a feed.

The issue of bandwidth has come up recently as RSS feeds multiply and the readers draw down the feed data, often every hour. Publishers may provide a short description only as one way to reduce the amount of bandwidth required.

RSS readers have various ways of showing you the link. In Figure 3-9, you can see a link at the bottom of the pane that shows the content. The reader interface shown in this figure gives you a choice of either opening the rest of the content within the reader (which means that the reader is also acting as a browser) or connecting via your default browser to the source page. Use your browser if you want to see the page in a larger area instead of in the smaller reader's pane or if you think that you'll want to surf through the originating site more fully.

Making sure that you have the latest news

RSS readers generally look for updated feeds every hour or two. You can usually change this setting. Sometimes you can change the setting per feed. For example, you may want your political news every hour but your recipes can wait for 24 hours. (How often do new recipes come out, anyway?)

Nevertheless, to make sure that you have the most up-to-date news, click the Update, Refresh, or Get button — the name of this button varies with the reader — to download the latest items in all your feeds. If you have a lot of feeds, this could take a few seconds.

Getting alerts — or not

Most software RSS readers have pop-up boxes that materialize seemingly out of nowhere in the vicinity of your system tray, the area at the right side of the Windows taskbar. Some readers also play a sound when new news comes in. Do you want these popups distracting you throughout the day? Of course, your answer will depend on how urgent the news is to you. You can choose whether you get the notification in the Options dialog box in RssReader and you find a similar feature in other programs, as shown in Figure 3-10. RssReader lets you decide whether you want the sound and even gives you two sounds to choose from.

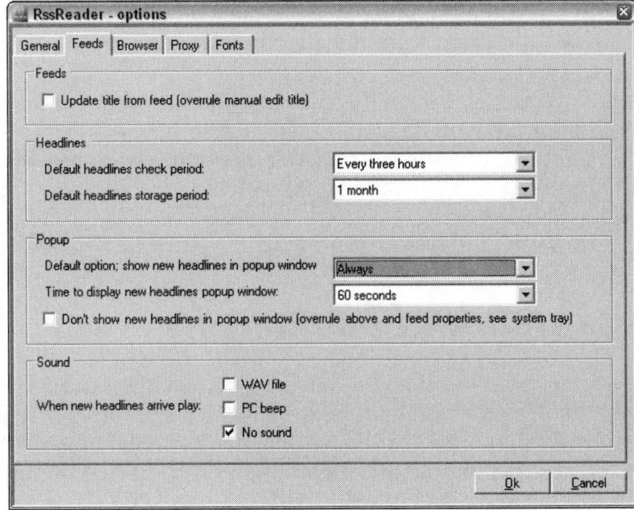

Figure 3-10: You can choose whether you get pop-up alerts.

Mark as read or important

If you look back at Figure 3-9, you can see that some of the feed titles are in bold text and some are not. What's that all about? Your e-mail program provides you with a way to distinguish between e-mails that you have read and those that you haven't, and feed readers do the same. In RssReader, bold titles are items that you haven't read, and as soon as you click an item, the text loses its bold font and changes to regular text. To avoid rereading news items that you've already seen or if you know that certain items don't interest you, you can mark them as read even though you haven't yet read them.

In RssReader, choose Edit⇨Mark as Read to get rid of the boldface for the selected title. Conversely, you can choose an item that you've read and mark it as unread. (Perhaps you want to go back to the article later.)

In SharpReader, for example, you can right-click the selected title and choose Mark Read to eliminate the boldface. This may seem a little silly at first, because to mark a headline as read, you need to select it, at which point it instantly becomes shown as read. So why go to the point of marking it as read? The value is twofold, as follows:

- You can select a range of headlines by selecting the first, pressing Shift, and selecting the last. Then you can mark them all as read or unread.
- You can select a feed title (that is, the name of the entire feed) in the left pane and mark all its news items as read or unread.

For example, in Sharpreader, you can right-click any item and choose Mark All Read or Mark All Unread from the shortcut menu.

Another handy feature is the ability to flag an item as important or give it a ranking. RssReader lets you flag an individual item's headline (but not an entire feed) as important and puts an exclamation point to the left of the headline. In SharpReader, you can flag items with a number so that you can rank their importance.

Using search and bookmarks

If you subscribe to many feeds, you may sometimes need to find an item in the midst of a lot of news, so many readers let you search your feeds. You can find this feature in some browser-based readers as well. In fact, some browser-based readers let you search all the feeds that they monitor. Feedster, shown in Figure 3-11, offers this feature.

These search features work like every standard search feature you've encountered. Of course, the more feeds you have, the more you need to search. Remember that you can often organize your feeds themselves into categories to help you find the items that you want.

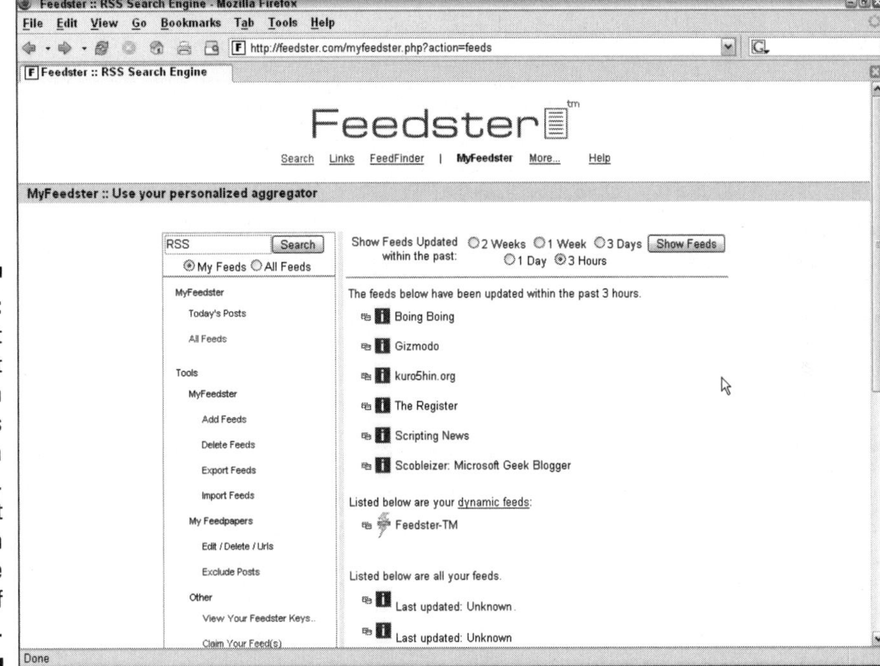

Figure 3-11: Most readers let you search your feeds for a keyword. Some let you search an entire directory of feeds.

Sending a feed as e-mail

You've just read the most fascinating (and improbable) RSS feed on the newly discovered health benefits of chocolate. Now you want to let your chocoholic (and RSS-clueless) sister know about it pronto. Some readers have a feature to quickly send a link to an article to someone by e-mail. In SharpReader, for example, you can right-click any item and choose Send as Email to open a new e-mail in your default e-mail program with the item headline as the subject and its URL in the body of the e-mail, as you see in Figure 3-12.

Configuring the view

All software readers allow at least some configuration. For example, you can drag the border between panes to adjust the size of each pane. Sometimes you can change fonts or font colors. Newz Crawler has a Make Newspaper feature that lists news items vertically in a separate window as if they're in a newspaper or newsletter.

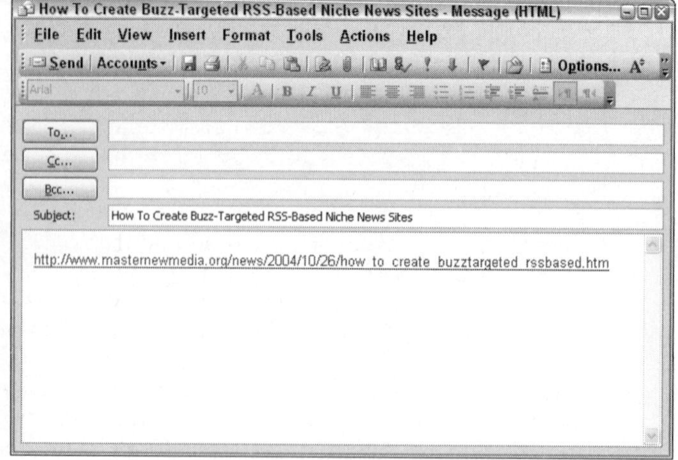

Figure 3-12: You can send the URL of a news item to a friend.

Some readers offer tools for collecting news items in one place. The idea is to "clip" the news that interests you. You can then quote the content in your own feed, comment on the items on your Web site, or save articles for future action.

Bloglines has a nice feature for creating clippings. You just click the Clip/Blog This link on any news item to copy that item to a special Clippings area. The clippings are then listed for you on the left, just like news feeds. You can click any clipping to view it on the right, as shown in Figure 3-13.

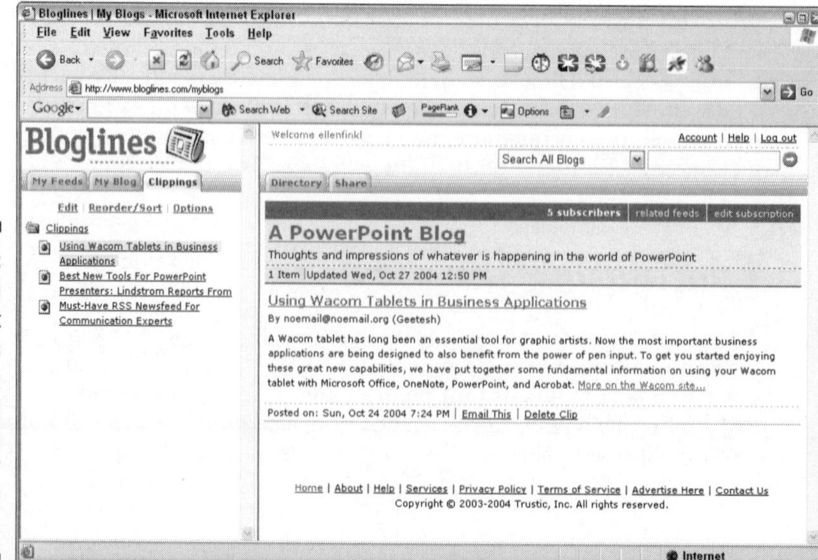

Figure 3-13: You can collect news items in one place so that you can read them or comment on them later.

Unsubscribing to RSS Feeds

You can easily unsubscribe to RSS feeds that you don't want. In fact, if you use a reader that comes with a large number of preinstalled feeds, you may spend quite some time deleting feeds before you get settled in because they clutter up your nice, clean view.

Generally, you select the feed in the reader window and then click a Delete button or right-click the feed and choose Delete. You may have to confirm the deletion (which is very annoying when you're deleting several). Some readers allow you to select a bunch of feeds and delete them all in one fell swoop.

Interestingly, you can sometimes delete individual items in a feed. I've seen this only in software readers. Deleting items you don't want is a great way to reduce clutter. Use the same technique that you use for deleting feeds.

Getting RSS on Your PDA or Mobile Phone

Never be away from the news! If you have a Web-connected PDA or mobile phone, you can now get your RSS feeds while you're on the move. RSS feeds are great for keeping up to date on your PDA or mobile phone, because you can download them and then read them offline.

For the Pocket PC, some of the available news readers are as follows:

- A4News
- PocketRSS
- Egress
- Mobile News

Figure 3-14 shows an example of one of my feeds on a Pocket PC device. You can also check out the following additional services:

- A new service at `www.mobilerss.net` transforms any feed to an HTML format that you can synchronize with your PDA.
- Mobile RSS Reader (`www.dace.fi/website/index.php`) is an application that you download to your Web-enabled mobile phone. You can then download RSS-feed URLs and read them on your phone.

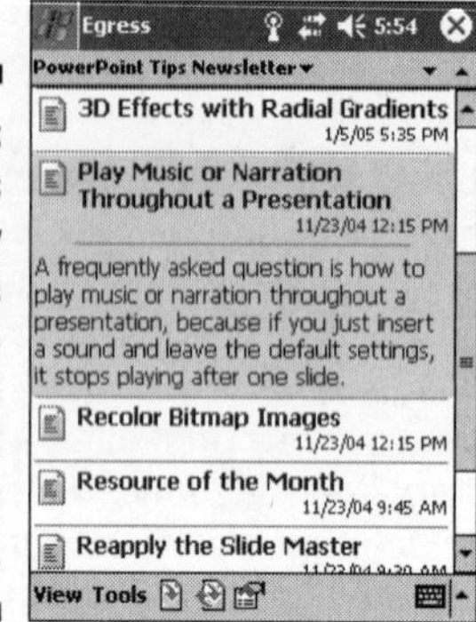

Figure 3-14: Egress lets you view RSS feeds on a Web-enabled Pocket PC hand-held device.

The news can follow you everywhere!

Part II

Developing Great RSS Content

"I'm sorry Mr. Garret, a 35 year old tattoo doesn't qualify as a legal trademark for 'Mother.com'."

In this part . . .

In Part II I explain what you need to create great RSS feeds for any type of content. I provide an overview of blogging, because blogging has been instrumental in the fast growth of RSS feeds. This is also the part where you discover some of the major blogging software out there and how to publicize your blog with RSS.

Eager for more? I also explore how to get the results you want from your feed by fine-tuning your writing for your audience. I steer you towards the many resources you can use to gather content for your feed, and discuss how you can use RSS to market your Web site.

Chapter 4

Using RSS to Spread Your Blog

In This Chapter

- Understanding just what a blog is
- Creating the blog and the feed
- Using your RSS reader
- Creating a blog using HTML
- Maintaining your blog
- Publicizing your blog with RSS

What's a blog, after all? *Blog,* short for *Web log,* is just a Web site with a series of dated entries, with the most recent entry on top. Those entries can contain any type of content you want. Blogs typically include links to other sites and online articles with the blogger's reactions and comments, but many blogs simply contain the blogger's own ramblings.

Unquestionably, the popularity of blogging has fueled the expansion of RSS feeds. According to Technorati, a company that offers a search engine for blogs in addition to market research services, about one-third of blogs have RSS feeds. Some people who maintain blogs are publishing an RSS feed without even knowing about it, because some of the blog Web sites automatically create feeds (more about how this happens shortly). If you think that blogs are only personal affairs, remember that Microsoft has hundreds of them, and businesses are using them more and more to keep employees, colleagues, and customers up to date.

In this chapter, I give a quick overview of blogging and how to use RSS with your blog to gain more readers. If you want to start a blog, this chapter explains where to go next. If you already have a blog, I explain how you can create an RSS feed and use it to publicize your blog.

If you're totally not interested in blogs, feel free to skip this chapter. You won't hurt my feelings, honest.

Bloggers Unite!

Blogging has become a movement. Blogs have become influential, and even the mainstream media are taking notice — and reading. Web sites have been around for a long time. How did a few daily entries balloon into millions (yes, millions) of blogs and an entire industry?

Blogging is the back to our roots part of the evolution of the Internet. The Internet started as a tool for researchers, scientists, academics, and the government. The early days of the World Wide Web (which grew out of the Internet) contained lots of personal sites and free information, as people discovered they could post anything they wanted. Still, the great expansion of the Internet was driven by commercial uses.

However, people never forgot those earlier days of personal interests, and they still had more to say. People discovered that they could *publish,* meaning that they could create a Web site whose main purpose was to provide ongoing updates on anything — current events, social mores, technical advances, and so on — including their opinions on these topics. It was the opinions — well-researched, smartly written, often funny — that hooked people on reading blogs.

A history of blogging

The earliest blogs were simply updates on the early history of the Internet. In early 1992, Tim Berners-Lee (the inventor of the World Wide Web and now Director of the World Wide Web Consortium (www.w3c.org) regularly posted the progress being made on the development of what would become the Internet. In 1993, Marc Andreesen, known for his creation of the Mosaic and Netscape Web browsers, created a "What's New" log at the National Center for Supercomputing Applications. These were mostly news items to keep colleagues up to date.

A very early site that is recognizable as the kind of blog we know today contained Justin Hall's daily ruminations. You can still see his first daily page at www.links.net/daze/96/01/10/. It's more like free poetry than prose. He starts, "daily thoughts, a useful notion" and ends with "sounds like a good idea to me, I think I'm gonna have a little somethin' new at the top of www.links.net every day."

Dave Winer, whom we could call the father of RSS, started a news page in 1996, also for techies, but he added personal commentaries, in true blog fashion. Slashdot (www.slashdot.org) started its "news for nerds" in 1997. Jorn Barger coined the term *Weblog* in December 1997 for his own Web site. By 1998 and 1999, a couple of people created lists of Web logs, of which there were 20 to 30 at the time. By 1999, Peter Merholz had shortened *Web log* to *blog.* Rebecca Blood, who maintains a history of blogging at www.rebeccablood.net/essays/weblog_history.html, started her well-known blog in 1999. Blogging was limited to people who knew how to create Web sites until 1999, when Pitas (www.pitas.com) started the first free build-your-own-blog Web tool. Other tools soon followed. These tools allowed bloggers to edit their blogs right in their browser, without any knowledge of HTML or Web design. Blogging became easy, and the number of blogs grew exponentially.

A few incidents helped to make the blogging world an important phenomenon. A story about White House intern Monica Lewinsky broke in Matt Drudge's blog (www.drugereport.com). One of the best examples of the influence of blogs occurred after Senator Trent Lott made a comment at Senator Strom Thurmond's 100th birthday that seemed to be a favorable reference to Thurmond's earlier support for racial segregation. While the mainstream media virtually ignored the comment, bloggers, including www.talkingpointsmemo.com, pounded the issue. People read the blogs, and within a few days, TV and newspapers picked up the issue. After two weeks, Lott had to resign as U.S. Senate majority leader.

The war in Iraq and the 2004 U.S. presidential campaign (which started in 2002) were also hot blog topics. Democratic candidate Howard Dean started the first campaign blog by a presidential candidate. Now, several mainstream media outlets have their own blogs, including *The New York Times* and *The Washington Monthly.*

So when will you join the march of blog history?

Figure 4-1 shows a blog that contains many typical features of blogs, as follows:

- **Main content:** A regular, often daily, entry.
- **Link to RSS feed:** A link to the RSS feed, so the visitor can subscribe.
- **Date:** The entry's date, with the most recent entry always on top.
- **PermaLink:** A permanent (nonchanging) URL that contains the same content as the entry. The blog's main URL changes whenever the blog is updated.
- **Comments:** A way for readers to comment about the entry. Many blogs don't have this feature, because it requires a lot of time on the part of the blogger to respond to the comments.
- **Trackback:** A list of other sites that link to the entry. The more trackbacks, the more popular the entry.
- **Blogroll:** A list of the blogger's favorite blogs.
- **Archives:** A list, often by month, of previous entries.

Bloggers discovered that it was fun to write about what they thought. They felt they had something to say, and now anyone, anywhere in the world, could read it. They didn't have to get a job as a reporter or write a book. Blogging is the true democratization of publishing.

Keep in mind that you don't need a blog to create an RSS feed. An RSS feed can contain press releases or computer tips (that's what I use mine for) that are not based on a blog, because the format of the source content on the Web site is simply not blog-like.

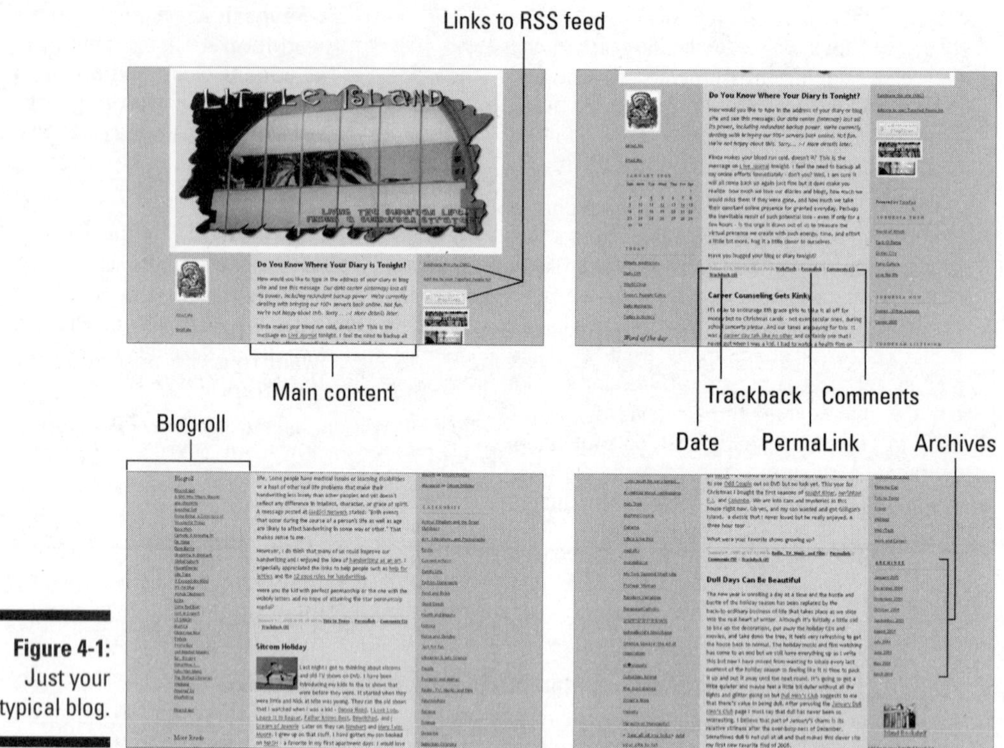

Figure 4-1: Just your typical blog.

Who started the first blog? Of course, it's hard to know, but for the curious, see the sidebar "A history of blogging."

For lots more on blogging see *Buzz Marketing with Blogs For Dummies,* by Susannah Gardner from Wiley Publishing.

Creating a Blog

If you want to create a blog, you need to decide which type of service or technology you want to use. Your choice of blogging tools is an important decision — after all, you'll probably use that tool almost every day.

The easiest way to start a blog is to use a Web-based service. You don't need your own Web site, because the Web service hosts your blog for you. This means that the blog resides on their computers, not yours. You just enter your content into a Web form in your browser and click a button to post your blog.

If you want to run your own Web server, you can. Several blogging programs work on a server. The disadvantage is that you need more technical skills. The advantage is that you have more control over your blog. Also, you don't have to worry about your blogging service going under or its servers crashing. In this section, I emphasize programs that host your blog for you. In the next section, I explain how you can create a blog without a blogging service.

Choosing a blogging service

Blogging services offer a bewildering array of features. Before you start, you should think about the type of blog content you want to create so you know which features you'll need. Here are some questions to ponder:

- Do you want to be able to include images? How about audio and video? Some services let you upload files; others don't.
- Many blogs create a *community* by allowing readers to respond to blog entries. A community is an amazing animal — if you have the time for it. After all, you'll want to read all the comments and perhaps reply to them. Do you want to allow readers to comment on your entries? If so, will the service you choose allow you to control spam comments?
- Do you want to put out an RSS feed? Of course you do! What kind? RSS? Atom? Which version? Is the creation of the feed automatic? If you have comments, are they included in the RSS feed or do you want a separate RSS feed for the comments?
- Do any restrictions exist on content? A few services restrict you to noncommercial use. Hosted services don't allow you to post certain types of content (adult, racist, and so on) to your blog.
- Does the service place ads on your blog pages? If so, can you opt out by paying a fee?
- Can you write in any language (as opposed to just English, for example)?
- Can you create more than one blog?
- Can you customize the look of your blog? If so, how much can you customize it, and is it easy to do?
- Can you make your blog private if you want? Can you require a password? (This option is important for groups that want to limit accessibility to specific individuals, such as employees or family members.)
- Can you get statistics on how many people are visiting your blog page?
- How much does the blogging service cost, if anything?
- Does the service offer more than one level of features? Some offer a free version as well as an upgraded version that you pay for. Compare the feature sets to decide which level you want. Remember that you may want to upgrade in the future. Does the service allow that?

- How good is the support in case you have questions? Can you call? What are the support hours? Is the documentation helpful?
- Is there a backup system in case the service goes under or you decide that you aren't satisfied with the features and you want to transfer your blog to another blogging service?
- Does the blogging service restrict the amount of traffic to your blog? For example, if your blog is reviewed by *The New York Times* and millions of people come to visit your blog, do you have to pay extra?
- Can you view sample blogs that use the same service?

In the next few sections, I delve into some specific blogging tools that you may want to use. However, there are many options out there, so don't feel that you need to limit yourself to these choices. Some blogging sites are so easy to use that you can try them out and then go on to another one if you decide to: In other words, getting in with these sites is simple and getting out is too.

Blogger.com

Blogger.com (`www.blogger.com/start`) was one of the first major blogging tools and is probably the best-known blogging site. As of this writing, Blogger.com hosts over 292,000 blogs. It's owned by Pyra.com, Ltd., which was itself recently bought by Google. (This suggests that Google may soon follow Yahoo into the news feed world.) Blogger.com creates Atom feeds. (For more information on Atom feeds, see the section "How RSS Started," in Chapter 1, as well as Chapter 7, "Creating RSS Feeds from Scratch".)

You work in your browser to write, manage, and post your blogs. If you don't have your own Web host, Blogger.com hosts your blog on its servers, using its BlogSpot service.

Blogger is free — so the price is right. BlogSpot is free but puts ads on your blog. Figure 4-2 shows the Blogger.com home page.

To sign up for Blogger.com, go to the Blogger.com home page and perform the following steps:

1. Click the Create an Account Now button.

   Fill out the form that appears, including your name, password, e-mail address, and so on.
2. Check the Acceptance of Terms check box to agree to the Blogger.com terms. These include not using your blog for anything illegal or offensive.
3. Click Continue.
4. Enter a blog name and URL, as shown in Figure 4-3, or click the Advanced Blog Setup link if you want to put your blog on your own Web site.

Figure 4-2: Blogger.com is an easy place to start blogging.

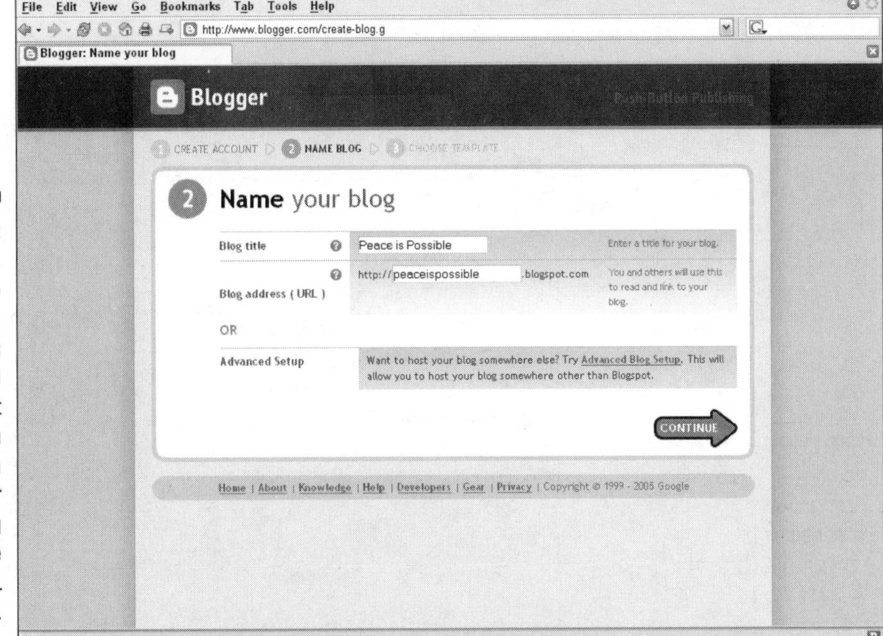

Figure 4-3: When you sign up to create a blog using Blogger and its Blogspot server, you create a name for your blog and choose the URL as well.

5. If you want to use the Blogspot server, click the Continue button.

   If you choose the Advanced Blog Setup link, you need to provide the information that Blogger.com needs to upload the blog. This is not hard to do, but the site doesn't offer much help; I had to change my publishing settings a couple of times before I got the blog to work properly.

6. Choose a template from the choices provided, as shown in Figure 4-4.
7. Click the Continue button.
8. Click the Start Posting button to starting creating your blog.

Once you've followed these steps to create the blog, you can immediately start writing anything you want, using the posting text box shown in Figure 4-5. Click the Publish Post button and you've posted your first blog content.

You can allow comments on your blog if you want to create a conversation. Just select the Yes option button under the Allow New Comments on This Post label. But be forewarned: you have to be prepared to answer these comments!

Blogger offers some other helpful options for posting. You can post by e-mail, use Blogger's BlogThis! browser button to post from any Web site, post photos with Blogger's Hello add-on, or even use AudioBlogger to post audio files by phone. You can create a group blog — this would work well for a family or even a business group. For information about these features and others, click the Help link.

Figure 4-4: Designing your blog's look is as easy as choosing a template.

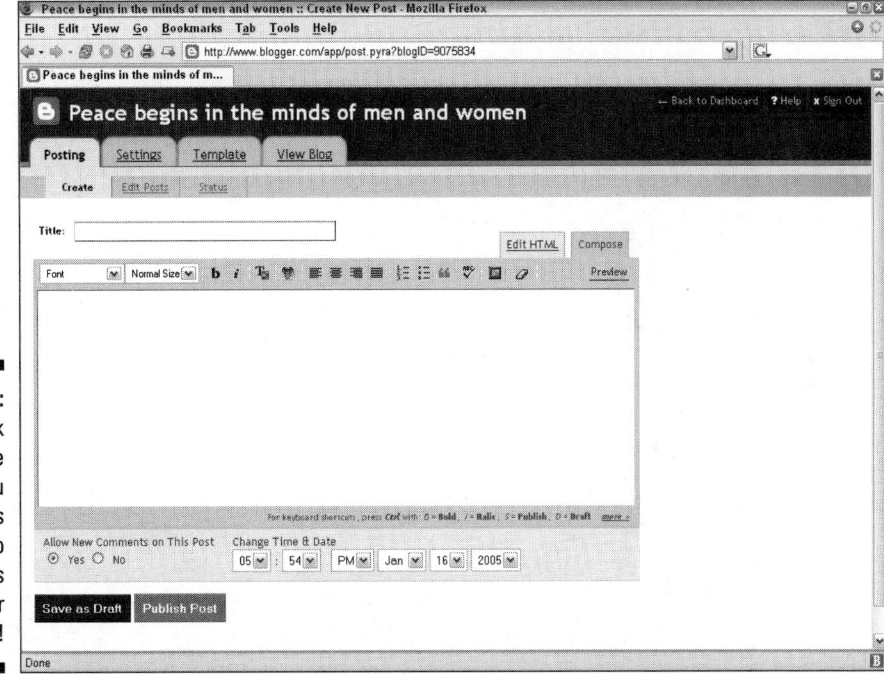

Figure 4-5: The blank box before you challenges you to express your creativity!

Figure 4-6 shows my first blog created with Blogger. I chose to create it on my own Web host's server. The blog took just a few minutes to create.

Publishing your blog creates the Atom feed by default, although you can turn off the feed. (Now, why would you want to do that?) The default filename is `atom.xml`, which I found unhelpful. You can change the name — I chose the same name as my HTML file so that I had `peace.html` and `peace.xml` files.

Of course, I immediately subscribed to my feed. Figure 4-7 shows it in Feedreader. It's just a short feed, but I like it anyway!

LiveJournal.com

LiveJournal.com (`www.livejournal.com`) has over 2 million active blogs as of this writing. This Web-based service is also free, although you can also buy into an upgraded version of the service.

LiveJournal was started by Brad Fitzpatrick in 1999, based on a system he had been using for his own journal. The software is open source, which means that anyone can use the software, view the source code, and contribute to its development. LiveJournal doesn't offer the option of hosting your blog on your own site, although if you have your own Web server, you could use the software on your server — but that would require some advanced configuration.

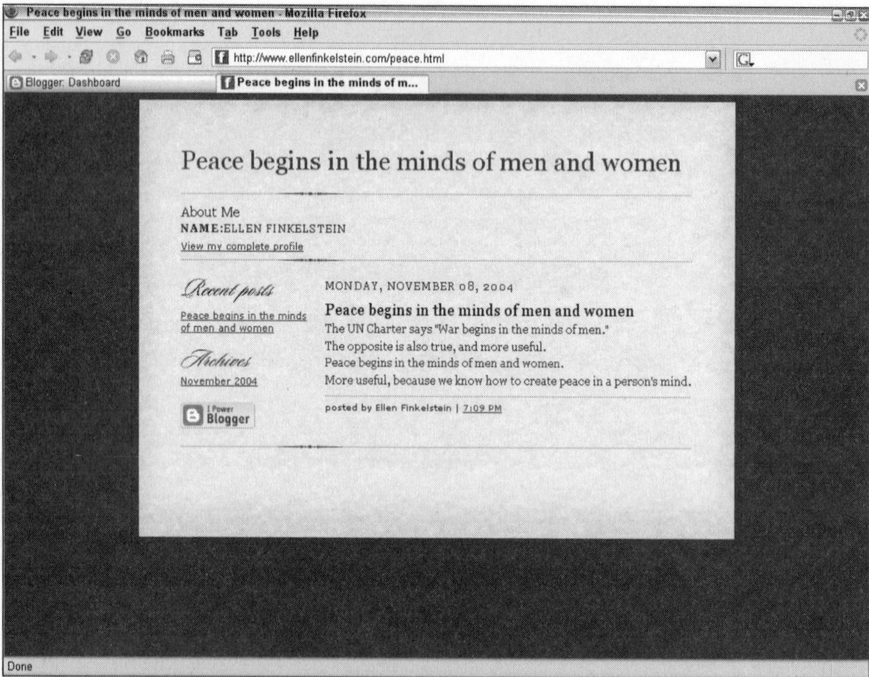

Figure 4-6: My first Blogger.com blog!

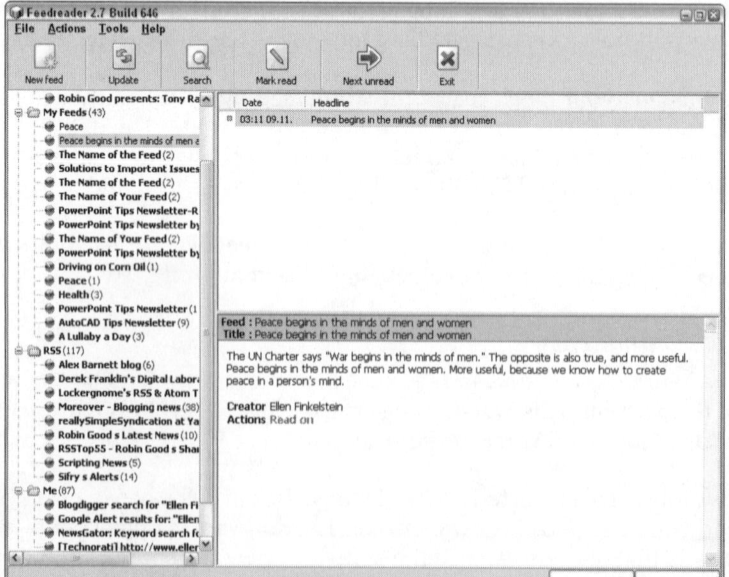

Figure 4-7: My blog in Feedreader.

LiveJournal creates both RSS 2.0 and Atom feeds automatically. Interestingly, LiveJournal.com is also an RSS Web-based reader, providing you with a personal Web page where you can subscribe to and read news feeds.

LiveJournal offers both personal blogs — that is, journals — and *communities,* which are blogs in which a number of users can post entries about a topic.

To create your blog in LiveJournal, do the following things:

- Register by providing a username, password, and e-mail address.
- If you want, you can choose a paid account, which offers some additional features, including a shorter domain name and a LiveJournal e-mail address.
- Confirm your e-mail address by responding to an e-mail that you receive immediately after signing up.

After you are all set up, you can customize your layout by choosing a template and setting text colors, background, and colors of other elements on the page. You can choose a mood icon as well.

Figure 4-8 shows my blog in LiveJournal, after choosing the Notepad template and changing the background and text colors. (I admit, I just copied and pasted from my Blogger.com blog. I can think only so many deep thoughts in one day!)

Finding your feed is not that easy — the URLs for both the RSS and Atom feeds are buried in FAQ 149 (choose Support➪Frequently Asked Questions➪Syndication➪Where can I get an RSS or Atom feed of my journal?). After I found the URLs, I was able to subscribe easily.

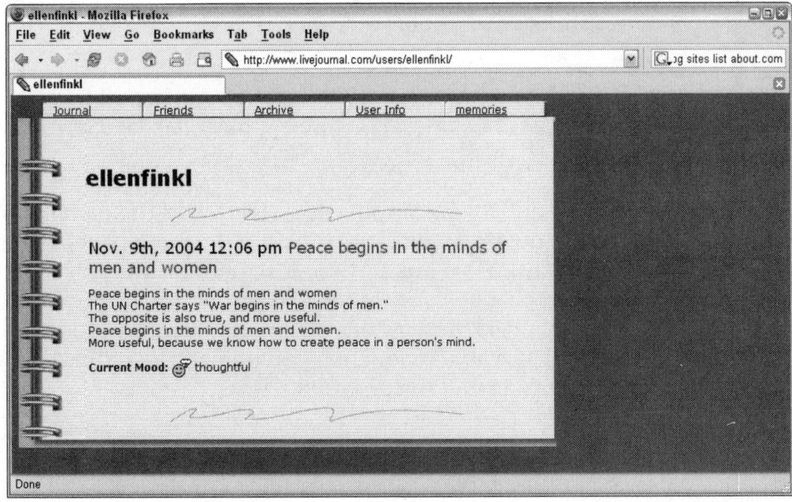

Figure 4-8: My blog in LiveJournal.

Movable Type and TypePad

MovableType (www.movabletype.org) is different from Blogger and LiveJournal because MovableType is software that you download and use on your own Web site. (Therefore, in case you were wondering, you need a Web site.) On the other hand, TypePad (www.typepad.com) is the hosted version (like Blogger and LiveJournal) and doesn't require that you have your own Web site. Six Apart (www.sixapart.com), the owner of both MovableType and TypePad, is coy about its exact user numbers, but it estimates that it has over a million users worldwide.

MovableType is free only for personal use and with a limit of three blogs. If you want to have more authors and unlimited blogs, you'll pay one-time fees ranging from $69.95 to $99.95. Fees for nonprofit, educational, or commercial use range from $39.95 to $199.95. (The fees may change over time, of course.)

You'll have to meet the following requirements to use MovableType:

- **A Web host that allows you to run custom CGI scripts:** CGI scripts are little pieces of code that run between a browser and a Web server. You need to check with your Web host to find out if they allow this. My Web host (at my subscription level) does *not* allow custom CGI scripts, so that would immediately stop me from using MovableType. However, many Web hosts do allow these scripts. Contact your Web host's technical support to determine whether the host supports custom CGI scripts. Often, you can upgrade to a level of service that allows you to run CGI scripts.
- **A Web host whose servers run Perl:** Perl is the programming language that's often used to create and run CGI scripts. You need version 5.004_04 or later. If you're not sure about the version, ask your Web host.
- **An FTP program to upload files to your Web server:** You currently may use an FTP program to upload files to your Web site. If not, you can get one; two well-known tools are Cute FTP (www.cuteftp.com, $39.99) or WS_FTP (www.ipswitch.com, $34.99).
- **A Web browser with JavaScript enabled:** Almost all browsers support JavaScript; just check that you haven't disabled JavaScript in your browser.

When you download MovableType, you need to find the installation instructions. (Hint: Click the Documentation link on the home page, and then click the Installing MovableType link.) These instructions are very specific (and long). You need to change some of the CGI scripts to specify where your Web host's server keeps Perl (here again, you'll probably have to ask) and where you plan to install MovableType. Then you upload the required files to your Web host's server to install the program.

After configuring the files, you go to the Web location where you have installed MovableType and you see the MovableType program in your browser. You can start your blog. MovableType comes with templates, but you can customize them.

While configuring MovableType seems difficult, the advantage is customizability and top-notch features.

MovableType's sister product, TypePad, makes creating a blog simpler. TypePad uses MovableType, but TypePad keeps everything on its own servers, so you don't have to install or configure anything. TypePad costs from $4.95 to $14.95 per month, depending on the level of features you want. You can also download a 30-day free trial.

Signing up for TypePad is similar to signing up for Blogger and LiveJournal. Because TypePad uses the MovableType software, signing up for the trial is a great way to see whether you would like to eventually upgrade to MovableType. Figure 4-9 shows my blog (you must be getting bored with it by now) in TypePad.

You can see some useful features of TypePad in Figure 4-5. For example, viewers can comment; I've already added a wisecrack comment. (The other blogging sites also allow comments.)

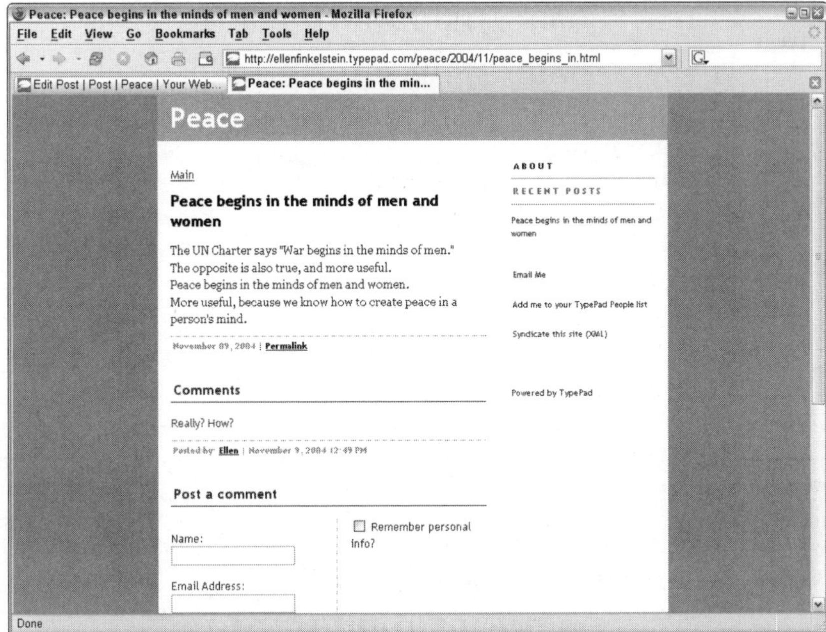

Figure 4-9: Now for the third time — the same blog in TypePad.

Note the Syndicate This Site (XML) link, which allows viewers to add your feed to their readers. Obviously, TypePad creates the feeds automatically — in both RSS and Atom formats. Again, you need to search in TypePad Help (look for "Syndicating Your Weblog") to find the URL.

Of course, you can also right-click the link in your own blog and choose Copy Shortcut or Copy Link Location from the shortcut menu. Then copy the URL into your RSS reader to subscribe to your own blog. (I always subscribe to my own feeds so that I can check them when I update them.)

Bloglines

Bloglines (`www.bloglines.com`) is an interesting mix of a blogging tool and an RSS Web-based reader. Bloglines claims tens of thousands of users. I discuss Bloglines in Chapter 2 (see Figure 2-1) as a reader. Here I cover it as a blogging tool.

Bloglines is simplicity incarnate, as shown in Figure 4-10. What you lose in customizability, you gain in ease of use. You just type inside the box and click the Post to Blog button. That's all there is to it. If you know some HTML, you can format your blog. For example, you can add hypertext links.

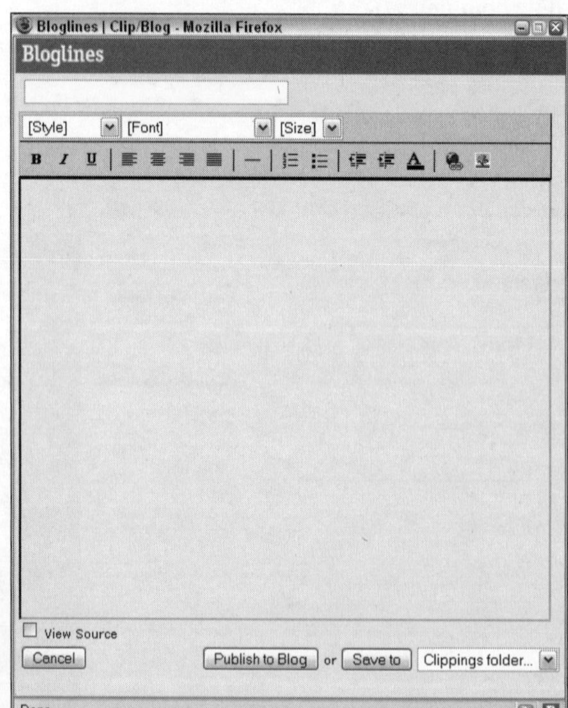

Figure 4-10: Bloglines' blogging window.

Figure 4-11 shows my first blog in Bloglines. (Thank goodness, I finally came up with something new!)

Notice the Sub Bloglines button in the upper-left corner above the calendar. This is the RSS feed that Bloglines automatically creates for your blog. Clicking this button subscribes you to the blog's RSS feed. In Figure 4-6, you can see the list of the RSS feeds that I've subscribed to. A list of links to other blogs is called a *blogroll* (but don't eat it for breakfast with coffee).

Bloglines has a unique Clip Blog feature that takes advantage of its dual nature as both an RSS reader and a blog tool. Many blogs are collections of links and content from other feeds or blogs. The blogger then comments on content and provides the links for further reading. Bloglines facilitates this process of collecting information (usually by reading RSS feeds) and reorganizing it into another source of information (which is also an RSS feed).

Here's how you add items to your blog and publish comments with Clip Blog:

1. **When reading your feeds in Bloglines, if you see an item that you want to put into your blog, click the Clip/Blog This link, as shown in Figure 4-12.**

   A small window opens with the item's title and URL.

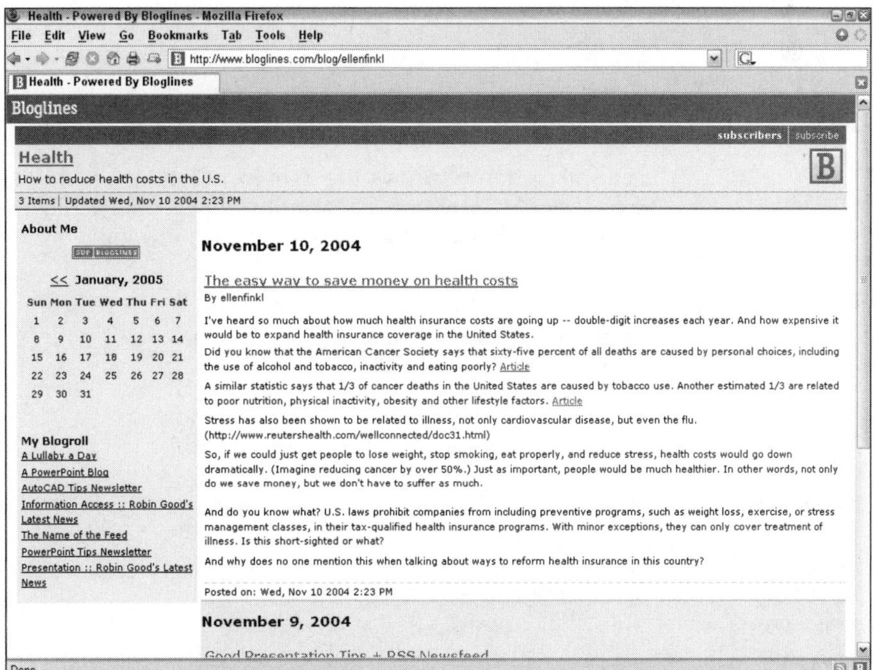

Figure 4-11: My first blog in Bloglines.

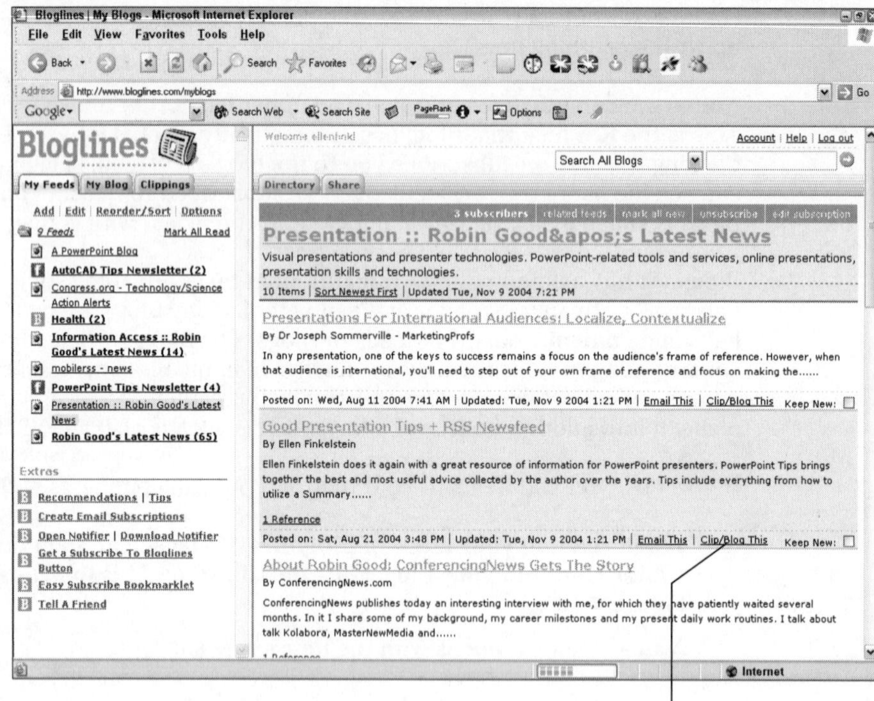

Click this link.

Figure 4-12: To clip a blog, click the Clip/Blog This link for an item.

2. **Click the Publish to Blog button to add the item's title and URL to your blog, as shown in Figure 4-13.**

   You can also choose to save the item to a Clippings folder, where you save material for later use. The window now displays the message, "The item has been blogged" and has a Close Window link.

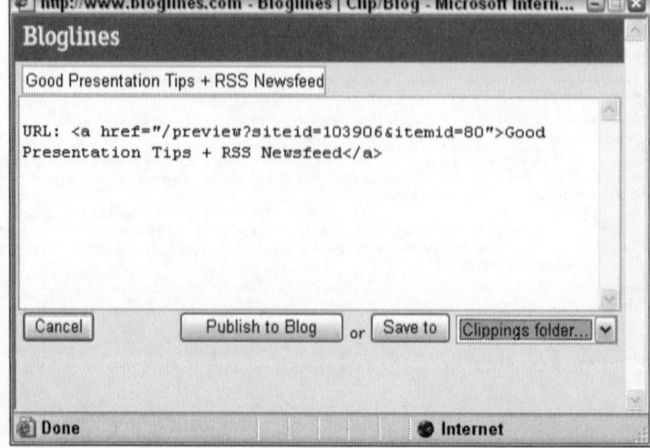

Figure 4-13: You can add any feed's title and URL to your own blog.

3. **Click the Close Window link to close the window.**
4. **Click the My Blog tab in Bloglines (see Figure 4-12) to go from your feeds to your blog.**

   In the Edit Posts section, you now see the new post that you saved. You usually want to add some more content.
5. **Click the new post to open its editing window and add any content that you want.**
6. **Click the Resave to Blog button.**

   You've just created a new blog entry!
7. **Click the View Blog link on the My Blog tab to see your new entry.**

You can see my entry in Figure 4-14. I diverged from the topic of health, as you can see, and started showing off, adding an item announcing one of my own feeds.

MSN Spaces

The new kid on the block is MSN Spaces (`spaces.msn.com`), Microsoft's blogging service, which opened for business while I was writing this book. You can see this home page in Figure 4-15.

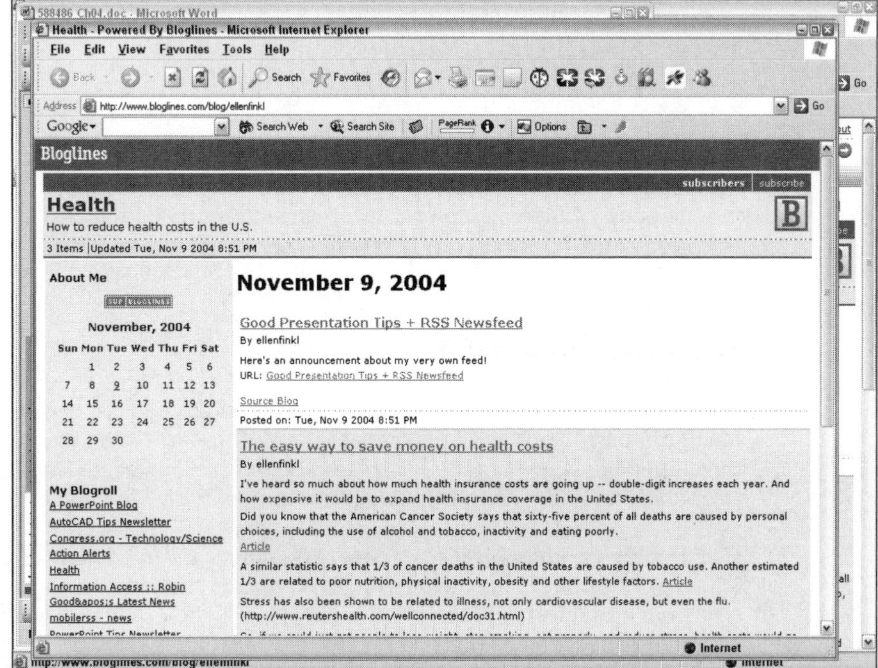

Figure 4-14: My new entry consists of the URL of an item from another feed plus some text that I added.

Figure 4-15: The home page for MSN Spaces, a new blogging service from Microsoft.

MSN Spaces is free and allows you to:

- make your blog public or private
- upload images
- allow comments

You should be aware that MSN Spaces is somewhat integrated with MSN Messenger. For example, if you make a blog private, you must start by choosing the people who can view your blog from your MSN Address Book. After that, you can add other people one-by-one.

Getting started

Obviously, once you have chosen a blogging tool, you'll be eager to start writing. Perhaps you already know what you want to say — in fact, maybe fully developed ideas are practically exploding out of your head. But for most people it's a good idea to think a bit about how their blog will develop:

- **Decide on your blog's purpose.** You may want to write a mission statement that describes what you are trying to accomplish and why. Include your expected audience. For example, are you creating a blog to promote yourself or your product? Are you trying to rally support for a cause? Are you sharing information about a topic of interest? Is your blog just a water cooler for your family members to swap stories?

- **What kind of content will you include?** Do you just want to create a diary-type blog and write off the top of your head? Will you need a source of inspiration? If so, where will you get it? Or, do you want to collect news and comments from other sources and then remix them with your own thoughts to create something new? If you're the organized type, try listing the main points of your first few blog entries.
- **What is the focus and format of that content?** Will you focus on one topic or let yourself write about anything that interests you? Will people read your blog because you're a very interesting person, because you write well, or because they're already interested in a topic that you're covering? Will they come for information, opinions, or both?

On the other hand, you may be blogging for purely personal reasons and not care if anyone else is interested. That's fine, too.

- **Consider your schedule.** How much time will it take you to write a regular blog entry? How much time do you have every day to blog? Many blogs are started and abandoned (like the ones I started for this chapter). Good blogs are updated daily or almost daily.

If you're considering a blog for your business, and you're already spending lots of time communicating your thoughts via e-mail, blogging probably won't take you any more time.

Blogging can be very fulfilling for personal use and very useful for business use — blogging is a great way to communicate. So give it a try and see what happens!

Creating a Blog with Your HTML Editor

If you already have a Web site and maintain it, and you don't need fancy blogging bells and whistles, you may not need a blogging tool at all. For example, perhaps you don't want to allow comments or responses — this requires some sophisticated programming, which the blogging services offer but which you may not be able to do easily on your own. If you don't need this kind of feature, you may choose to create a blog on your own.

After all, what is a blog? It's just some text on a Web page, listed by date. If all you want to do is create a daily entry, you can create one in the same way you create any other Web content.

Figure 4-16 shows how I put the content of the two blogs I started earlier in this chapter (which you can see in Figures 4-9 and 4-11) on a page of my Web site. Here I'm working in Microsoft FrontPage and displaying the blogs in Preview mode.

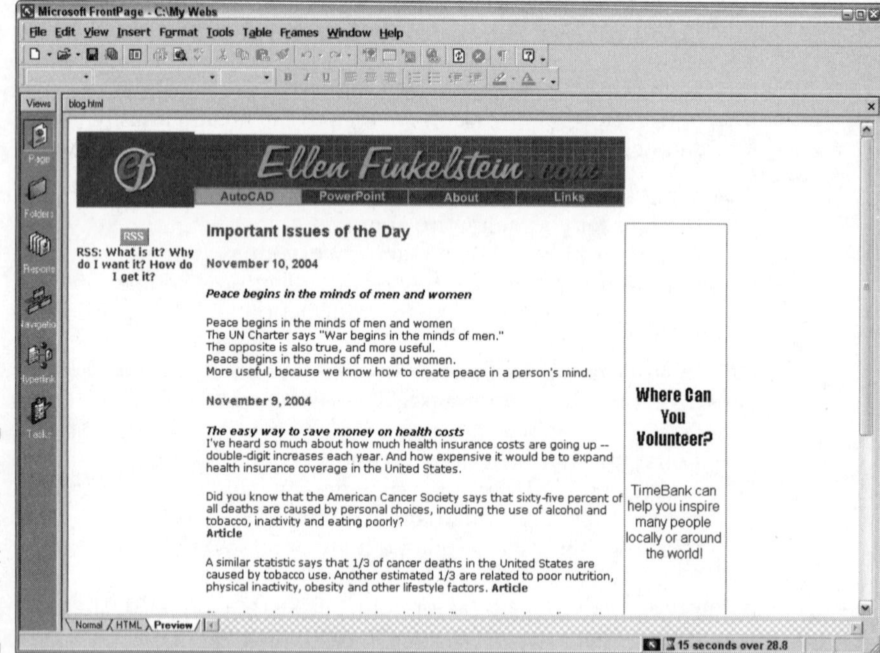

Figure 4-16: You can create a blog right on your Web site.

You can put each entry on a new page or put several entries on one page. Your choice may depend on the length of your blogs.

The only remaining step is to create your RSS feed. Part II of this book is all about creating your own RSS feeds.

Maintaining Your Blog

After you've created and posted a few blog entries, you'll establish a routine of maintaining your blog every day or so. The most popular bloggers put aside a few hours each day, usually at the same time, to blog. Of course, that's not considering those bloggers who seem to post 24/7. In this section I provide some ideas for efficient blog maintenance.

You may want to follow the example of one blogger gets all his entries out of the way in the morning but uses an automated system to post them throughout the day so that it seems as if he's always working — meanwhile, he's out having a good time!

Archive this!

Most blogs archive older issues to preserve their wisdom for posterity. In fact, in the sidebar "A history of blogging," I include links to the earliest blogs that go back to the mid-nineties; these are still available on the Web.

To archive older issues, decide how many blog entries you want on a page, and then follow these steps:

1. **When your entries on a page exceed the number you want to include, create a new page.**

   Name and title the page according to the dates of the blogs. For example, you could name the page `2004-11.html` for all your November 2004 entries.

2. **Select older entries that you want to archive, and cut and paste them into the new page.**
3. **Add a link on the archive page to your current page, the one that always contains your latest entries.**
4. **Put a link on your current page that sends the reader to the archived page.**

   You can create one area that includes links to all your archived pages.

Getting input for your blog

Although many people write entries based on blogs or news stories that they've read, don't forget that you should add something meaningful to other peoples' content. Work on developing your own voice and your own point of view.

When you mention an outside source, provide not only a link but also a mention of the author and title. In other words, be generous about giving credit to your sources.

Maintaining your blog is more than just posting. If you allow people to add comments, you should comment on some of those postings. (You may want to delete some of them, too! Blogging tools allow you full control over your content.)

Comments from your readers can be a major source of content. Readers may bring up a source or idea that really gets your juices flowing. On the other hand, you will probably get a fair number of spam comments.

If gathering information is part of your plan for obtaining content for your blog, you need to find resources that you can read each day. Perhaps you're responsible for keeping your company or department informed on issues that affect them. Other blogs are probably not enough. You should also look at RSS feeds, news (which may or may not be available via RSS feeds), and Web sites (which also may or may not be available via RSS feeds).

In Chapter 3, I cover ways to find resources using RSS. In the section "Using RSS directories," I explain how to search RSS directories for RSS feeds in your area of interest. In the section "Creating a new feed from a search," I show you ways to create a new feed from a keyword search.

Although the practice is somewhat controversial, you can also create a new feed from a Web site. Converting HTML to an RSS feed is called *scraping.* There is controversy over the question of whether you need to ask permission to do this. In Chapter 8, I explain methods of scraping RSS feeds from Web sites. A number of tools are available to help you accomplish this task.

Adding ads

Here's another consideration for maintaining your blog — do you want to make some money from it? If your blogging service is not free, you may want to at least make up some of the cost of using it.

The main way to make money is to place ads on your blog. Opportunities for including ads will certainly proliferate in the future — lots of people are trying to figure out how to make money from their blogs. You can expect to see more tools become available that help you make your blog financially — as well as personally — worthwhile. However, right now, ways to include ads with your blogs are limited.

You may not be able place ads on your blog if it's hosted. However, Blogger is now offering the opportunity to place Google Adsense ads on your blog. Adsense ads are like the ads you see to the right of your browser when you do a search on Google, except that they appear on your Web site. The ads are specifically chosen (automatically) to relate to the content of your site. So if you have a blog on health, you'll see ads related to health and health products.

If you create your blog on your own Web site, you can use Google Adsense, too. Go to `www.google.com/adsense` to sign up. You get paid a small amount for each time someone goes to your site and clicks one of the ads. Because the ads are appropriate for your site's content, people are likely to click the ads. Okay, so you probably won't make thousands of dollars per month, but if you work carefully at publicizing your blog and a few hundred people read it each day, you could make a few hundred dollars a month — certainly enough to pay for your blog.

A similar option is Blogads (www.blogads.com). Advertisers sign up and choose the blogs they want to advertise on. You can sign up to be listed as one of those sites.

Depending on your topic, you may attract sponsors. For example, if you blog about how to use a computer program, the software company that makes that program may sponsor you.

On the other hand, it's perfectly all right to keep your blog ad-free. In spite of the commerciality of the Internet, a strong culture also exists for keeping information and opinion noncommercial. Some topics lend themselves more to ads than others. You may feel that your blog will be corrupted by ads. If you're blogging because you love it, why bother with ads?

Finding other ways to make money

You can ask for donations. Some bloggers use Amazon's Honor System program, which allows site visitors to donate to your site. (Go to www.amazon.com and scroll to the bottom of the page. Click the Join Honor System link.)

If it's appropriate for your blog's topic, you can become an Amazon associate and recommend books that relate to your blog. If readers buy the books, you get a small percentage. (Go to www.amazon.com and click the Join Associates link at the bottom of the page.) Some blogging tools, such as TypePad and WordPress, include support for selling books via Amazon. Many readers will appreciate your recommendations for further reading and won't think of these links as advertising.

Publicizing Your Blog with RSS

If you feel that no one is reading your blog, it can be disheartening. But you can't just sit back and wait for the masses to come to you; you need to let people know about your blog. Just having an RSS feed doesn't guarantee that people will subscribe. And most people still read blogs by going to the blog's Web site.

The first step is simply to let people know about your blog. Tell them the URL of the blog and of your RSS feed. Send an e-mail to all your friends and colleagues. Put the URL on your business card. Explain to them the advantages of subscribing to your feed. (Give them this book!) Chapter 11 is all about how to promote your feed, so you can find more useful tips there.

If you used a hosted blog service, such as Blogger or LiveJournal, remember that they only list your blog on their sites. Therefore, you need to go out and make your blog and its RSS feed visible elsewhere on the Web.

If you can find other blogs on similar subjects that accept comments, feel free to make constructive comments and include a link to your own blog. Perhaps you can write some articles for online or offline publications and mention your blog in them.

Quite a few sites function as directories just for blogs, regardless of whether they have RSS feeds. People come to these sites to search for blogs on topics that interest them. You can list your blog on some of these sites to help people can find it.

Chapter 15 includes a list of the ten best RSS directories, but here, in Table 4-1, I include a list of some of the best blog directories. These directories list the Web site URLs of the blogs, and these blogs may or may not have RSS feeds. You can add your own blog's URL to these sites.

Table 4-1 Blog Directories

Site Name	*URL*
Blogdex	`www.blogdex.net`
Blog Search Engine	`www.blogsearchengine.com`
Blogwise	`www.blogwise.com`
Blogstreet	`www.blogstreet.com`
Web Portal	`http://portal.eatonweb.com`

Use a combination of blog directories and RSS directories to publicize your blog. Keep your blog interesting, relevant, updated, and useful, and people will come knocking at your door.

Chapter 5

Writing for Results

In This Chapter

- Picking an audience
- Deciding what you want to say
- Finding content resources
- Adding value
- Using RSS to market your site
- Creating a Web site based on RSS feeds

No matter what type of content you want for your RSS feed — blog, press releases, news, industry updates, tips, and so on — you need to write something to get the results you want. What results do you want? Decide on your goal, and the means to attain the goal become much clearer.

In this chapter, I don't talk about good writing in the traditional sense. That is, I don't talk about using active voice versus passive voice or creating an outline before you write. Instead, I explain how to develop content that takes you where you want to go. Because RSS feeds can have many purposes, this chapter takes a broad-based approach. In fact, you'll find the information here useful for many other communication tasks, such as writing Web site copy, creating presentations, designing marketing materials, and more.

I've included some great tips and tricks for finding hard-to-get information from Web sites.

At the end of this chapter, I discuss how an RSS feed can help you market your Web site and get more traffic to it. Finally, I throw in some thoughts about creating a Web site that is totally based on RSS technology.

Picking an Audience

The first step in deciding what you want to write is to identify your audience. Sometimes your audience is obvious. For example, if you are a sales manager and want to create an RSS feed to keep the sales reps in the field up to date, you already know your audience.

However, if you have a site that sells software, you need to think more carefully about your audience. Are you writing for potential customers or existing customers? For instance, I've seen RSS feeds on software sites that anyone can subscribe to, containing FAQs about support issues. I was searching for the best software, and the information offered was all about problems people were facing with the software! Not a good first impression, to be sure. With this in mind, you may want separate feeds for potential customers and existing customers.

Part of the process of identifying your audience includes deciding what you want to get from your audience or what you want your audience to do. Do you want your audience to buy something? If so, your RSS feed should be constructed differently from an RSS feed designed to support existing customers.

You should also consider what your target audience knows and what they don't know. Many RSS feeds are designed for the developer community — programmers who want to keep up to date on the latest software programming tools. These feeds don't bother to explain terms that might be gobbledygook to you and me, because they assume that the readers understand those terms.

On the other hand, if you're targeting new customers, you don't want to use terms that they may not understand. (What potential buyer wants to feel stupid?) You can't even assume that these readers have read your previous news items where you defined technical terms. Therefore, each item in such a feed needs to be as self-explanatory as possible.

Using Full Text or Links?

An RSS feed can consist of a short description with a link to a site or the full content of an article. The relative advantages of these two structures are hotly debated among people who think deeply (and loudly and in many words) about RSS feeds.

Some say that subscribers are annoyed by having to click a link to go to the Web site (which you can often view right in your reader). It's an extra step. Why not provide the reader with the full story right up front? Figure 5-1 shows a feed that includes the entire entry within the feed.

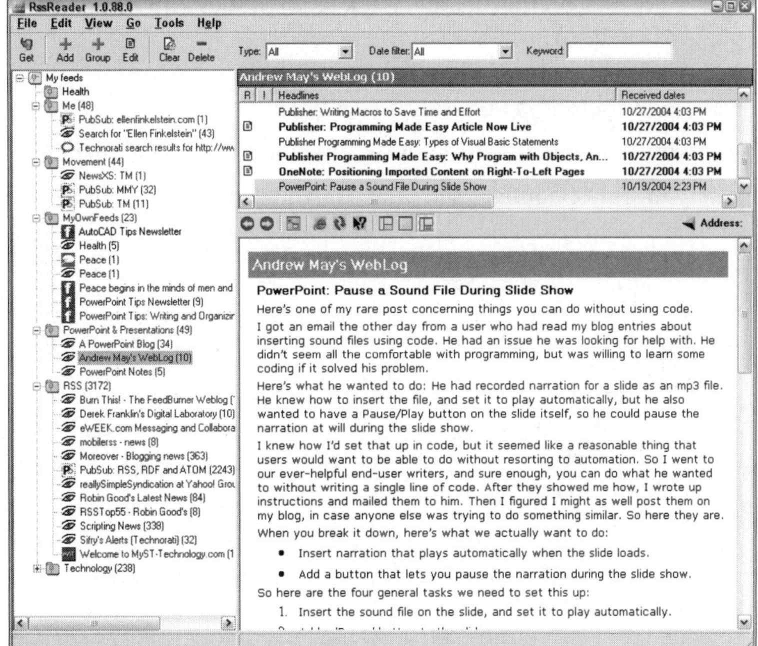

Figure 5-1: This RSS feed gives you the whole story right away.

Others say that the descriptions help readers decide whether they want to read a story. Descriptions can act as a filter to help subscribers choose when to dig deeper. Also, full-text feeds definitely involve more bandwidth. The bandwidth problem can slow the feed just as an image-heavy Web page slows the display of a Web site. The Web server may be overloaded with the increased demand for its resources. Finally, if you're selling a product or service, you probably want to use a link to your site to increase traffic to your site. (See the section "Using RSS to Market Your Site," later in this chapter.)

The contents of RSS feeds are typically mirrored on a Web site, but they don't have to be. You may not have any of the content of the feed on your site. The feed doesn't have to be a repetition of your Web site, just as an email newsletter doesn't have to be on a site.

Sometimes you see an RSS feed that includes titles only — no description or content at all (see Figure 5-2). I discuss this practice more in Chapter 10 in the "Deciding on description length" section. I don't recommend using titles only; it's very frustrating to the subscriber.

Here's my take on this debate. Look at the issues and decide for yourself. If:

- **bandwidth is an issue,** use descriptions only.
- **your content is text only,** use full text.
- **you don't want your content on your site,** use full text.
- **you want people to see your Web site,** use descriptions only.

For example, my RSS feeds offer tips on AutoCAD and PowerPoint, two software programs. Both programs are very graphical in nature, and I often need to show images of the program to make the tip clear. I also want readers to see the result of using the tip, such as some cool effect in PowerPoint. Also, I want people to come to my site and see the rest of my tips — and perhaps buy my books. I'm not so concerned with bandwidth, because I don't imagine that the number of people reading my feeds is that great as to affect my Web host's servers. Therefore, I use descriptions that link to my Web site, where subscribers can see the entire tip.

On the other hand, if you are writing a blog, your entry is probably mostly text, and your feed can probably contain your entire entry. If you have a loyal audience, hopefully those folks want to read what you have to say each day, so why not make your full blog available up front?

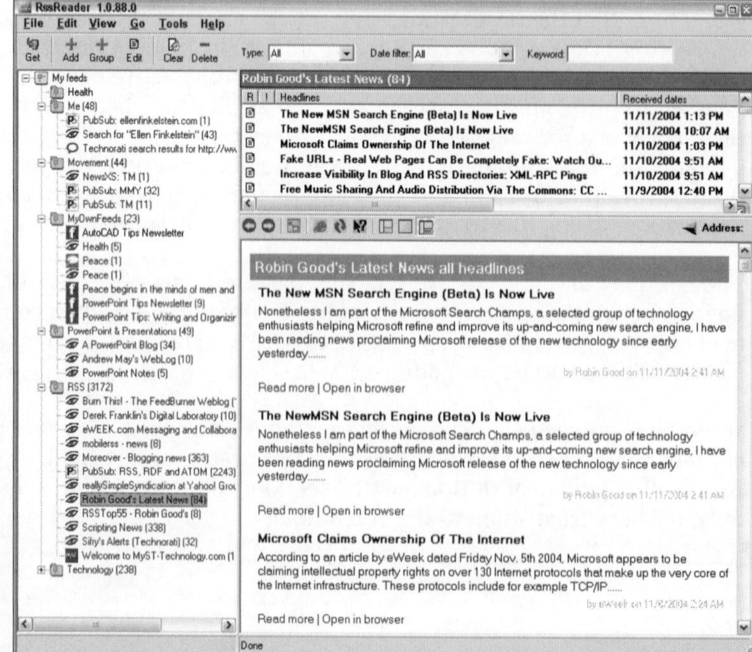

Figure 5-2: This RSS feed shows you the beginning only. If you're interested, you click to go back to the Web site for more.

Deciding What You Want to Say

When you have decided on your audience and feed structure, you should think about what you want to say. You probably have plenty to say, right? If you are already sending out an e-mail newsletter and want to convert it to an RSS feed, you already have your content. Remember, an RSS feed doesn't need to be updated on a daily basis. On the other hand, you do want to consider how often you want to publish your feed and organize your content for regular updates. If you create a big burst for your first feed, you may not have much to say later on!

If your RSS feed is a new communication — perhaps you want to reach out to customers or you want employees to be more aware of updated content on the company Web site or intranet — you may not have existing content to put in it.

In Chapter 4, I discuss some ideas for developing content for blogs in the section "Getting Started."

If your RSS feed represents your company, make sure that it meets the editorial standards of your company, like any other type of communication. If someone in your company edits printed reports, PowerPoint presentations, and Web site pages, you should also get a review of RSS feeds. You want to make sure that you don't publish any material that could harm the company or violate any confidentiality agreement you may have signed.

Attracting new customers

If your goal is to attract new customers, you probably want your content to be about your product or service. Because new customers don't know much about the product or service yet, you need to emphasize the features and their benefits, just as you would in an ad. You would also let them know about new products or services and updates to existing ones. Success stories and testimonials would also be appropriate. You may also want to add information about your company and its accomplishments, such as press releases, awards, reviews, articles, and so on. In other words, you may as well admit it — this feed is advertising.

An RSS feed, like an e-mail newsletter, can establish your reputation as an expert and bring people back to your site via links, perhaps to buy your products or services. Unlike an e-mail newsletter, an RSS feed doesn't end up in the spam folder, and each time subscribers open their RSS reader, they see your feed. Because they probably open their reader most days, you attract their attention much more often than you would be with a weekly or monthly newsletter, but with less work on your part.

Keeping current customers happy

You also need to keep current customers happy, especially because they are your best source of future customers. You can offer them tips on how to best use your product or service, offer special deals for existing customers, or provide training. You might want to include news of interest to people in your field, such as trade shows and legislative initiatives. Including stories about how other customers used your product or service to solve a business problem can be compelling.

Figure 5-3 shows Macromedia's RSS feed on Flash, its program for creating Web animation. On its site, Macromedia states that its feeds include technical notes, security bulletins, information about product updates, and information for developers.

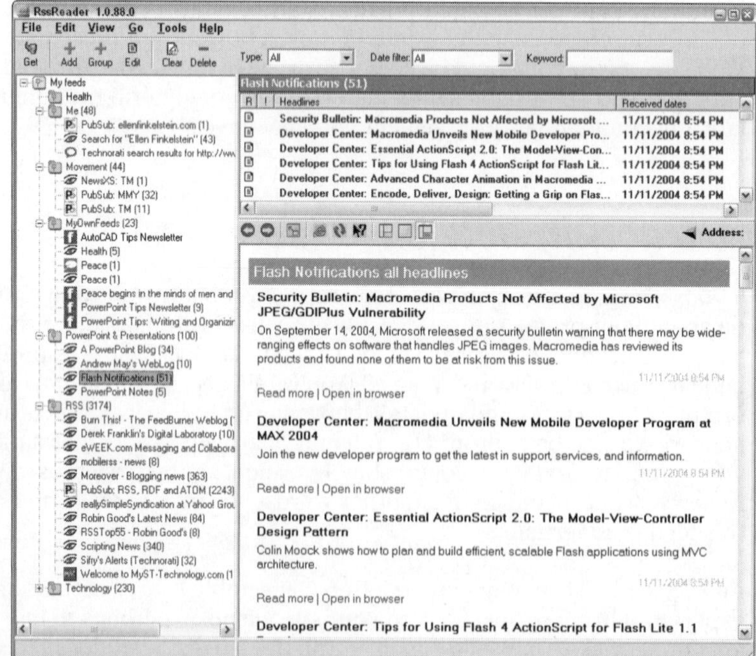

Figure 5-3: Macromedia's RSS feeds offer information for customers on its software products.

Links to support resources are helpful and appreciated. News of planned updates can keep customers interested. You can also offer the following items:

- A link to a location where customers can offer ideas for new features
- A way to submit bugs, suggestions, kudos, or complaints
- The opportunity to ask questions

In fact, just keeping in contact makes customers feel more comfortable. So go ahead and communicate!

Communicating with employees or colleagues

Communications to employees or colleagues can run the gamut from general and motivational to technical and informational. You may be able to be fairly informal, unless you're writing an employee newsletter in a very large company.

The possibilities are endless, and you may find that you can create several RSS feeds for different audiences or purposes. For example, you may be the director of Human Resources. Perhaps you want one feed for all employees that contains the following items:

- Updates on benefits
- New policies
- Company accomplishments
- Introduction to new hires
- Promotions and transfers

Another feed can be internal, just for the members of the Human Resources department. This feed may discuss only issues that the department needs to know, such as employment law changes — as well as notices about holiday parties, vacation schedules, and so on.

A third feed could be for managers, to let them know what your department can do for them, recent successes, changes in laws and employee benefits, changes in policies that they may need to explain to their subordinates, and so on.

If you're a sales manager consider creating a feed for sales reps on the road. RSS feeds are especially useful when your employees are in far-flung places.

Are you intrigued by the idea of using company-internal RSS feeds? If so, check out Chapter 1, in the section "Controlling information flow," where I discuss using RSS on an intranet or extranet and describe how RSS facilitates document management within a company.

Providing news

Many RSS feeds are news based. After all, something new is always happening, so lots of news is always available. Constantly changing situations are the perfect medium for an RSS feed.

Some feeds cover general news, of the kind that you would see in a newspaper. The major newspapers and news services all have RSS feeds now, so you can get your news fix easily. To make the choice more interesting, these organizations have created dozens of specialized feeds. Figure 5-4 shows part of the list of the feeds at *The New York Times.*

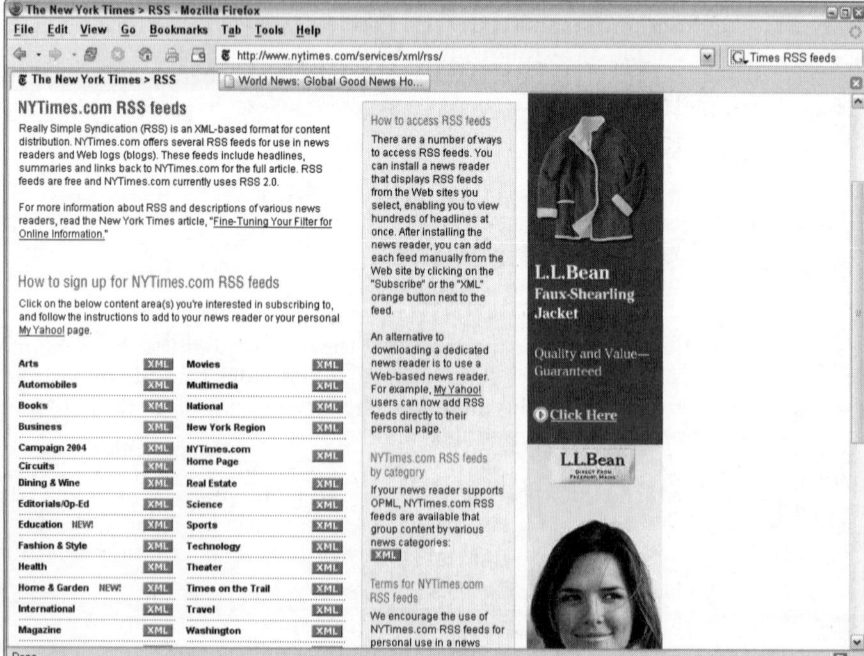

Figure 5-4: *The New York Times* offers specialized feeds on many topics.

Assuming that you are involved with an organization that offers less news than *The New York Times'* "All the news that's fit to print," what news do you want to offer? More likely, you want to collect news about a narrow subject, such as genetically modified foods or LCD projectors. People often collect news about their field and then redistribute that news to their colleagues.

Nonprofit organizations that work on a particular issue, such as efforts to combat a disease or furtherance of family values, often send out newsletters containing news on that issue. Often, they are also trying to raise money to support their efforts. The organizations collect the news from numerous sources and pass it on to their subscribers. RSS is ideal for this type of communication.

Of course, your organization doesn't have to be nonprofit to have a newsletter. Whatever the reason, providing relevant, current news is a way to keep your members, customers, prospects, colleagues, and others interested in what you have to say.

Holding forth on your opinions

Are you a pundit? Do you have opinions you're bursting to share? Of course you do! Many blogs are based on their authors' opinions, and people read the blogs to help them make their own decisions on issues. But opinions are not just for blogs. The technical community is full of people with strong opinions — even on RSS. If you know a lot in a certain discipline, you can put your opinions on the related matters of the day in an RSS feed.

Offering your expertise

If you're a smarty, other people may want to know what you know. People lap up tips about every conceivable subject — computers, cars, house repair, investment — you name it, people want useful information about it. As Web site owners who send out e-mail newsletters have known for a long time, people love free information.

Whenever someone asks you a question you can put the answer in your RSS feed (and on your Web site or in your blog). You can then simply reply to the person with the link to your answer. In this way, your answer is now available to others who may have the same question. Many of the tips in my RSS feed come from questions that people e-mail to me.

You can offer your expertise for many reasons. You may have a consulting company and want to spread your reputation as a knowledgeable person in your field. The same situation applies if you sell a product. Figure 5-5 shows the Web site of a computer security training and certification company. The company offers an RSS feed to help further establish its status in the area of its expertise.

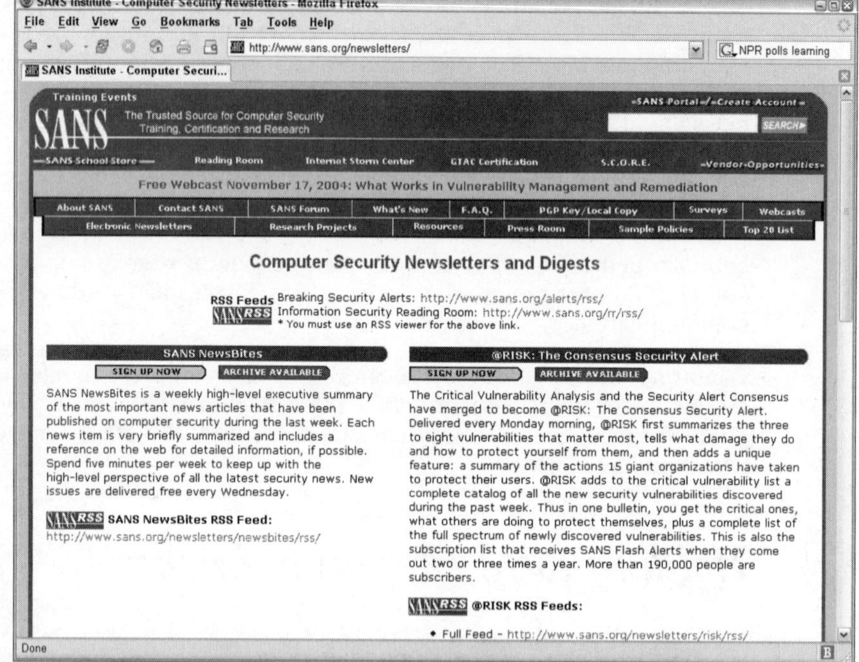

Figure 5-5: If you're an expert, an RSS feed helps you tell the world about your expertise.

Finding Content Resources

You may be a great writer, but odds are at some point you'll find that you can't possibly create all the content you need for your feed from thin air. At some point, you have to collect some resources as the basis for your feed. For example, in my RSS feeds on AutoCAD and PowerPoint tips, I get content from the following sources, among others:

- Questions that readers send me
- Content in my books
- Tips that I read about — a few of which are also available in RSS feeds
- Other experts

Developing a rich and thorough collection of content resources is really the secret to creating RSS feeds with great content. You can easily collect dozens or even hundreds of resources. Your job is to find, digest, filter, analyze, summarize, and finally spit out a whole that is more useful than all its original pieces.

As you collect bits and pieces of data, you need to watch out for copyright issues. For example, *The New York Times* allows you to use its feeds — and even put them directly on your site — but for personal use only. Some people encourage the republishing of their news; others don't.

However, you can always use published news in the following two ways:

- If the information is public, you can take the content and rewrite it in your own words. For example, news about a politician is public, so you can restate the content and comment on it, as long as you are really doing your own writing. However, it's still good form to credit your source.
- You can write a comment about the news and provide a link to the original source. For example, you can say, "Today I read that the President said such and such. Here's what I think about this issue . . . You can read the original story here." Readers could then click the underlined hyperlink to read your source.

In the next few sections, I discuss some common sources for news and information and explain how you can find them.

Using blogs and RSS feeds

Obviously, a great way to collect information for your feed is to find other feeds on the same topic you want to cover. Finding the feeds is a snap. In Chapter 2, in the section "Finding News Feeds," I explain how to search for feeds on appropriate sites as well as for RSS directories. You can search by topic or keyword. Some RSS readers have an auto-find feature. When you go to a site, the reader automatically finds any feeds.

If your reader doesn't have an auto-find feature, go to any search engine and do a search on "RSS" along with your topic-specific keywords. For example, if you're looking for material on floral ribbon, enter **RSS floral ribbon** in your favorite search engine.

You can do the same type of search by topic or keyword at blog directory sites to find blogs on topics that interest you. Chapter 4 lists a few blog directories to get you going.

One of the best ways of finding news and Web-based information is to create a custom feed from a search. For example, if you have a feed on the floral ribbon industry, you could do a search on "floral" and one on "ribbon." Unfortunately, many of the services don't allow you to put words together (as in "floral ribbon") the way you can in a standard Web search engine. These tools are still in the early developmental stage. You should try a number of keywords for your searches. One of the wonderful things about RSS readers is that you can easily handle a few dozen feeds. In Chapter 3 in the section "Creating a new feed from a search," I list some of the sites that offer this search feature.

Create search feeds from several resources using the same keywords. In my experience, the different sites provide very different results. Each service seems to use quite different methods of searching and culls data from different resources.

Do you want to search through blogs that don't have a feed? If going from blog site to blog site is an inefficient way to gather the information you need, you can create an RSS feed from the blog. You can try BlogStreet (`www.blogstreet.com`), which offers a service of creating an RSS feed from a blog. In Chapter 8, I discuss other methods of creating RSS feeds from Web sites that don't have a feed.

Using e-zines and discussion groups

Of course, not all resources are available as RSS feeds. One idea is to sign up for e-mail newsletters from relevant sites. (At the same time, e-mail the sites and ask them to put the content of their newsletters into an RSS feed.)

In the example of a floral ribbon newsletter from the previous section, you would go to Web sites that serve florists, such as the Independent Florists' Association's site, to see whether they have a newsletter. You should also look at local and regional sites that serve florists.

For many topics, you can find relevant newsgroups and discussion groups to gather content. Yahoo Groups (`www.groups.yahoo.com`) has discussion groups on every conceivable subject — and some that you can't conceive of. If the archives are public (as noted on each group's page), you can just click the RSS button to get a feed of the discussion. For newsgroups, you need a news reader (not to be confused with an RSS feed reader), such as Outlook Express. Your Internet service provider probably has an arrangement with a server that maintains newsgroups, and you can search for newsgroups that cover your area of interest.

Using the news

Newspaper sites have evolved into a great resource for your RSS feed content. You can search for news on these sites, often over a long period of time, taking advantage of their incredible archives, as shown in Figure 5-6. Many newspapers offer RSS feeds, although these often aren't targeted to a specific topic.

Crayon (`www.crayon.net`) lets you "create your own newspaper." It's just a way to collect links to newspaper sites all in one place, but it can be useful for doing research, especially on regional topics.

MyYahoo! has a great service for creating RSS feeds from news stories. I discuss the MyYahoo RSS feed feature in more detail in Chapter 2, in the section "Web-based readers."

The Moreover site (`http://.moreover.com/categories/category_list_rss.html`) has over 300 free news feeds. One of the topics may be just what you need. The site also offers custom feeds for a fee. This site has an excellent base of news resources.

Scouring Web sites one by one

Many Web sites have their own search feature. Unfortunately, Web sites may update their content without letting you know — which is why they should have an RSS feed. These search features vary in quality, so try more than one set of keywords. When all else fails, see whether you can find a site map to dredge up the nuggets of information that may be hiding there.

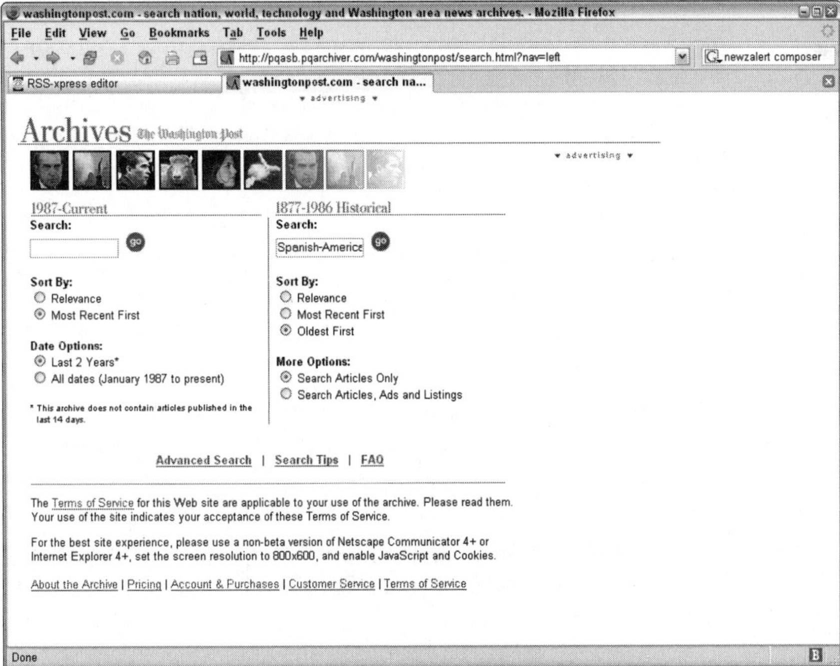

Figure 5-6: *The Washington Post* offers archives (for a fee) back to 1877!

Many of the RSS search feeds that I previously mentioned are essentially Web site searches. But what if you need information from a specific site?

Would you like to create an RSS feed from a Web site? You can do this, although it is somewhat controversial to do so without the permission of the site owner. This process is called *scraping,* and I discuss it in Chapter 8. Scraping works best for sites that are structured with dated news items. Several services are available to provide scrapes for you and then you can subscribe to the resulting RSS feed.

Making news personal

What can you add to your RSS feed from your own personal resources? Have you ever thought about creating your own news?

If you do your own research, the results are news, even though you created the results yourself. For example, if you want to know what percent of people who browse the Web are fed up with pop-up ads, you can do a survey. Speak to everyone you know and ask them. The results may not be as scientific as a survey done by scientists or professional pollsters, but as long as you explain your methods, you can say that it's news: "my own nonscientific survey."

You have probably seen surveys on Web sites. Many of the news organizations' sites have regular surveys. Why not take a survey on your company's Web site? You ask a question about the topic of the day, people answer it, and you click a button to instantly see the tally of all the answers. If your company's IT department can't help you with this, perhaps you can find Web site polling software that you can put on your company's server. Some Web host companies offer polling tools.

If many people visit your site, you can poll them on issues that you — and they — are interested in. You can then report the results of your survey. Other resources that you can add to your feed are as follows:

- Market studies
- Analyses of your experience with a wide range of customers
- Graphs showing results from projects you've completed
- Testimonials that you've collected over the years

You can probably think of more sources of information, depending on your field, experience, and the purpose of your RSS feed.

Using nonelectronic sources

In this electronic age, we shouldn't forget that books (real, paper ones) still exist. When was the last time you went to the library? (At least, you should check out whether your local library still exists!) You may be surprised at what you can find, especially in older books and historical records.

Also remember that people still communicate in ways other than e-mail and instant messaging. In person or phone conversations with people, whether customers, potential customers, colleagues, or experts in your field, are often valuable resources for your communication effort.

Your company probably maintains archives of physical documents that you can rummage through. Not all documents have been transferred to electronic format. At least you'll get some exercise opening all those dusty boxes!

Adding Value

After you have collected all the information that you can — and perhaps cannot — manage, how do you add value? You don't want to overwhelm your readers with disorganized and unrelated contents. Your job is to make the information useful and meaningful.

The first step is to organize your material. You can do the following things:

- Filter out the junk
- Sort items in order of importance or relevance
- Categorize so that related items are near each other
- Put opposing points of view side by side to provide balance

All these activities take data and turn it into information that people can find and use more easily.

The next step is to think about the material and write about it. One important task is to make the news readable, by using clear and logical expressions. But then you can add more. Here are some ideas of what you can contribute:

- An explanation of the relationships between various items or between the items and your main topic or field
- A clear step-by-step method of accomplishing a task
- Your opinions, of which you certainly have many
- An analysis of the news

The information that you gather is just a lot of noise until you give it organization and meaning.

Using RSS to Market Your Site

If the main point of your RSS site is to bring readers back to your site, you are using RSS to market your site — or your product or service. You can write your RSS feed so that you encourage readers to click the link to go to your site.

In the section "Full text or links?" earlier in this chapter, I discuss the advantages of creating an RSS feed that uses short descriptions with links to a site. (See Figure 5-2 for an example.)

Using links to get readers to your site is not some kind of trickery (as bloggers may tell you). Selling a service or product from a Web site is perfectly legitimate, and you can create an RSS feed that provides real value, rather than just advertising, for your site.

If you don't sell anything, you may be using ads to help pay for your site. By bringing readers back to your site, you can make some income even from an informational site.

You can register your feeds with the RSS directories to make the feeds available to a much wider audience than may already be on your mailing list. See Chapter 3 for a list of RSS directories.

You can create several feeds, directed at slightly different groups. For example, if you sell handicraft kits, you could create one feed on the topic of handicrafts and another on gift ideas. In this way, you can attract a wider audience.

Coordinating with your e-mail newsletter

If you have an e-mail newsletter, you can use your RSS feed as an alternative for the following people:

- Those who want the convenience of getting your information at any time — rather than when you happen to send out the newsletter
- Those who feel that they already have more than enough e-mail
- Those who like to get all their information consolidated in their RSS reader

If your newsletter is in HTML format, you probably already include links to your site. After all, you can't put everything in your newsletter — it would be too repetitive. In the same way, you can put those links in your RSS feed.

Your RSS feed can be advance notice for the content of your e-mail newsletter, which then consolidates your feeds. For example, you can create a feed for software tips and update the feed weekly. Then you can send out an e-mail newsletter at the end of the month containing all the new tips for the month.

Delivering promotions and other marketing content

You can use your RSS feed to announce promotions, discounts, new products or services, and so on. Most of these communications need to convey more information than you would put into a feed. Therefore, you would create a catchy headline as your title, and provide enough information in your description to encourage people to click the link to read more.

Used in this way, an RSS feed is a low key way to market. People get a chance to decide whether they're interested. If they are, they'll click.

Sending out press releases

You can use your RSS feed for all your press releases. You may not want to include the entire press release in your feed; then again, you may. It's really up to you. In fact, you can create some feeds with descriptions and links and others with the full text, to suit your needs. Media organizations, who are overwhelmed with faxes and e-mails of press releases, would probably be happy to sign up for your RSS feed instead.

By linking to your Web site's press release page, you may be able to entice the press to go to your site and learn more about your company.

Creating a Web Site Based on RSS Feeds

Are you an extreme news freak? Would you like to create an entire Web site based on news only? You can create a Web site that focuses on a narrow niche interest or even the latest fad or buzz. Start by collecting RSS feeds on a topic, using the techniques that I explain in this chapter; you can quickly amass a huge amount of content for the site on a narrowly focused or timely topic. One of the most important of these techniques is the use of search feeds, which I discuss in the section "Using blogs and RSS feeds," earlier in this chapter, and in Chapter 3 in the section "Creating a new feed from a search."

Once you tap into all those feeds, using the methods that I discuss in Chapter 11 for displaying news feeds on your site, you can turn RSS feeds into HTML pages, and thus quickly and easily create a Web site on your topic. Of course, you would need to filter and organize the content, as I explain in the section "Adding Value," earlier in this chapter.

Because the content on your site is so focused, you should be able to get a fairly high relevance rating on search engines. This means that when people search for your topic, they're likely to find your site. The number of links to your original sources would also enhance the site's ranking.

You could then use ads from Google AdSense (`www.google.com/adsense`), related Amazon Associate books and other products (go to `www.amazon.com/associates`), and perhaps other sources of ads to create an income, based just on the news.

Finally, you can create an RSS feed from your site and register it on the various RSS directories. People looking for feeds on your topic can register for your feed and come back to your site. The feed brings traffic to your site from people who are not doing searches, but instead are looking for news via RSS feeds.

I provide a visual overview of this process in Figure 5-7.

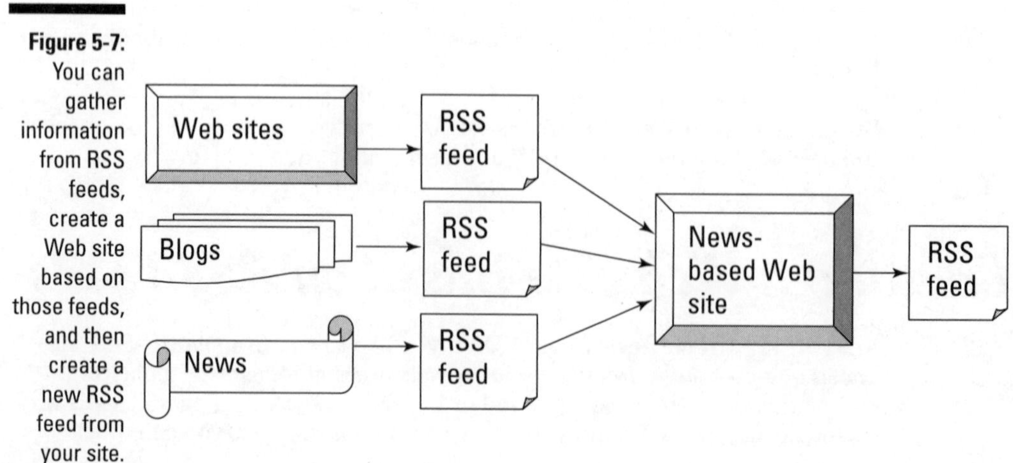

Figure 5-7: You can gather information from RSS feeds, create a Web site based on those feeds, and then create a new RSS feed from your site.

Catch a Shooting Star

Stephan Miller (www.webpronews.com/authors/stephanmiller.html), an internet marketer, calls this type of site a "shooting star" site, meaning that it's based on a phrase, name, or term that's the current buzz. In his article "Nuthin' New Except Search Terms," Mr. Miller describes the process of searching for current top search terms using Wordtracker (www.wordtracker.com/). Wordtracker is a service that keeps track of the most commonly used search terms. The idea is to focus a Web site on those search terms. He then expanded his list using the keyword tool at Overture (www.inventory.overture.com/d/searchinventory/suggestion/). Overture is Yahoo's Web marketing program. (Its home page is found at www.overture.com.) Then he gathered related RSS feeds and placed them on his new site. He was able to create a site that got a significant amount of traffic using this technique.

This continuing cycle of Web site to RSS feed to Web site to RSS feed can create opportunities for even small organizations to ingest, interpret, and communicate information. Whether you have a specific product or service to sell or you consider yourself primarily an independent publisher, you can write content that provides great results.

Part III

Launching Your RSS Feed

"As a Web site designer I never thought I'd say this, but I don't think your site has enough bells and whistles."

In this part . . .

In Part III I describe the many ways to create RSS feeds. I start by explaining the RSS formats and show you the quickest way to create an RSS feed, using an on-line form. I also review some RSS creation software.

Are you the kind that likes to build things from the ground up? For you I explain how to create an RSS feed from scratch by writing the XML code. I'll make it easy as pie, I promise you. Finally, I cover ways to automate the creation of RSS feeds.

Chapter 6

Creating Your First Feed

In This Chapter

- Understanding feed formats
- Optimizing your site for RSS
- Using an online editor or software
- Editing your feed
- Reading your first feed

You're ready to create your first RSS feed and there's just one thing you want to know — how? If you have a blog and your blogging tool creates your feed automatically, you don't need this chapter. But if you need to generate your feed yourself, read on. In this chapter, I help you choose a format, prepare your Web site, and then get you started creating the feed using one of the simplest methods: an online editor or software.

Both online editors and software provide you with the structure you need to easily create RSS feeds. You enter information in some text boxes and presto, you have an RSS feed. Okay, it's a little more involved that that, but these tools really do make creating an RSS feed fairly painless.

Before you know it, you'll be reading your own first feed!

Understanding the Formats

As of this writing, the latest RSS format is 2.0. However, you don't need to use that version and some people use an earlier version, either because that's what they started with or because it's simpler. (See the sidebar "How RSS Started" in Chapter 1 for more information about how RSS evolved into the various formats).

In Chapter 7, I go into the details of the three major versions, but here I just discuss the generalities and give you enough information to choose a version.

From 0.91 to 2.0 and Atom, too

RSS has progressed through several versions. Then you have the Atom format. For example, Blogger (www.blogger.com), a major blogging service, creates Atom feeds by default. Most people who create Atom feeds do so because the tool they use creates Atom feeds, not because they have chosen Atom. Many bloggers don't widely register their feeds — not to speak of the fact that many bloggers don't even know that they are creating feeds.

Confusing as it sounds, the successor to the 0.91 version is version 2.0 (not 1.0). However, many people still use 0.91 because of its simplicity. It's a nice place to start if you're writing RSS feeds from scratch. (In Chapter 7, I explain how to create an RSS feed from scratch.)

All the newer tools create 2.0 RSS feeds. However, a number of older tools still exist that create earlier version-based feeds. Figure 6-1 shows the distribution of the various RSS versions that are registered at Syndic8 (www.syndic8.com) as of this writing. As you can see, most people use .91, 1.0, or 2.0, with version 2.0 having the largest share. You can expect that percentage to grow over time.

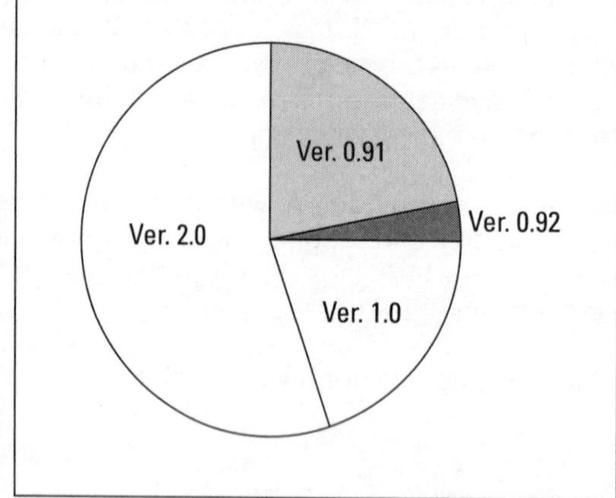

Figure 6-1: The distribution of RSS feed versions registered at Syndic8.

Picking the format that's right for you

Because RSS comes in several versions, you need to decide which version you want to use. Your choice depends on several issues, as follows:

- **How many bells and whistles you want:** If you want advanced features such as enclosures (for example, an audio file) or if you want to keep track of as much data about your feed as possible, you probably should use 2.0.

- **Which tool you use to create your feed:** Most tools create feeds using only one version, so your choice of tool may determine your version. Some blogging sites let you choose between RSS 2.0 and Atom feeds. Older tools create .91 or 1.0 feeds, while new ones create 2.0 feeds.
- **Your knowledge of XML:** If you're a programmer and want to take advantage of more advanced features, you'll want to use 1.0 or 2.0, or perhaps Atom.

Table 6-1 compares the main versions of RSS (not including Atom).

Table 6-1 Comparison of the Main RSS Versions

Version	*Advantages*	*Comments*
0.91	Simplest format.	Officially superseded by 2.0, but still popular. Easy to upgrade to 2.0.
1.0	Offers additional features via modules that are being developed.	Based on RDF, so it's useful if you have RDF applications or if you need the features of its modules.
2.0	Offers additional features via modules that are being developed. Has many more features than 0.91, including unique identifiers (GUID) and enclosures (such as audio files).	Latest version, allowing for namespaces, which are a way to add new tags, defined elsewhere (usually on a Web site).

The attraction of Atom is that it offers features that make it easier to manipulate the data that make up the feed. This advantage is generally not especially important to the person creating the feed, but it allows programmers to create software that can organize and filter the content.

Optimizing Your Site for RSS

If your main content is on your Web site and you want to create an RSS feed from that content, you can organize your site to make the transformation to a feed easier and make it so that the feed picks up content more accurately, especially if you want to automate the process. Some of these changes are also useful for optimizing your site for search engine placement, so you get two benefits in one.

Deciding on the Web page structure

What is the relationship between your Web site and your feed? That depends on the purpose of your Web site and the purpose of your feed. Here are some possibilities:

- Your feed announces changes throughout your Web site; in this case the Web site is primary. These changes can occur all over the place, so the feed will not be related to a specific page. Each item may link to a different location, and each location may also contain other content. In this situation, you don't change your Web site because of your feed, rather the feed changes when the Web site does.
- You want to communicate a series of articles on your Web site that are in one place, such as a blog, press releases, product updates, or tips. In this situation, the Web site's structure should be divided into well-organized — and perhaps dated — items, much like a feed. You also want to consider archiving old items so that readers can find them for a long time to come. For more information on archiving, see the following sidebar "What is a permalink?"
- Your feed is self-sufficient, more like a newsletter. No specific location on the Web site may match the content of any item. You may be providing the full text of your feed items in the feed and linking to a more general location on your site. For example, your feed may discuss company achievements and personnel changes. In this case, the connection to your Web site is limited. The information may or may not be contained somewhere on the site.

Many people put each item on a different Web page and then link to that Web page in the RSS feed. You may decide to use a separate page for each item for the following reasons:

- You find it easier to create small, short pages instead of organizing fewer, longer pages.
- Shorter pages load faster.
- Each page's URL can use words that relate to the content, such as `www.sitename.com/3d_in_powerpoint.html`. Search engines count the name of the page in their rankings, so these pages might help increase your traffic.
- If you want to include ads on your site to generate income, you have more pages to put ads on!

With this type of organization, you may find yourself with an awful lot of Web pages, but if you use some type of Web content management software, this may not be a problem. (See Chapter 8 for information on content management software that creates RSS feeds.)

What is a permalink?

If you want to archive old items, you should consider using *permalinks.* Permalinks are used in blogging software, but they can be appropriate to any regularly updated content items, such as press releases. A permalink is a permanent URL that contains the item. The item originally appears on a current page that changes constantly. For example, your current page may contain this month's press releases — or your last five blog entries. However, these items will not stay on this page because new items will take their place. Therefore, you can specify a permanent location for each item and link to that URL instead. In that way, if someone reads your RSS feed a month later (or ten years later), the link still takes the person to the related item instead of to your current page, which by then is totally different.

By structuring your Web site with permanent locations for all your items, you can set up your feed to link to your permanent locations, rather than the page where they first appear.

If you want to put several items on one Web page, you can create a bookmark for each item and then link to that bookmark. A bookmark URL looks like this:

```
http://www.sitename.com/pagename.html#bookmarkname
```

You can place a bookmark anywhere on your page, using the following HTML syntax:

```
<a name="bookmarkname"></a>
```

Maintaining relations between your feed and your site

Like HTML, RSS feeds contain tags, although RSS tags are specific to the RSS format and version. When creating a feed, you should think about how you'll use a number of these tags. Some tags are required, while others are optional. For example, the feed as a whole always has a tag containing a link that appears in the feed. This link is in addition to the tag contained in individual news items that links to the full item on the Web site.

The tags go in your feed, but if they link to your Web site, they also relate to your Web site. Before you can create your feed, you need to figure out how your feed connects with your Web site.

Figure 6-2 shows the main features of a 0.91 RSS feed. Here you can see that the feed link goes to a main tips page, but the first item's link goes to a page that is specific to that item.

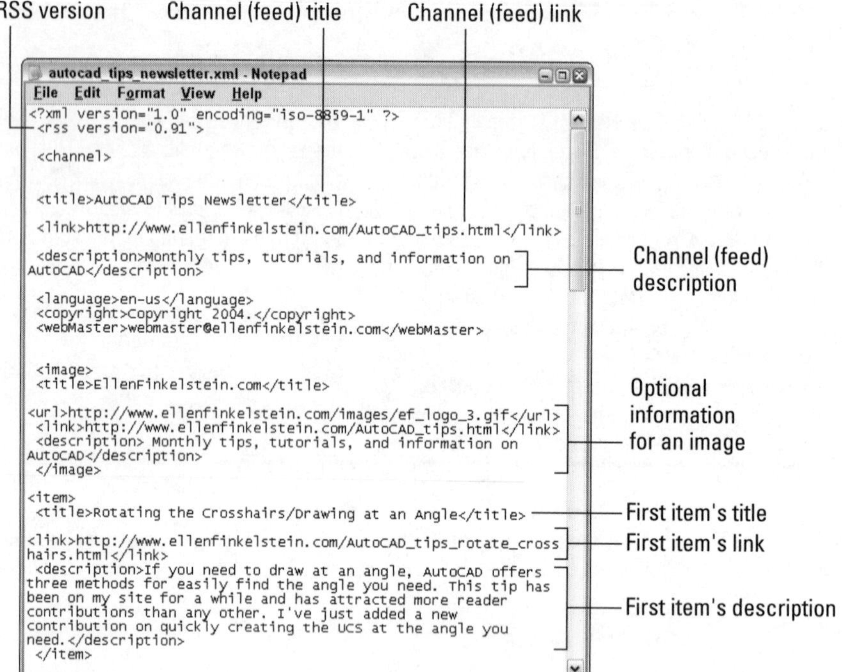

Figure 6-2: The features of a 0.91 RSS feed.

Notice that the RSS feed, which is an XML file, looks a little like an HTML file. The feed uses tags enclosed in angle brackets (< >), and each tag has a matching closing tag that contains a forward slash (/). For example, there's a `<title>` tag, and then you see the title of the feed. Following the title's text, you find a `</title>` closing tag.

In the next chapter, I explain the features of the RSS syntax in more detail. Here I discuss how the parts of your RSS feed relate to your Web site. These components apply specifically to a 0.91 RSS feed, but they are similar for the other versions. Later versions have more tags and therefore more options.

Channel (feed) title

All feeds must have a channel tag. Technically, you can have more than one channel in a feed, but almost universally, feeds have one channel and most RSS readers only support one channel per feed. You use the `<channel>` and `</channel>` tags to enclose your channel. A channel must have a title, and therefore the channel title is the same as the title of the feed. The channel title is therefore the name of your overall topic. If you have a blog, the channel title would be the name of the blog. Perhaps you have a feed for software support issues, and your software is called Silly Software. In this case, the channel title would be "Silly Software Support Issues." This title may be the same as the heading on the Web page that contains the content that you want in your feed. Figure 6-3 shows the same feed as Figure 6-2, but in an RSS reader, SharpReader.

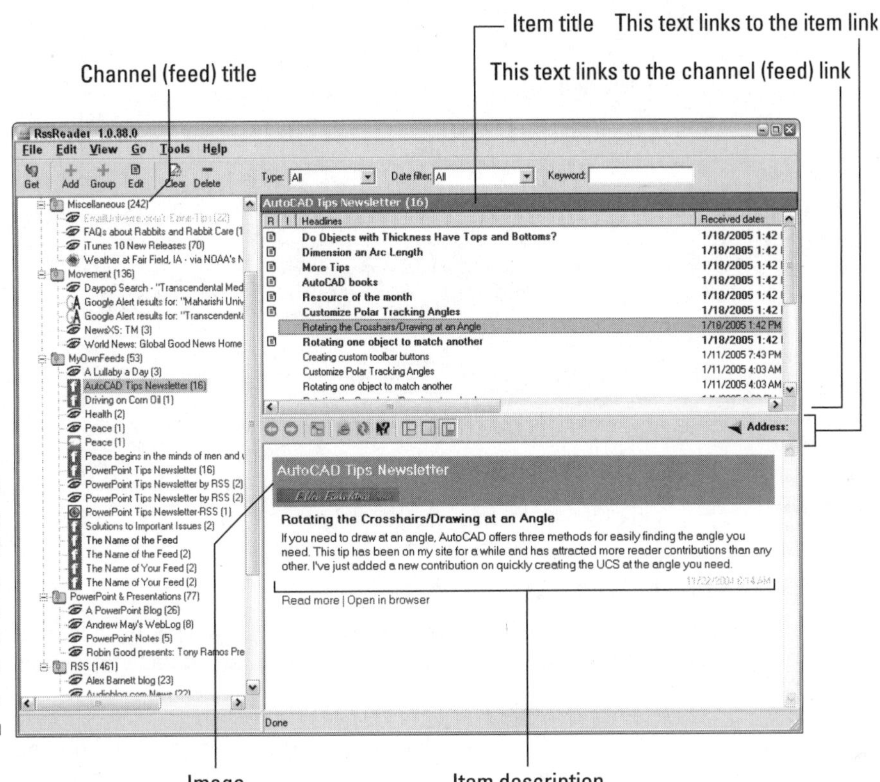

Figure 6-3: A 0.91 RSS feed in an RSS reader. Compare this feed to Figure 6-2.

Channel (feed) link

Each channel must have a link. While this may be a link to your home page, if your RSS feed relates to another part of your site, you should link to that part of the site, as shown in Figure 6-2. Consider seriously which URL you want to use for your feed link. Many feeds link to the site's home page, but that isn't always ideal. Readers are frustrated when they click a link and then can't find any content related to the topic of the feed, which may be in a different part of the site. For example, if you have a feed containing software support issues, link to your main support page rather than to your home page.

Channel (feed) description

Each channel must have a description. This description is an overall description of the topic of your feed. In the previous software support issues feed example, the description could be "Regularly updated FAQs, version releases, and related software issues for Silly Software." The description is generally not shown in an RSS reader. However, most readers let the viewer display the properties of the feed, and the description is often included there, as you can see in Figure 6-4.

Figure 6-4: Some RSS readers let you display feed properties, where you can find the feed description.

Channel (feed) language

You can enter the language of your feed. This allows RSS readers and other RSS-related software to group feeds by language, in case someone is looking for all feeds in Sanskrit.

You need to use official XML language and country codes. You can find language codes at `www.loc.gov/standards/iso639-2/langcodes.html`. Country codes can be found at `www.iso.org/iso/en/prods-services/iso3166ma/02iso-3166-code-lists/list-en1.html`.

Channel (feed) image

Optionally, you can include an image with your feed, as you can see in Figures 6-2 and 6-3. (This image is a little too large for a feed, so some readers squish the image.) Adding an image helps you to brand your feed and connect it to your Web site's logo. Therefore, you probably want to use the same logo that you use on your Web site. The only change may be to make the logo a little smaller.

The image has the following four components:

- **Title:** The title appears as a ToolTip when you hover the mouse cursor over the image. This is similar to the `<alt>` tag for images in HTML.
- **URL:** The URL indicates the location of the image. Be sure to include the `http://` so that the RSS reader can find your image on your server. You can use the same location that you use for your Web site.
- **Link:** This link can go to your home page or the same location as your feed link. Here you have a little more latitude, because one Web site convention is that logos link to the home page.

- **Description:** I've never seen this appear in a feed. You can just copy the feed description here, if you like.

Optionally, you can add `<width>` and `<height>` tags to specify the dimensions of the image in pixels. The maximum width should be 144 (the default is 88), and the maximum height should be 400 (the default is 31). You can see why my logo sometimes gets squished — its 506 pixels wide!

Additional optional channel (feed) elements

You can add other tags if you want. These tags specify further information about your feed. Some RSS readers can use this information for sorting or filtering operations. The major ones are as follows:

- **Copyright:** You can add a copyright symbol and notice of up to 100 characters.
- **Managing Editor:** The `<managingEditor>` tag is an e-mail address. The suggested format is `username@domain.com` (Full Name). This e-mail address should represent the person to contact if readers have questions or comments.
- **Webmaster:** Use the `<webmaster>` tag for the Webmaster of the RSS feed, which may also be the Web site's Webmaster. This would be the person to contact regarding technical problems.

You probably shouldn't include a very private e-mail address in these tags, as that address can be used by spammers.

- **PICS rating:** The `<rating>` tag is a Platform for Internet Content Selection rating that you may have received. This rating is specified by the World Wide Web Consortium (`www.w3c.org`). The purpose of this rating is to control access to adult content by minors. This tag is rarely used.
- **Publication date:** Use the `<pubDate>` tag to indicate the official publication date.
- **Last build date:** The `<lastBuildDate>` tag specifies when the content of the feed last changed. This would be the date of your last news item.
- **Text input:** If you have a CGI script that can accept input, you can use the text input tags to allow readers to send comments back to you. I've never seen this tag used in practice, but I list it here because you see it in some RSS creation tools.

There are a few more optional elements out there, but these are the most notable.

Item title

The next section of your feed contains your actual news items. Some RSS-creation tools have a limit of 15 items per feed (which the 0.91 format specified), and you usually don't want more. If you try to create a feed with hundreds of items, RSS readers may not display all of them. Each item starts with an `<item>` tag and ends with an `</item>` tag.

The item title is your headline. If you have separate items on your Web site, you may put an `<h2>` (heading 2) HTML tag on these items in your Web page's code, because they're important, but not as important as the heading for the entire page. The feed title is similar to these headings because it labels individual items in your feed.

Item link

Each item needs a link. If you are using permalinks (see the earlier sidebar "What is a permalink?"), this link goes to your permalink for that item. Either way, the link takes the reader to the full article, which is especially important if you don't provide the full text of the article in the feed.

Item description

The item description is different from the feed description. The item description provides the reader with enough information to decide whether to read the article. For example, it may be the first paragraph of your complete article. If you choose to include the full text of your article, the description is the full article. So your description can be short or very long!

You can often copy the item description straight from your Web site, although you may prefer to write up a little teaser instead.

The feed stands alone

For example, perhaps you want to send out a newsletter — on the lost art of sculpting pudding or any other topic that catches your fancy. You may already be sending out an e-mail newsletter, and perhaps you have a mailing list of students or clients that you gathered not from a Web site, but from your regular business or teaching activities. You want to stay in touch with this group but would like to switch from e-mail to RSS.

Why? Maybe you really, really like RSS feeds.

Whatever the reason, you can certainly start with your feed. When your feed is done, you can convert it to HTML to create the Web site based on your feed. In Chapter 11, I describe tools to convert RSS feeds to HTML. You use these tools to put the content of RSS feeds (whether your own or those of others) on your site. Use one of these tools and you have created a Web site that is nothing but a conversion of your feed to HTML.

As you can see, the relationship between an RSS feed and a Web site can take many angles.

Creating an RSS Feed the Easy Way

The previous sections of this chapter gave you an idea of how you can relate your Web site and your RSS feed and the components of a feed. In this part of the chapter, I show you some of the easiest ways to create an RSS feed.

The tools I cover here, both online and software based, ask you to fill in the blanks to complete the components that I discussed in the previous section. Once you understand these components, creating an RSS tool is easy (so if you didn't read the previous section, hop back there now and give it a quick scan). The online tool doesn't provide much in the way of help, but most software tools provide some explanation and a wizard-like interface to help you along.

Filling in the blanks with UKOLN

One of the earliest tools for creating RSS feeds is still around: UKOLN's (UK Office for Library Networking) RSS-xpress RSS Channel Editor (`http://rssxpress.ukoln.ac.uk`). This editor creates 1.0 RSS feeds and is free. However, no help is provided, so it's really important that you have a good understanding of the components of a feed.

UKOLN also maintains a directory at the same location and an excellent resource page at `www.ukoln.ac.uk/metadata/resources/rss/`.

In the following steps, I show you how to create a feed using UKOLN's tool:

1. **From** `http://rssxpress.ukoln.ac.uk`**, click the New button.**

   You see the editor, as shown in Figure 6-5.

2. **Enter the channel title, channel link, and description in the appropriate text box.**

   The title is the name of your feed. The link is simply a hyperlink that people can click to go to your site. You can use your home page or a page that is more closely related to your feed, depending on how your site is structured. Include `http://` in the link's URL.

3. **Enter a copyright notice, a Webmaster's e-mail address, and a language in the next set of text boxes.**

   You can see the result in Figure 6-6. By default, the language in this box is en-gb, which is British English. For more information on this option, see the "Channel (feed) language" section earlier in this chapter.

4. **Scroll down to the section labeled Item 1.**

   Don't bother to complete the Text Input section, which is rarely used.

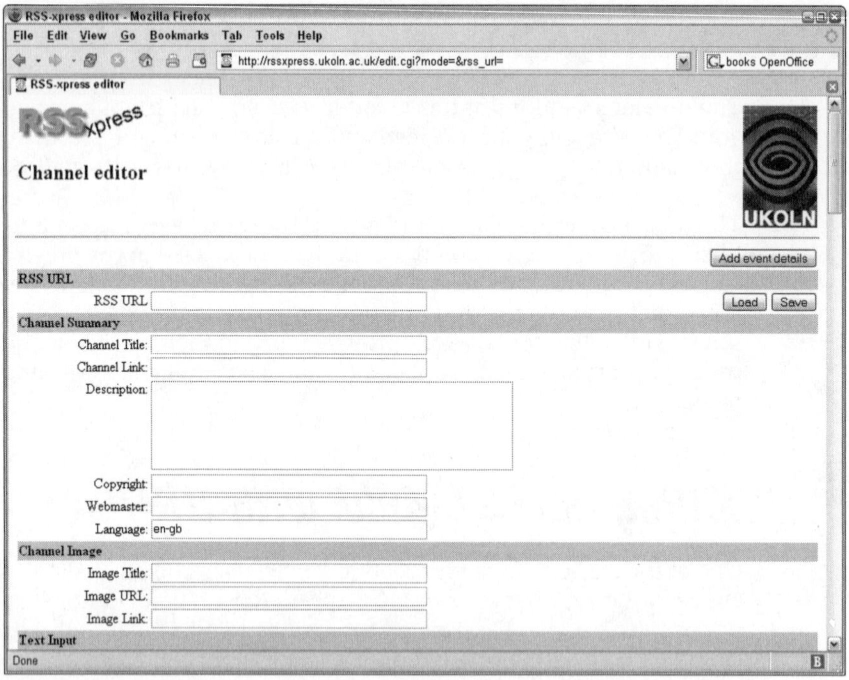

Figure 6-5: UKOLN's channel editor.

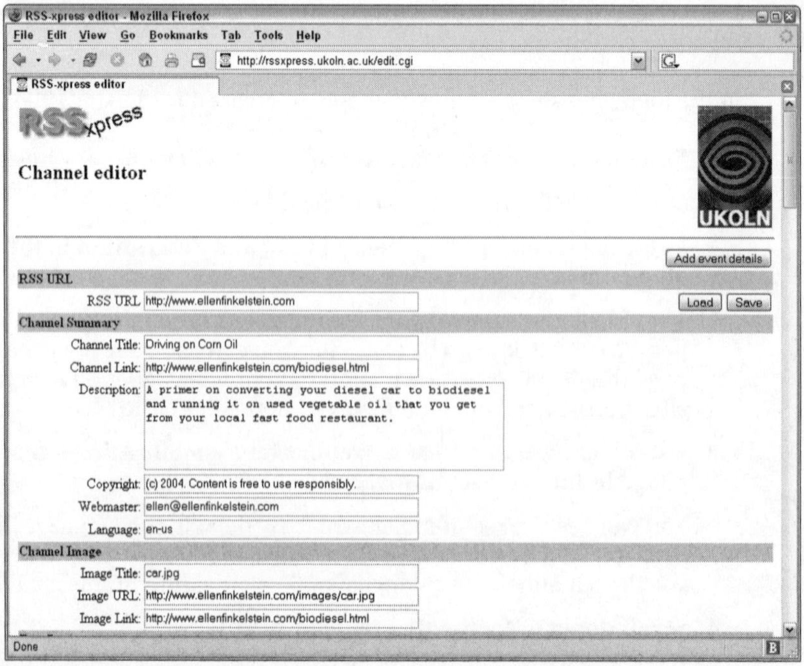

Figure 6-6: The top portion of the channel editor is complete.

5. **In the Item 1 section, enter a title, a link, and a description.**

   The link should be a URL of a location that contains the same content or the full content on your Web site. Include `http://` in the link's URL. The description can be a short account of a full article or the full article itself.

6. **Continue to add more items, up to 15 total, as shown in Figure 6-7.**

7. **Scroll up to the top of the page and click the Save button.**

   A dialog box opens allowing you to download the XML file.

8. **Download the file to a convenient location on your computer, perhaps where you save your other Web site files.**

When you save the file, the default filename is always `rss.xml`. If you are saving a second feed in the same location, the file becomes `rss-1.xml`. These names are not very helpful and could even be confusing. You should therefore rename the file right away before creating a new feed.

Figure 6-8 shows most of the `biodiesel.xml` file. If this is the first time you have seen an RSS 1.0 file, do not despair! RSS 1.0 looks a little more complex than the other versions. That's why you may want to use UKOLN or another service or program to create your files so you don't have to create this type of file from scratch! In Chapter 7, I explain the RSS versions in more detail.

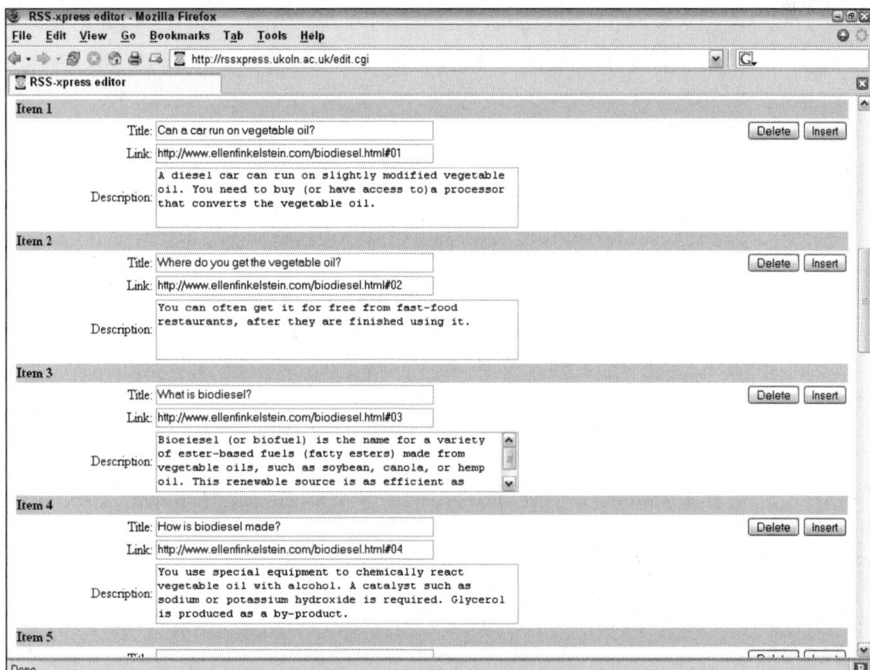

Figure 6-7: Each feed item has a title, link, and description.

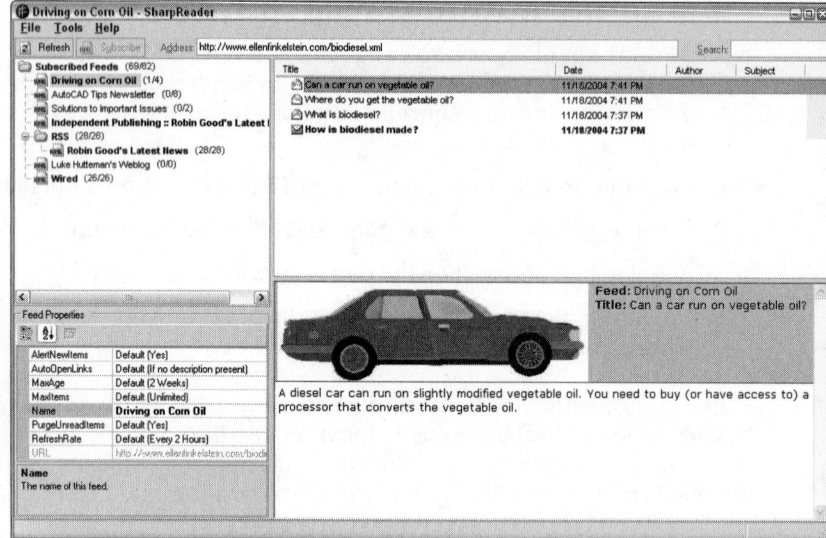

Figure 6-8: The feed created with UKOLN's service in Sharp Reader, an RSS reader.

Figure 6-8 shows you what a feed looks like in a reader. (I made the image too large again!) In the section "Reading Your First Feed," later in this chapter, I explain what you need to do to get your feed into your reader.

Note that although the feed has links to a Web site, I created this feed without creating any Web pages. In other words, the links don't work. I'm pointing this out to emphasize that a feed can have an existence separate from a Web site.

You can use UKOLN to edit your feed as well. See the section "Editing Your Feed," later in this chapter.

Several other on-line tools for creating RSS feeds are available, as follows:

- **WebReference's RSS Channel Editor:** An older tool that creates 0.91 feeds and includes some simple help — you just click a question mark next to an item to display an explanation of that item. Go to `www.webreference.com/cgi-bin/perl/rssedit.pl`.
- **WebDevTip's RSS Headliner:** This tool creates 0.91 RSS feeds. Go to `www.webdevtips.com/webdevtips/codegen/rss.shtml`.
- **IceRocket:** This newer tool creates 2.0 feeds. IceRocket maintains your feed on its server. Go to `http://rss.icerocket.com`.
- **Shared RSS:** This online tool hosts the feed for you. Go to `www.sharedrss.com`.

- **My RSS Creator:** This RSS creation service is very new, as of this writing. It maintains your feed on its server. As far as I know, this online service is the only one that supports enclosures, which are necessary for *podcasting.* (See Chapter 9 for more about podcasting.) This tool also submits your feed to RSS directories. After the 14-day free trial, you pay $19.95 per month. Go to www.myrsscreator.com.

For my list of favorite RSS creation tools, see Chapter 14.

Using NewzAlert Composer

Castlesoftware's NewzAlert Composer is software that you can purchase for $29.95. The company offers a free 15-day trial at www.castlesoftware.biz/NewzAlertComposer.htm. NewzAlert Composer creates RSS 2.0 version feeds. You create the feed in the program and then upload it using the included FTP feature. Composer is one of the few RSS creation tools that supports enclosures, which are necessary for podcasting. In Figure 6-9, you see the main NewzAlert Composer window.

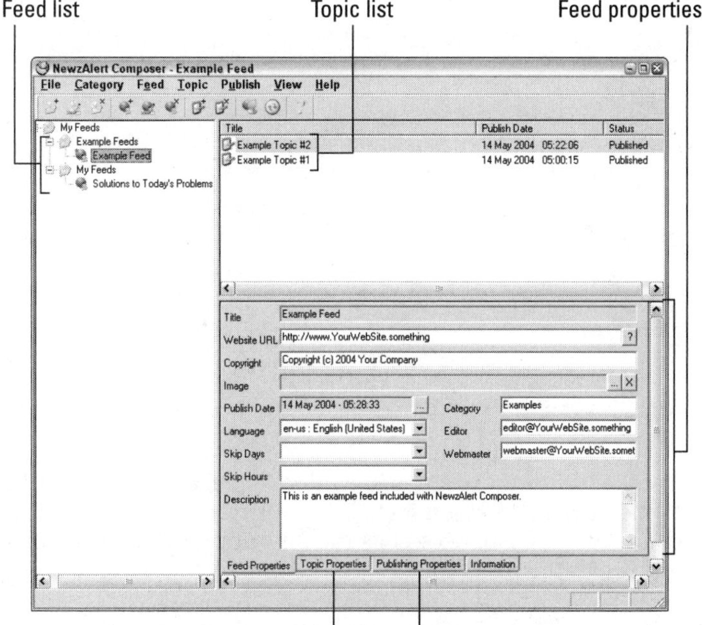

Figure 6-9: NewzAlert Composer is a program for creating 2.0 RSS feeds.

NewzAlert Composer is set up like most RSS readers, using the familiar three panes. The left pane contains the list of your feeds, in case you have several. The top pane shows the items (topics) for the selected feed. The bottom pane has the following four tabs:

- **Feed properties:** Here you see properties that apply to the feed as a whole, including the title, URL, description, image, language, and so on. This corresponds to the channel data that I describe in the section "Relating your feed to your Web site," earlier in this chapter.
- **Topic properties:** This tab contains properties that are specific to the selected topic (item) in the feed. These include the title, link, publish date, and description.
- **Publishing properties:** These properties contain the information necessary to FTP (upload) your feed to your Web site.
- **Information:** This tab contains a brief overview of NewzAlert Composer.

You can use the main window to create a feed on your own or use the wizard shown in Figure 6-10. In the following list, I describe the wizard, which is ideal for first-time users. (The wizard may start automatically the first time you open the program.) You can easily change any information later, using the tabs.

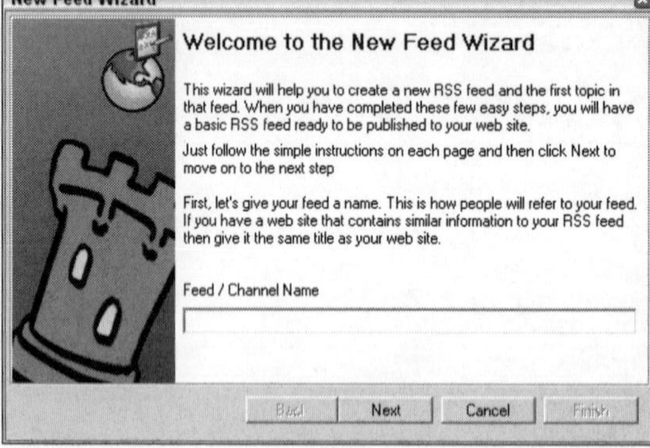

Figure 6-10: Start the NewzAlert wizard by entering the feed title.

To follow along with these steps, download the free trial at the URL given at the outset of this section and install the software by double-clicking the downloaded file. Then double-click the NewzAlert Composer icon on your desktop to open the program.

To create a new RSS feed using the wizard, follow these steps:

1. **Choose File⇨New Feed Wizard.**

   The Welcome panel opens. If the wizard starts automatically, you can skip this step.

2. **Read the explanation and enter your feed title, as shown in Figure 6-11. Click the Next button.**

   In this example, I use the same information as I did for the UKOLN feed. You can compare Figure 6-10 with Figure 6-6. After you click the Next button, you see the Feed Category screen.

3. **In the Feed Category screen, choose a category for your feed from the list provided. For now, just choose the My Feeds category and then click the Next button.**

   The purpose of categories is only to help you organize your feeds. You can create new categories if you have a number of feeds on a variety of topics.

4. **On the Feed Details screen, enter the feed URL and description. Then choose a language from the Language drop-down list, as shown in Figure 6-11. Click the Next button.**

   The feed URL can be your home page or, preferably, a page directly related to the topic of your feed.

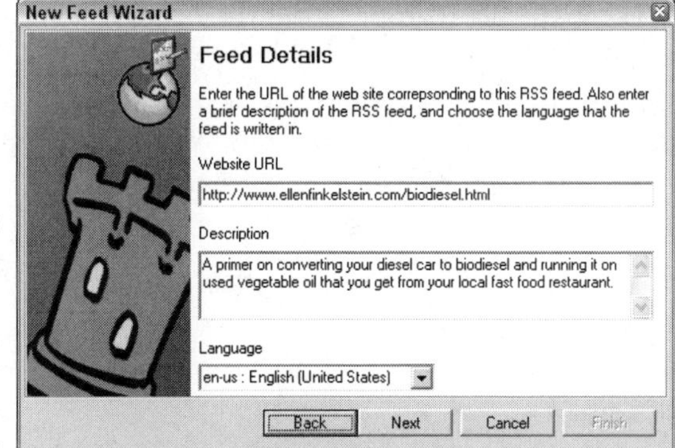

Figure 6-11: Fill in basic details about your feed.

5. **On the second Feed Details screen, fill in an e-mail address for the feed editor and a copyright notice. Click the Next button.**

   You can omit these details if you want.

6. **On the First Topic screen, enter a title, URL, and description, as shown in Figure 6-12. Click the Next button.**

   Compare Figure 6-12 with Figure 6-7, which showed the same information in the UKOLN Channel Editor. A topic in NewzAlert Composer is the same thing as an item in UKOLN.

   The description can contain only a summary of, or introduction to, a fuller topic that you have on the Web site at the location represented by the URL. On the other hand, the description can be the entire item.

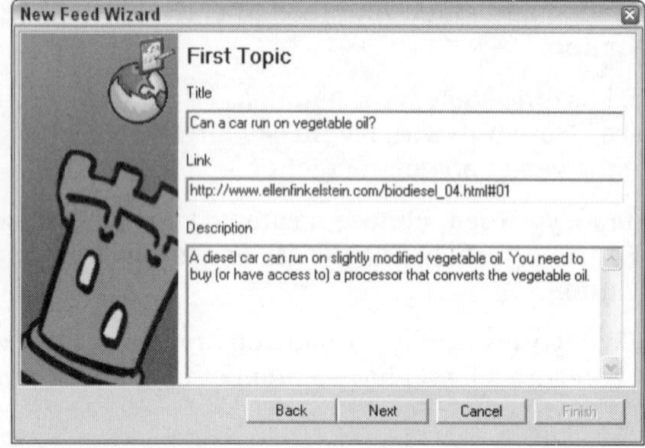

Figure 6-12: The first topic is complete with a title, URL, and description.

7. **On the Publishing Information screen, complete the information you need to upload your feed. This information includes your server name, username, and password. Click the Next button.**

   You also have the option to use the NewzAlert Composer server to host your feed or to save the file on your hard drive and upload it using your own FTP tool. To save the file to your hard drive, choose File on Disk from the Method drop-down list of the Publishing Properties tab.

8. **On the second Publishing Information screen, enter the location where you want to save the RSS feed on your Web server (or Web host's server). Also enter the RSS feed filename, as shown in Figure 6-13. Click the Next button.**

   If you want the file to be in your root folder, just type a forward slash (/).

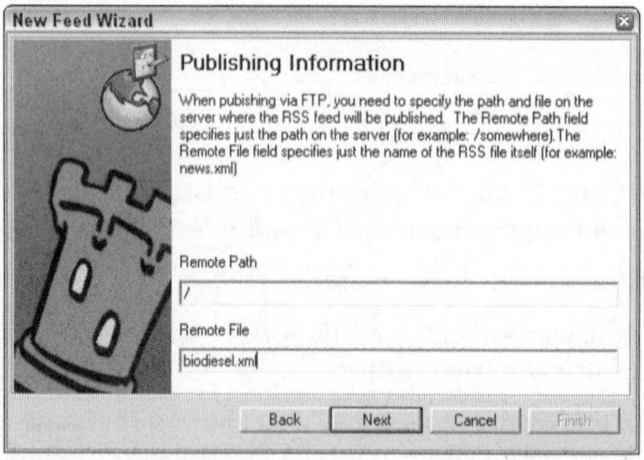

Figure 6-13: You need to specify the location and filename for your feed.

9. **If you're satisfied with the feed, click the Finish button.**

   You can add more items before you upload the feed. I explain the procedure in the section "Editing Your Feed," later in this chapter.

You're done! You can see the result in Figure 6-14. Compare this to Figure 6-8, which shows a similar feed created with UKOLN's tool. In this case, I created only one feed and didn't add an image. You can add an image using the Feed Properties tab.

I explain how to upload the feed in the section "Reading Your First Feed," later in this chapter.

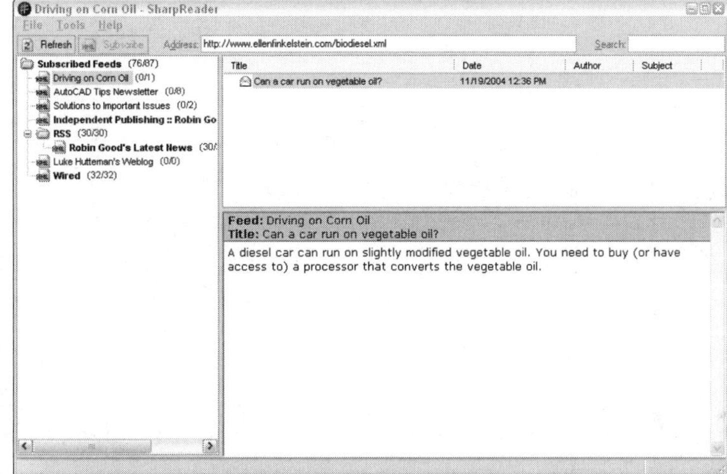

Figure 6-14: My one-item feed viewed in SharpReader.

Using FeedForAll

NotePage's FeedForAll is a direct competitor to NewzAlert Composer. FeedForAll has a few more features and is therefore a little more expensive, at $39.95. To check it out before you buy you can download a 30-day free trial at `www.feedforall.com/download.htm`. FeedForAll also creates 2.0 feeds. Some of the additional features offered by FeedForAll are as follows:

- The ability to repair older feeds
- The ability to export to HTML, CSV (comma-delimited format), or text files
- A simple image editor
- HTML and XML editors

FeedForAll has a wizard, just like NewzAlert Composer. Choose Feed⇨Wizard to start creating your feed with the wizard. Figure 6-15 shows the main FeedForAll screen.

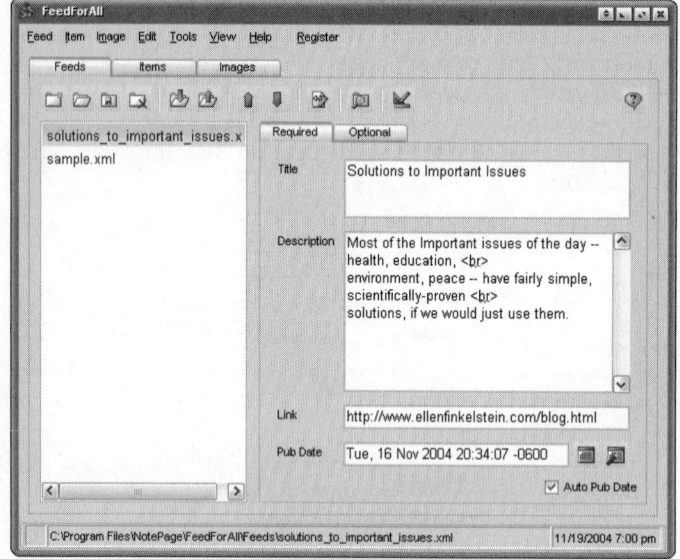

Figure 6-15: NotePage's FeedForAll creates RSS feeds.

You use the three tabs at the top to create and edit feeds, items (the equivalent of NewzAlert's topics,) and images. Choose a feed on the Feeds tab, and then click the Items tab to choose one of the items listed there.

In RSS 2.0, you can add HTML tags in your description to get a more precise result. I wanted to control the line wrapping, so I inserted break tags (`<br>`), as you can see in Figure 6-15.

If you are writing an RSS feed from scratch, you need to be more careful. Any HTML tags that you use must conform to XML rules. In this case, you would need to use the self-closing form of the <br> tag, which is <br />. However, most RSS feed creation tools make this conversion for you.

On both the Feeds and Items tabs, the right pane has Required and Optional tabs, so you can keep it simple or try your hand at some of the more advanced features of RSS 2.0.

A free (and open source) option for creating RSS feeds is ListGarden. Go to `www.softwaregarden.com/products/listgarden` to download this software.

Editing Your Feed — Again and Again

Of course, as you add items, you need to edit your feed to accommodate them. Part of publishing an RSS feed is the constant updating to add new items. Mostly, editing a feed means adding new items and deleting old ones.

Occasionally, you may want to change a feed property. Of course, if you make a mistake, you can always correct it and republish your feed.

If your feed is tightly integrated with your Web site, remember to update your feed whenever you change your Web site. For example, if you add a new tip to your Web site, add it to your RSS feed as well.

RSS readers automatically sense that the feed has changed and display the new feed information. (This feature is one of the wonderful characteristics of RSS feeds. In contrast, if you sent out an incorrect e-mail, you would have to resend it and notify everyone of the mistake.)

Editing feeds and items in UKOLN

To edit a feed in the UKOLN Channel Editor, enter the full URL of the RSS feed and then click the Load button. The feed loads into the form and you can then change it in any way you want. When you've made your changes, save it again.

UKOLN has a major gotcha. If you have loaded a feed with a large number of items and then you load another feed with fewer items, the additional items from the first feed remain in the form. Be careful to delete them by clicking any such item's Delete button before you save your second feed because those items come from a different feed!

Editing feeds and items in NewzAlert Composer or FeedForAll

In both NewzAlert Composer and FeedForAll, to change existing data, you choose your feed from your feed list and make changes in the text boxes.

To add topics in NewzAlert Composer, choose Topic⇨New Topic or click the New Topic button on the toolbar.

To add items in FeedForAll, click the Items tab and choose Item⇨New or click the New Item button.

In both cases, be sure to upload the feed again, as I explain in the next section.

All the RSS-creation tools that I have discussed in this chapter greatly facilitate the creation, editing, and updating of your RSS feeds. The required information is clearly laid out. In the case of Composer and FeedForAll, you also have Help features available in case you have questions.

Reading Your First Feed — Finally!

You've created your first feed, and you're ready to send it out to the world — the World Wide Web, that is — for all your many future subscribers to read. Here's how.

Uploading your RSS feed

Just as you upload your Web pages, you need to upload your RSS feed. The feed is usually a simple text document with an `.xml` filename extension. Depending on the tool you use, you may have a choice to upload from the program or to save to your hard drive and then upload using your own FTP program.

Depending on the program you use, do the following:

- With UKOLN's Channel Editor, click the Save button and download the file to your hard drive. Then upload the file separately, as you would your Web page files.
- With NewzAlert Composer and FeedForAll, you can save to your hard drive or use their FTP feature.

Validating your RSS feed

Your next step is always to check that your feed is valid. A valid feed conforms to very strict XML rules. If your feed is not valid, RSS readers won't be able to display it. Luckily, with most RSS-creation tools, you don't usually have a problem, but occasionally something can come up.

You can use either of the following two free online services to provide the validation you need:

- **Feed Validator for Atom and RSS (**`www.feedvalidator.org`**):** This service is nice because it offers some help when your feed doesn't validate. You can see Feed Validator in Figure 6-16.
- **RSS Validator (**`www.rss.scripting.com`**):** This service is bare-bones, but it works.

I encountered one problem with my UKOLN Channel Editor feed. Apparently, the date was not in an acceptable format. You can see the result of this validation in Feed Validator for Atom and RSS, shown in Figure 6-17.

This site not only shows you where the error is, but it also provides some rudimentary help, usually a link to the source of the format's specification. If you still have a question, it might help to look at some other valid feeds.

Feed Validator for Atom and RSS - Mozilla Firefox
File Edit View Go Bookmarks Tab Tools Help
http://feedvalidator.org/
Feed Validator for Atom and RSS
FEED Validator
FOR ATOM AND RSS
http:// Validate
Now supports Atom 0.3! (more)
Home · About · News · Docs · Terms
Copyright © 2002-4 Mark Pilgrim and Sam Ruby
Find: self-closing Find Next Find Previous Highlight Match case
Done

Figure 6-16: Feed Validator is simplicity incarnate. You'll need no instructions here!

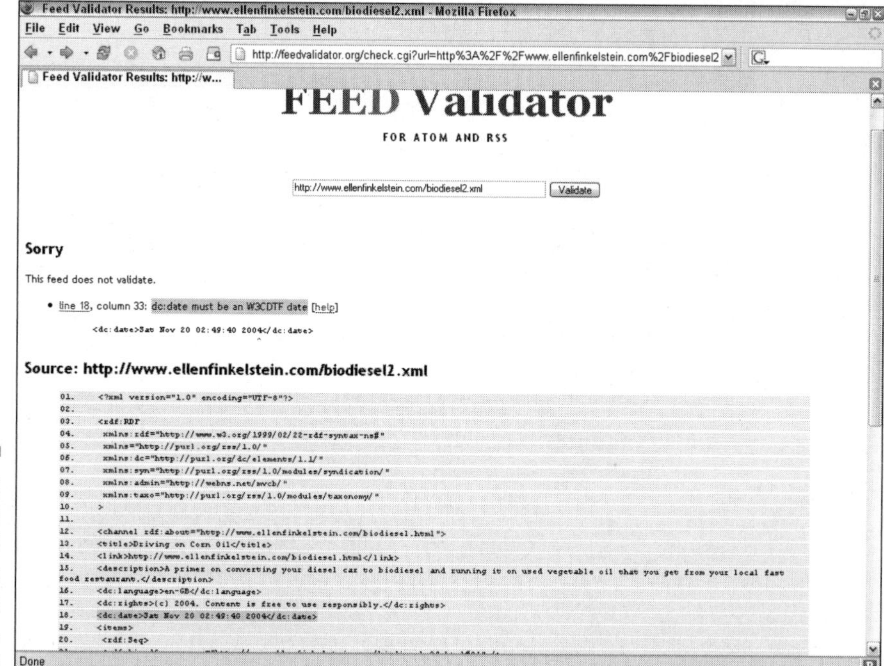

Figure 6-17: If you have an invalid feed, you need to correct it.

Subscribe!

Your feed is uploaded, validated, and ready for prime time. All you need to do is to subscribe to it using your favorite RSS reader. If you've been reading other people's feeds for a while and have just created your own for the first time, you will get quite a thrill seeing your feed in your reader. Remember the first time you saw your Web site in your browser? It's almost like that. You've been published! Anyone can subscribe to your feed now and read your immortal words.

But wait. Who will see your feed if no one knows about it yet? You still have some work to do. In Chapter 10, I explain how to promote your feed so that everyone in the entire world knows about it. Well, almost everyone.

Chapter 7

Creating RSS Feeds from Scratch

In This Chapter

- Understanding the RSS file structure
- Creating your own RSS file
- Testing your feed

If you're the type of person who likes to change the oil in your car, or when you cook noodles you start by mixing the flour and the water, then you like to get things done with your own two hands. If that's the case, you may want to create your RSS feed from scratch. I can promise you that your hands won't get dirty!

Creating an RSS file, which is just a variety of XML file that uses RSS syntax, from scratch is pretty easy. It's a simple text file, so you can use Notepad or any other plain-text editor to create the feed. If you start from a template or existing feed, your job is even easier.

You can also use a special XML editor. Later in this chapter, in the section "Creating Your Own RSS File," I show an example of an XML editor.

First, What is XML?

All RSS files are in XML format. XML stands for Extensible Markup Language. The "Extensible" part means that it is more flexible than HTML. With all its flexibility, XML is still a very specific format and your RSS feeds must follow that format perfectly to be valid.

XML files look a lot like HTML files, and use angled bracket tags. You use the tags to give your data attributes or descriptions. The difference is that in XML, you can make up your own tags, whereas in HTML all possible tags are predefined. An example of a tag in an RSS file is the `<item>` tag, along with its closing `</item>` tag. This tag surrounds each item in your feed.

Another difference between HTML and XML is that HTML describes presentation (the display that you see in your Web browser), whereas XML describes data or content,

Because each component has a tag, you can write programming code that uses these tags to display the content between the tags. In fact, this is exactly what the creators of RSS readers do. You could also create a database from your feed, using the tag names as fields in the database. In other words, by giving data attributes, you can manipulate it in many ways, which makes the data more useful.

The RSS versions are special varieties of XML files, with a specific syntax. By defining a syntax, which is like a grammar, RSS readers and other RSS-related programs can know what type of data to expect inside a certain tag and can reliably use the data to display your RSS feed. Without this syntax, a program would not be able to display your feed properly. The RSS reader can also check for changes within any feed by looking inside the relevant tags.

Understanding the RSS File Structure

In fact, the only difference between creating an RSS feed from scratch and using one of the services or programs that I mention in Chapter 6 is that you need to type the tags that define each component.. Typing the tags is not very hard when you understand the syntax of the version of RSS that you are using. If you want to use some of the extended capabilities of RSS, your job is a bit more complex. In this chapter, I keep things simple and provide you with some resources to help you if you want to dig deeper into extended capabilities.

If you are a programmer and want more technical details, a good start is to go to the O'Reilly XML.com site, and read an article called "What is RSS?" (`www.xml.com/pub/a/2002/12/18/dive-into-xml.html`).

Declaring the XML version and encoding

Because the RSS file is an XML file, it is good form, but not necessary, to declare the XML version (which at this time is always 1.0) at the top, as shown here:

```
<?xml version="1.0"?>
```

In addition, you can optionally declare the type of *encoding* that you are using. Encoding basically defines how each character that you type should be interpreted. You may think that an *a* is an *a,* but what if the language is Russian? If you don't include information about encoding, an RSS reader makes an assumption based on an assumed default.

Two common types of encoding are iso-8859-1, which is the Latin/West European character set, and UTF-8 (or UTF-16), which is a form of *Unicode*. Unicode is a character set that allows the representation of a wide range of languages. Here's an example of a declaration at the top of the file that includes both the XML version and the encoding information:

```
<xml version="1.0" encoding="iso-8859-1"?>
```

If you omit the declaration, you can expect the RSS reader to assume that you have used a UTF-8 encoding. UTF-8 encoding is a good choice if you're not sure which one to use.

Dealing with illegal characters

Certain characters are reserved by XML format for its own purposes. For example, the < and > characters are used to surround tags. If you use one of these characters in the content part of your news feed, your feed can't validate. You need to *escape* these characters (and you thought you were trying to get to it, not away from it). To escape means to use a workaround so that you don't have to use the character. Table 7-1 shows the illegal characters in XML and what you need to type to display them.

Table 7-1 Illegal XML Characters and How to Escape Them

Plain-Text XML	*Encoding*
&	&
<	<
>	>
' (apostrophe / single quote)	'
" (double quote)	"

Don't forget to include the semicolon after each escape character.

Beware of using the ampersand (&) and the apostrophe (') in your headings! These two characters are common and can easily invalidate your feed.

For example, if you want your title to read "Bicycles & More," you would type the following:

```
Bicycles &amp; More
```

Choosing a file type

When you save your file, you need to decide which file type extension to use. Most RSS feeds use an XML file type, which means that you name the file something like `myfeed.xml` when you save it. However, you may be able to use an RSS file type (myfeed.rss), which would make some sense. RSS readers don't have any trouble with an RSS file type, but your Web host may not allow it (mine doesn't). Also, you want to make sure that browsers treat the RSS file properly. When a potential subscriber clicks your RSS or XML button, you want the browser to open the file and display it on-screen. When browsers have to deal with an unknown file type, they may instead open a dialog box asking if you want to download the file. This will confuse people to no end. If you want to use an RSS file type, test it carefully.

If you are using RSS 1.0, you can also use an RDF file type. The filename would be something like `myfeed.rdf`. Again, make sure that your Web host and typical browsers handle this file type properly.

Staying simple with RSS version 0.91

If you're writing a feed for the first time, I recommend starting with RSS version 0.91. All readers read 0.91, and it's the simplest of all the RSS versions. If you're knowledgeable about XML, you may find all versions easy, but for the rest of us, 0.91 is definitely the place to start. You can always change versions later. Switching from 0.91 to 2.0 is especially easy. I used 0.91 when I created my first feeds (which is why I am definitely not objective).

Looking at the 0.91 structure

Listing 7-1 is a simple template for RSS 0.91. You can download this template at `www.dummies.com/go/syndicatingwsfd`. This template includes only the most basic tags, although additional tags may be included. For a description of most of the additional tags, see the section "Additional optional channel (feed) elements" in Chapter 6.

For the official document that specifies RSS version 0.91, go to `http://backend.userland.com/rss091`.

Listing 7-1: RSS Version 0.91 Template

```
<rss version="0.91">
  <channel>
    <title>The Name of Your Feed</title>
    <link>http://www. put_website_url_here.com</link>
    <description>Feed description</description>
    <language>en-us (or other language)</language>
    <item>
```

```
      <title>Title of First Item</title>
      <link>http://www. put_website_url_here.com</link>
      <description>The item 1 content.</description>
    </item>
    <item>
      <title>Title of Second Item</title>
      <link>http://www. put_website_url_here.com</link>
      <description>The item 2 content.</description>
    </item>
  </channel>
</rss>
```

In Chapter 6, in the section "Relating your feed to your Web site," I explain the terms used in the tags of RSS version 0.91. However, even without that explanation, you can understand the bare-bones structure of the feed template, which is as follows:

1. **Declare the RSS version, using the `<rss>` tag and the version attribute in the format shown in Listing 7-1.**

   As I explain in the section "Declaring the XML version and encoding," earlier in this chapter, you can optionally declare the XML version before you declare the RSS version.

2. **Use the `<channel>` tag.**
3. **Use the `<title>`, `<link>`, and `<description>` tags to provide information about the feed as a whole. The `<language>` tag is optional.**

   End each tag with its closing tag: `</title>`, `</link>`, `</description>`, and `</language>`.

4. **Start each item with the `<item>` tag.**
5. **Within each item, add a title, link, and description, each enclosed in tags of the same name.**
6. **End each item with the `</item>` tag.**
7. **When you finish adding your items, end the channel with the `</channel>` tag.**
8. **End the feed with the `</rss>` tag.**

If you use the text shown in Listing 7-1, you get a valid RSS feed (if you are careful with special characters and if you validate it; see the section "Validating your RSS feed" in Chapter 6 for instructions on how to do this). Your URLs don't need to work or be real.

Figure 7-1 shows the result of using this feed. On the left, you see the RSS feed itself in Notepad. (Notepad is ideal because it doesn't insert any non-text characters.) On the right, you see the feed after I've uploaded it and subscribed to it in my RSS reader.

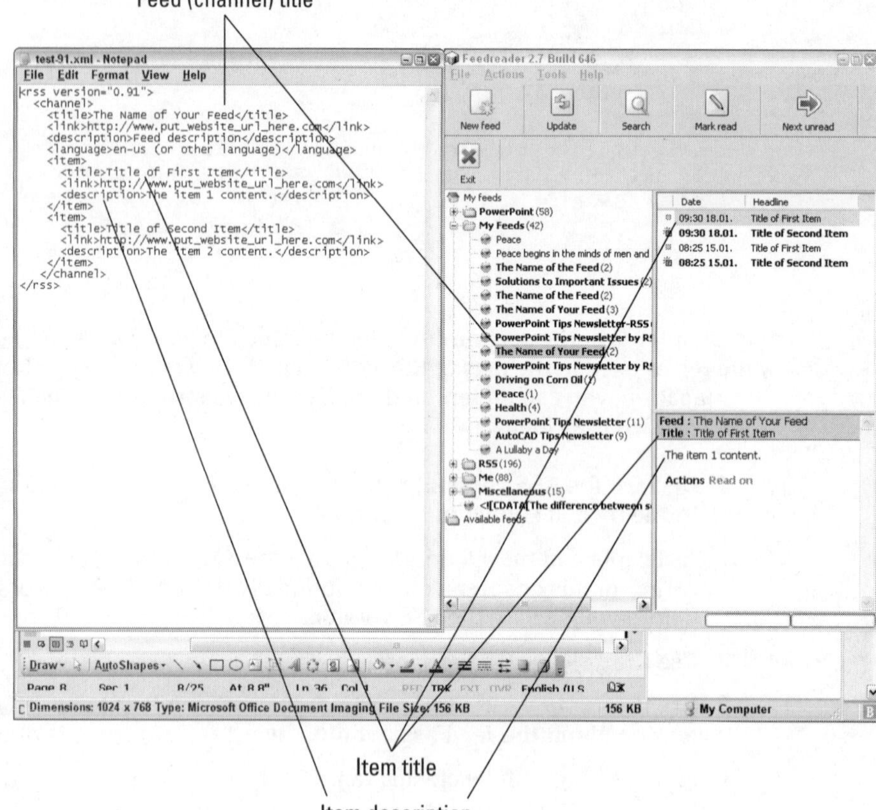

Figure 7-1: This template creates a very boring feed. Hopefully, you'll find something more interesting to say!

You can't have more than 15 items in a channel in a 0.91 version RSS feed. I suppose that way back then (in 1999), people didn't write as much as they do today! The latest version, 2.0, removes this restriction.

Using the 0.91 template

You can use a template to create your own feed. You just need to edit the content between the tags. To use this template, follow these steps:

1. **Download the template from** `www.dummies.com/go/syndicatingwsfd`.
2. **Open the template in Notepad or another text editor.**

   Don't use a word processor that adds code to text. Certain formatting, such as new line characters and smart quotes, is not acceptable. You can use a word processor if you are careful to save your file in a text-only format.

You may customarily use Macromedia Dreamweaver or another Web site creation program to create text files that relate to your Web site. However, these programs may expect HTML instead of XML and may remove some of your tags!

3. **Change the content between the tags.**
4. **Save the file as an XML file.**

   For example, save the file as `myfirstfeed.xml`.
5. **Upload the file to your Web site.**
6. **Validate the feed.**

   See the section "Validating your RSS feed" in Chapter 6 for instructions. If your feed doesn't validate, edit it, save it, and upload it. Test the file again (and again, if necessary) until it validates.
7. **Open your RSS reader and subscribe to your feed.**

   When you enter the feed URL in your RSS reader, you would use `http://www.myfirstfeed.xml` if you uploaded the file to the root directory of your Web site.

That's all there is to it! You should now be able to read your feed in your reader. Of course, you probably want to add an RSS button that links to the XML file. Then people can subscribe to the feed from your Web site.

Maintaining your RSS feed

After you have published your feed, you just edit the XML file in your text editor to make changes. For example, to delete an item, delete all the content from an `<item>` tag through an `</item>` tag.

To add an item to the feed, follow these steps:

1. **In Notepad or your XML editor, select an existing item, including both the `<item>` and `</item>` tags.**
2. **Copy the text to the Clipboard and paste it wherever you want it.**
3. **Edit the content between the tags.**
4. **Follow Steps 4 through 6 of the previous list to save, upload, and validate your feed.**
5. **Open your RSS reader and refresh your feeds.**

   You should see the changes you just made reflected immediately.

Remember that you probably don't make that many changes to your feed — perhaps one or two a day. Using a template and a text editor is easy enough in this situation. After all, if you used one of the RSS-creation programs that I discuss in Chapter 6, you would still have to delete any unwanted items, type new items, save, upload, and validate. The RSS-creation programs provide more of a structure because of their interface, but the actual steps are about the same.

Graduating to RSS version 1.0

RSS version 1.0 is completely different from version 0.91. RSS 1.0 is an RDF file. RDF is a type of XML file that was developed to represent information about data on the Web. RDF is perfectly suited for RSS feeds and provides some tools that some developers like.

In Chapter 1, in the sidebar "How RSS started," I discuss the history of RSS versions, including some information on RDF and version 1.0.

An in-depth discussion of RDF is beyond the scope of this book. If you want more information about RDF in general, go to `www.w3.org/RDF`, `www.w3.org/TR/rdf-primer/`, and `www.xml.com/pub/a/2001/01/24/rdf.html`. For details on RDF specifically for RSS feeds, go to the official specification for RSS version 1.0 at `web.resource.org/rss/1.0`.

Listing 7-2 shows the same RSS feed as Listing 7-1, but in version 1.0 format. You can download this template at `www.dummies.com/go/syndicatingwsfd`.

Listing 7-2: RSS Version 1.0

```
<rdf:RDF
  xmlns:rdf="http://www.w3.org/1999/02/22-rdf-syntax-ns#"
  xmlns="http://purl.org/rss/1.0/"
  xmlns:dc="http://purl.org/dc/elements/1.1/">
  <channel rdf:about="http://www. put_website_url_here.com">
    <title>The Name of the Feed</title>
    <link>http://www. put_website_url_here.com</link>
    <description>Feed description.</description>
    <language>en-us</language>
    <items>
      <rdf:Seq>
        <rdf:li rdf:resource="http://www.
            put_website_url_here.com/page1.html" />
        <rdf:li rdf:resource="http://www.
            put_website_url_here.com/page2.html" />
      </rdf:Seq>
    </items>
  </channel>
  <item rdf:about="http://www.
            put_website_url_here.com/page1.html">
    <title>Title of First Item</title>
```

```
    <link>http://www. put_website_url_here.com</link>
    <description>The item 1 content.</description>
    <dc:creator>Author</dc:creator>
    <dc:date>yyyy-mm-dd</dc:date>
  </item>
  <item rdf:about="http://www.yoursite.com/page2.html">
    <title>Title of Second Item</title>
    <link>http://www. put_website_url_here.com</link>
    <description>The item 2 content.</description>
    <dc:creator>Author</dc:creator>
    <dc:date>yyyy-mm-dd</dc:date>
  </item>
</rdf:RDF>
```

If you use the text shown in Listing 7-2, you get a valid RSS feed — except that you need to add a valid date in place of `yyyy-mm-dd`.

Figure 7-2 shows this feed in Feedreader. The feed looks the same as you see in Figure 7-1, except that the feed indicates the author because the template includes that information.

Obviously, the version 1.0 feed is more complex looking and longer than the version 0.91 feed. Notice that at the beginning, between the `<items>` and `</items>` tags (notice the plural), the two items are listed together, before being specified individually. This section defines the order of the items. RSS version 1.0 offers the following special features, which you can see used in this template:

- **The addition of the author and publishing date for each item:** Version 0.91 does not support this information. This is a feature of one of version 1.0's extensions, Dublin Core.
- **The listing of sources for the syntax of the code:** These listings are called *namespaces.* The namespaces are the first three URLs in the template.
- **A different placing for the `<channel>` tag:** The `<channel>` tag closes before the items are listed, rather than at the end of the items. This isn't especially significant — it's just a difference in the structure of version 1.0.

The process for using the version 1.0 template is the same as for version 0.91. You still create your feed in a text editor and edit it in the same way. For details, see the previous section in this chapter.

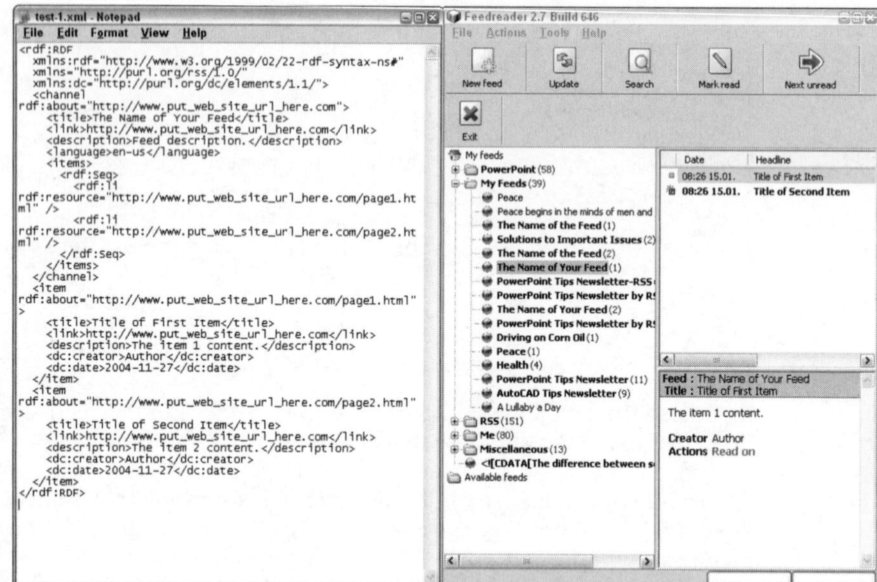

Figure 7-2: The version 1.0 template in Feed-reader.

Getting current with RSS version 2.0

The most recent version of RSS (not including Atom) is version 2.0. Version 2.0 is a direct descendent of 0.91 and is not an RDF format. Version 2.0 offers some new features compared to 0.91 that developers asked for. Some of these new features are as follows:

- **The `<guid>` (Global Unique Identifier) tag.**

  This tag uniquely identifies each item, in case two different items exist with the same name and content. It also helps a reader avoid presenting the same item more than once. The GUID is usually a permalink but doesn't have to be. (For more about permalinks, see the sidebar "What is a permalink?" in Chapter 6.) The `<guid>` tag has an attribute, `isPermaLink`, that can be true or false. Set it to false if you are not using a permalink for your GUID, as follows:

  ```
  <guid isPermaLink="false">2004-11-30-01</guid>
  ```

- **Explicit provision for namespaces.**

  I explain namespaces in the previous section of this chapter.

- **The `<enclosure>` tag.**

The tag is the source of much excitement in the RSS world because it allows you to attach a media item, such as an MP3 file. You need the following three attributes:

- `url`: The location of the enclosure
- `length`: The size in bytes
- `type`: The type of file, which must be a standard MIME type

An example of the enclosure tag is as follows:

```
<enclosure url="http://www.yoursite.com/sounds/sky.mp3"
        length="5588242" type="audio/mpeg"/>
```

- **An** `<author>` **tag so that individual items can specify different authors.**
- **A** `<category>` **tag so that you can assign a category to each item.**

Furthermore, version 2.0 does not have a 15-item limit per channel, as does version 0.91.

For more information on the official details of the RSS version 2.0 format, go to `.blogs.law.harvard.edu/tech/rss`.

Listing 7-3 shows the same RSS feed I've used for Listings 7-1 and 7-2, but in version 2.0 format. I've used some of the additional tags in this version. You can download this template at `www.dummies.com/go/syndicatingwsfd`.

Listing 7-3: RSS Version 2.0

```
<rss version="2.0">
<channel>
  <title>The Name of the Feed</title>
  <link>http://www. put_website_url_here.com</link>
  <description>Feed Description.</description>
  <language>en-us</language>
  <copyright>Copyright notice</copyright>
  <pubDate>Tue, 30 Nov 2004 13:43:03 CST</pubDate>
  <lastBuildDate>Tue, 7 Dec 2004 09:41:01 CST</lastBuildDate>
<managingEditor>you@domain.com</managingEditor>
<webMaster>webmaster@domain.com</webMaster>
  <item>
    <title>Title of First Item</title>
    <link>http://www.put_website_url_here.com</link>
    <description>The item 1 content.</description>
    <author>you@domain.com</author>
    <pubDate>Tue, 30 Nov 2004 13:43:02 CST</pubDate>
    <enclosure url="http://www. put_website_url_here.com/
          filename.mp3" length="0001" type="audio/mpeg"/>
    <guid isPermaLink="false">id_01</guid>
  </item>
  <item>
```

Listing 7-3: *(continued)*

```
    <title>Title of Second Item</title>
    <link>http://www. put_website_url_here.com</link>
    <description>The item 2 content.</description>
    <author>You@domain.com</author>
    <pubDate>Tue, 30 Nov 2004 13:50:02 CST</pubDate>
    <enclosure url="http://www. put_website_url_here.com/
          filename.mp3" length="0001" type="audio/mpeg"/>
    <guid isPermaLink="false">id_02</guid>
  </item>
</channel>
</rss>
```

The above feed validates, but of course you should replace the existing dates and times with current dates and times. Also, if you include an enclosure, be sure to use actual data for the files you're enclosing. Figure 7-3 shows this feed.

You can find permitted formats for the date in the `<pubDate>` tag at `asg.web.cmu.edu/rfc/rfc822.html#sec-5`. Look for the section on "Date and Time Specification." Most RSS-creation tools automatically create this tag for you based on your computer's clock.

As you can see, version 2.0 is not much different from version 0.9, except that version 2.0 has more tag options. The channel only requires the title, link, and description tags. Each item must have a title or a description, but if you include the entire text in your description, you don't need a link. Note that you can put HTML coding into your item descriptions (with the required escape codes as described in Table 7-1), as in the following example:

```
<description>What's important is
          &lt;b&gt;you!&lt;/b&gt;</description>
```

This code looks pretty fierce, but the result would simply look like the following:

```
What's important is you!
```

In HTML, this would look like the following:

```
What's important is <b>you!</b>
```

In other words, you have to escape the angled brackets by including the appropriate substitute.

To use the 2.0 template, follow the same procedure I describe in the section "Using RSS version 0.91," earlier in this chapter.

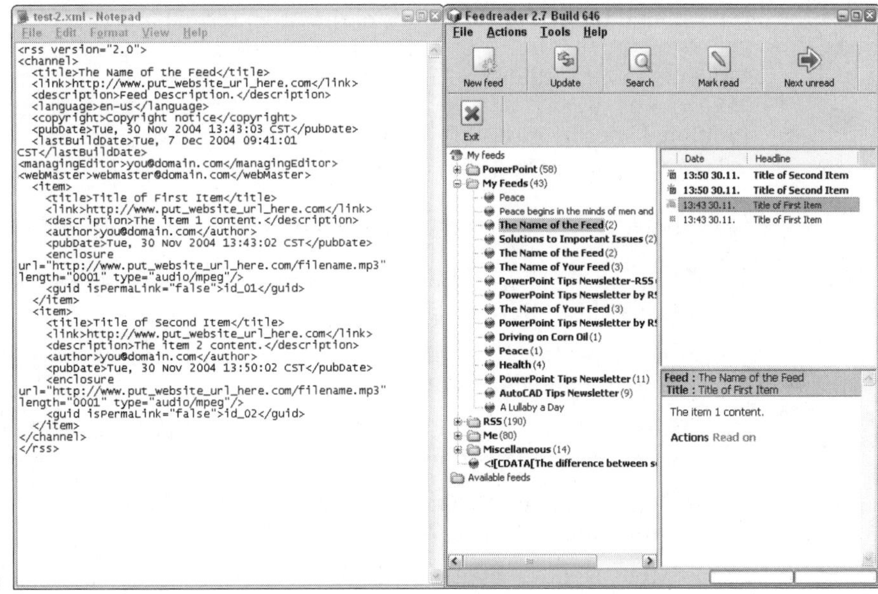

Figure 7-3: The version 2.0 feed in Notepad and Feedreader.

If you want to take RSS 2.0 to the max, read "Looking for the perfect feed: RSS 2.0 Templates" This article by Mike Golding is the clearest I've read on the topic. The article starts with a bare-bones 2.0 feed, using only required tags, and then moves on to explain more complex options that include namespaces and reference the Dublin Core and Syndication modules. Go to `www.notestips.com/80256B3A007F2692/1/NAMO5P9UPQ`.

Splitting the Atom

Talking about Atom can be confusing. What do you call it? Technically, it's a news feed but not an RSS feed, but "RSS" has become a general term for news feed. You can say that an Atom feed is another syndication format.

As far as I'm concerned, you can call it whatever you want as long as you understand that the two formats are different — and I'll probably do the same.

Not to be outdone, Atom has version numbers, too. The current version is 0.3. Like true RSS feeds, an Atom feed is an XML file. The tags have slightly different names, but the basic idea is the same. You have to give credit to RSS readers that can read all versions of RSS plus Atom, given the fact that each version is slightly different and needs to be interpreted accordingly.

You can find the technical details of the Atom format at www.ietf.org/proceedings/04aug/I-D/draft-ietf-atompub-format-01.txt. A slightly more readable specification is at www.atomenabled.org/developers/syndication/atom-format-spec.php. You can read additional specifications of the values allowed for some of the tags at bitworking.org/projects/atom/draft-gregorio-09.html.

Some of the main differences between RSS 2.0 and Atom are as follows:

- RSS news items are called items, whereas in Atom they're called entries and use the <entry> tag.
- Atom feeds don't use the <channel> tag, which is just as well, because it doesn't really have any purpose.
- Instead of using a <guid> tag, in Atom you use an <id> tag to uniquely identify each entry (item).
- In Atom, you refer to a namespace to identify allowable tags, as shown in the third line of Listing 7-4.
- In Atom, all links must include the rel, type, and href attributes. See Listing 7-4 for examples. The rel tag is always "alternate", the type tag is almost always "text/html", and the href tag is the URL for the link.

Listing 7-4 shows an Atom feed template you can use like you use the previous listings in this chapter. You can download this template at www.dummies.com/go/syndicatingwsfd.

Listing 7-4: An Atom Feed

```
<feed
     version="0.3"
     xmlns="http://purl.org/atom/ns#"
     xml:lang="en-us">
   <title>The Name of the Feed</title>
   <link
      rel="alternate"
      type="text/html"
      href="http://www. put_website_url_here.com"/>
    <modified>2004-11-30T18:30:02Z</modified>
    <author>
      <name>You</name>
      <email>you@domain.com</email>
    </author>
    <copyright>Copyright 2004</copyright>
    <entry>
       <title>Title of First Item</title>
       <link
          rel="alternate"
          type="text/html"
          href="http://www. put_website_url_here.com"/>
```

```
        <id>tag:yoursite.com,2004:3.2397</id>
        <issued>2004-11-29T08:29:29-04:00</issued>
        <modified>2004-11-30T18:30:02Z</modified>
        <content>"The item 1 content.</content>
      </entry>
      <entry>
        <title>Title of Second Item</title>
        <link
           rel="alternate"
           type="text/html"
           href="http://www. put_website_url_here.com"/>
        <id>tag:domain.com,2003:3.2398</id>
        <issued>2004-11-28T08:29:29-04:00</issued>
        <modified>2004-11-29T18:30:02Z</modified>
        <content>"The item 1 content.</content>
      </entry>
</feed>
```

This feed validates, but of course you should update the dates and times.

Overall, although the Atom format is more verbose and complex than RSS 2.0, you should find it understandable and familiar — after looking at all those other RSS formats! Figure 7-4 shows this feed in Notepad and, after I validated and uploaded it in Feedreader.

To use the 2.0 template, follow the same procedure I describe in the section "Using RSS version 0.91," earlier in this chapter.

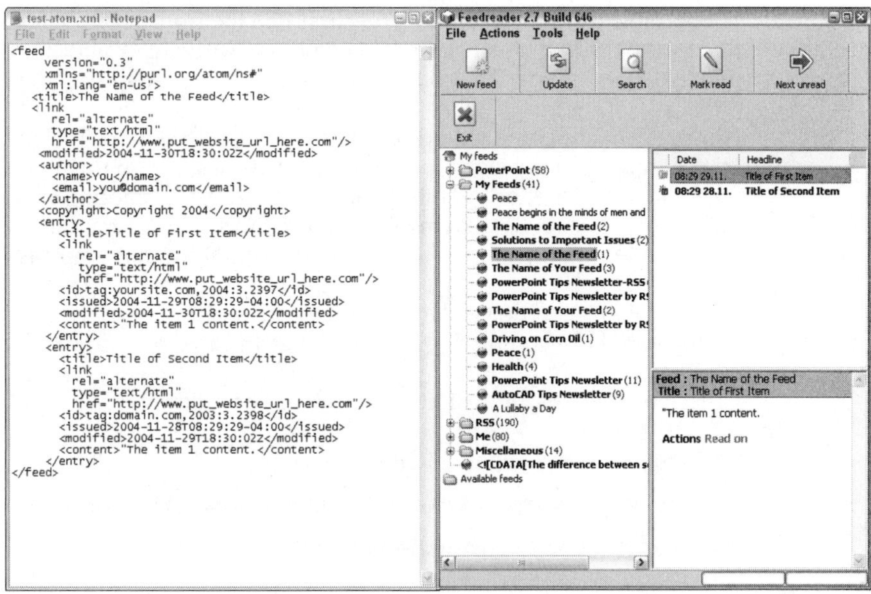

Figure 7-4: An Atom feed in Feedreader.

What difference does it make?

By now, you may have realized that regardless of the format, feeds look about the same in an RSS reader. As a matter of fact, the differences are more important to developers of the readers than to the people who create the feeds. Developers are trying to include features that publishers will find useful, but when you're starting out, you mostly want to choose a format that is easy to work with.

If you use an online service or program, as I discuss in Chapter 6, or an automated method, which I cover in Chapter 8, you simply use whatever your tool creates. End of story. But if you want to create your files from scratch, you obviously have more choice. If you're a developer, you can scrutinize the specifications of the various versions and decide which version is best for you.

If you simply want to make sure that everyone can read your feed, choose RSS version 0.91 or 2.0. No self-respecting RSS reader fails to read those — and I've never found one that didn't respect itself. For the ultimate in simplicity, use version 0.91. To be sure that you're up to date and can most easily make the transition to more features, should you decide to add them later on, choose RSS version 2.0.

Creating Your Own RSS File

You've analyzed the various RSS versions and decided on the one you want to use. Now it's time to create your first RSS file from scratch. Some people like to start with a clean slate. You can open Notepad or another text editor and just start typing. That blank white page may be inspiring to you.

However, most people would probably prefer a little help. Typing an RSS file from scratch is just asking for little syntax errors to pop up all over the place, which means you'll be spending lots of time troubleshooting when you try to validate your feed. So take my word for it: Start with a template or an existing feed, and let your inspiration focus on your content, not your tags.

An XML editor can be very helpful. The XML editor color-codes your tags, for example, to help you distinguish your tags from your content.

Other common features of XML editors are as follows:

- Indenting and aligning tags
- Showing the structure of the XML in a hierarchical format
- Allowing you to customize the font

An easy-to-use freeware XML editor is firstobject XML Editor, shown in Figure 7-5. You can download this XML editor at `www.firstobject.com/dn_editor.htm`.

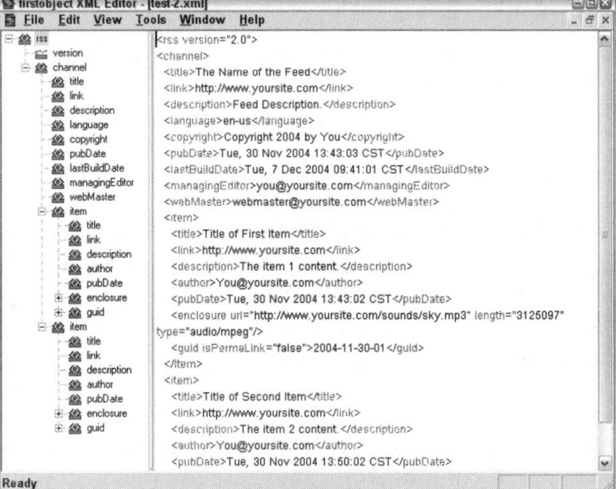

Figure 7-5: You can use an XML editor, such as firstobject XML Editor, to create your RSS feeds.

Because Figure 7-5 is shown in black and white, I should probably explain that the tag names and attributes are in red, the angled brackets are in blue, and the content is in black on-screen. Viewing your feed in color in this way helps you spot problems more quickly.

Starting from a template

A template is a good way to start, because it's simple and the content usually functions as a hint to tell you what goes between which tags. I've made the templates in this chapter available on the Dummies Web site. For the specific files, see the section for each RSS format earlier in this chapter.

Download the template and open it in your text editor. Immediately choose File⇨Save As and save the file as a new XML file, using the name that you want for your feed. This procedure leaves the template unchanged so that you can use it again for your next feed — and your next, and your next.

If your Web host requires that filenames have no spaces, remember not to add spaces to your filename when you save. Using an underscore (_) can help make the filename readable while avoiding spaces.

Now, go through your feed and change the boilerplate to your own content. To add an item (or entry, if you're using Atom) based on an existing item, follow these steps:

1. **Select and copy one of the existing items (or entries) — including both the beginning and ending tags.**
2. **Place your cursor where you want the new item, usually after the last existing item.**
3. **Paste the text.**
4. **Edit the content for your new item (or entry).**

After you've added lots of items, you may want to delete some. Usually, you delete the earliest entries because they get out of date. They're probably in order, but you may find publish and modified dates useful to help you figure out what you wrote when. Just select the items you no longer want and delete them. All gone!

Deleting an item doesn't affect your Web page, where the item may also reside. However, if you have a system of permalinks and you have a Web page that matches your feed content, you can delete the items on your main Web page but leave the items on their own page at their permalink URL.

For more information on permalinks, see the sidebar "What is a permalink?" in Chapter 4. If you don't use permalinks, what you do with a Web page that contains the same content as your feed is up to you. You may want to archive your older content in some way (which is one purpose of permalinks).

My templates don't include every possible tag and include some tags that you may want to delete. To find out which tags are required and which are optional, look at the specifications or simply experiment. If you take out a tag and your feed doesn't validate, you know that the tag is required.

Using existing feeds as an example

Another method for creating a feed is to use an existing feed as an example. You can easily find zillions of feeds by looking in one of the RSS directories. (Chapter 15 provides a good list.) Click some RSS or XML buttons and open the XML file. Find one that you understand and that uses many of the tags that you want to use. Then copy and paste the file to your own text editor or XML editor and use it as a template.

When you use an existing feed, remember to change *all* the content. For example, be sure to change any dates. Often the person who originally wrote the feed used a program that created the dates automatically. The date and time formats are somewhat complex — they include seconds! They also want your time zone. Sometimes the time zone is written as the number of hours plus or minus GMT (Greenwich Mean Time). The specification for each of the versions provides a syntax (or a link to one) for dates. In each section of this chapter where I've discussed the individual versions of RSS and Atom, I've provided links where you can find the specifications.

An existing feed may use tags that you don't need or may omit tags that you want to use. Of course, the same is true of a template. Look at several existing feeds to see how they use tags and how the tags appear in your reader. Then decide which ones are important to you.

Taking Your Feed for a Test Drive

You've completed your first feed from scratch. Congratulations! Now you want to get it out there in cyberspace so that people can read it. Look it over carefully, and see whether you can find any errors or omissions. When you think it's perfect, you're ready for the next step.

Make sure that you've saved the file. You'll probably save the XML file where you save your Web files, or you may choose to create a separate folder for the file. Then back up the file in the same way that you back up your Web files. (You *do* back up your files, don't you?)

Uploading your RSS file

To test your feed, you need to upload it to your Web site. At this point, you don't need to make any changes to your Web site pages. You just want to make sure that your feed works. Upload the file to the folder on your Web site where you want to keep your feeds. You can organize your feeds in a separate folder or put them with their corresponding Web pages — just be consistent.

If you use Microsoft FrontPage, Macromedia Dreamweaver, or other Web-page software and you usually upload pages using that program, you can do the same for your feeds. If you usually use an FTP program to upload files, you can use that program for your RSS feed, if you prefer.

Validating your feed

The next step is to validate your feed. Validating simply means to make sure that the file complies with XML and RSS rules. Do not do anything else before validating your feed! (Do not pass Go. Do not collect $200. And absolutely do not link to it from your Web site or register it with any RSS directories.) If you are creating feeds from scratch, the possibility of errors increases dramatically, especially the first time you create a feed.

In the section "Validating your RSS feed" in Chapter 6, I provide a couple of free validation Web-based tools that you can use. Use them! If your feed doesn't validate, you need to correct it. Some feed validators provide an explanation of what might be wrong. Even if you use a feed validator that provides such an explanation, you may still have trouble figuring out the problem. A computer program is analyzing your feed, not a person. And guess what? — computer programs can be pretty dumb sometimes! For example, if you forget to add the > symbol at the end of a tag, the validator thinks that everything else in your feed is inside the tag and goes wild. With a little persistence, you'll soon have a perfect feed, as shown in Figure 7-6.

Figure 7-6: Ahhh, the joys of a valid feed.

Troubleshooting feed problems

If you have problems getting your feed to validate, you're not alone. Here are some tips that I picked up during my efforts:

- Close all tags.
- Check exact tag names, for example, `<pubDate>`, which needs that uppercase D.
- Check the date syntax.
- Only use tags in the specification; if you add a namespace; only use those allowed in the namespace.
- Use the simplest text editor you can find to avoid adding nontext characters, or use an XML editor, such as the one I show in Figure 7-5.

Subscribing to your feed

Now that your feed is perfect, open your RSS reader and subscribe to it. If you haven't yet created an RSS or XML button for your feed on your Web site, type the URL into your reader's text box. Your feed should appear immediately.

Doesn't your feed look nicer in your reader than in your text or XML editor? Happy reading!

Hopefully, you are now inspired to continue to maintain your feed. Perhaps you'll even create multiple feeds! Now is the time to start promoting your feed. Read Chapter 11 for lots of great ideas about how to do so.

Chapter 8

Automating RSS Creation

In This Chapter

- Choosing an RSS-creation tool
- Using blogging software
- Using content-management tools
- Scraping from HTML
- Converting e-mail to RSS
- Using advanced tools

You want to create RSS feeds, but the methods that I discuss in Chapters 6 and 7 are not for you? Not only are you not the "do it from scratch" type, but you also don't want to even think about your RSS feeds, right? You just want them to happen. If you have too much else to think about to contemplate creating RSS feeds, you need automation.

After all, your focus may be on your Web site or marketing, rather than on creating and maintaining your RSS feeds. Perhaps your feeds are just an adjunct to your e-mail newsletter. You may not want RSS to be the center of your world. I accept that.

Good news! If you're looking for ways to automate the creation of your RSS feeds, you have some options. In this chapter, I explain some of the options and help you choose the one that's right for you.

Choosing an Automated RSS Tool

The New York Times has dozens of RSS feeds. Do you think that the editors of the *Times* manually enter all the text into an RSS-creation program? Probably not. Like the editors of the *Times,* you may also need some way to make this RSS thing happen by itself — or it may not happen at all.

If you're creating a blog, you just need to choose a tool that creates your RSS feeds for you, as I explain in the next section. But if you aren't creating a blog, you need another solution. A number of Web content management systems can now output RSS feeds for you. You may already be using one of them.

You can also *scrape* your site. Scrapers are software tools that try to figure out which part of your page should go where in an RSS feed. I give you some tips for making that process come out the way you want it to.

A couple of tools turn e-mail into RSS feeds. I threw those into this chapter because RSS feeds often replace or complement e-mail newsletters.

Finally, a number of advanced tools can help you create RSS feeds, especially if you're willing to develop a database for your Web pages and try your hand at some programming.

Using Blogging Software

Most blogging tools create RSS feeds. Blogs are ideally suited for RSS feeds because their format naturally contains discrete, dated items — blogs practically scream, "RSS me, RSS me!"

The major blogging tools all create RSS or Atom feeds. Here are some examples:

- **Blogger:** Atom feeds
- **LiveJournal:** Both RSS 2.0 and Atom feeds
- **MovableType/TypePad:** Both RSS 2.0 and Atom feeds

For more information about blogging tools, see Chapter 4. If your main goal is to create a blog, you should have no problem with your RSS feed because the blogging tool creates it for you.

Using Content Management Tools and Databases

If you have a complex Web site with many pages, you may use a Web content management system to manage it all. Most of these systems now create RSS feeds, although you may have to search to find this feature.

RSS is new enough that you may get some virtual quizzical stares if you ask about it. For example, when I first sent a query about the Lotus Workplace Web Content Management system and asked whether the program created RSS feeds, I got a reply asking what RSS was. But, when I explained, customer service confirmed that the system does indeed create RSS feeds.

Even many of the lower-priced content-management systems (CMS) now offer the ability to create RSS feeds.

Content management systems are basically databases — albeit complex ones. To output an RSS feed, you need to include the proper fields so that the program can create the feed. These fields are usually the same as the tags in the RSS feed, such as the title and description fields.

If you can't find anything in the CMS documentation, try technical support. An update may be available that allows you to create RSS feeds.

If your content is contained in a database, you can use a tool to extract that data and put it into an RSS feed. You can find an article on using Active Server Pages (ASP) to create an RSS feed from data in a Microsoft Access database at this Web site: `www.purplepages.ie/site/articles/article.asp?faq=6&fldAuto=76`. The article explains that you could also use data from other databases. Of course, this method requires detailed knowledge of programming using ASP.

Another article, at `www.lowendmac.com/tech/php16.html`, explains how to create an RSS tool using PHP and a MySQL database.

The point is that, if you can program, you can take content from almost any structured source and turn it into an RSS feed. See the section "Using Advanced Tools," later in this chapter, for other sophisticated tools for creating RSS feeds.

Scraping from HTML

Wouldn't it be wonderful if you could find a program that would just take your Web page that contains the content you want in your RSS feed and create your RSS feed automatically? Of course, the program would have to make some assumptions, but it may just provide what you need.

Or, for more precise results, perhaps you could create your Web site so that a program would know what content to put where in an RSS feed. Maybe you could add some HTML tags that would indicate which text was an item title and which was a description.

Now here's a wonderful daydream: How about creating an RSS feed from someone else's Web site? Perhaps you want to find out when your stocks go up or when your competitor sends out a press release. Could that be done?

To some extent, your dreams have been answered. The process is called *scraping,* and it means culling content from the HTML code of a Web page. In this chapter, of course, I stick to scraping tools that create RSS feeds from Web pages.

You can find a variety of tools to scrape your site for you. Some are more automated, meaning that you don't have to fiddle with your HTML. However, depending on the organization of your site, the results may not be exactly what you want. Other tools suggest that you put certain HTML tags around the parts of your site that you want to use as items, and the scraping tools then look for those tags. Some tools are Web-based services, and others are software.

Using FeedFire's online service

In general, tools that simply create a feed without requiring you to do anything create simpler feeds. Obviously, if you want to create a feed from someone else's site, you can't modify the underlying HTML code, so you would use a tool that takes the existing text and creates a simple feed from it. One example of such a tool is FeedFire (`www.feedfire.com`), shown in Figure 8-1.

To create an RSS feed, you only have to provide a URL, and you instantly have an RSS feed. This feed lists the links on the page and creates an item for each link, using the text of the link. No descriptions are added, so you get a feed with item titles only. Nevertheless, for providing the means to quickly following up on a site that you're interested in, the feed is very helpful.

To create the feed, follow these steps:

1. **Go to** `www.feedfire.com`**.**

   Feel free to take the time to read the home page, which describes the service.

2. **Click the Create a Channel link.**

   The URL text box appears.

3. **Enter the URL of the Web page that you want to create an RSS feed for.**
4. **Click the Create button.**
5. **Click the Test button to see the links that the RSS feed will include.**
6. **If you like the results, click the RSS button to subscribe to your feed.**
7. **If you want, choose up to three categories for the feed, and specify whether you want the feed to be public or private.**

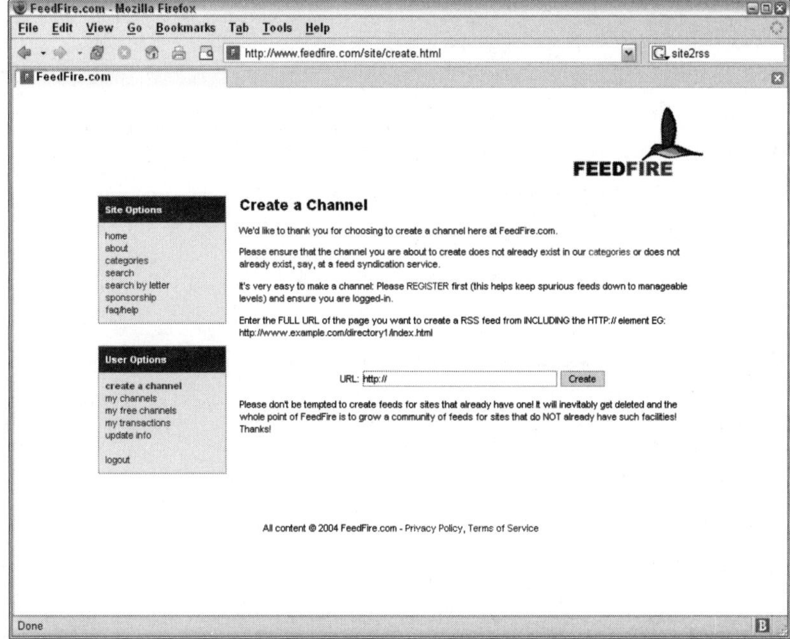

Figure 8-1: FeedFire creates a simple RSS feed for you in no time.

To give you an idea of how this works, look at Figure 8-2, which shows a simple site on rabbits, `www.rabbit.org`. You can clearly see all the links listed on the site's FAQ page. A site with distinct elements like this one is ideal for scraping.

To provide an example, I subscribed to the feed that I created. Figure 8-3 shows this feed in RssReader.

Can you see the connection between the Web page and the feed? The feed items are not in exactly the same order, but for the most part, you can clearly see the relationship. Each link becomes an item title. In this case, the titles are meaningful enough that you can easily tell whether you want to follow up and click the link to read more.

This service is free, but FeedFire has various paid levels that let you control which links you want to include in the feed (by specifying keywords to include or not include), and you can even sponsor the feed by putting your name in front of the feed's title. FeedFire tacks on some ads to its free RSS feeds.

You may have noticed that FeedFire's feed creates only titles. That's because the HTML underlying the page doesn't provide enough information to determine what content should go in the description area of an item in a feed. A simple tool can only create a simple feed from other peoples' sites.

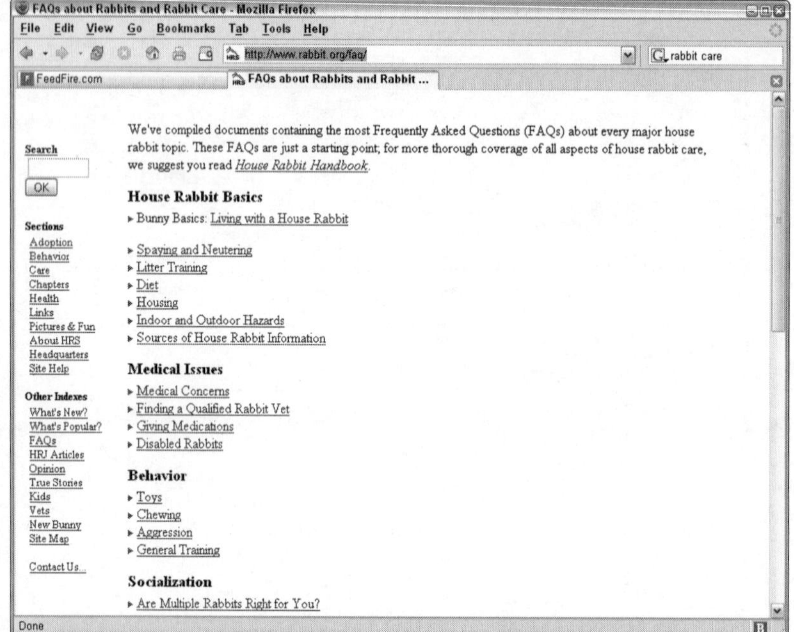

Figure 8-2: Everything you ever wanted to know about rabbits, but were afraid to ask.

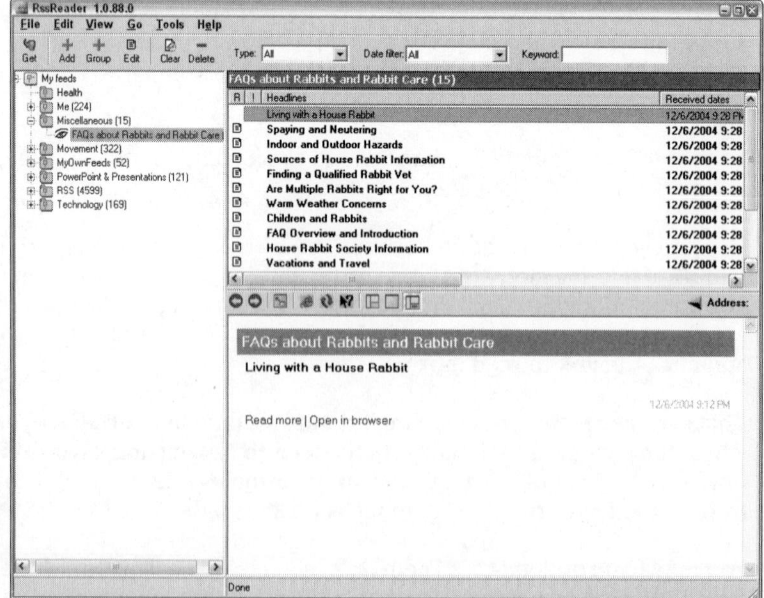

Figure 8-3: This feed was created from the Web site shown in Figure 8-2.

Using W3C's online service

I had hoped to find more automatic online services, but unfortunately most of them have been removed or are no longer supported. As of this writing, if you want to create a full-featured feed for your own Web site, you only have a few choices. Two of these are BlogStreet's Go XML and Site Summaries in XHTML.

BlogStreet's Go XML service (`www.blogstreet.com`) identifies permalinks and creates an RSS feed. If you don't use permalinks, however, it probably won't work for your site, because it identifies the blog posts based on the permalinks.

Site Summaries in XHTML is an online service that uses hints in an XHTML document to generate a feed. It is hosted by W3C, the World Wide Web Consortium, which is an organization that develops and supports Web standards. You need to start with an XHTML document, but fortunately W3C has an online service, called Tidy, that converts an HTML document to an XHTML document.

XHTML is HTML that's expanded to be usable as an XML document. The purpose of XHTML is to provide HTML with more flexibility and extensibility. XHTML is designed to be familiar to HTML users, while providing the advantages of XML.

Though it's possible to convert your HTML page to XHTML and then convert the XHTML to an RSS feed, it's not as easy as I'd like a so-called automatic tool to be. But, it's not terribly difficult either.

If you work with HTML code directly, you may want to use this method. You don't need to change the HTML pages on your Web site. Rather, the conversion process happens on the W3C Web site, and in the end, you just get a nice RSS feed that you can use. This service creates RSS version 1.0 feeds.

To use the Site Summaries system, follow these steps:

1. **Go to `www.w3.org/2000/08/w3c-synd/#`, shown in Figure 8-4.**
2. **Following the explanation of the tags that you need to use, as shown in Figure 8-5, create the tags in your HTML document as follows:**
   - The title of the page becomes the title of the channel, so you don't need to do anything there.
   - Surround each item with a `<div class="item">` tag at the beginning and a `</div>` tag at the end.
   - Within each item, surround the item's title with `<h2>` and `</h2>` tags.

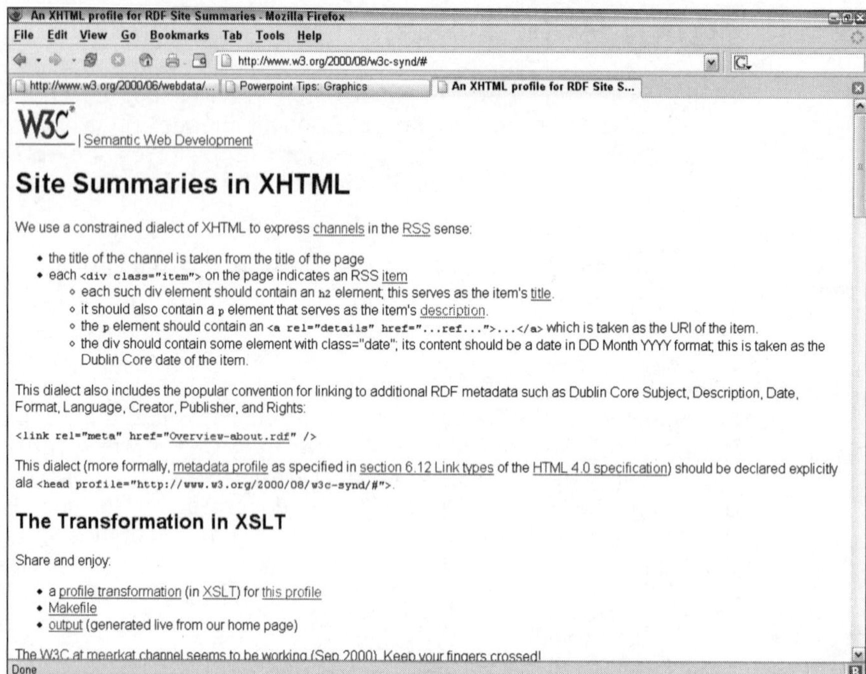

Figure 8-4: The Site Summaries in XHTML Web page.

Thanks to Dan Connolly and Max Froumentin for helping me with the use of this service.

- Within each item, surround the description with the <p> and </p> tags.
- Within each item's description (between the <p> and </p> tags), add the following, where the link is the link for that item:

```
<a rel=details" href="http://www.ellen
 finkelstein.com/powerpoint_tip.html">
```

- Within each item, you can add to some element the following attribute, whose content is a date in the `DD Month YYYY` format. For example:

```
<span class="date">28 Feb 2001 13:30:25 CDT</span>
```

3. **Save your page and upload it to your Web site.**

   Figure 8-6 shows the resulting page. As you can see, the page contains only one item, for the sake of simplicity.

4. **Go to Tidy page (`http://cgi.w3.org/cgi-bin/tidy`) to convert your HTML to XHTML, as shown in Figure 8-7.**

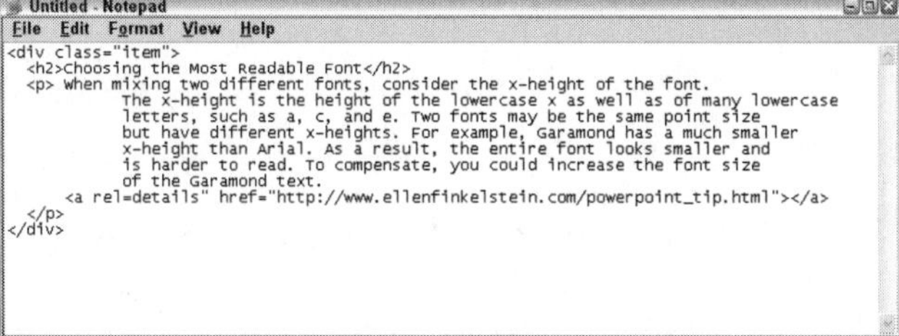

Figure 8-5: A sample item marked up as required by the W3C online service.

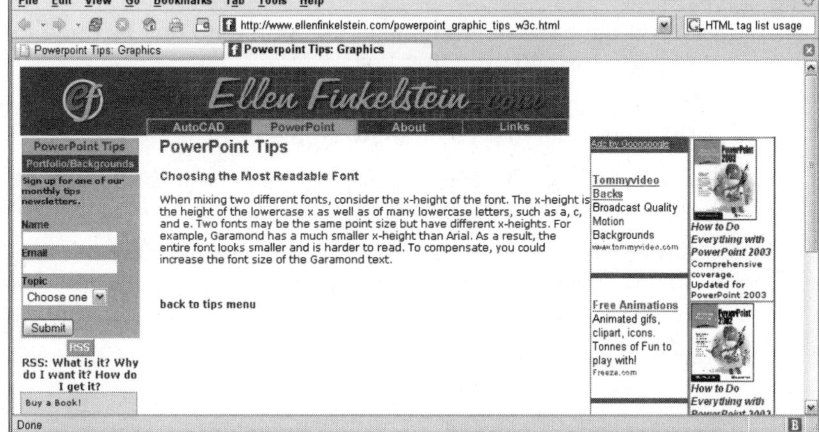

Figure 8-6: This page has the proper tags for the conversion from HTML to RSS.

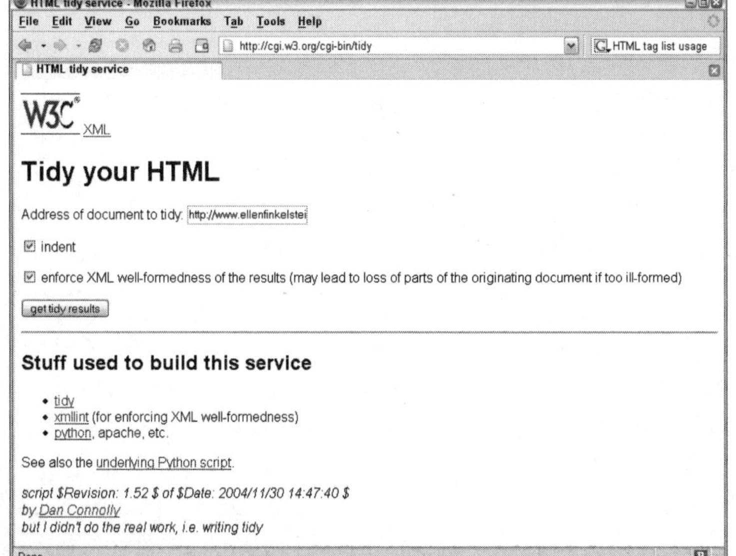

Figure 8-7: The Tidy page tidies up your HTML and turns it into XHTML.

5. **Enter the URL of your page in the Address of Document to Tidy text box.**
6. **Click the Get Tidy Results button. You can see the result in Figure 8-8.**

   Whoa! What's that? Well, it's your HTML page minus the images, style sheet, and so on. It looks like a mess, but don't worry. This is just an intermediate stage. Note that you have a huge, unintelligible URL in the browser's Address text box.
7. **Select the entire URL in your browser's Address text box and press Ctrl+C to copy it to the Clipboard.**
8. **Return to** `www.w3.org/2000/08/w3c-synd/#` **and scroll down to the Try It section of the page.**
9. **Select the current contents of the XML Data text box and press Ctrl+V to paste the URL into that box.**

   Although the name of that text box is confusing, this is where you put the source file that you want to convert to XML.
10. **Select the current contents of the Page text box and press Ctrl+V to paste the same URL in that box.**
11. **In the Base text box, enter a base URL, perhaps the home page of your site or a page that is related to your feed.**

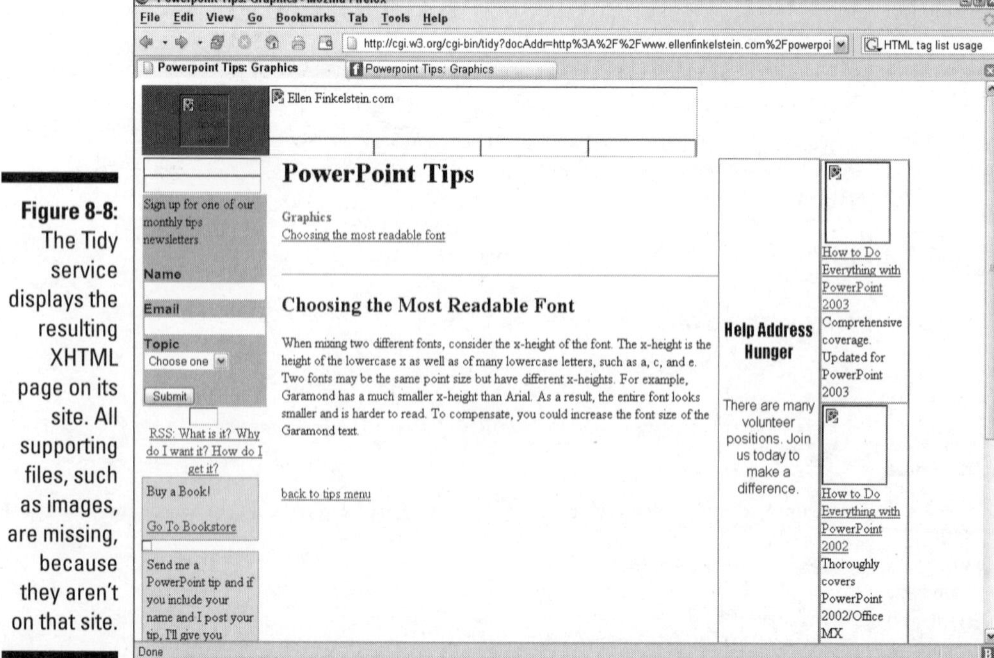

Figure 8-8: The Tidy service displays the resulting XHTML page on its site. All supporting files, such as images, are missing, because they aren't on that site.

12. **In the Channel text box, enter the URL that you want for your feed.**

    This is the filename of your feed. You can see the completed text boxes in Figure 8-9.

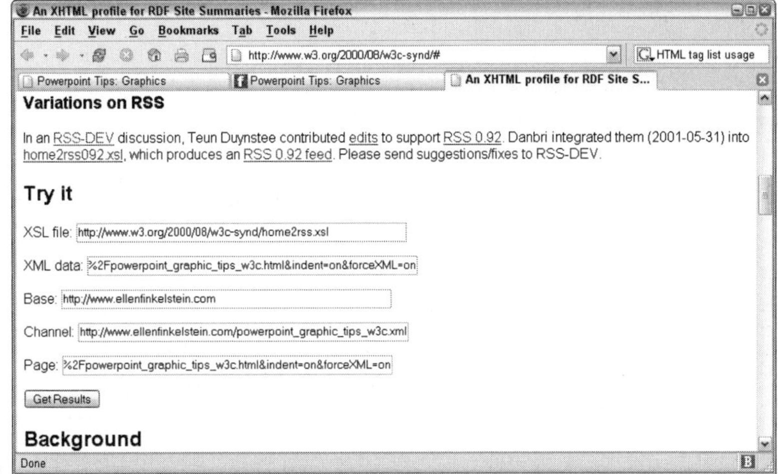

Figure 8-9: The completed text boxes contain the information that W3C's online RSS conversion service needs to convert an XHTML file to an RSS file.

13. **Click the Get Results button.**

    You can see the results in Figure 8-10. Another strange-looking page! Don't lose hope!

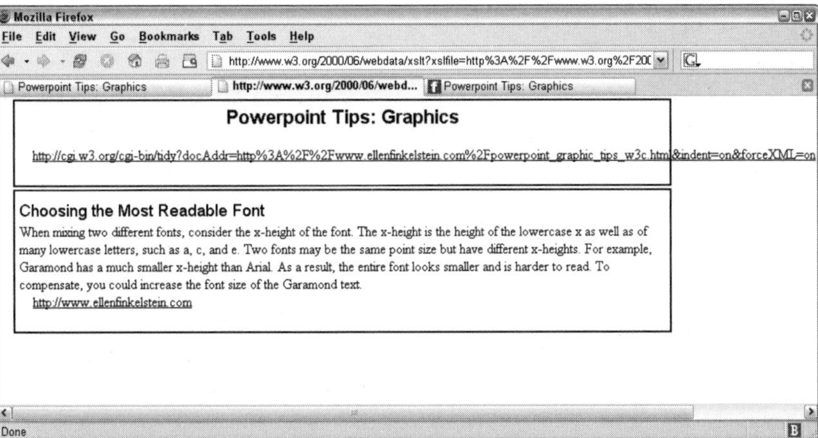

Figure 8-10: The result of the conversion looks strange. The URL is so long that it could string around the world!

14. **In your browser, choose View➪Source or Page Source to see the underlying code. You see the result in Figure 8-11.**

Finally, you have an RSS feed.

Figure 8-11: You now have a feed in RSS 1.0 format.

15. **Select the text of the feed, and then copy and paste it into Notepad or an XML editor. Save the file and upload it to your server.**
16. **Go to your favorite RSS reader and subscribe to the feed. Figure 8-12 shows the result of the example used in these steps.**

You're done. I'm the first to admit that this supposedly automatic method is not all that automatic. It takes lots of steps. But it works, and it may be just the solution for you. It's free, too. Hopefully, someone will come up with a more direct service that involves fewer steps.

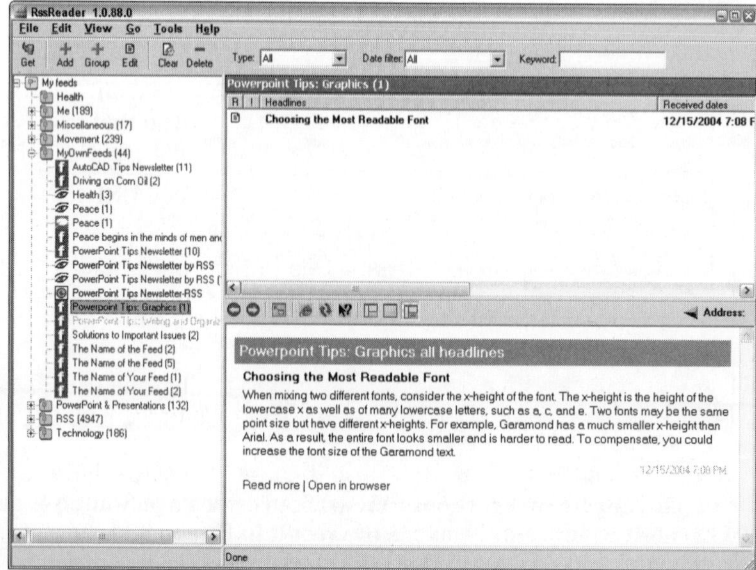

Figure 8-12: The feed in my Rss-Reader.

Converting E-Mail to RSS

If you have an e-mail newsletter that you would like to convert to an RSS feed, you may want a tool to convert e-mail to RSS. While most RSS feeds are based on Web-site content, feeds can be self-sufficient. If you think of RSS as a way to communicate with your clients, potential clients, colleagues, and so on, and you already have an e-mail newsletter for that purpose, you can see that a tool to convert e-mail to RSS makes a lot of sense.

An RSS feed doesn't have to replace your newsletter; instead, it can complement your newsletter. You can send out your e-mail newsletter but also offer an RSS feed for those who prefer it. Giving your subscribers a choice is always a good idea.

NewslettersByRSS

NewslettersByRSS (`www.newslettersbyrss.com`) is a free service that enables you to output an RSS feed for your e-mail newsletter. You send an e-mail to a special (long) e-mail address that the site gives you and the site turns it into an RSS feed.

Follow these steps to set up this service:

1. **Click the Publishers tab.**
2. **Click the Sign Up or New Account link.**
3. **Fill out the form, including your RSS feed's title, description, and link (on your site), and click the Sign Up button.**

   You will get a confirming e-mail in your inbox.
4. **Add the e-mail address that NewslettersByRSS.com provides you in the confirming e-mail to your subscriber list so that each time you send out a newsletter, you automatically create an RSS feed.**
5. **When you send out an e-mail, use the RSS feed URL (which ends in `.nbrss`) to subscribe to your new RSS feed.**

   Of course, you should mention this URL in your e-mail so that people can subscribe. You can add a button that people can click on to subscribe on your Web site, too.

Figure 8-13 shows the feed in my RssReader. The link goes to a page on NewslettersByRSS's Web site that contains the entire e-mail.

You don't have to use this service in the way it suggests. For example, you can use it to create a one-item RSS feed whenever you want. Just send an e-mail to the address the site provides you, and you have an RSS feed. It's very simple!

iUplog

I originally planned to write about MailByRSS, a free service from iUpload (www.iupload.com/product/mailbyrss.asp). The service was similar to NewslettersByRSS. However, when I contacted the service with a question, I was told that it was moving to a new service, iUplog (www.iuplog.com). (Moral: things are constantly changing in the world of RSS!). iUplog is a blogging service for people who want to blog via e-mail or their cell phone. The service lets you post text, images, audio, and video from wherever you are.

iUplog has a six-month free trial and then costs from $2.95 to $16.95 per month, depending on the amount of control you want over the look of your blog. The service hosts your blog and automatically creates an RSS feed for you.

In this context, I'm interested in the feature that lets you create an RSS feed via e-mail. (Of course, if you like the blogging idea, take a look at it.) iUplog assigns you a Web URL that you choose, with its domain name after it. For example, I chose PowerPointTipsNewsletter.iUplog.com. The advantage of the blogging aspect of the service is that you can edit and format your content, whether you think of it as a blog or as a complement to your e-mail newsletter. The basic service offers a number of templates that you can choose from, a place to store links (a blogroll), and an About page with information about you, including a photo.

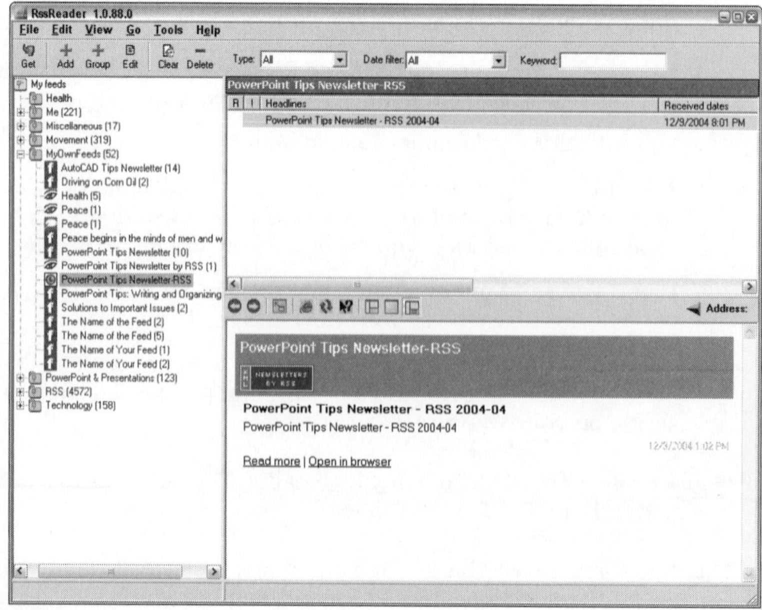

Figure 8-13: Here's the feed that I created using NewslettersByRSS.

Put an RSS button on your opt-in and opt-out pages (where people subscribe or unsubscribe) to help you attract and retain subscribers who may prefer to receive your newsletter via RSS rather than via e-mail.

After you sign up, you receive an e-mail confirming the Web site URL that you chose, confirming your login information, and providing you with the e-mail address that you use to send in content. Add the e-mail address to your subscriber list or just send an e-mail.

E-mail does not necessarily arrive as quickly as a direct upload to a Web site. You may have to wait for the e-mail to arrive before you see the results on the Web site.

When you log in, click the View Blog link to see your entries. You can see my test blog in Figure 8-14.

Click the RSS Subscribe button to subscribe to your RSS feed. In Figure 8-15, you can see the feed in my reader.

As you can see, your feed is really just a link to the Web site. But then again, lots of feeds are like that.

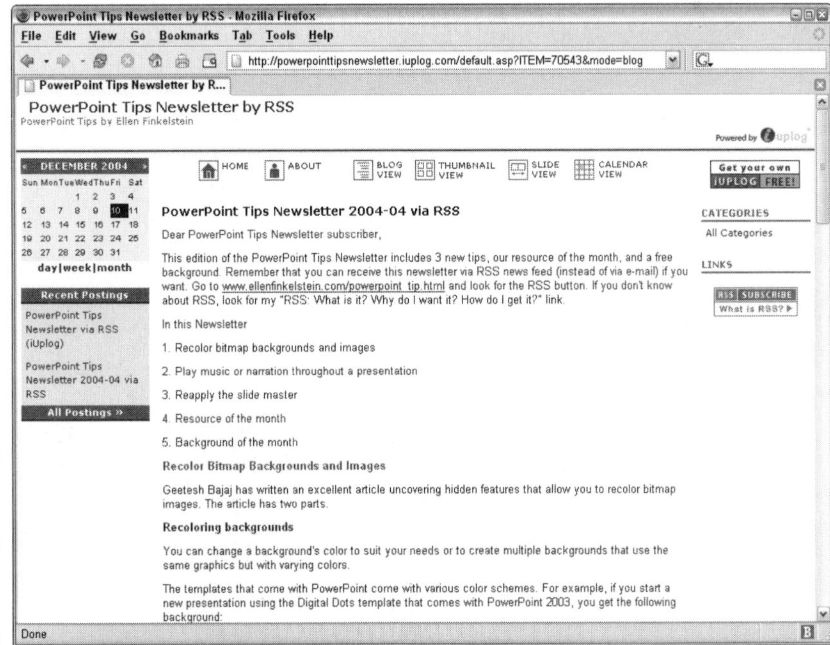

Figure 8-14: I created this blog by e-mailing iUplog.

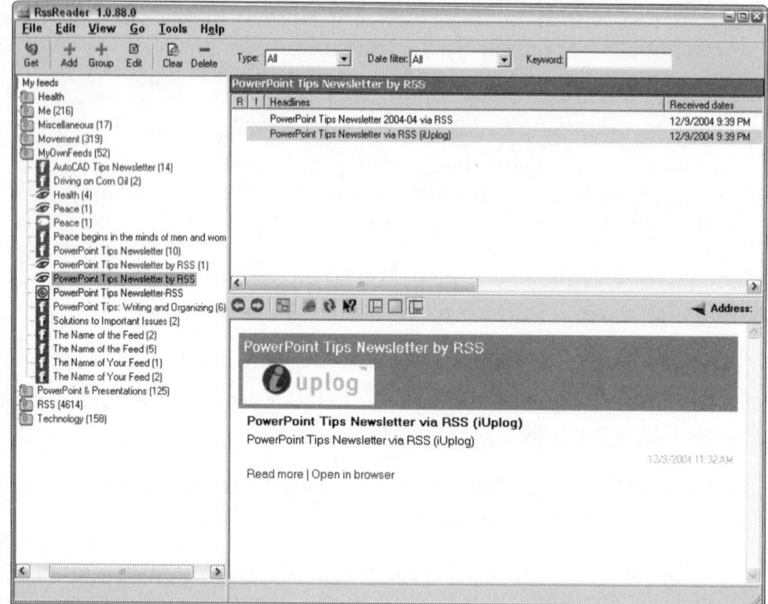

Figure 8-15: My feed created by e-mailing to iUplog.

All the e-mail–posting services warn that you need to keep the e-mail address that they provide private to avoid having others post spam on your blog and feed! Therefore, don't share this e-mail address with others.

A number of blogging tools (MovableType and Blogger are two examples) offer the ability to post via e-mail. You can therefore use them in a similar way to create an RSS feed for your e-mail newsletter.

Using Advanced Tools

If you have some programming or at least configuring skills and can upload some scripts or programs to your server, you may consider some more advanced tools. These tools generally use *regular expressions* to define which text goes in the feed. A regular expression is a way of specifying which text you want to work with. For example, if you want to create an RSS feed from someone else's site, you may notice a pattern that puts useful content after a specific heading and before a second heading. So, you could specify that you want to scrape text between those two headings. (For more information about scraping, see the "Scraping from HTML" section earlier in this chapter.)

Most of these tools were created with the idea of scraping someone else's Web site, because they try to figure out the structure of that Web site.

Here are some popular scraping tools that create RSS feeds. They all require some programming expertise.

- **xpath2rss:** A tool for scraping Web sites using XPath expressions (a method of selecting parts of HTML and XML documents). Address: `www.mnot.net/xpath2rss`
- **Script4rss:** Creates scripts in Perl to convert HTML pages to RSS feeds. Address: `sourceforge.net/projects/script4rss`
- **Grouper:** Takes search results and Web pages and converts them to RSS feeds. Address: `www.geckotribe.com/rss/grouper`
- **RSS.py:** A Python tool for generating RSS feeds. Address: `www.mnot.net/python/RSS.py`
- **RssHarvest:** Address: `www.bitworking.org/RssHarvest.html`

You won't find many services that scrape your site for you and output an RSS feed because of the economic, technical, and even legal issues involved. So you may have to roll up your sleeves and set up an automatic method for creating RSS feeds. However, once you set up this system, it should be easy and fast.

If you're technically minded, you can find a good step-by-step article on the process of creating a scraping tool at `weblogs.asp.net/rosherove/articles/29509.aspx`.

Chapter 9

Podcasting: Adding Multimedia to RSS Feeds

In This Chapter

- Understanding podcasting
- Receiving a podcast
- Listening to a podcast
- Creating a podcast
- Finding out more about podcasting

Podcasting has caused a great deal of excitement lately. But just what is it? *Podcasting* is simply the delivery of an audio file in an RSS feed. Actually, you can put any type of file in the feed, but right now, most podcasters are using audio files.

Why are people hopping up and down about podcasting? From the point of view of the creator, just as the World Wide Web made it possible for everyone to publish content at a very low cost — no printing costs and almost no distribution costs — podcasting gives everyone the ability to distribute multimedia files; not just to one or two people via e-mail but to the public. You could call it the democratization of radio. All you have to do is create the file, upload it to your Web server, and list it in your RSS feed — and off it goes around the world (or at least to your subscribers).

From the point of view of the listener, you now have the option to listen to the shows or music you want, when you want them. Just as RSS gives you control over how, when, and where you read information, podcasting gives you the same control over audio content. Podcasting is sometimes compared to TiVo, which lets you listen to television content you want at any time. And like content on the Web, the ease of creation means that you can find lots of interesting content.

Well, perhaps podcasting is a little more than that, so that's why I wrote this chapter. If you want to create your own podcast, read on, because by the end of this chapter, you'll have all the tools you need. And, it's fun!

For information on where the word *podcasting* came from, see the sidebar "The origin of podcasting."

Understanding Podcasting

To create a podcast, you start by recording an audio (or other multimedia) file, such as a talk show or music. Then you reference that file in your RSS feed. That makes you a podcaster. Your subscribers receive your feed and download the audio file. They can play your podcast in several ways, but it's usually done using a portable MP3 player or the software on their computer that they use for playing MP3 files.

Podcasting is the child of RSS version 2.0, which includes an `<enclosure>` tag. The purpose of this tag is to allow you to enclose a file with the RSS feed. You can think of an enclosure as being similar to a file attachment in an e-mail message. When you receive an e-mail with an attachment, your e-mail program displays that attachment and allows you to download the attached file so that you can open it. The same is true for an RSS enclosure.

You place the enclosure within any item in your feed so that each item can have its own enclosure. I explain the syntax for enclosures in Chapter 7 in the section "Using RSS version 2.0." You need the following three elements:

- The URL of the file.
- The file's size in bytes (not the length of time that the file takes to play, although the attribute is called "length").
- The file's MIME type. For MP3 files, the MIME type is audio/mpeg.

For the file type, you use standard MIME types. You can find a list of acceptable MIME types at `www.fileformat.info/info/mimetype/standard.htm`.

Here you see a sample item from an RSS 2.0 file, similar to the template that I used in Chapter 7. As you can see, the `<enclosure>` tag contains three attributes: the URL, the length, and the type. All of this information goes within the `<enclosure>` tag in the format you see here:

```
item>
    <title>Title of Second Item</title>
    <link>http://www. put_website_url_here.com</link>
    <description>The item 2 content.</description>
    <author>name@put_website_url_here.com</author>
    <pubDate>Tue, 30 Nov 2004 13:50:02 CST</pubDate>
        <enclosure
          url="http://www.
           put_website_url_here.com/sounds/leaf.mp3"
```

```
            length="663968"
            type="audio/mpeg"/>
      <guid isPermaLink="false">2004-11-30-02</guid>
    </item>
```

In Windows, you can determine the length of a file by right-clicking the file in Windows Explorer and choosing Properties, as shown in Figure 9-1. You can see that the size is 663,968 bytes.

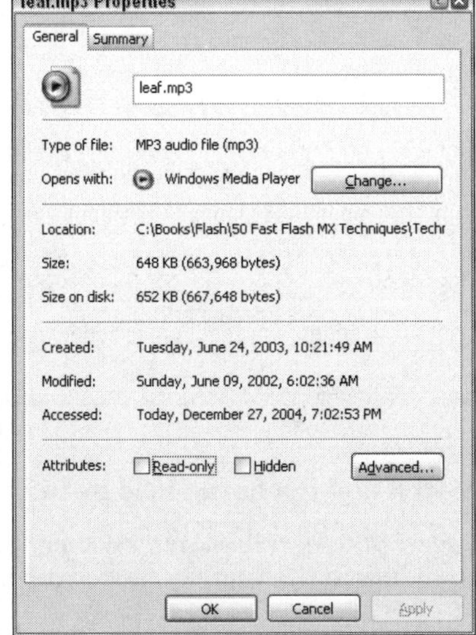

Figure 9-1: The Properties dialog box for a file shows its size in bytes.

How podcasting works

Because podcasting is a method of delivering files, it involves both the producer and the receiver of the file.

Here's how podcasting works:

1. **The podcaster creates a file, usually an audio file.**

   The MP3 audio format is most often used, because it provides excellent quality in a small file size. If you have an existing audio file that you have permission to publish, you can skip this step.

2. **The podcaster creates (or updates) an RSS feed and specifies the file in the feed, using the** `<enclosure>` **tag.**

3. **The podcaster uploads the RSS feed and the MP3 file to a Web site.**

The origin of podcasting

Podcasting is based on the RSS 2.0 `<enclosure>` tag but was developed by Adam Curry, a former MTV DJ, along with Dave Winer, the developer of the RSS 2.0 format. The two met in New York and discussed a concept that would allow computers to download content overnight so that it would be available when the user wanted to use it. When Winer incorporated the `<enclosure>` tag into the RSS 2.0 format, this concept became a real possibility.

Adam Curry wanted an application that would download the MP3 files to his iPod (hence the name *podcasting,* which is meant to be a cousin to *broadcasting*). He started to develop the application and then made it open source so that others could contribute to its development.

Soon people started to realize how useful this concept was and began to create their own shows. The Web site iPodder.org listed many of these productions. Adam Curry himself started a site, The Daily Source Code (`www.dailysourcecode.com`) for his own podcasts.

For history buffs, the term *podcasting* was first suggested by Ben Hammersley in the February 12, 2004 article "Audible Revolution" in *The Guardian* (read it at `www.guardian.co.uk/online/story/0,,1145689,00.html`) and then first used in context by Dannie J. Gregoire in a Yahoo! group post (read it at `http://groups.yahoo.com/group/ipodder-dev/message/41`). Adam Curry then popularized the term on his site.

4. **A person subscribes to the feed and opens the feed in an RSS reader.**

   You need to use a reader that supports enclosures. At this point, only a few do. I list some of these readers in the section "Receiving a Podcast," later in this chapter.

5. **The RSS reader either automatically downloads the enclosed file to a folder or displays a link that downloads the file when you click on it.**

6. **The person listens to the file directly from the computer or transfers it to a portable device, such as an MP3 player, and plays the file on that device.**

Actually, radio shows such as WebTalk (`www.webtalkradio.com`) and KenRadio (`www.kenradio.com`) have been offering MP3 downloads for years from their Web sites. The difference here is the means of delivery, which is via RSS feeds, rather than from Web sites.

How podcasting is being used today

Podcasting is now being used almost solely to deliver MP3 files. Most of these files are either audio blogs or some type of talk/music show. People are having lots of fun creating their own shows, and their enthusiasm shines through.

In my experience, the people who are creating podcasts are a different crowd from those creating plain RSS feeds. The podcast group is akin to the Web radio tradition and is definitely a small subset of those using RSS feeds.

As more people are getting involved in podcasting, the variety is increasing. For example, the BBC has an experimental podcast, In Our Time, which is a discussion of ideas throughout history. This is great content with a great method of delivery, and I hope it is a sign that the future will hold lots of valuable audio material.

I've also seen a software company, Ipswitch, which sells FTP software, start to use podcasting to deliver knowledge base articles that explain how to use its software and FTP in general. Go to `http://blogs.ipswitch.com/archives/2004/12/were_podcasting_1.html#more`.

It will be interesting to see what uses people find for podcasting — whether for information or entertainment — in the future.

The endless possibilities of podcasting

How could podcasting be used? Let me count the ways. Remember that you can use any type of file for the enclosure. Podcasting is actually a limiting term because it refers only to broadcasting using the RSS technology. Remember that the great advantage of RSS is that it sends updates automatically. Any content that changes or is updated regularly is a likely match for RSS. To broaden the discussion, consider how the `<enclosure>` tag in RSS could be used.

A few examples are as follows:

- **Video:** Video could include trailers of the latest movies, messages to customers, product demonstrations, software technical support (showing how to accomplish a task), displays of new products, and more.
- **Software:** Software companies could deliver software updates.
- **Text:** If you want people to get text, you could attach text documents — in plain text or HTML, for example — such as manuals, procedures, and anything that you update regularly.
- **Images:** You could send pictures of your latest vacation or your latest products.

As you can see, you can use enclosures in many ways. Use your imagination and you can start to see some of the possibilities in your field.

Podcasting, relating as it typically does to audio files, also has many uses. While current uses are mostly just for fun, the delivery of regular audio updates has great promise. Here are some ideas you might explore:

- **The same content as the feed description, but spoken:** This may be great for people who have limited or no sight; it may also just be a more interesting way to get the content of the feed. Also, you can listen to content when you can't read it, for example while you're driving.
- **Background commentary on the feed:** Examples include the source of the content, how it was obtained, additional details, and so on.
- **Outtakes, or sample content:** For example, you could include an audio trailer with the announcement of a new movie or song.
- **Source documentation for a news item:** Perhaps a reporter interviews a politician, and a news organization puts the story in an RSS feed. The enclosure could include the original interview.
- **Brief talks by the CEO or testimonials by customers.**
- **Language lessons.**
- **Instructions for tasks that require the use of hands:** Cooking lessons or software tutorials are good examples.
- **Walking or museum tours.**
- **Any type of speech or debate.**
- **Recordings of meetings.**
- **Short stories, fairy tales, songs, and so on.**

Some of these ideas come from Amy Gahran's blog at `http://blog.contentious.com/archives/2004/10/29/what-is-podcasting-and-why-should-you-care`.

I've been a busy podcaster . . .

For this chapter, I created a podcast called "A Lullaby a Day." This podcast is for technosavvy moms who can't sing and whose babies won't go to sleep. (Talk about niche podcasting!) Each day I offer a new lullaby. I would expect Mom to bring the baby to the computer to listen to the songs, or she could play them on a portable device with speakers attached — no, I don't recommend putting headphones on the baby!

I've created a few items, using songs I wrote when my first child was very young. If you read through this chapter, you'll see how I was able to create this podcast without spending a penny. (Okay, I took advantage of at least one 30-day trial offer, so it may not be free forever.) If you decide to seriously get into podcasting, you should buy some better equipment, editing software, and so on. I briefly discuss the process of creating the audio file in the section "Creating a Podcast," later in this chapter.

Don't expect to find this podcast anywhere online. It's just an anecdote for you to read in this book! The point is to show how easily you can create a podcast.

As you can see, the possibilities are endless. Podcasting creates many types of opportunities for communicating in a more personal, immediate way than mere text. Because the costs are so low, podcasters can create content for niche audiences.

You should note that a possible cost relates to the bandwidth that the enclosed files use as RSS readers download them from your Web site. If lots of people receive your RSS feed, your Web host may charge you if you go over the bandwidth limit that you pay for. Sometimes charges for bandwidth overages can run quite high.

Receiving a Podcast

If you are interested in podcasting, whether to receive them or create them, the first step is to try some out. Although it's easy to get a podcast, you need the right tools. Podcasting is new, and only a few RSS readers support the `<enclosure>` tag required to receive podcasts. I'm sure that this will change as existing RSS readers introduce new versions.

Finding the reader meant for you

Surprisingly, only a few RSS readers support enclosures and can therefore receive a podcast, but when you find one that does, the process of receiving a podcast is easy and painless. In some cases, the process happens automatically, perhaps only requiring you to configure the software to download any enclosures. In other cases, you see a link that you click to download the enclosure, just as you would to download a file from the Internet.

Here are some RSS readers that you can use to receive podcasts or enclosures:

- NewsGator: Both the program (which works within Outlook) and the online version support enclosures. You can find this program at www.newsgator.com. Figure 9-2 shows an enclosure in the free online version.

  Figure 9-3 shows my podcast in the Outlook version of NewsGator.
- **Bloglines:** As far as I know, Bloglines was the first online RSS reader to support enclosures. Figure 9-4 shows my podcast in Bloglines. Click the Enclosure link to download the enclosure. Go to `www.bloglines.com`.
- **iPodder:** This free program is specifically designed for subscribing to podcasts. Figure 9-5 shows iPodder in the process of downloading the MP3 from my podcast. You can get it at `www.ipodder.org`.

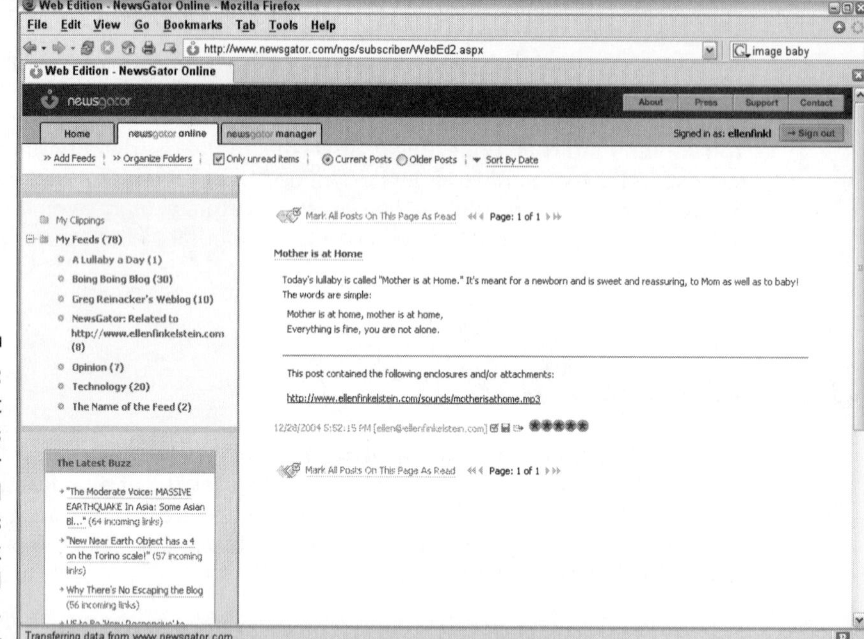

Figure 9-2: My podcast in News Gator online. All you do is click the link to download the MP3 file.

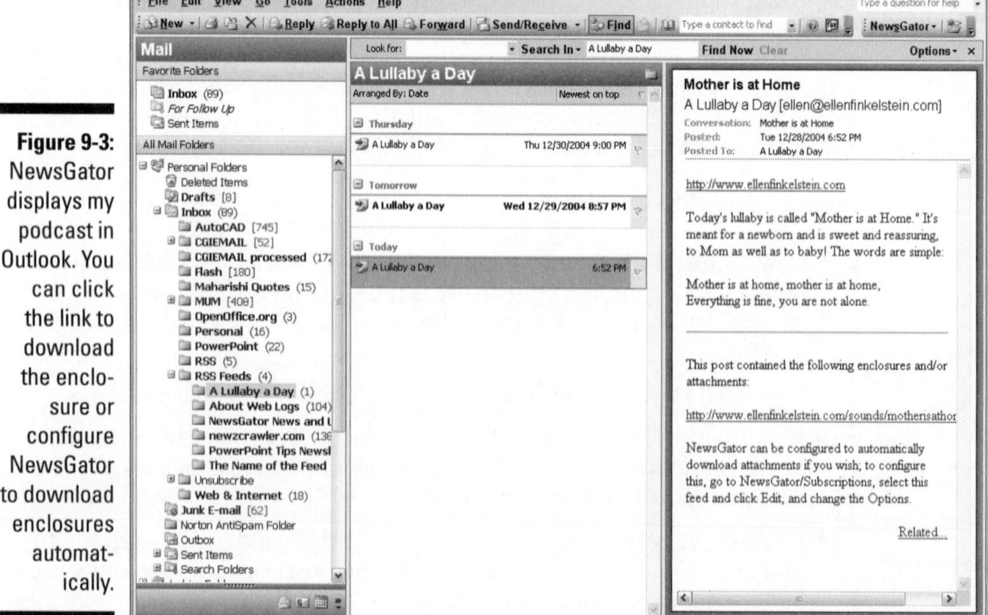

Figure 9-3: NewsGator displays my podcast in Outlook. You can click the link to download the enclosure or configure NewsGator to download enclosures automatically.

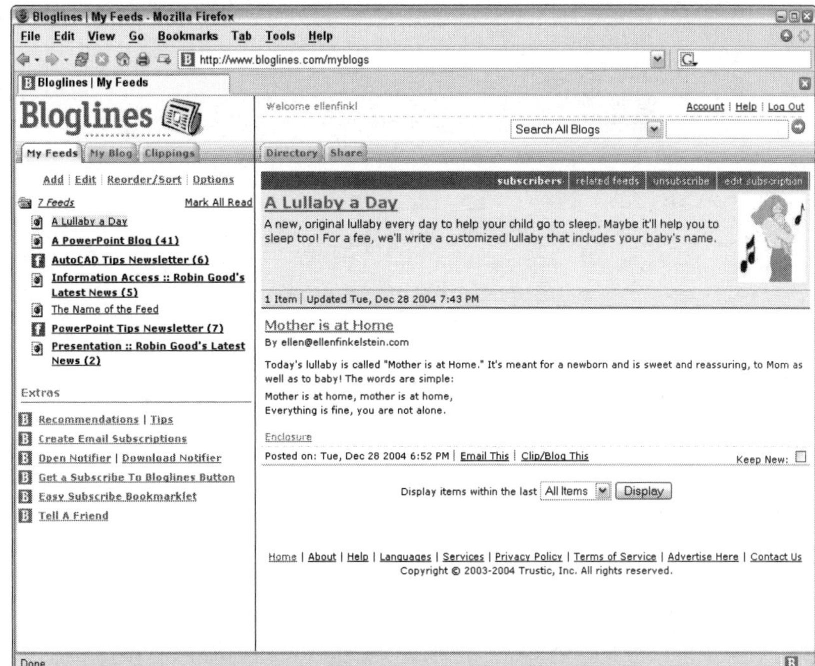

Figure 9-4: Here you see my podcast in Bloglines. Just click the link to download the enclosure.

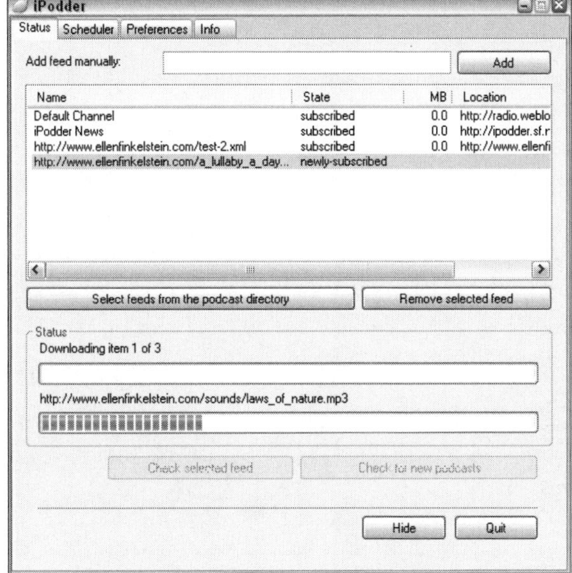

Figure 9-5: iPodder is downloading one of my lullabies.

- **BlogMatrix Jäger 1.6:** An RSS reader that supports enclosures, this program automatically downloads enclosures and adds them to your iTunes or Windows Media Player play list. Jäger does not have a built-in Web browser but instead uses your browser to display content, taking up just a column on the left of your screen. Figure 9-6 shows my podcast in Jäger. Go to `www.jaeger.blogmatrix.com`.
- **Vox Lite:** A free, stand-alone RSS reader that supports enclosures, Vox Lite sets up a default folder for the downloads, which you can change. Downloads are automatic. Go to `www.stevenwood.org/stories/2003/06/08/voxLite.htm` for information and `www.download.com/3001-9227_4-10257684.html` to download the program. You can see Vox Lite in Figure 9-7.
- **Doppler Radio:** This is a free program that is devoted to retrieving podcast enclosures. Go to `www.dopplerradio.net`.

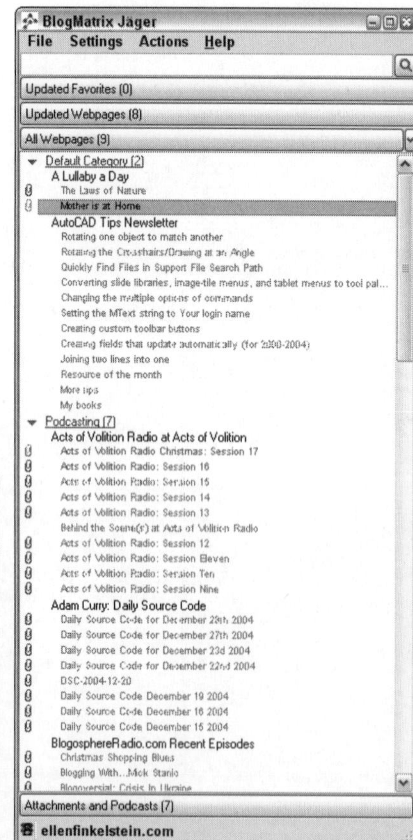

Figure 9-6: My podcast is listed in Jäger. The paper clip indicates an enclosure, which downloads automatically.

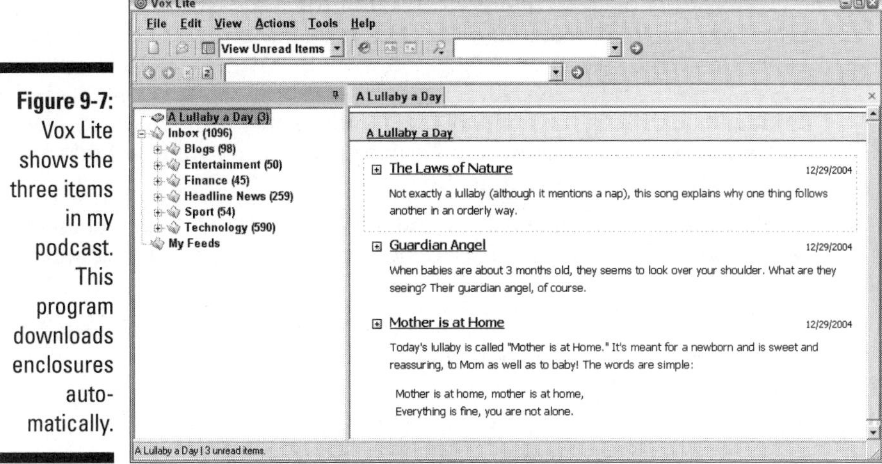

Figure 9-7: Vox Lite shows the three items in my podcast. This program downloads enclosures automatically.

I've shown so many readers here because the RSS readers that support enclosures are quite different from each other. Perhaps these figures can help you choose the one that suits you best, without having to download them all and try them out.

By the time you read this book, I expect that other RSS readers that support enclosures will be available. Choose one of these RSS readers for your podcasts and you're ready for the next step — finding podcasts to listen to.

Finding the podcast for you

As you may expect, the people who create podcasts want you to listen to them, so they try to make them easy to find. As with RSS feeds, you can find podcasts on the Web sites that create them.

Sometimes you see the familiar RSS or XML button, but other times, you may see different buttons. Figure 9-8 shows a few samples. As you can see, a standard convention hasn't been developed yet, so you need to look carefully.

Figure 9-8: Web sites use a variety of buttons and links for their podcasts.

For now, the easiest place to find podcasts is at the podcast directories. These directories seem to pop up daily. Here are a few podcast directories worth checking out:

- **iPodder:** This site is the home of the iPodder software, which was developed by Adam Curry and others. Besides a directory, you can find general information on podcasting. Go to `www.iPodder.org`.
- **PodcastAlley:** These podcasts are rated. You can also find a podcast forum and a list of software that's useful for podcasting. You can add your own podcast. Go to `www.podcastalley.com`.
- **Podcast.net:** Here you can find podcasts by category — and the site has lots of categories. You can add your own podcast. Go to `www.podcast.net`.
- **Digital Podcast:** This is another directory categorized by subject. Go to `www.digitalpodcast.com`.
- **Podcasting News:** This site offers news about podcasting. Its directory is at `www.podcastingnews.com/forum/links.php`. You can add your own podcast.

Before long, you'll have a list of your favorite podcasts, and your main problem will be finding time to listen to them all!

Downloading a podcast

When you have chosen software and found a podcast that you want to hear, subscribing to it is easy. Remember that the podcast is an RSS file, usually in XML format. The same techniques that work for subscribing to RSS feeds apply to podcasts. Each program is slightly different, but they all exist to let you subscribe to feeds, so they make it easy.

For more information about subscribing to RSS feeds, see Chapter 3.

You can get the URL for a podcast in several ways, but two of the most common are as follows:

- Click the RSS button, XML button, or podcast link to open the XML file in your browser. Select the URL and copy it to the Clipboard.
- Right-click the link and choose Copy Link Location, Copy Shortcut, or something similar.

In your software, you see a command such as Add a Feed or Subscribe. When you use this command, you see a URL text box. Just paste the URL that you copied into this box to subscribe.

Some RSS readers provide wizards that walk you through the process of subscribing. Some can import OPML feed lists that contain all the feeds you've subscribed to. (I explain OPML files in more detail in Chapter 3.) Several readers synchronize feeds with Bloglines, one of the online readers that supports podcasting.

Of course, the main point is to get that MP3 file that contains the podcast. To get the MP3 file, you often don't need to do anything. Some of the RSS readers automatically download the file to a folder on your hard drive. Otherwise, you find a link in the reader that you can click. A download dialog box opens, and you can then save the MP3 file.

Remember where you downloaded the file so you don't lose it! If your reader downloads the file automatically, you can generally customize the location.

The legend of podcasting describes the following scenario: You choose some podcasts in the evening and start the downloads, leaving your computer on all night. As you sleep, the podcasts download. In the morning you transfer the files to your MP3 player and then listen to them on your way to work or school.

Listening to a Podcast

When you have subscribed to a podcast and downloaded an MP3 file, you're ready to listen to it. The first time you do this, try listening to the file right on your computer.

The coolest people, I suppose, listen to podcasts on an MP3 player, whether it's an iPod or another device. Being of a certain age, I have to confess that I've never even seen an iPod (except in ads), although I do know someone who has one.

The important point is that you can listen to your podcast wherever and however you want. It's your choice.

Listening on your computer

You can usually just double-click the MP3 file in Windows Explorer (if you're using Windows) to play it. Windows can usually find an appropriate program to play the file. Or, you can open the file in a program that plays MP3 files. In Windows, that program could be Windows Media Player or iTunes. On a Mac, it would probably be iTunes. Other possibilities are Winamp, RealPlayer, and QuickTime Player. Figure 9-9 shows one of the MP3 files in my podcast playing in Windows Media Player.

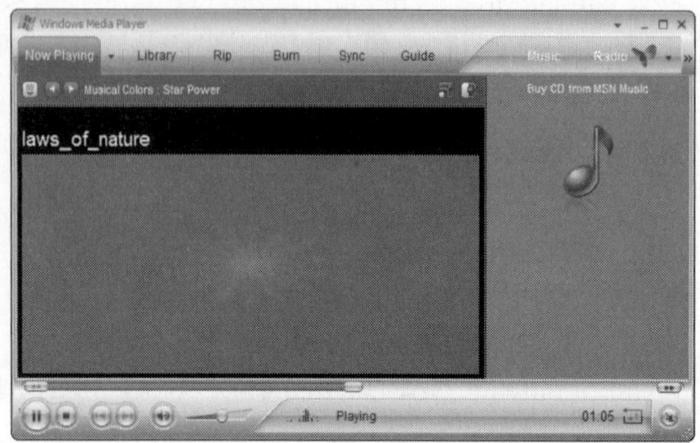

Figure 9-9: My lullaby playing in Windows Media Player. Seeing it is not the same as hearing it. (Well, maybe seeing it is better than hearing it.)

In iTunes, you can add the entire folder that contains your podcasts by choosing File⇨Add Folder to Library. Figure 9-10 shows several podcasts listed in iTunes.

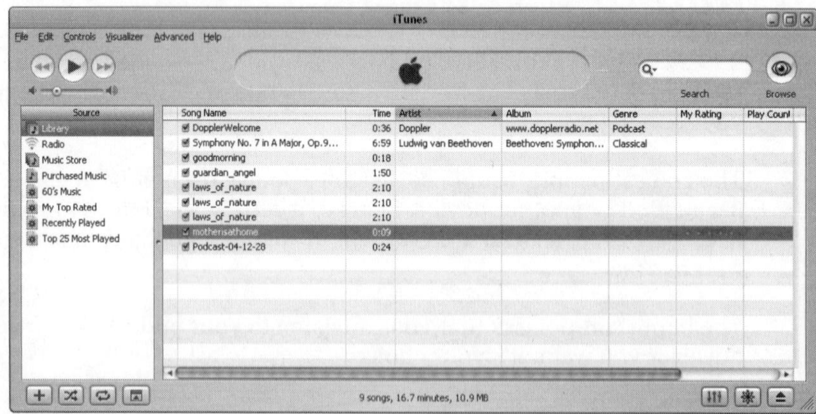

Figure 9-10: Podcasts in iTunes.

Now you have more options for listening than just MP3 music while you work at your computer. You can listen to the podcasting version of radio — which can be anything at all.

Listening on an MP3 player

Perhaps you have an MP3 player and you use it while you commute to work or go out jogging. Wouldn't it be nice to transfer your podcasts to your MP3 player and listen to them wherever you go?

Of course, this is a cinch. You probably already transfer MP3 files from your computer to your MP3 player, and podcasts are no different. Not all MP3 players are the same, but here I describe how this process works with an older MP3 player that I was able to beg, borrow, (but not steal) — an Archos Jukebox 6000.

If you're using the player for the first time, you probably need to install drivers. Follow the instructions that come with the player to do this. Then plug the player into your computer using the USB (or other) connector that comes with the player. When I did this, Windows automatically recognized the device and ran me through a wizard to set everything up. This process created a new drive that I could see in Windows Explorer.

After that, I followed these steps to download and play my MP3 file:

1. **From Windows Explorer, I dragged my downloaded MP3 files to the new drive.**

   Actually, my son had lots of music on it already, so I created a new `Podcast` folder for my podcasts.

2. **I turned on the player and figured out the menu, and my podcast opened in my new folder.**
3. **I moved through the menu and chose Adam Curry's Daily Source Code podcast of December 28, 2004.**
4. **I pressed the Play button, and now I'm listening to his podcast on the MP3 player!**

   He's talking about his in-laws leaving and his mom's successful operation. He also discusses the Firefox and Safari Web browsers. Then I listened to my own podcast. I am sitting here listening to myself on an MP3 player. Cool!

Your MP3 player may be a little more automatic depending on its version — for example, you may be able to plug it in and have the MP3s transfer without dragging them. Most MP3 players have a synchronization feature that copies files. You can also make play lists to automatically play your podcasts in sequence, one after another.

Creating a Podcast

Are you ready to create your own podcast? You don't have to be an audio engineer or a programmer. I won't give you details about how to create the best-quality audio files; that's beyond the scope of this book. But read on to get all the information to create your first podcast. You can refine your technique later.

Creating the audio file yourself

You should start by creating your audio file, which should be in MP3 format. You can create MP3 files in several ways:

- **Use sound-recording software:** This is the least expensive method, and you can find a list of sound recording programs at `www.mp3-recorder.net`. You attach a microphone to your computer, open the software, and click the Record button, and start talking, singing, or playing (or all three). You then save the file.
- **Use a digital voice recorder:** This is the kind of recorder that businesspeople use to dictate letters. (Does anyone do that any more?) Do a Web search for "digital voice recorder" and you'll find lots of options.
- **Convert existing audio content to MP3:** For example, you can convert CD files to MP3 files. If you have files in WAV or other formats, you can convert them as well. For an open-source option, you can use LAME. You can find more information, including the download, a short list of interfaces for LAME, and software that incorporates LAME at these sites:
  - `www.mp3-encoders.com/lame_encoder/`
  - `sourceforge.net/project/showfiles.php?group_id=290`
  - `www.mp3-converter.com/encoders/lame_encoder2.htm`

You need to be aware of two issues when creating MP3 files. First, you obviously shouldn't use copyrighted material without permission. Second, the MP3 format is patented. Software that creates MP3 files should have a license. The LAME software gets around the patent by using its own formula to create files that MP3 players can play.

If you want to get more professional, you need to invest in a high-quality microphone, audio-editing and -mixing software, and so on. Even so, your investment will be a lot less than starting your own radio station!

For information on Web-based services for creating audio files, see the section "Creating audio Web content with a service," later in this chapter.

Creating the feed

When you have your MP3 file, you're ready to create your feed. Because you now have two components, the feed itself and the audio (or other) file, you need to take two steps, as I describe in the following two sections.

Including the enclosure tag information

You can use an RSS feed-creation program (see Chapter 6) or write the feed from scratch (see Chapter 7). Here I explain how to use NewzAlert's Composer, because it supports enclosures and is easy to use. I explain the basics of creating a feed using Composer in Chapter 6, so these steps just explain how to add an enclosure:

1. **Create your feed and at least one topic, as shown in Figure 9-11.**

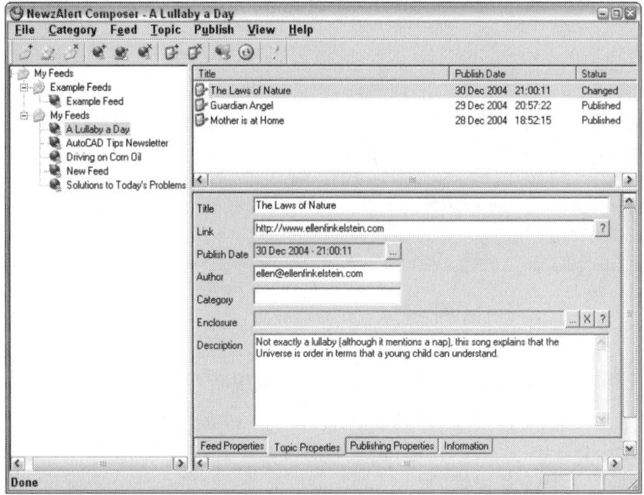

Figure 9-11: NewzAlert's Composer enables you to add enclosures to an RSS feed. Here you see an item (they call it a topic) that doesn't yet have an enclosure.

2. **Click the Ellipsis button (...) to the right of the Enclosure field to open the Enclosure Information dialog box, shown in Figure 9-12.**

3. **In the URL text box, enter the URL for your MP3 file.**

   The first time you create an enclosure, you need to decide where you will put your MP3 files. For example, you may have a folder called `Sounds` for all your sounds, just like you may have a folder called `Images` for all your images. Or, you may want to keep each sound with its XML file. Don't forget to create the folder structure you want on your Web site, and use that structure when specifying the URL for your MP3 file.

4. **To obtain the file size, click the Ellipsis button to the right of the File Size text box. In the Open dialog box that opens, locate and select the MP3 file (on your hard drive) and click the Open button.**

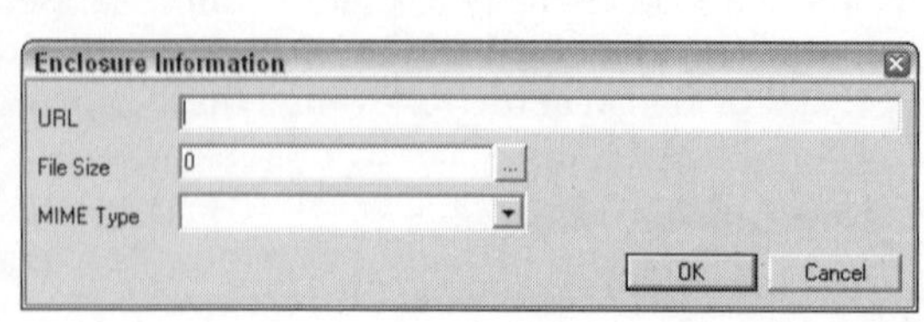

Figure 9-12: You complete the enclosure information in the Enclosure Information dialog box.

The file size is automatically entered into the File Size text box.

5. **From the MIME Type drop-down list, choose the file type.**

   For an MP3 file, choose audio/mpeg, as shown in Figure 9-13.

Figure 9-13: All the enclosure information is now entered.

6. **Click the OK button to return to Composer's main window.**

   That's all there is to it! Publish your feed and you're done. (I explain how to publish a feed in Composer in the section "Using NewzAlert Composer" in Chapter 6.)

To create the feed from scratch, see the section "Understanding Podcasting," earlier in this chapter. You simply fill in the URL, length (size in bytes), and type inside the `<enclosure>` tag, following the structure that I provide in that section.

Uploading the MP3 file

Your podcast won't work unless you remember to upload your MP3 file to the location you specified in your feed. If you specified a new folder for the MP3 files in your feed, you need to create that folder on your Web host's server. Then upload the file to that folder.

Creating audio Web content with a service

A couple of services enable you to create podcasts if you use established blogging software. You phone the service and talk (or sing) on the phone. Your phone call is recorded and saved as an MP3 file, thereby creating the audio content. You can then download the file or post it to one of the listed blogging programs or online services. If you publish to a blog, you are not directly creating an RSS feed, but your blogging software or service creates the feed for you, which then displays the audio content.

One of these services is Audioblog. Figure 9-14 shows an example of an RSS feed that includes an Audioblog feed. You click the Play button to play the audio file.

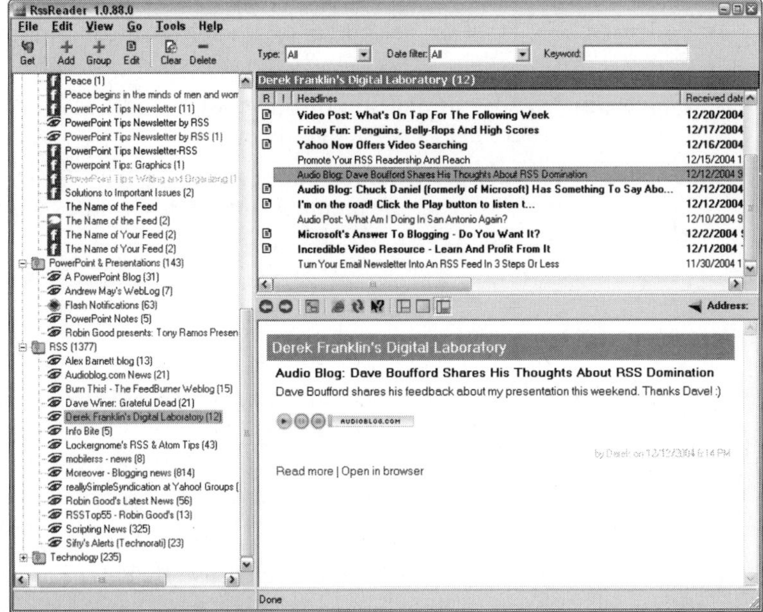

Figure 9-14: An RSS feed with an Audioblog sound attached.

One of the nice features of this system is that you can call from anywhere, so you can create the blog while you travel. Some audio services are as follows:

- **Audioblog:** Address: `www.audioblog.com`
- **Audlink:** Address: `www.audlink.com`
- **Audioblogger:** This is Blogger's audio service, so it works only with Blogger. Address: `www.audioblogger.com`
- **Rizzn's Podcaster:** Address: `www.rizzn.net`

If you don't have a Web server or are concerned about the amount of space that you'll use when you podcast — MP3 files can get huge — you may want to use a podcast hosting plan such as Liberated Syndication (www.libsyn.org).

Finding Out More about Podcasting

Because podcasting is so new and everybody's got something to say about it, I suggest that you read some articles. Some of these articles are general raves; others are more specific. These articles can give you an idea of the excitement that podcasting is generating. I've divided them into general articles and how-to's.

Here are a few of the best general articles:

- **Podcasts:** New Twist on Net Audio, by Daniel Terdiman. Address: www.wired.com/news/digiwood/0,1412,65237,00.html
- **Podcasting invades newsprint:** By Steve Rubel. Address: www.micropersuasion.com/2004/10/podcasting_inva.html
- **'Podcast' your world:** Digital technology for iPod does for radio what blogs did for the Internet, by Stephen Humphries. Address: www.csmonitor.com/2004/1210/p12s03-stct.html
- **Podcasting:** Address: http://en.wikipedia.org/wiki/Podcasting

Here are some how-to articles:

- **How-To:** Podcasting (a.k.a. How to get podcasts and also make your own), by Phillip Torrone. Address: www.engadget.com/entry/5843952395227141
- **Podcasting How-To:** By Jordan. Address: www.podfly.com/mambo/content/view/21/57
- **How to Podcast with Blogger and SmartCast:** By Peter Forret. Address: www.forret.com/blog/2004/10/how-to-podcast-with-blogger-and.html
- **How to podcast in three (relatively) easy steps:** By Michael Lehman. Address: www.howtopodcast.org
- **Random Thoughts from HowardGr:** By Howard Greenstein. Address: www.howardgreenstein.com/blog/2003/10/05.html
- **Podcasting on a Budget:** By Phillip Cairns. Address: cairns.servehttp.com/mudsongs/Poor-mans-podcast.htm

- **Skype + Podcast Recorder = SkypeCasters:** By Stuart Henshall. Address: www.henshall.com/blog/archives/001056.html
- **Help for Podcast Pingers:** By Dave Winer. Address: www.ipodder.org/2004/10/19#a255

Of course, Yahoo! has a discussion group on podcasting. Go to http://groups.yahoo.com/group/podcasters.

Yahoo has just come out with Media RSS (its name for RSS with enclosures). Yahoo! is even encouraging publishers to syndicate RSS feeds with video content. For more information, go to http://tools.search.yahoo.com/mrss/mrss.html. The idea is that you can list your feeds and then visitors to Yahoo! can find the feeds using the new Video Search feature at http://video.search.yahoo.com.

Part IV
Getting the Most Out of RSS Feeds

In this part . . .

Part IV takes RSS feeds to the next level — making them top quality, promoting them, and reusing them. First I give you the lowdown on RSS best practices, so that you don't get sloppy. Then I cover ways to promote your feed so that the whole world knows about them. That's what you want, isn't it?

Finally I get into how to turn an RSS feed into a Web page so that you can republish RSS feeds on your Web site. Placing the content of an RSS feed on a Web site is an important part of syndication.

Chapter 10

Incorporating Best Practices

In This Chapter

- Validating all feeds
- Supporting the technology
- Keeping up to date on formats
- Staying on topic
- Choosing the best structure
- Being timely

When you have figured out how you will create your feed, you need to settle down and focus on your procedures and content, and decide how to make your feed most effective.

For example, you want to make sure that your feeds display properly in the RSS readers that your subscribers use. You also need to consider the effect that your feed can have on your Web server — will so many RSS readers checking for changes every hour overwhelm it? You should consider some of the technical aspects of the RSS format to make sure that your feed doesn't look like gobbledygook.

At the same time, you want to focus on effective writing. What's the best feed title? How should you word your item titles? How much of your news should go in the description? As with any Web site, timely, up-to-date content is paramount. How do you make sure that your feed doesn't get stale? What do you do with old items?

How you decide all these issues is the topic of this chapter. May you have the best RSS feed possible!

Validating All Feeds

You validate a feed to make sure it's in the proper format and works properly. I've mentioned the importance of validating feeds a couple of times before in this book, but I'll say it again — in case this is the first chapter you're reading or if you forgot: Validate all your feeds!

If you write your feeds from scratch, errors can creep in. Leave out one angled bracket and your feed will not validate. In Figure 10-1, I removed the last angled bracket from the end of a version 1.0 RSS feed. In other words, instead of ending the feed with the following:

```
</rdf:RDF>
```

the feed ended this way:

```
</rdf:RDF
```

Figure 10-1 shows the result when I tried to validate the feed.

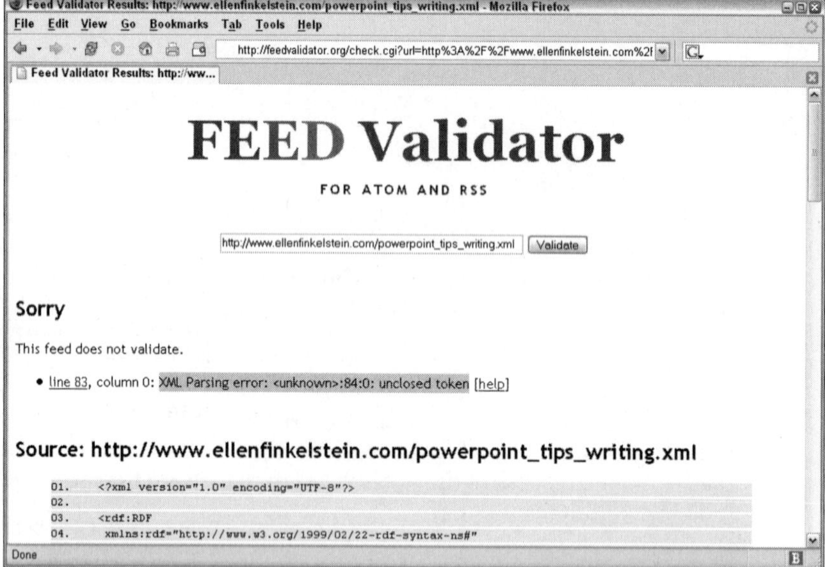

Figure 10-1: Change one jot or title, and your feed isn't valid.

It's a fact of life: People can't subscribe to a nonvalid feed. When it happens, it can be pretty embarrassing. Figure 10-2 shows what the invalid feed looks like in an RSS reader. Is my face red?!

If you've edited an existing feed and let an error creep in, those who have already subscribed simply cannot see your changes. Your feed stays stuck in the past and never gets updated. Bad news!

If you use an RSS-creation tool, you'll be less likely to get errors, but cyberspace isn't perfect — you never know what can happen between your hard drive and your Web host's server. So, after you upload either a new feed or any changes, validate that feed! It's part of practicing safe RSS creation.

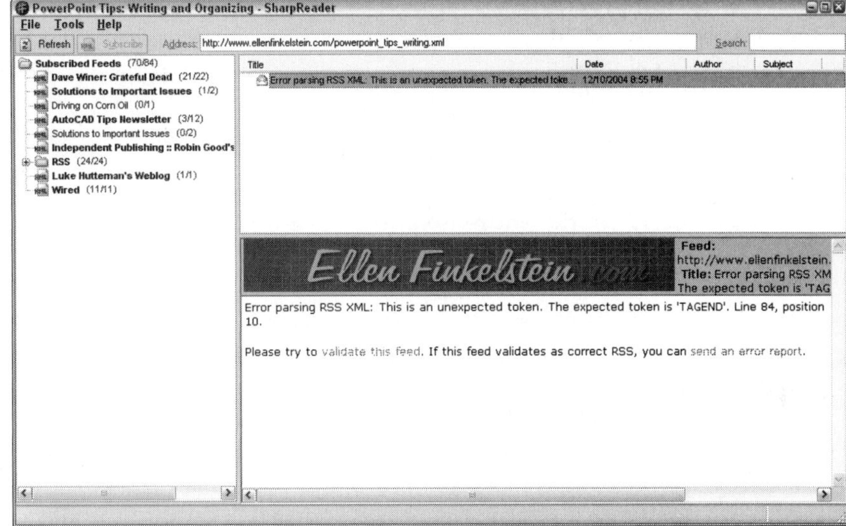

Figure 10-2: An invalid feed in Sharp Reader. It's not a pretty sight.

Supporting the Technology

RSS is a fairly new technology, and as far as its growth towards widespread use, it's still in its adolescence. People are still figuring out the consequences of using RSS. For example, here are some questions people are asking:

- Will all the requests for updates from RSS readers overwhelm Web servers?
- Does an RSS feed increase Web site traffic? If so, by how much?
- Will the content be as compelling outside the context of your site and its branding?
- How many people are using RSS anyway? How many are subscribed to my feed?
- If I switch from an e-mail newsletter to RSS, will I increase or decrease the attention I get from my subscribers?
- Will nontechnical people start using RSS in droves, just like they use e-mail and instant messaging?

Some of these questions are technical, such as the issue of Web server overload. Others are marketing related. The last question requires a crystal ball. Nevertheless, the answers to these questions are important for the future of RSS and its usefulness to you. Not all of these questions have firm answers yet, but they're worth discussing.

Caching your feed

If you have your own Web server and are concerned about the extra traffic that an RSS feed may create — or if your Web host limits the amount of traffic on your site — you can take the following actions to make your feed Web server–friendly:

- **Don't put the entire item in the feed.** Most bloggers put the entire entry in their feed. Some feel very militant about this. But if server overload is a problem, instead put only the first paragraph or an overview into each item's `<description>` tag.
- **Don't include links to images in your descriptions.** Because you can include HTML code in your item descriptions, you can add links to images. These greatly increase the size of your feed.
- **Encourage users to set their readers to update less often.** You can evangelize about this if it's important to you. Most readers allow you to customize this setting. Figure 10-3 shows this setting in RssReader. Note that a person can update manually more often than the default setting.

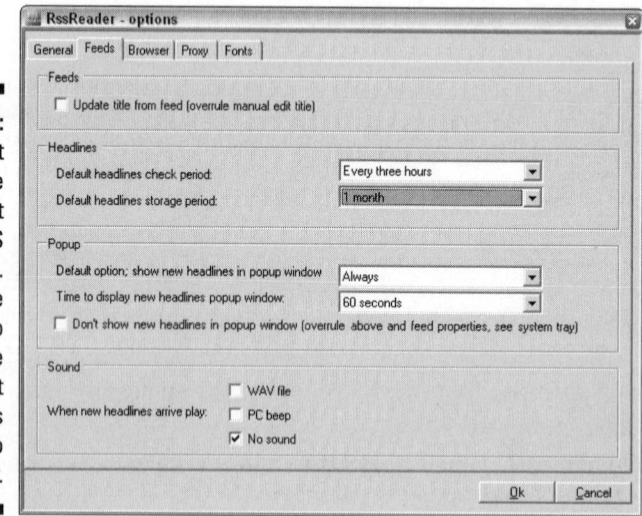

Figure 10-3: You can set the update time in most RSS readers. Here the time is set to every three hours. Most readers default to every hour.

- **Use a caching service.** An online service, such as the new and free RSSCache (`www.rsscache.com`), can help you reduce bandwidth requirements. This service stores your feeds on its servers. You use its server's address as the URL for your feed. When RSS readers request updates, RSSCache's servers download only the changes.

Luckily, RSS feeds are mostly text, at least for now. RSS 2.0's `<enclosure>` tag allows you to include media content, and as this feature becomes more common, the bandwidth requirements may grow to become a serious problem. For more information on using the `enclosure` tag, see Chapter 9.

Publishing without losing Web-site traffic

A lot of discussion on RSS has centered on the issue of how a feed affects Web-site traffic. Before I go on, I should say that not everyone is interested in Web traffic. Many bloggers don't care how many people visit their site — only how many people read their blog. If people can read bloggers' content without visiting their sites, as they can in an RSS feed, what's the problem?

On the other hand, many Web sites exist to sell a product or a service. These sites need traffic to make sales. Although bloggers and other noncommercial types may stick up their noses, the truth is that selling from a site is not evil!

Some people have reported that their Web traffic has increased after they've introduced a feed. This is anecdotal evidence at best. The articles I read were trumpeting the value of RSS, and if other people experienced no change or even a decrease in traffic, they probably didn't write about it. So in the end, you have to see for yourself.

My experience was that I found no significant change in the level of Web traffic. I also didn't experience hordes of viewers unsubscribing from my e-mail newsletter to switch to RSS. But I do know that people appreciated the alternative channel of communication and used it.

Remember that your feeds are a new way for people to click through to your site. Each item, sitting in each person's reader, contains a link where readers can find out more. In this way, an RSS feed is similar to an e-mail newsletter, except that you don't have to e-mail it. In fact, each time you update your feed (daily or even more often), you give your subscribers another opportunity to click.

One of the wonderful things about RSS is the opportunity for syndication. This means that not only are you syndicating your content to people who subscribe but also that others may pick up your content (if you allow them to) and display it on their Web site or incorporate it in their blog or feed. Obviously, this only adds to the places where people can click a link and end up on your Web site.

Providing compelling content

The best practice of all is to provide compelling content that attracts people. Great content is:

- useful.
- accurate.
- up to date.
- well-written.

Making your feed useful

There are several sources you can look to for feedback on the quality of your content. If you use your Web site statistics (provided by your site host) wisely, you can analyze what topics your readers find most valuable and act on that information to make your feed content more useful. If you have a comment feature on your Web site, you can read people's comments. When you write an article and get a huge response, you know that you've hit a chord.

The truth, the whole truth, and nothing but the truth

Verify all your facts and don't state opinion as if it is a fact. Remember that the Internet contains lots of dubious sources, so don't be too quick to believe what you read. In your feed, pass on only what you are pretty darn sure is accurate. Your subscribers will learn to trust you as a result.

Keeping at it all the time

Keeping up to date is also important, but it isn't hard; it just takes time. Of course, you don't want to add an item every day if you don't have anything to say. If you read blogs regularly, you've certainly seen entries that scream, "I just need to write an entry today, even though I don't know what to write about." However, getting into the routine of publishing regularly is important for a successful feed. Keep a list of ideas for future entries for those days when your inspiration fails you.

One reason for the connection between success and timely content is that RSS readers usually pop up with new items every day (or every hour). So, if your feed has a new item, it will be on that list, and people are much more likely to click through, especially if the item title seems immediately relevant. Those pop-up lists are important for getting the attention of your readers. Remember that some users subscribe to dozens of feeds and that you're competing with all those feeds for attention.

Making it clear

How do you make your feed easy to read? You need a balance of brevity and meaningfulness. The feed itself is just an item title and description. If the description is short, you need to concisely express the content in a way that gives readers enough information to decide whether they want to read the rest. Well-crafted titles are especially important.

Good writing principles for any medium apply here as well, regardless of the length of your feed description. Basic principles are as follows:

- Know the main point you're trying to make, and write around that point.
- Be clear, concise, and consistent.
- Write for your audience in tone and level.
- Use examples and analogies to explain your points.
- Review and edit for grammar, spelling, and punctuation.
- Use a lively, engaging tone to avoid boring your readers.

Principles that are specific to Web writing apply here as well, although some of these principles apply mostly for longer content. These principles are as follows:

- **Break content into chunks.** Segment text into easily readable pieces, using headlines, short paragraphs, and lists (bulleted or numbered). Isn't it nice that RSS feeds automatically break your content into titles and short descriptions?
- **Put the most important content first.** This means starting with an overview, breaking down into the details, and then summarizing. Your short description is the perfect overview.
- **Use a variety of formats.** In addition to straight paragraphs and lists, use some of the following formats:
    - Questions and answers
    - Examples
    - Called-out quotes, including testimonials and summaries
    - Checklists
    - Case histories or customer experiences
    - Lists of resources and links
    - Frequently asked questions (FAQs)
    - Diagrams, charts, and graphs
    - Price lists
    - Polls or quizzes
    - Images and easily recognizable icons
- **Be concise.** (Did I say that already? It bears saying again.) The rule of thumb is to write 50% on a Web page of what you would write for print. Try to delete any unnecessary words. Okay, delete any unnecessary words. Better yet, delete unnecessary words.

Chapter 5 offers lots of specific resources and techniques as well as advice on how to find content and add value to it.

Just how many people read your feed?

One disadvantage of RSS is that you don't have a list of subscribers the way you do for an e-mail newsletter. Many people use the number of subscribers as an important statistic for determining the success of their newsletter, but what about RSS?.

If you have access to sophisticated Web-development techniques, you can create a database by keeping track of the number of clicks to your pages. Of course, you won't get names, but you can get a count. Some ways to get a count of clicks are as follows:

- Collecting cookies and tracking the IP addresses from the cookies
- Using link-tracking software
- Linking your feed to a CGI script that logs the IP address and source address of visitors and then redirects visitors to the Web page
- Using special URLs for your feed that you know are linked to only by your feed and then using your site statistics to track those URLs
- Using FeedBurner (`www.feedburner.com`), which hosts RSS feeds and provides statistics for you

You can't assume that every click indicates a person reading your feed. Those "clicks" may be robots (programs that automatically search the Web). RSS readers also contact your feed to look for updates, regardless of whether a person is looking at the results.

In the end, you may not be able to get an accurate count. You'll need to make your decision based on the end results — for example, sales or comments submitted by readers.

For example, the *Christian Science Monitor* created RSS feeds when other newspapers were hesitant to provide news for free, especially out of the context of their Web sites. Since then, the *Monitor*'s print circulation is up, and its Web-site traffic has grown fourfold. Its RSS file accesses have doubled, into the tens of thousands. The cost to the *Monitor:* almost nothing. If people pick up on the content, they consider it a way of getting their name out to potential customers. The *Monitor*'s site has an RSS feed button (they use an XML label on their button). On the left of their page, they list all the blogs, all of which have RSS feeds.

Getting attention

Some people worry that RSS leaves the initiative up to the subscriber. Whereas e-mail is delivered to a person's e-mail program and shoves itself in the person's inbox, an RSS feed must wait until a reader decides to open the RSS reader. Then that feed may compete with a number of other feeds.

Actually, one of the main reasons for RSS's popularity has been that e-mail newsletter publishers have been so frustrated by the fact that their well-written, well-meaning newsletters are considered spam by various spam blockers. The result is that many of their subscribers don't see the newsletter.

In addition, it's reasonable to consider the preferences of your subscribers, who are overwhelmed with e-mail and want to get their news all in one place. By subscribing to an RSS feed, they are choosing that medium and are therefore motivated to check their feeds.

Remember that most RSS readers include a pop-up notification that lists new items. I often find myself distracted (from the writing of this book!) by going to look at new feeds. I can turn off the notification, but I don't, because I really do want to see what's new (perhaps some new RSS feature that I should be writing about). So, don't hesitate to offer RSS feeds along with your e-mail newsletter.

Some Web-site owners don't like the idea that people can see their content outside the context of their Web site. I mention this in the section "Publishing without losing Web-site traffic," earlier in this chapter. Remember that for people to see your Web-site content, they have to go to your Web site. Usually, they get there by doing one of the following things:

- Typing your URL in their browser
- Clicking a link from another site
- Clicking a link in your e-mail newsletter

But just as people can click a link in your e-mail newsletter, they can also click a link in your RSS feed. The feed is a way for you to bring people to your site that may not otherwise come. And you don't even have to bring them to your site to sign up! If you register your feed with directories, people who are interested may subscribe to your feed — people who may have never been to your site. Other sites may syndicate your feed and display it there — more opportunities for people to click through to your site.

What spurs people to go to your site? How do they even remember that your site exists? Some people like to keep track of many sites, but how can they remember them all? People may keep a list of favorites or bookmarks in their browser, but those lists quickly get too long. The RSS reader automatically notifies subscribers of new items and keeps the list nicely organized in categories, too. People can easily scan the new items and click the ones that they're interested in. So RSS is just one more tool in your arsenal to get attention. If you update your feed regularly, you'll get the attention of your subscribers.

Signing on, now or later

Some publishers are holding back to see whether RSS is just a fad or whether it will become more widespread. Right now, most people who subscribe to RSS feeds are highly attuned to information, whether for their work or for fun. RSS hasn't attained the level of use of e-mail and chatting — at least not yet.

But what have you to lose? RSS feeds are so easy to create. They're quick and they're cheap. Those are pretty attractive qualities. If you want to reach people who want the information that you have — whether it's about a product or the cost of tea in China — you can reach them with an RSS feed.

Yes, people are writing RSS feeds about tea. Two examples are Tea News Feed (`www.teanews.it/rss.xml`) and Just for Tea Lovers (`www.just-for-tea-lovers.com/index.xml`).

Keeping Up to Date on Formats

Although creating an RSS feed is easy, the base formats have their complexities. Educating yourself about the various versions and their features can open new possibilities for your feed. For example, version 2.0 lets you include an `<enclosure>` tag that references an audio or video file — in fact, any type of file. For more information, see Chapter 9.

Understanding the encoding

The better you understand the RSS format, the better you can make proper use of it, without having to tear out your hair. For example, as I explain in Chapter 7 in the section "Dealing with illegal characters," you'll get frustrated fairly quickly unless you know how to escape the illegal characters, which are & (ampersand), < (less than), > (greater than), ' (apostrophe or single quotation mark), and " (double quotation mark). Several times I tried to use an ampersand in my item titles, only to discover that the feed didn't validate. (Finally, I got the point!)

Similarly, if you want to use characters from languages other than English, you must use a character set that supports your language. In Chapter 7 in the section "Declaring the XML version and encoding," I explain the various character set encoding types you can use. If you find that some RSS readers are displaying some of your characters incorrectly, the readers may be using Windows character sets. Changing your encoding set may solve the problem.

Using the format properly

Remember that a program is interpreting your feed to display it in a reader. Therefore, while the XML format may seem flexible to you, you should use it as it was designed so programs can display your feed correctly. This means that you should use the various tags according to their obvious purpose. So, put publish dates in the `<pubDate>` tag, not in the `<lastBuildDate>` tag, and put descriptions or item content, not copyright notices or "Click here for more," in the `<description>` tag.

When your feed is out there, others may try to pick it up and display it on their Web sites. I explain this process, called *parsing,* in Chapter 11. When you know that your feed may go through several processes by several different programs, you get the idea that you should toe the line with standard usage practices. Otherwise, you don't know how your feed may get mangled. People who may otherwise further syndicate your content may hesitate if your feed looks downright weird, due to unusual practices.

An important part of marketing your feed is to brand it with your logo. (Chapter 10 is all about promoting your feed.) For this, make sure that you take advantage of the `<image>` tag. For your feed's image to appear properly, you should keep its width within the recommended limits — width=88 and height=31 — and certainly not more than the maximum allowed limits — width=144 and height=400. If you use a large logo, it may appear squished, and Web sites that want to pick up your feed may choose not to do so because the size of the image may crowd out other content.

Make sure that you use your links so that software can distinguish between different items. Readers may use any number of clues to determine which items they've already downloaded. For example, they may use a combination of the date and the title. However, if you use the same title twice, one of your items may not get updated. Another clue to software is the link. If the links are different, an RSS reader can usually interpret the item as different. But many feeds use identical links for several items because they are all on the same Web page. Again, this can create a situation where your feed isn't properly updated. You can use several techniques to ensure unique items, as I describe in the following sections.

Unique links

Many people put the content of each item on a separate HTML page. If you follow this procedure, all your links are unique. But if the thought of creating all those pages scares you and you prefer to put all the content for your feed on one Web page, place bookmarks in the HTML code and link to the bookmarks. In the HTML code, a bookmark looks like this:

```
<a name="BestFont">Choosing the Best Font</a>
```

The link in your feed looks like this:

```
http://www.put_website_url_here.com/#bestfont
```

If you put your content on one HTML page, using bookmarks not only helps your items appear to be unique, but it also brings your subscribers to the exact place on the page that contains the content they want to read. That makes for satisfied people!

Permalinks

Permalinks (permanent URLs for Web site content) are a fixture of blogging, but you don't need to use blogging software to use the concept of permalinks. (For more about permalinks, see the sidebar "What is a permalink?" in Chapter 6.) You can permanently archive each item on a separate page, while leaving your current items together on one main page. Then you can link to the permalink, which is always unique.

GUIDs

Global Unique Identifiers (GUIDs) are stored in the `<guid>` tag of RSS version 2.0. I explain this tag in Chapter 7 in the section "Using RSS Version 2.0." The GUID is often a permalink, which, as I explain in the previous section, is always unique. However, you can just as easily use a date-time stamp. Unless you publish two items within the same second, this technique creates a unique identifier. Another possibility is to use a simple index system. Start from 1 and count up. This method gives you the fun benefit of keeping track of the total number of items you've published.

Staying informed

If you're involved in RSS, you should keep up to date on what's happening in the field. A lot — but not all — of the chatter is technical. People are writing articles on how to use RSS for marketing, creating intercompany communications, delivering audio and video, delivering software updates, and more. In Chapter 14, I list some excellent resources on RSS, including (of course) RSS feeds on RSS.

Staying on Topic

One of the best practices you can use is to stick to your topic, more or less. I say more or less because, in the blog world, rambling, dithering, meandering, wandering, and circumambulating is often considered a salutatory quality, (much to be praised). This technique works if people come to your feed (or blog) because you're a great writer; have creative, funny, and deep thoughts; and have a fascinating personality.

Unfortunately, that description doesn't fit all of us! Most feeds have a topic, and people come to read about that topic. Therefore, except for a few minor diversions, you should stick to that topic.

Chapter 5 is all about ways to ensure that you write to get the results you want from your RSS feed.

Staying on topic is not hard. Here are some basic principles:

- **Keep it simple.** Don't try to cover everything in one feed. Design a feed to have a simple purpose and topic.
- **Focus on your audience.** Understand what your audience wants (perhaps by doing some surveys). Then provide the content that is most useful to your readers.
- **Know the purpose of your feed.** Write a mission statement for your feed. Knowing why you're writing can help you stick to the point.
- **Provide multiple feeds.** If necessary, create multiple feeds for different purposes. Some feeds may be technical in their purpose, such as a place for employees to find out about newly updated software tools. Another feed may be about company accomplishments. Still another may list company job openings. If you keep these feeds separate, readers can find what they need much more efficiently.

Using the Structure to Your Advantage

Although the basic structure of the feed is set, you can use that structure for better or for worse. Deciding how to use your RSS feed to get the best results is not much different than deciding how to word an ad. As with an ad, you want the following three components:

- **An attention-getter:** Your feed and item titles get the attention of your readers — or potential readers. For example, people searching through a directory of RSS feeds may decide whether to subscribe based on your feed's title. They generally have no more information than that. After people have subscribed, they decide whether to read an item based on its title.

- **Enough supporting information for people to make a decision:** The supporting information is the description, which expands on the title and explains what the full article is about — if you're not including the full entry in the description.
- **A way for people to act:** Clicking your link is the action you want people to take. Make sure that when they do click, they find useful, appropriate information on the other end.

Deciding on description length

You can structure your feed in several ways, depending on your needs. Different feeds can have varying structures, but you should follow some best-practice guidelines. In Chapter 5 in the section "Full text or links?" I discuss the various ways that you can structure your feed items. Basically, you have the following three choices:

- Include only titles and forget the descriptions
- Include the full text of your entries in your descriptions
- Include short descriptions

I discuss these three options further in the next three sections.

Including titles only

If you include only titles and no descriptions, your readers must click to your site for every article they want to read. This technique can cut two ways. On one hand, you may think that readers will certainly click to your site to read the article. On the other hand, they may click nothing, especially if your headings aren't compelling. Figure 10-4 shows an example. (Figures 5-1 and 5-2 in Chapter 5 show feeds with short descriptions and full-text entries.)

Feeds that are comprised only of titles are usually created using an automated method, such as a Web content management system, because the description part can be difficult to extract from Web-page content.

From the point of view of best practices, using only titles goes against the purpose of RSS feeds, which is to enable readers to view a large amount of material in one place and sort through it quickly. A title-only feed is not really a feed at all; it's just a collection of favorite links in one place.

If you need to create a title-only feed, make sure that your titles are clear and explicit so that readers can make informed choices. Instead of writing "New Discounts!" you could say "30% off on Product A until January 30."

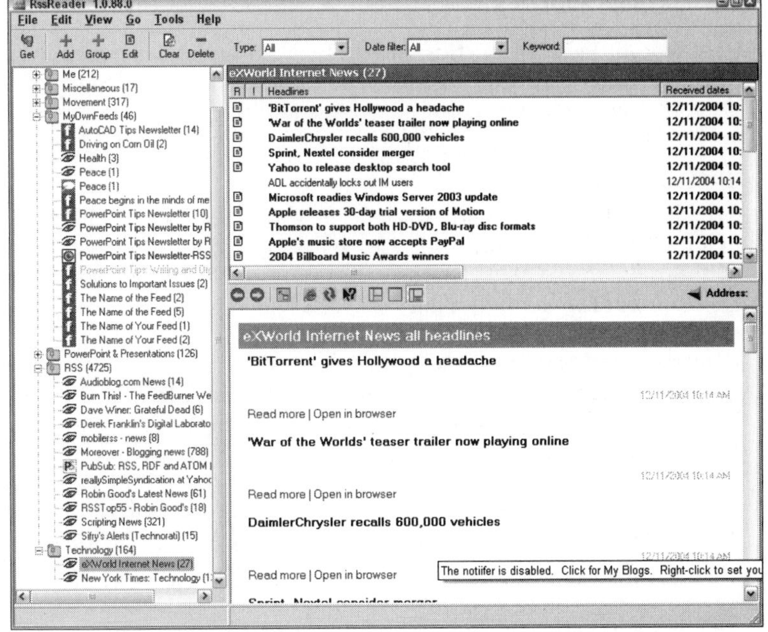

Figure 10-4: This feed shows only titles, with no descriptions.

Because a title-only feed requires readers to click through for every article, Web-site traffic statistics don't provide much information about what topics are interesting and valuable to visitors.

Some Web-site owners feel strongly that they want users to view their content only in the context of their site. Perhaps they have ads that they want viewers to see (and click). They may also have links on their site to other areas of the site, where they sell their products or services.

I think that title-only feeds will slowly die as the following things happen:

- Web-site owners see that their traffic doesn't drop
- Web-based companies see that their sales don't diminish
- Web-site owners find that their feed is a great communication device and actually brings motivated buyers to their site
- Automated tools improve to better create good descriptions (or people learn to use these tools more effectively)

Even if you include descriptions, some RSS readers ignore the descriptions and display only the titles. Your feed may appear, on a Web site with only the titles.

For this reason, you should make sure that your titles are meaningful when viewed out of context of their descriptions — or even out of context of the rest of your feed. Your titles should be as complete as possible and convey the topic clearly, without getting too long. Also, try not to use too much jargon. If possible, write out acronyms and use general terms.

Including full-text entries

Full-text entries are mostly for bloggers who don't care about Web traffic or bandwidth. This format is nice for readers who want to read the full entry without having to click. On the other hand, it doesn't provide a quick way to selectively scan through many entries.

Another good use for full-text entries is press releases. If you're trying to get people to read your press release, you don't want to make them think about whether they should click (to click or not to click, that is the question), you just want them to read.

Some content-management systems create full-text entries when they create feeds. Not able to ferret out a short description , they include the entire page's content.

Of course, if you want to bring people back to your site, full-text entries may have a negative impact, because readers have less impetus to click — all the content is right there.

Because your feed can end up anywhere, including on someone else's site or alongside another related feed, avoid language that is relative only to your feed and site, such as "on this site" or "at this link." These expressions may not make sense out of context.

Including a short description

The middle ground is to include short descriptions. Just as Goldilocks found one chair too big, one too small, and one just right, a short description is a great option for many reasons. Your descriptions can be a teaser: the first paragraph or an overview of the full text of the entry. This technique still requires your readers to go to your site to read your content, but it gives them enough information to decide whether they're interested. This win-win value gives this approach my vote of approval.

Short descriptions ideally fulfill the purpose of RSS feeds. These descriptions allow the reader to skim over large amounts of information and quickly decide what they want to read.

As the publisher, you get a good balance, too. Readers who are interested click through, and they're obviously motivated to get your information. There they are, on your site, having chosen to be there. Aren't these your best potential customers? And you're not using up bandwidth on people who click through, discover that they're really not interested, and then immediately leave.

You can also track which Web pages your readers click through to. For example, if you have a feed that contains information on your various products, by analyzing the results of your traffic statistics, you can get valuable information about the relative popularity of your products. With titles only, unless your titles are very explicit, readers are mostly clicking blindly; therefore, the clicks don't reflect their interests as clearly.

Deciding how many entries to include

RSS version 0.91 limits the number of items in a feed to 15. The RSS 1.0 specification allows more but recommends a maximum of 15. Version 2.0 has no limit. However, you probably shouldn't include more than 100 items in a feed. Consider your subscribers' point of view and how your feed will appear in various types of readers and other contexts, especially on Web sites.

Figure 10-5 shows a feed with over 150 entries, a full month's worth. This feed, which aims to include everything about blogging, puts out many entries each day.

The more entries you include, the less likely your readers will scan through all the headings — it takes too long and appears overwhelming.

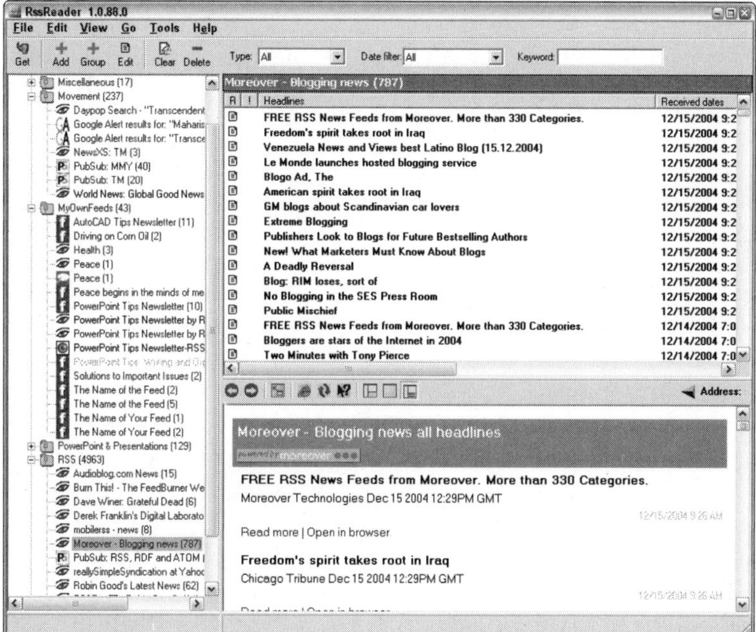

Figure 10-5: This feed has dozens of entries.

Remember that some browser-based readers show feeds in a column; examples are MyYahoo! and AmphetaDesk. Imagine 150 items for one feed! You would have to scroll down forever to get to your next feed.

Also, feeds can be imported into Web sites. Here again, the structure is a vertical column. Sites that may pick up your feed will not do so if that means importing a long HTML page and crowding out other material that they want their viewers to see.

I don't think there's a magic maximum number of feeds items, because the best practice would depend on how often you update your feed. However, the basic principle is to allow people to quickly scan the feeds items to decide what they want to read. If they have to scroll down too much, you've lost them.

Decide how old is old. For example, if you update every day, an item that is two weeks old is ancient. On the other hand, if you update every week, you may decide to keep items that are up to two months old. Then remove older items from your feed on a regular basis.

Being Timely

The main point of RSS feeds is to keep people up to date on the latest news. Therefore, your responsibility is to keep your feed regularly updated. Moreover, you want your feed to be the place to go to find all the information on its topic. So, keep at it and make it a permanent record of the news that's relevant to the feed's topic.

Don't start a new feed every week. People don't want to constantly subscribe to a new feed. Instead, make your feed long-lasting and timely, and people will gravitate to it. Archive older items and make them easily accessible. For example, you could keep one permanent item in your feed that links to the archives. Your subscribers will soon learn that they can get the up-to-date information they want by going to your feed.

Chapter 11

Promoting Your Feed

In This Chapter

- Registering your feed with directories
- Linking to your feed
- Letting your visitors know what RSS is
- Telling others about your feed
- Promoting your feed with your e-newsletter

Creating a feed is not enough — not if you want people to read it. You need to let people know that your feed exists and try to get them to subscribe to it.

Promoting a feed is similar to promoting a Web site or an e-mail newsletter. You have to work at it a bit. Luckily, some easy-to-use tools are available to help you.

This chapter explains the many ways to get the word out.

Registering Your Feed with Directories

The number one way to let people — those outside your usual range of contacts — know that you have a feed is to register it with as many directories as possible. This concept is similar to registering your Web site with Web-site directories such as Yahoo!. But it's usually a simpler process, except for one fact — you can find a lot more RSS directories than Web-site directories.

Of course, you should also promote your Web site content itself. When you get people to your Web site, if they like the content, they may look for your feed so that they can keep up to date on any changes that appear on your site. See Chapter 14, which lists ten great ways to market your Web site, for more ideas.

The reason for all the directories? Nobody really knows, but here are some possibilities:

- Searching for RSS feeds on Web-site search engines, such as Google, is not very effective. For example, you may search for XML files by entering **Web marketing filetype:XML** in a search engine. But, although most RSS feeds use an XML file type, lots of XML files are not RSS feeds. XML is used for many other purposes, so your results often include lots of irrelevant information. If you enter **filetype:RSS**, you'll get RSS feeds, but only a fraction of those that exist. Also, not all feeds are directly based on Web-page content, which is what Web search engines look for.
- RSS is a new technology that's causing a lot of excitement, and many people want to get in on the act — so they start directory sites.
- Some sites hope that you'll come for the free feeds and stay to buy customized, specialized feeds or other RSS-related services.

Perhaps as the technology of RSS spreads, simpler and more effective methods of finding (and marketing) RSS feeds will emerge.

So, you need to do the legwork and register with as many directories as you can. To get you going, Figure 11-1 shows CompleteRSS.com, an RSS directory where you can search for and subscribe to RSS feeds.

Chapter 14 has a good list of RSS feed directories to give you a head start.

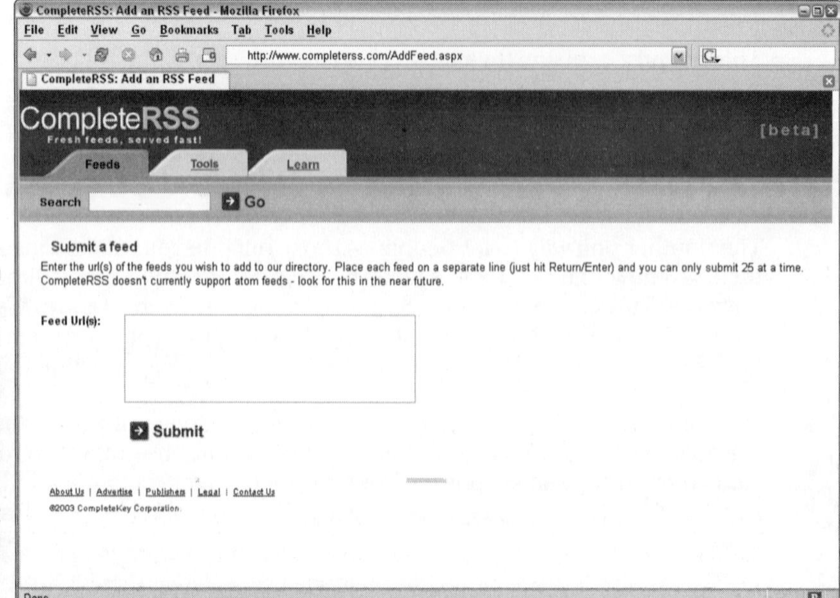

Figure 11-1: CompleteRSS.com is an example of an RSS directory where you can submit your RSS feed.

If your feed is based on a blog, you can still register at all the RSS directories, but you should also register at blog directories. Blogging is a whole world unto itself. In fact, more blog directories exist than RSS directories. Do a Web search using the keywords *blog* and *directory,* and you'll find what seems like millions of listings. (A year from now, after you've finally registered at all of these directories, I hope you'll come back and finish reading this book!)

RSSSubmit is a site that automates the process of registering your feed at a number of well-known RSS directories. For more information, go to `www.dummysoftware.com/rsssubmit.html`. Some directories allow you to pay for a featured listing. For example, Syndic8 (`www.syndic8.com`) will list your feed on its busy, highly ranked site for $25 per week.

Directories may use spiders (software that searches the Web automatically) to check out your feed, but they operate on their own schedule. You can proactively let them know when you have updated your feed by a process called *pinging.* Pinging simply contacts a specific Web server and makes sure that it's functioning. An easy-to-use service is Ping-O-Matic at `pingomatic.com`. The service is free and pings over a dozen directories. You simply enter the URL of your Web page (not your RSS feed) in the Blog Home Page text box and click the Submit Pings button.

Registering with directories is a broad sweep type of marketing. The people who go to directories are specifically interested in RSS feeds and search for feeds on topics that interest them. From the point of view of outreach, you may reach anyone that way, which is why you can get such a diverse group of people. Although you're reaching people who just want RSS feeds, these people are obviously quite interested in information and news. They are highly motivated to go out and find those feeds.

To reach those who aren't as RSS savvy or as motivated to find feeds, check out the sections "Explaining What RSS Is" and "Telling Others about Your Feed," later in this chapter.

Linking to Your Feed

Of course, when people do find your site, you want your Web-site visitors to subscribe to your feed, so you need to put an RSS or XML button on your site. (For my very opinionated opinion about which button to use, see the section "Looking for the orange or blue button" in Chapter 3.)

To get your button, you can copy one from any site that has one. Right-click the button and choose Save Image As. You can also do an image search on Google by entering **RSS** or **Atom** in the search text box. If you choose Atom, you'll get Atom buttons as well as pictures of atoms. You won't have any trouble figuring out the difference because atoms are MUCH tinier.

Although the convention is pretty well set, you don't have to use the typical button. Figure 11-2 shows Derek Franklin's big RSS button, which he makes a big deal about. He's trying to plug RSS and decry the standard tiny button, both at the same time.

If you want to have fun with feed buttons, try G.T. McKnight's Web site at `www.gtmcknight.com/buttons/feeds.php`. Here you can find everything *except* the typical RSS button.

Add a hyperlink to the button, linking to your RSS feed's file. To add a hyperlink to a button, select the button, and use your Web creation software's hyperlink command. In the HTML code, the result looks something like the following:

```
<a href="autocad_tips_newsletter.xml"><img
          src="images/rss_btn.gif"></a>
```

Now visitors can easily subscribe to your feed.

You need to make clear what the RSS feed is about. If you have a page that includes many different types of content, label the RSS button with the name of your feed. Figure 11-3 shows a good example.

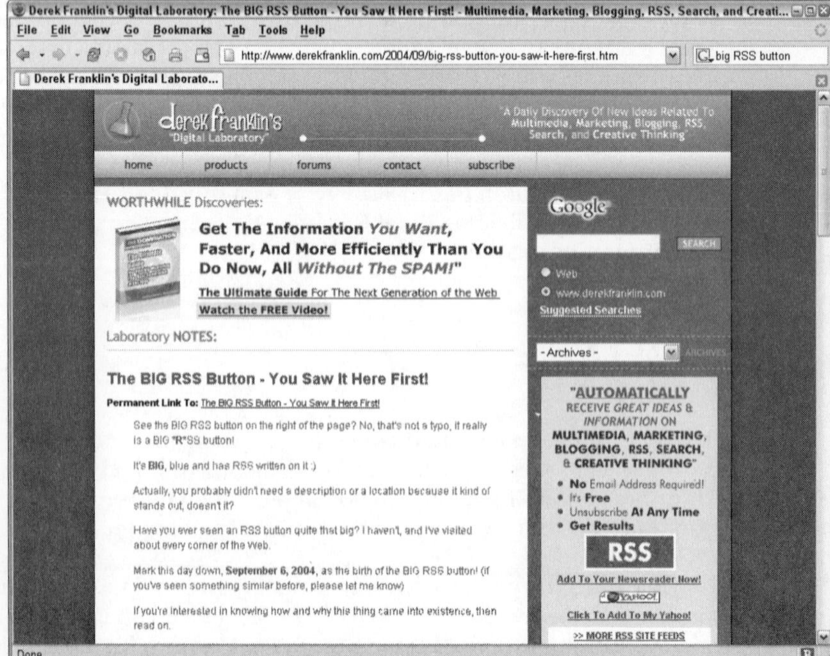

Figure 11-2: You can use a BIG RSS button instead of the usual small one, if you want.

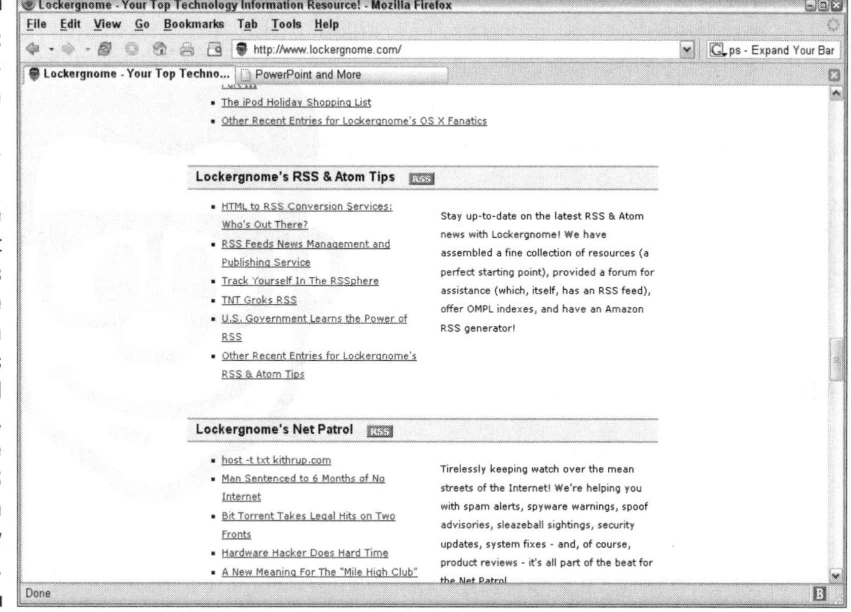

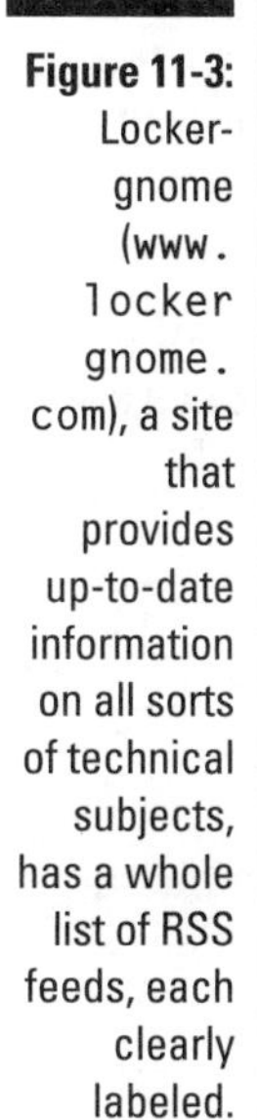
Figure 11-3: Lockergnome (`www.lockergnome.com`), a site that provides up-to-date information on all sorts of technical subjects, has a whole list of RSS feeds, each clearly labeled.

If you have a place on your site for visitors to sign up for an e-mail newsletter, that's a good place to put your RSS link. Then people can choose which way they want to receive information from you. Another good place is on an unsubscribe page. Maybe people will sign up for your RSS feed while unsubscribing to your e-newsletter.

Getting Auto-Discovered

Some RSS readers can automatically find RSS feeds on a Web page. This feature is called auto-discovery. (No, it's not when you finally discover that antique 1966 VW you've been searching for.)

You can ensure that this auto-discovery works by using the link HTML tag and the code on any Web page that contains an RSS feed. You place this code in the `head` section of your page, which means between the `<head>` and `</head>` tags. Here's the code:

```
<link rel="alternate" type="application/rss+xml" title="RSS"
          href="http://www.your_URL_here.com/feedfilename.
          xml">
```

You can put anything you want for the title attribute, but it should relate to your feed, because some browsers display this text. If you have more than one feed on a page, create a separate link tag for each feed, giving each one a different title.

For an Atom feed, the type should be "application/atom+xml".

If you use a template to create new Web pages, put this code in the head section of your template. In this way, all your new pages will automatically include the auto-discovery code.

Explaining Just What RSS Is

Let's face it — not everyone knows what RSS is yet. I know that from personal experience, as I describe in the following conversation:

"Guess what? I'm writing a new book."

"Congratulations! What's it on?"

"A Web technology called RSS. Ever heard of it?"

"Oh yeah. Isn't that Reading Short Stories?"

"No."

"Rapid Site Simulation?"

"No!"

"Registered Sixth Sense?"

"Oh, forget it!"

So, I've scientifically proven that not everyone knows about RSS. Therefore, unless your clientele is very geeky, you need to explain it to them. Most sites don't, but some do. Figure 11-4 shows what I put on my site. This is similar to what I've seen on other sites that explain RSS.

When explaining RSS, keep your explanation simple and appropriate for your audience. You don't really need to explain the technology, just what it means for them and how they can subscribe. If you want, recommend some RSS readers to make the process painless or refer them to a browser-based reader.

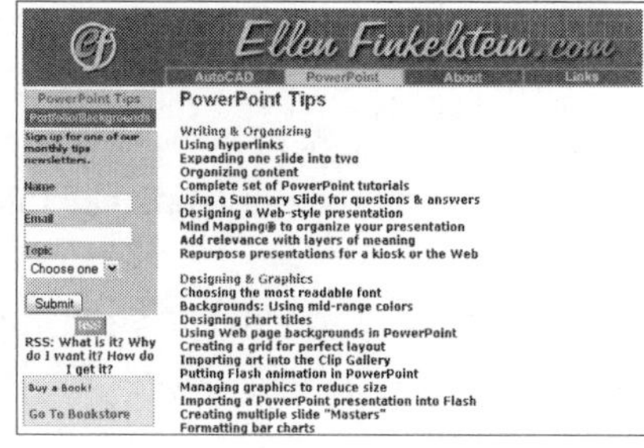

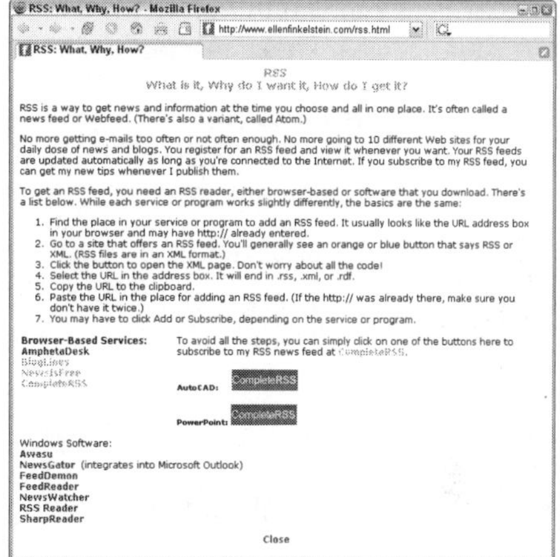

Figure 11-4: When you click the link below the RSS button, a window opens, explaining RSS.

Helpful text next to the RSS button can say something like "Subscribe to My RSS Feed on Widget Technology." In fact, any language that you may use for an e-mail newsletter would work, slightly modified, for your RSS feed. Here are some phrases that you can use:

- Get regular updates about widget technology
- Keep informed about widget technology
- Don't miss the latest news about widget technology!

More people are finding out about RSS every day, so even if they don't sign up right away, they may the next time they visit. Having an RSS feed shows that you're "with it." The implication is that if you are up to date enough to have a feed, you're similarly up to date in your field — and that's what your visitors want.

So evangelize a little, strut your stuff, and brag about being on the RSS bandwagon.

Telling Others All about Your Feed

To market your Web site, you do more than just register it and hope that people come. You probably proactively tell people about your site in many ways. Web-site marketing is a huge field. (Chapter 14 collects ten ways to market your Web site).

Some common ways to market a Web site also apply to marketing your RSS feed. These methods are:

- **Cross-link with other sites:** Ask sites that link to you to add a phrase about your RSS feed. Using the phrase "RSS news feed available" may be enough.
- **Send out press releases:** Because RSS is new, you can send out press releases about your news feed. That's right; the feed is news in itself, as shown in Figure 11-5.

You may have noticed that Figure 11-5 shows a blog. I've discovered that bloggers seem to be especially eager for content and often use anything reasonably newsworthy that you send them. Make sure that your news is relevant and recent, and you'll probably get a mention.

RSS feed links in your e-mail signature

A *signature* is text that automatically appears at the bottom of every e-mail you send. Almost all e-mail programs let you create a signature. You can often add links to this text. Your Web-site URL should be there. Why not a link to your RSS feed as well? Think of it as an RSS button in every e-mail! To subscribe, recipients can click the link to open the XML file and copy the URL from their browser's address text box. Alternatively, they can right-click and copy the URL to the Clipboard. Either way, they can then paste the URL into their RSS reader. Figure 11-6 shows an example.

Writing articles for other sites

A great way to get links to your site is to write articles for newsletters and sites that cover your field. The way others pay you is to link to your site. You probably don't want to substitute a link to your RSS feed for the link to your site (but then again, you may). However, other sites can also give you a byline. You can mention your RSS feed in the byline or perhaps even in your article.

Touting your feed in discussion groups

Some people regularly participate in discussion groups, newsgroups, and forums — or whatever you want to call them. Or, perhaps they often add comments to blogs. Just as you can mention your Web site in your comments (or put it as a signature below your name), you can mention your feed. People read your entry, realize that you're knowledgeable in your field, and go to your Web site or subscribe to your feed — or both.

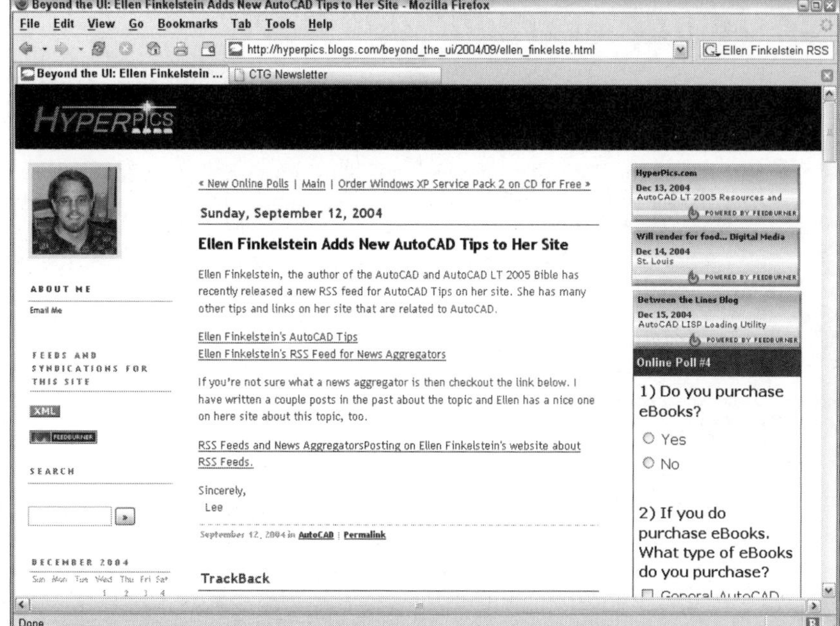

Figure 11-5: Just creating an RSS feed is often enough news to receive a mention on other sites.

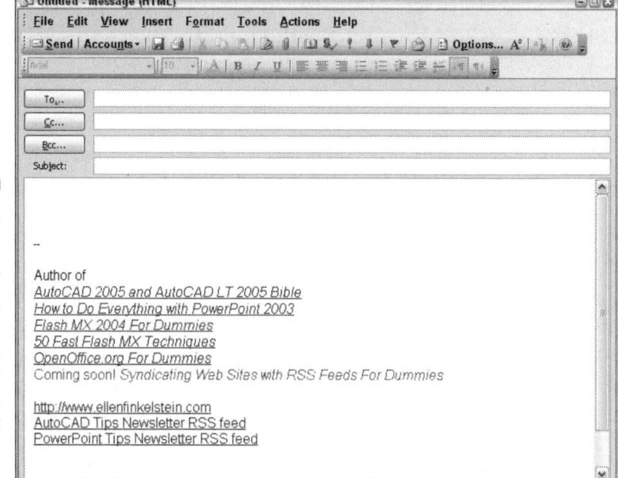

Figure 11-6: I shamelessly promote everything in my e-mail signature, including my RSS feeds.

This method brings you people who are intensely interested in the topic of the discussion group, but it can be time consuming. Those discussions can go on and on.

Telling everyone you know

"Hey! Guess what? I have an RSS feed! Pass it on." Wherever you go — conferences, business meetings, and so on — or whomever you talk to — friends, colleagues, and customers — let them know about your new RSS feed. They'll probably say, "What's an RSS feed?" and you can tell them all about it. It's a great way to break the ice at a party. (Well, you'll have to be the judge of that.)

Why not put the URL for your feed on your business card, stationery, or brochure?

Keeping Your E-mail Newsletter

If you have a successful e-mail newsletter, I don't recommend giving it up. E-mail is still the way that most people get their news. But you should definitely mention your RSS feed in your newsletter as an alternative way to get the same information, with a link to your site's explanation about RSS. I didn't experience a significant rush to unsubscribe to my newsletter. But I know that people look at my RSS description page, because I see the traffic statistics. At the very least, I'm educating people about RSS.

You can — and should — update your RSS feed when you update your Web site. If your newsletter is monthly, for example, and covers updates on your site throughout the previous month, people who subscribe to your RSS feed receive the news before your newsletter subscribers. You can plug this advantage to your readers. One of the major advantages of RSS is to notify your readers of changes as soon as they happen. By comparison, an e-mail newsletter is old news by the time you get it published.

Branding Your Feed

You probably hired a Web designer to make your Web site look beautiful, if you're not a designer yourself. You carefully use your logo on your site, your letterhead, your PowerPoint presentations, and all your publicity materials. Why not brand your RSS feed as well?

The `<image>` tag fits the bill perfectly for this purpose. Each feed can have only one image, so use it for your logo. I explain the details of the `<image>` tag in the following two places:

- Chapter 6, in the section "Relating your feed to your Web site"
- Chapter 10, in the section "Using the format properly"

Another way to brand your feed is to put your name in the RSS feed title. Figure 11-7 shows several examples in my RSS category of feeds, such as Robin Good's Latest News, Lockergnome's RSS and Atom Tips, and Moreover – Blogging News. Each of these examples uses the name of the person, company, or Web site in the title for branding purposes.

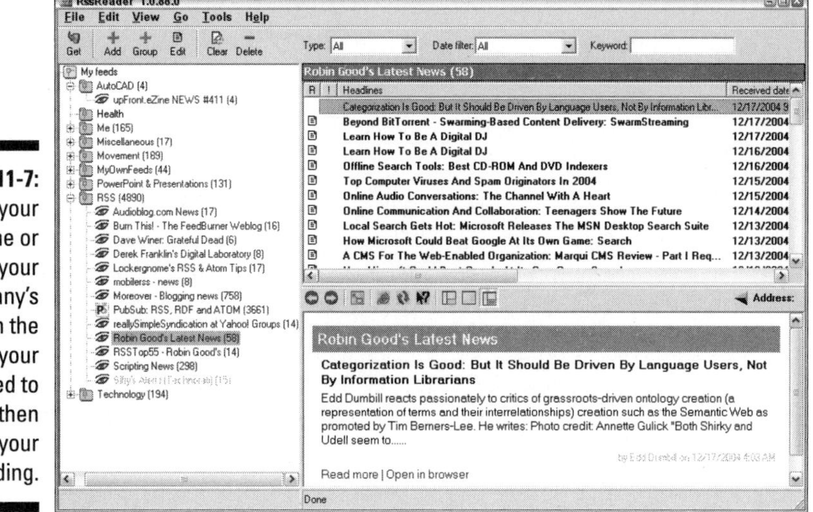

Figure 11-7: Use your name or your company's name in the title of your feed to strengthen your branding.

You could make up a little phrase and put it at the beginning of each item's description, such as "Home of the Best Widgets." People would soon start associating you with the best widgetry.

You can probably think of more ways to publicize your feed. Remember that publicizing your feed also publicizes your Web site and your business.

Chapter 12

Placing News Feeds on Your Web Site

In This Chapter

- Republishing RSS feeds on your site
- Choosing a conversion technology
- Using RSS-to-Web-site tools

Most of this book explains how to create an RSS feed from Web-based content. In this chapter, I explain how to do the opposite — turn RSS feeds into a Web page. This completes the cycle of the content, from Web page to RSS feed to Web page.

Anyone whose daily life involves finding, reading, understanding, filtering, analyzing, and publishing information needs to know about the tools and techniques that I describe in this chapter.

Republishing RSS Feeds on Your Site

For some people, publishing an RSS feed is enough. They simply want to make their content available to others in an easy-to-use format. These people have a blog or a Web site and want their customers or potential customers to know the latest information.

However, you may want your blog or Web site to collect information from other sources that people may want to read. For example, if you have a blog on politics, you may collect information from other blogs. In fact, some blogs may be interesting enough that you may want to put them in your own blog. Or, if you have a Web site that provides broad-based information on a specific topic, you may want to provide pages from other Web sites that also cover the same topic.

In short, if your content is actually an amalgam of other sources, wouldn't it be nice if you could somehow mesh it all together to create a Web site from those sources? Prior to RSS, collecting this information was difficult because you needed to go to so many sites. With RSS, you can subscribe to the RSS feeds of other sites and then reformat those feeds into HTML (or perhaps JavaScript) and display the results on your site. In some cases, you can filter the contents as well, to get exactly the type of information that fits your Web site. Figure 12-1 shows this process.

The reasons for republishing RSS feeds on your Web site are varied. Here are some sample scenarios:

- You want to provide current news on your Web site. For example, if your Web site is about health, you can include the latest health news on the site.
- You want to create a Web page that matches your feed. Perhaps you have a Web site of software tips. You also publish an RSS feed of your latest tips. On your Web site, you may put each tip on a separate page or collect them all on one page. The page probably organizes the tips by category, rather than date, because that structure is easier for people to find the tips they want. But you may also want a page of your latest tips for people who come back to your site and want to see what's new. Your RSS feed has that information. So, you republish your feed to a new page on your Web site, which now always contains your latest tips.
- You publish a private RSS feed that collects information about your industry. You make this available to sales reps and others inside your company. But some people may not want to use the RSS feed and may prefer to read the information on a Web site. So you create a Web page on your company's intranet that contains the same information as the RSS feed.
- To promote your Web site, you would like other sites to pick up your RSS feed content. People who manage these other sites may not know how to do this, but if you put your content on your Web site, you can give them permission to copy it, or perhaps link to it. If you create the Web page using JavaScript, you can supply Webmasters with the code.

As you can see, republishing RSS feeds as Web pages can be a solution in a number of situations. If you are ready to create a Web page from RSS feeds, whether they are your own feeds or somebody else's, you start by finding a software tool that can make the conversion.

Avoid legal entanglements! Before you take content from other Web sites, you need to get permission. Some sites make their policies clear, but others don't, so you need to contact the site's owner. Getting written (even e-mail) permission is always wise.

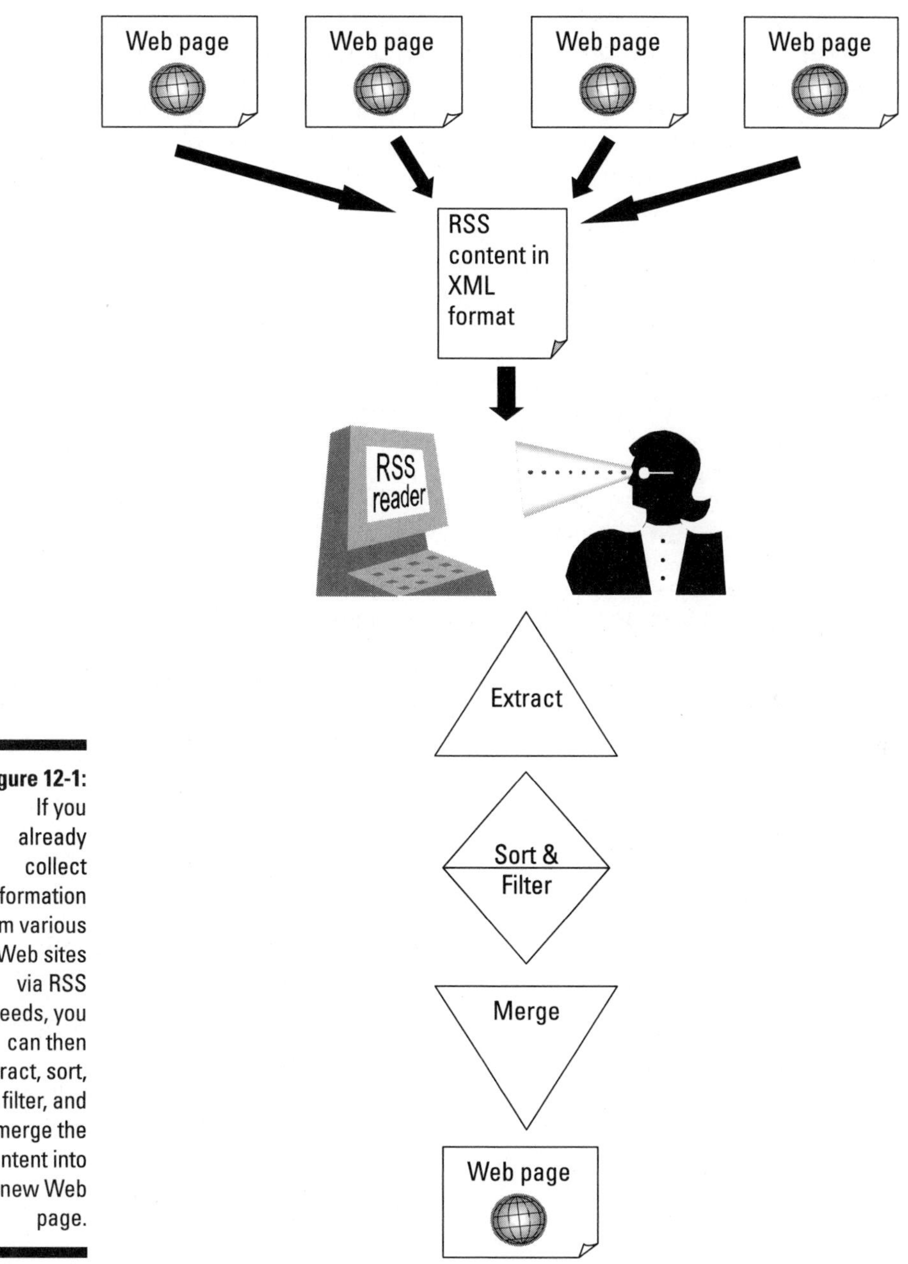

Figure 12-1: If you already collect information from various Web sites via RSS feeds, you can then extract, sort, filter, and merge the content into a new Web page.

Choosing a Technology to Convert RSS to a Web Page

Your choice of a technology to convert RSS to a Web page depends on your situation. Some tools require a fair amount of technological expertise, including uploading software to your Web server. Others are simple and automatic. Generally, the more control you want over a feed, the more you need a tool that requires some fiddling and configuring. You just need to find the tool that works for you.

I've discovered that programmers, just because they are programmers, seem to think that everyone else can handle code and its configuration. Many don't seem to understand that the rest of us get glazed-over eyes when we see a page of code. Programmers also seem to think that everyone can upload programs to their server. As a matter of fact, in many companies, employees aren't even allowed to install programs on their own computers without involving the IT department. Uploading software to the Web server? Not likely. Also, many Web hosts don't allow their customers to upload code, unless you subscribe to an expensive e-commerce package.

Nevertheless, you may have no restrictions on your Web server and may want the extra features that you can get by using software on your server. For example, you may want a solution that gives you full control over the look of the final Web page.

If you want a simpler solution, use a Web-based service that creates and perhaps hosts some code for you. Then you can simply refer to the code in your Web page to display the content you want.

You may also be choosy about whether the tool you use converts RSS to HTML or to JavaScript. Some people don't like the JavaScript solution because it's not readable by search engines. As a result, these pages don't rank highly and therefore are not as easy to find by users. Also, Windows XP Service Pack 2 blocks JavaScript by default, although viewers have the choice to display it.

In this chapter, I cover a wide range of solutions, with an emphasis on the simpler ones.

Using RSS-to-Web-Site Tools

Most Web-based services convert your RSS feed to JavaScript and simply give you the JavaScript code. The script itself resides on the service's Web server. As a result, you're dependent on that server maintaining the script and the content may load slowly as it references the service's Web server. The plus side is that this method is easy to use. I describe some features of Web-based services in the next section.

Software tools generally require you to upload code to your Web server, but the result is that you have more control over the code that way. These tools, called *parsers,* may be difficult for non-technical types to use. In this context, a parser analyzes text syntax and breaks it into chunks that it then reconfigures according to specific instructions. These tools analyze the structure of the XML in the RSS feed and then reorganize the feed into HTML code. I describe some software options in the section "Software tools."

Web-based services step-by-step

If you choose to use a Web-based service, you have a number of options, most of which are free. Hopefully, these Web sites will continue to offer their services for free.

RSSxpress-Lite

This service is on the UKOLN site from the University of Bath, the same site that has the RSS-creation tool mentioned in the section "Filling in the blanks with UKOLN" in Chapter 6. This service is the ultimate in simplicity and creates a line of JavaScript that you copy and paste into the HTML of your Web page wherever you want the feed to appear.

Go to `rssxpress.ukoln.ac.uk/lite/include` and read the explanation; then click the Try It link to see the page shown in Figure 12-2.

Then follow these steps to generate the content for a Web page:

1. **Enter the URL of an RSS feed into the URL text box or click one of the feeds on the right to enter that feed automatically.**
2. **Click the Get Script button.**
3. **On the following page, select and copy the JavaScript code.**
4. **Open the Web page where you want to place the JavaScript in the program you use to create Web pages (or any Web creation program).**
5. **Change to a view that displays the HTML code, and find the location where you want to put the converted feed content.**
6. **Paste the JavaScript code from the Clipboard.**
7. **In your Web creation software, return to your regular view of your Web page to see the result.**

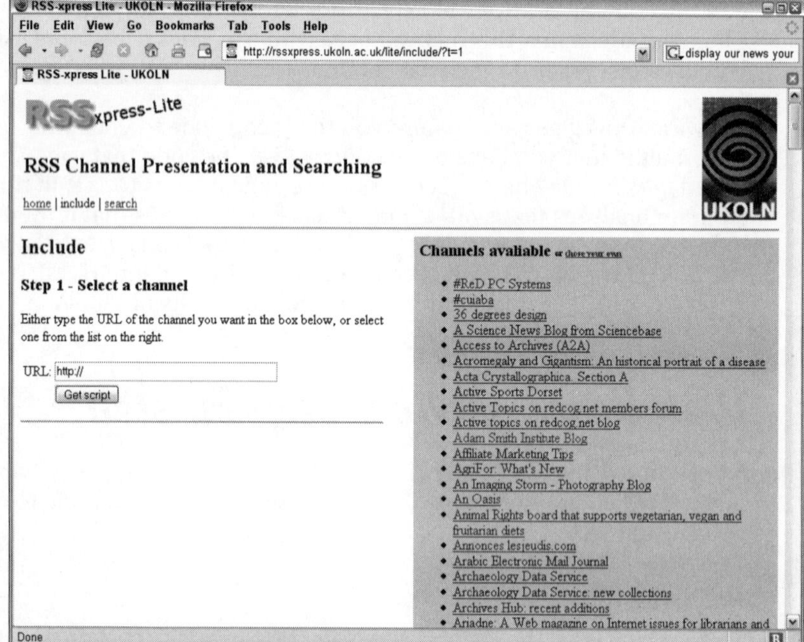

Figure 12-2: Simply enter the URL of an RSS feed into the URL text box.

Your Web-creation software may display the content or it may not display any content, depending on whether you're connected to the Internet, the capabilities of your software, the view you're in (your regular authoring view or a preview), the JavaScript settings, and other factors. The final proof is in the pudding — when you upload your Web page.

8. **Save your page and upload it to your Web server.**
9. **Open your browser and go to your new page.**

   You can see mine in Figure 12-3.

If you're conversant with style sheets, you can follow the instructions on the UKOLN site that explain how to get the look you want. You need to include the styles that the site lists in your style sheet and define them in the way you want.

Free RSS-to-JavaScript Service

An easy-to-use service is the Free RSS to JavaScript Service (`www.rss-to-javascript.com`). After you read the home page and click the Click Here link, you go to the Convert a Feed page shown in Figure 12-4.

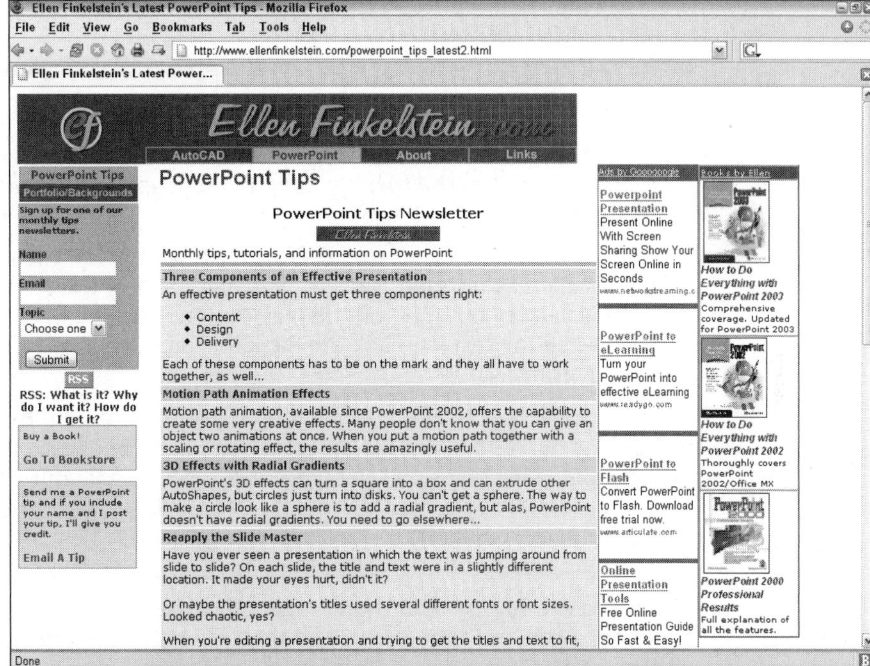

Figure 12-3: The result of my RSS-to-JavaScript conversion.

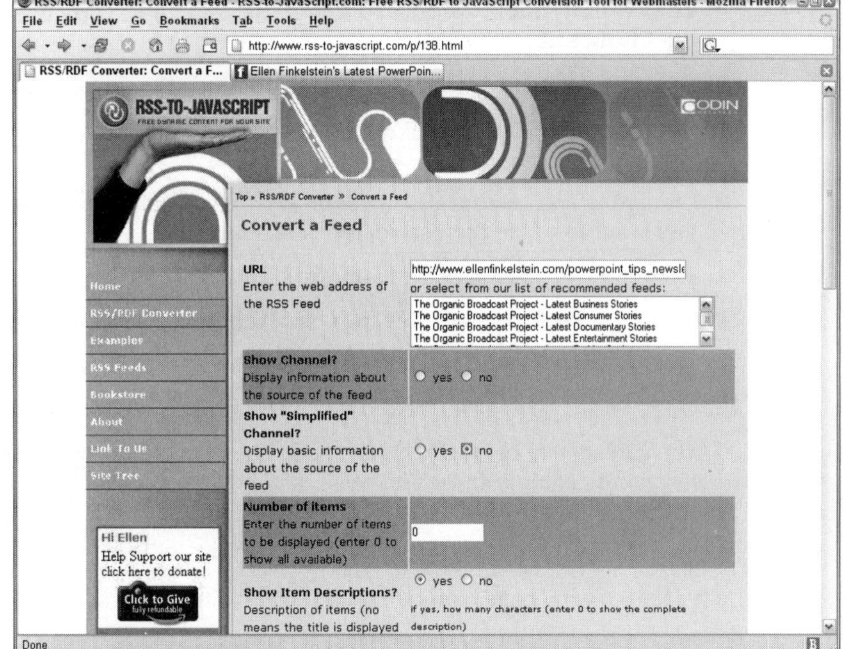

Figure 12-4: The Free RSS to JavaScript Service is easy to use and offers some flexibility.

Follow these steps to create a Web page from an RSS feed:

1. **In the URL text box, enter the URL of the feed that you want to convert.**

   It can be your feed or someone else's feed.

2. **Complete the rest of the form to specify the display options and click the Preview button.**

   At the bottom of the form (not all shown in Figure 12-4), you have a number of display options. Because you can preview the results so easily, you can try out different display options and see the results. If you don't like the results, click the Back button in your browser and try different settings.

   In my experience with this service, the preview is different from the final results on your Web site. This difference seems to be due to the fact that the resulting page takes on the style sheet (CSS file) of your site — which is probably what you want. If you don't have a style sheet, try changing the text color on the Free RSS-to-Javascript Web site form to differentiate the descriptions from the titles.

3. **When you are happy with the results, click the Back button in your browser to return to the form, and then click the Generate JavaScript button.**

   On the Feed Converter page, you see the JavaScript code.

4. **Click the Highlight All link to select the code, and copy the code to the Clipboard.**
5. **Open the Web page where you want to place the JavaScript.**

   Open the Web page in the program that you normally use for creating Web pages.

6. **Change to a view that displays the HTML, and find the location where you want to place the converted feed content.**
7. **Paste the JavaScript code from the Clipboard.**
8. **Return to your regular view of your Web page to see the result.**
9. **Save your page and upload it to your Web server.**
10. **Open your browser and go to your new page.**

    You can see my results in Figure 12-5. The display has taken on the format of my style sheet and fits in nicely with the rest of the page and the rest of my site.

The JavaScript puts a small "Powered by RSS-to-JavaScript.com" message at the bottom of your page, with a link to its Web site.

Without taking the time to go into step-by-step procedures, here are few other Web-based services that are worth a look.

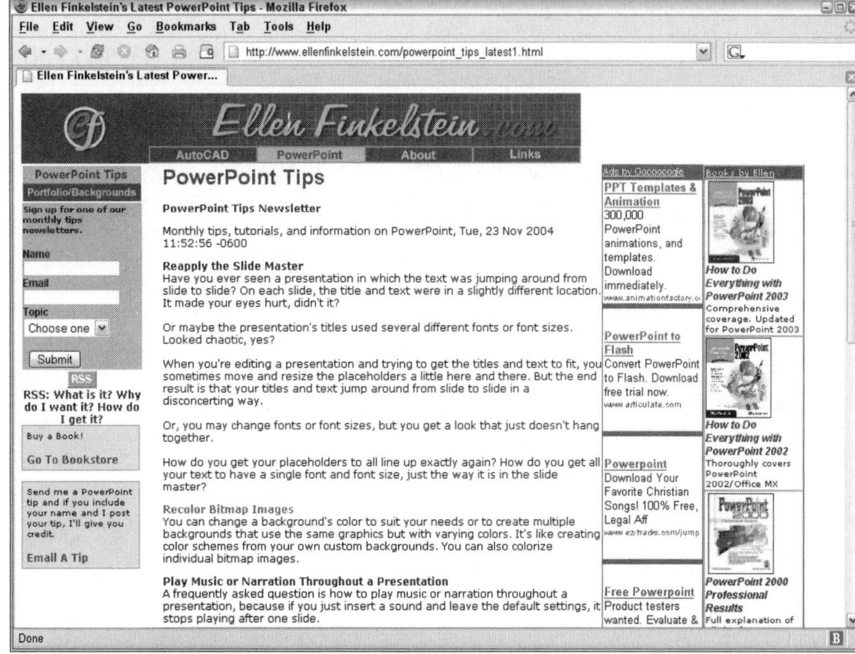

Figure 12-5: Here you see my feed as a Web page.

Feed2JS

This service is similar to the previous ones in this section except that the graphics are cuter and the service offers you the code which you can put on your own server. This site comes from Maricopa Community Colleges. The service is free, and the code is open source. You'll find this service to be user-friendly. Its motto is "Using RSS Feeds in your web pages is just a cut 'n paste away!" Go to `jade.mcli.dist.maricopa.edu/feed`.

If you put the code on your own server and create JavaScript files from your own feeds, you can offer the feeds to other Web sites so that they can display your feeds.

FeedRoll

FeedRoll is a nicely designed service, but you can only choose from a list of well-known RSS sources; you can't enter a URL. If you're interested in putting news from standard news sources on your site, this may work for you.

One nice feature is that you can choose from a number of display options. Click the Update button to see the preview to the right of the screen and get the JavaScript code that you need to copy and paste into your Web page. If you have a style sheet, you can configure it so that your feed looks like the rest of your Web page. Go to `www.feedroll.com/rssviewer`.

FeedSyndicator.com

FeedSyndicator (`www.feedsyndicator.com`) offers a simple way to convert any feed to JavaScript. If your Web server supports PHP (another popular language for the Web), you can use the available PHP code instead.

FeedSyndicator goes one step further than most services. You also get a button to put on your site that allows others to easily put your content on their sites. When they click the button it generates the code that they need in order to place the button onto their site. If you want others to pick up your content, this service is an easy way to make it easy for them do so.

You can also list your feed in the directory at FeedSyndicator. In return you can get a report that itemizes how many people click on your feed, who is syndicating your feed, and so on. A free trial is available, but you incur a monthly fee after the trial period ends.

You can specify the color and size of your text and configure several other display options. You can preview the result before you get the code. Take a look at the result in Figure 12-6.

Jawfish

This is another RSS-to-JavaScript converter. The site has some sample code that you can try out immediately to display a feed from the *Washington Post*. It works the same way as the previous tools that I discuss in this section. Go to `www.geckotribe.com/rss/jawfish`.

Software tools

Software tools involve uploading programming code to your server, because the code resides on the Web server, where it controls how your Web pages work when a viewer sees them in a browser. The program parses a specified RSS feed and displays it on a Web page.

The software tools that I have found require you to have complete and free access to your Web server and perhaps know how to change access permissions. If instructions like these make your eyes glaze over, just skip this section: "Remember to chmod this folder to 777." In other words, if you are using a commercial Web host that restricts what you upload or if you are in a large company environment where the IT department rules, you probably can't use these tools.

If your Web host lets you fiddle around or even have your own Web server, read on. If you've never uploaded PHP code before, you probably need to make full use of your Web host's technical support as well as the instructions on the sites that offer these tools. Some have forums where you can ask questions.

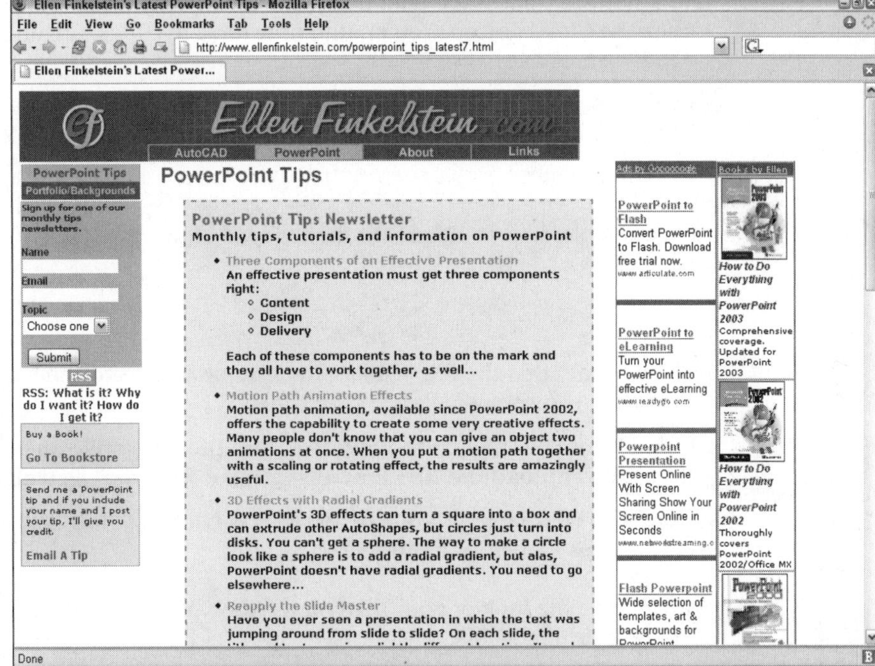

Figure 12-6: Feed Syndicator provides nicely formatted feeds on your Web page.

RSSlib

RSSlib comes in two flavors, PHP for servers that support the open-source PHP script language and ASP for servers that support Microsoft's Active Server Pages. Each of these flavors can create either HTML or JavaScript, so take your pick. Go to `www.2rss.com/software.php#rsslib` for more information and to get the downloads.

These tools are free. Unfortunately, the instructions are not very clear, so I provide basic instructions, with no bells and whistles, such as instructions to change the style sheet or limit the number of items in the feed. I got a prompt and helpful answer to my question from this service's forum and found this to be the easiest tool to use. (Your experience may differ.)

In this example, I use the tool that converts an RSS feed to HTML. To do this yourself, follow these steps:

1. **Go to** `www.2rss.com/software.php#rsslib` **and click the rsslib-php.zip link to download the file.**
2. **Create a new folder for the files.**
3. **Use WinZip or another decompression program to decompress the files into the new folder.**

You may see a message telling you to read `docs.htm` for instructions. Click the Close button. You should now have five files, including `rss2html.php` and `docs.htm`.

4. **Create (or edit) a Web page so that it contains a link to `rss2html.php` in the following format, where `rss_url` is the URL to your RSS feed:**

```
rss2html.php?rss_url=http://www.rss_url.xml
```

For example, you could create the following link:

```
<a href="rss2html.php?rss_url=http://www.ellenfinkelstein.
        com/powerpoint_tips_newsletter.xml">Link to my
        latest tips</a>
```

This format adds the RSS feed's URL as a parameter to the link so that the PHP file knows which RSS feed to use.

5. **Upload the Web page, the PHP files, and the CSS (style sheet) file. If necessary, upload the RSS feed (usually an XML file) as well.**

6. **Open the Web page in your browser and click the link. You should see the feed, as shown in Figure 12-7.**

You can change the look of your feed on the Web page by editing the CSS (cascading style sheet) file.

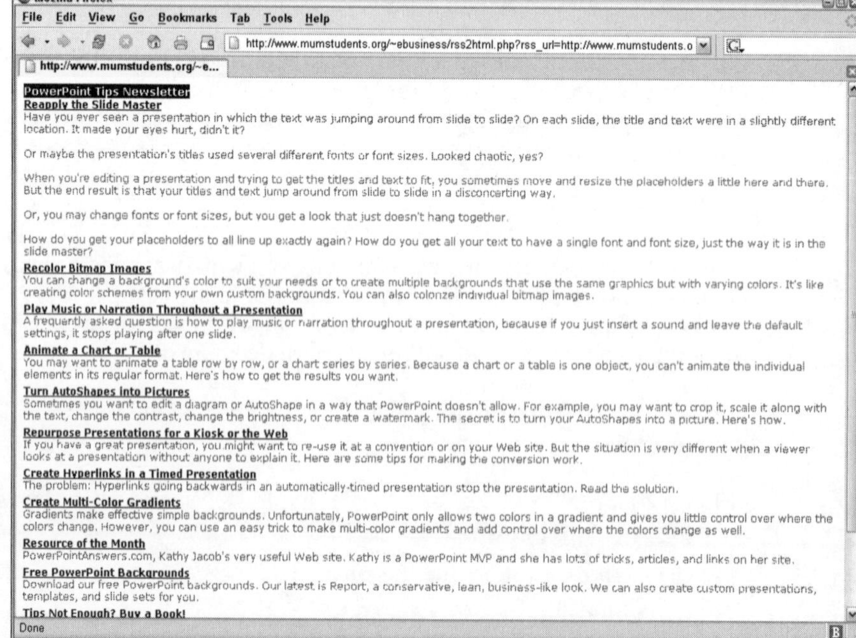

Figure 12-7: The 2RSS.com tool makes it easy to convert your RSS feed to HTML.

CaRP

CaRP is an RSS parser that uses PHP. You can find a free version at `www.geckotribe.com/rss/carp/docs/download.php`. CaRP also offers a commercial version.

The instructions for this program include changing some access permissions. If you're lucky, the automatic tool may work for you. If you're not, you need to do some manual configuring. If you get hung up here, turn to your Web host's technical support.

Part V
The Part of Tens

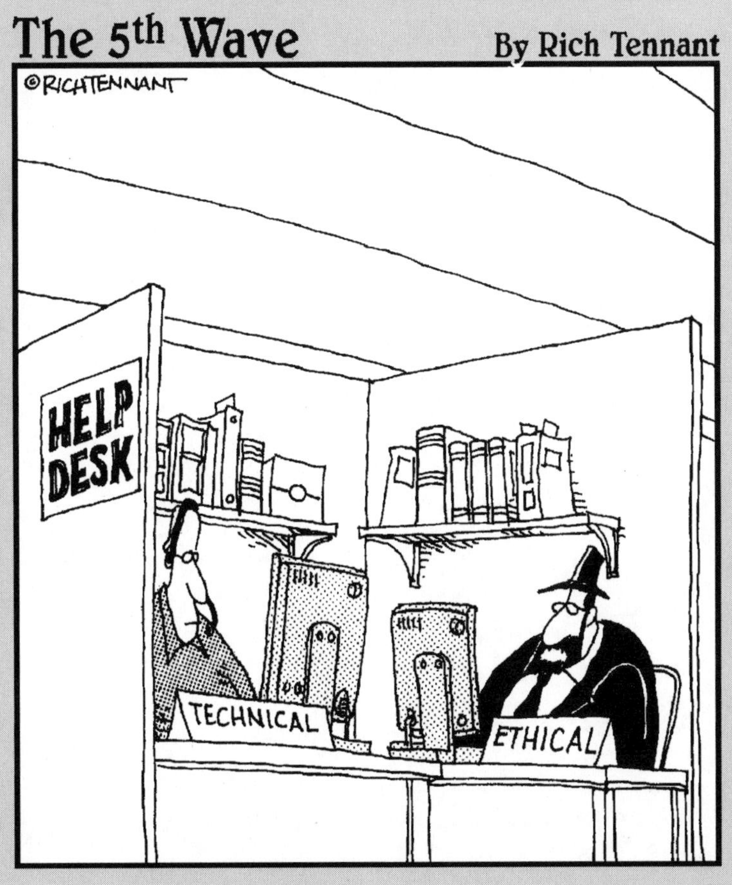

In this part . . .

Part V is the famous Part of Tens section included in all *For Dummies* books. Here I list the ten best RSS readers (in my humble opinion), ten ways to market your Web site, and the ten best RSS resources. Oh, and here's a little bonus: The Appendix explains the basics of setting up a Web site, just in case you don't have one yet.

Chapter 13

Ten Best RSS Readers

In This Chapter

- AmphetaDesk
- Bloglines
- FeedDemon
- Feedster
- NewsGator
- NewzCrawler
- Pluck
- RssReader
- SharpReader
- Yahoo!

Who cares if you call it a reader or an aggregator? You just want to read your RSS feeds as quickly and as efficiently as possible. Because your RSS reader is the basis of everything you do with RSS, you want it to be easy to use and free of hassles.

I tried lots of readers, and in this chapter, I list the best of the RSS readers. Most are free, but you need to pay for a few. (I used the trial version of the ones that came with a cost.) Your choice depends mostly on how you want to work — in a browser or outside of it — and whether you need some extra features. If you read a lot of feeds and use their contents as fodder for your own feeds, choose a reader that helps you integrate the reader and the publishing processes. (But don't try to feed your feeds to your animals as fodder, even if you live on a farm.)

The following list of RSS readers is alphabetical, not in order of quality, so read about them all and then decide which ones you want to try. After you try a few and see what you like, choose one and go with it.

Of course, my list is not exhaustive, and a number of other good RSS readers are out there. In fact, more seem to pop up each week. So if you find another reader and like it, it's probably the right one for you.

AmphetaDesk

AmphetaDesk (`www.amphetadesk.com`) was my first RSS reader, so I have a sentimental attachment to it. You can see it in Figure 13-1. AmphetaDesk has been around longer than most readers, even before Atom feeds, so it doesn't read Atom feeds (yet). Nevertheless, it's easy to use and works well.

AmphetaDesk is actually a hybrid, which is essentially a Web-based reader, with a small software component. You download a small program that sits on your desktop. Double-click the icon and you go to the Web site where your feeds are ready for you.

All your feeds are listed in a column; you scroll down to find the one you want or just read from top to bottom. While the column format means that you have to scroll, this method avoids constant refreshing of the page. As a result, AmphetaDesk is one of the fastest Web-based readers, and who can complain about reading your feeds more quickly?

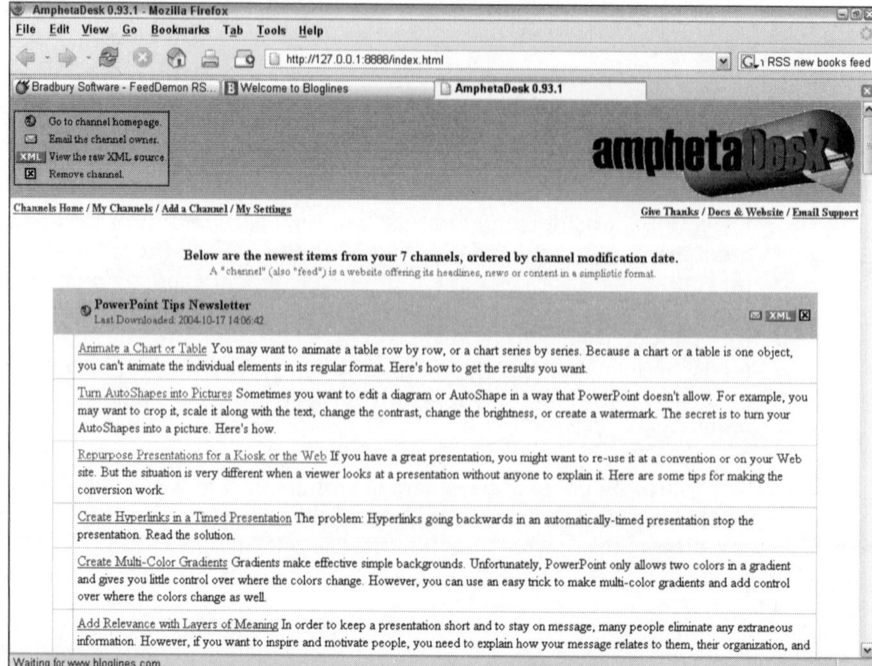

Figure 13-1: AmphetaDesk is tried but true.

If you want a more compact format, click the My Channels link. Then you see only the titles of your feeds. Clicking the title brings you directly to the feed's Web page.

On the AmphetaDesk main screen, click the Add a Channel link. In the text box that appears, enter a URL for a feed. Then click the Add This Channel button. AmphetaDesk also maintains a list of feeds that you can search alphabetically. In addition, you can add a little piece of software to your browser to automatically detect feeds on a site. You can find instructions for installing this software at `www.disobey.com/amphetadesk/finding_more.html`.

To delete a feed, click its Remove button. You can also send an e-mail to the Webmaster (if one is included in the feed) by clicking the envelope icon. Finally, each feed has its own XML button so that you can immediately view the source code of the feed. You can use this feature as a learning tool — if you like something about a feed, you can look at the code.

AmphetaDesk is simple and easy to use. Another advantage is that AmphetaDesk has versions for the Mac OS and Linux — it's one of the few cross-platform RSS readers.

Bloglines

Bloglines (`www.bloglines.com`) is a Web-based reader. You can see its interface in Figure 13-2., I discuss this reader more fully in Chapter 4, in the section "Choosing a blogging service." (You can see some of its features in Figures 4-6 through 4-9).

The unique feature of Bloglines is that it's also a simple blogging tool, and it allows you to easily copy material from your feeds into your blog. This integration of blogging and RSS feeds is valuable, and you should expect to see more of it in the future. The process of gathering information via RSS feeds, organizing and filtering it, and then republishing it in a new feed is useful to anyone whose livelihood is based on information.

Bloglines uses a two-pane layout, with your feeds listed on the left and their titles and descriptions displayed on the right. This is a good layout, but as with any Web-based reader, each time you choose a feed, you need to wait for the browser to display it.

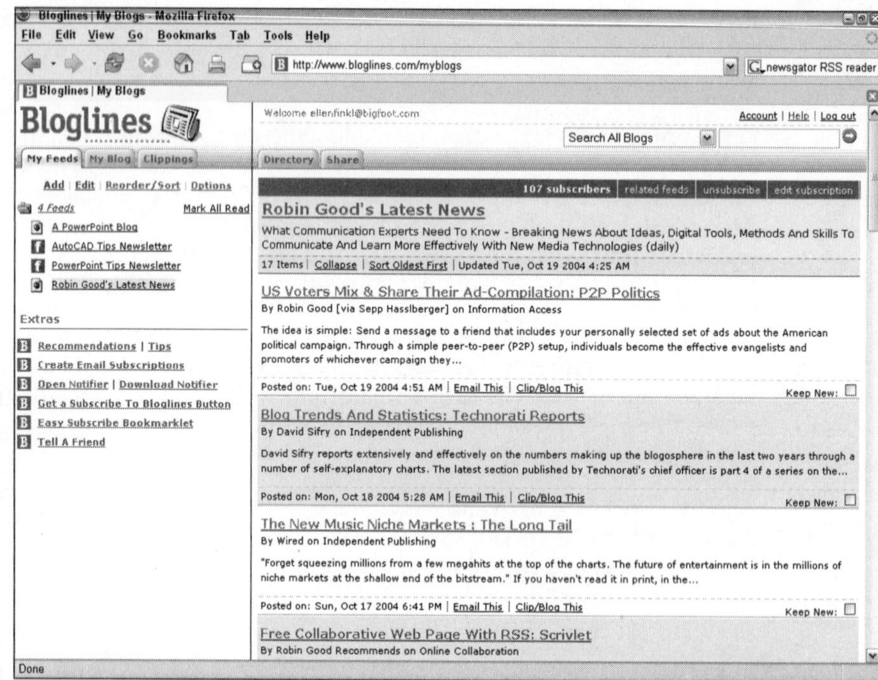

Figure 13-2: Bloglines combines reading and blogging into one Web-based tool.

FeedDemon

FeedDemon (`www.bradburysoftware.com/feeddemon/index.asp`) is an excellent software reader with some special features; it costs $29.95. A free trial version is also available. You can see FeedDemon in Figure 13-3.

Some of the extra features are as follows:

- A newspaper display of feeds for easy reading
- Watches that collect news from keyword searches
- A news bin to store nuggets of news that you want to save
- A built-in tabbed browser

The news bin is a nice feature, allowing you to collect information which you could then publish in a new feed if you want to. FeedDemon comes with a good list of RSS feeds preinstalled, and it mercifully allows you to choose not to subscribe to them when you install the program — which saves a lot of time deleting unwanted feeds.

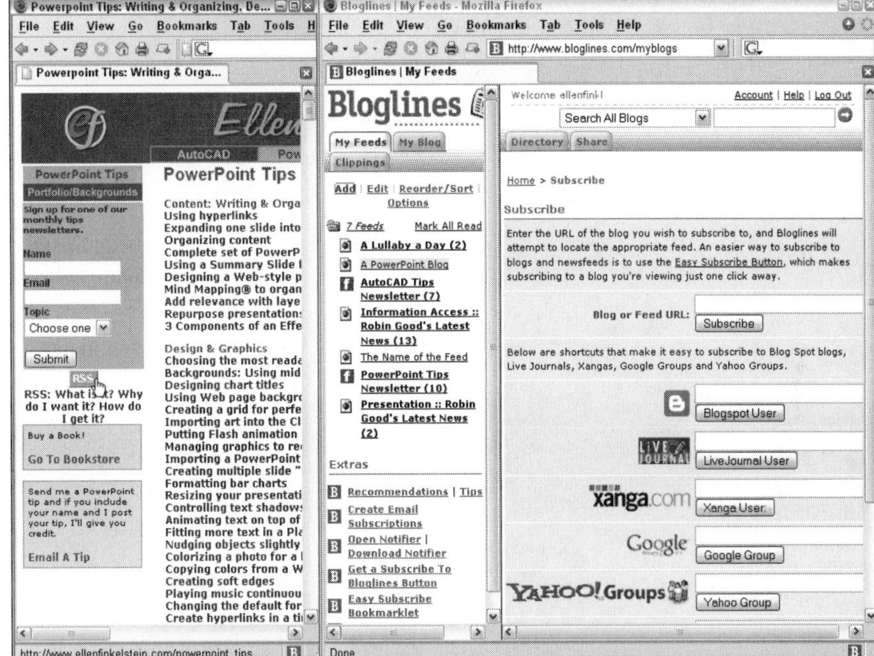

Figure 13-3: FeedDemon is a typical three-paned reader with some extra features.

Feedster

Feedster (`www.feedster.com`) is both a Web-based RSS reader and an RSS directory. I show the reader in Figure 13-4.

You click the MyFeedster link to read your feeds. Use the pane of tools on the left to add and delete feeds, and your feeds are then shown on the right. Click any feed in the left pane to display it in the right pane. You can then click the All Feeds link to see your list again, or you can click the handy Next Feed link to continue reading the next feed.

Feedster has a large selection of feeds in its directory that you can choose from. You can also submit your own feeds to this directory.

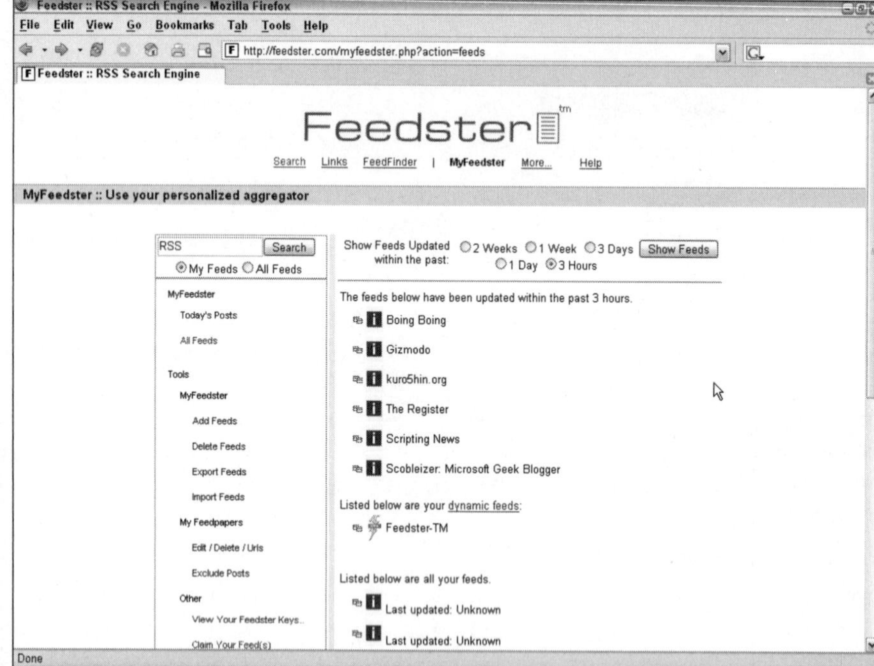

Figure 13-4: Feedster is an online reader but also has an RSS directory.

NewsGator

NewsGator (`www.newsgator.com`, $29; it offers a free trial) takes a different approach and integrates directly into Microsoft Outlook, so your feeds appear as a new folder in the left pane. In essence, NewsGator turns Outlook into an RSS reader, as shown in Figure 13-5.

If you use Outlook and have it open constantly, NewsGator is a good choice. Display is quick, and because you're in your e-mail program, you can easily copy content from your feeds and e-mail it to your friends or colleagues.

NewsGator also has a Web-based service, which offers additional services — some free and some for a fee. The online reader is free and includes auto-detect of feeds on a Web site and a directory of feeds. One of its fee-based services is search-based custom feeds.

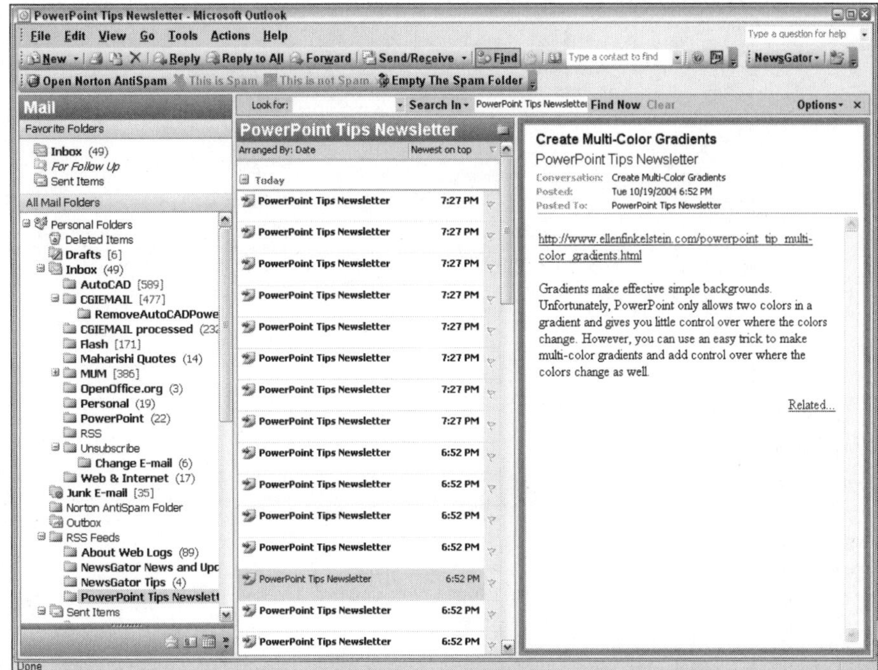

Figure 13-5: NewsGator displays your feeds in Microsoft Outlook.

NewzCrawler

NewzCrawler (`www.newzcrawler.com`, $24.95 with a free trial) is a full-featured reader. This reader uses the typical three-pane layout. One of its special features is the ability to post to blogs using Blogger, MetaWeblog, MovableType, Blogger, or LiveJournal — directly from within NewzCrawler.

To post feed content to your blog, you first configure your blog. Use the Help system for instructions. Then select an item and click the Blog This! button, as shown in Figure 13-6. Next, you simply click the Post button to post your entry.

In addition, you can add comments to blogs that you are reading, for any blogs that allow comments. (Go to the blog's Web site and read the instructions to find out if they allow comments). Click the Comment This! button to post your comment.

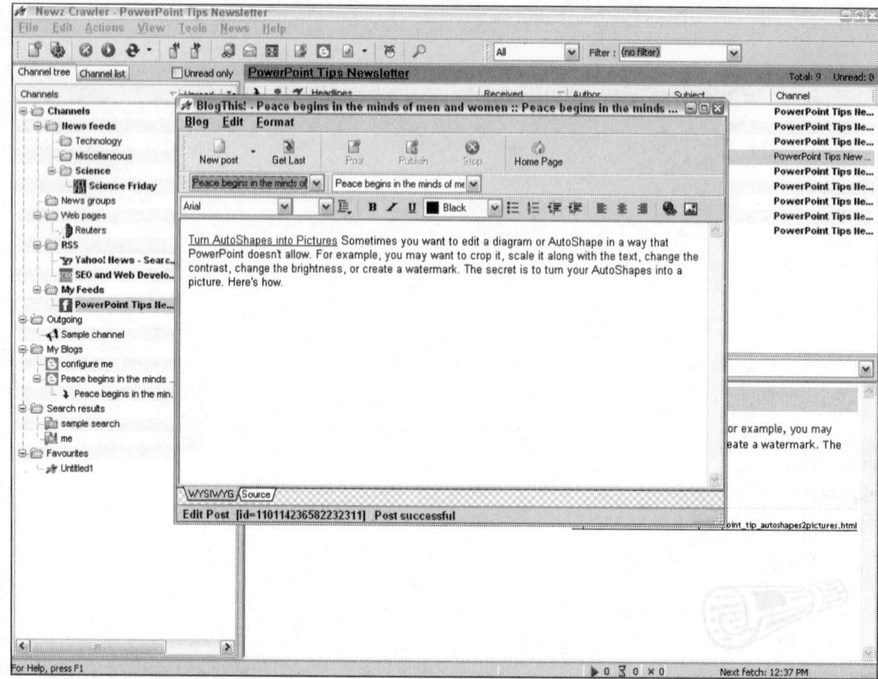

Figure 13-6: You can post directly to your blog from NewzCrawler.

NewzCrawler offers the following other useful features:

- A News Ticker that displays scrolling headlines as you work. You can click any headline to open it.
- A search feature, in case you have too many feeds to find what you want.
- A newsgroup reader to allow you to combine RSS feeds and newsgroups in one place.
- Search channels that collect the result of keyword searches.

If you're looking for a reader with some extra features, and especially if you are into both reading and publishing blogs, you'll be happy with NewzCrawler.

Plucky Pluck

Pluck (`www.pluck.com`) is a plucky newcomer and takes an unusual approach. It integrates as a plug-in with Microsoft Internet Explorer. Pluck appears in a pane on the left side of the browser screen, as shown in Figure 13-7.

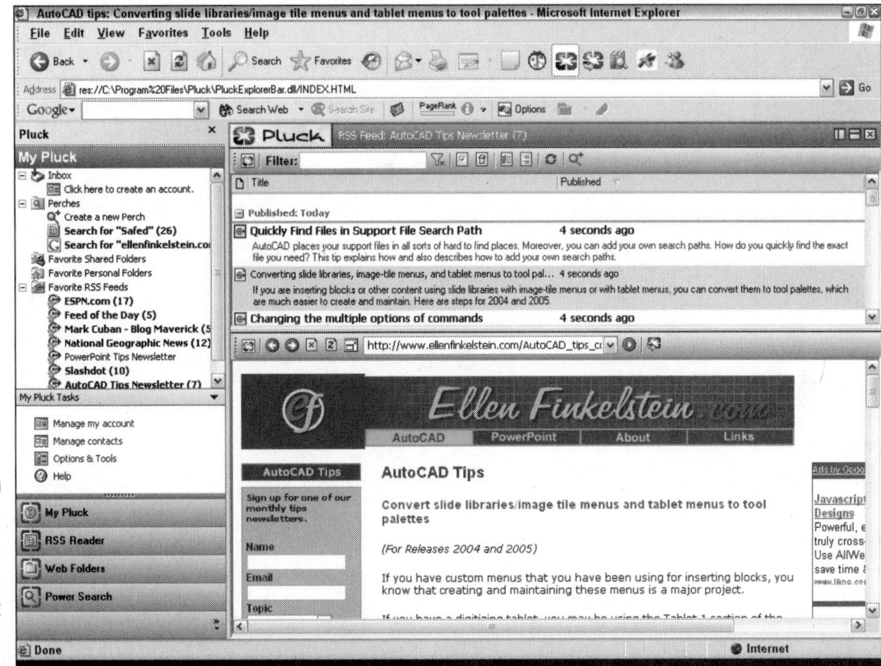

Figure 13-7: Pluck works within Internet Explorer.

You can open and close the pane as needed so that it's not in the way when you don't need it. Pluck is free but it inserts ads in certain places, such as its *perches* (which are watches for changes in the news, on Amazon.com, on eBay.com, or in a Google.com search). In spite of the ads, the perches are a nice feature. Obviously, Pluck conceives of RSS feeds as being intimately integrated with the Web sites that you are browsing.

Pluck auto-detects feeds on any page that you browse. If you often work in Internet Explorer, Pluck is a neat way to converge your RSS feeds with your browsing.

RssReader

RssReader (`www.rssreader.com`) is a simple, effective, and easy-to-use browser. This free reader has become my reader of choice among the free readers. I like the way it knows when I've copied a URL to the Clipboard and automatically loads it into the URL text box. You can see RssReader in Figure 13-8.

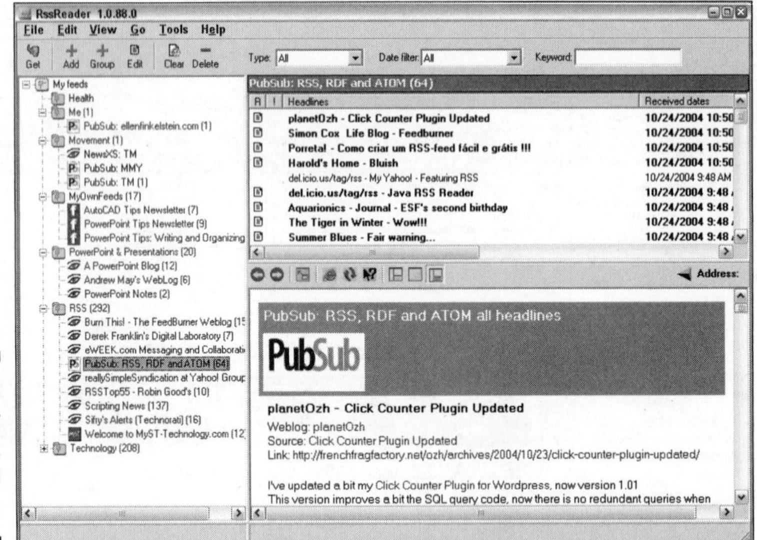

Figure 13-8: RssReader is a good, solid RSS reader.

The interface is the standard three-pane layout and is quite intuitive. RssReader doesn't have a lot of extra features, but I've found it to be completely up to the task of delivering RSS feeds. I like its pop-up notifier, which appears from the Windows system tray. RssReader has a couple of quirks, such as hanging out in the Windows system tray instead of as a button on the taskbar — making it sometimes hard to find. Overall, though, it's just what I need.

Simple Subscribing with SharpReader

SharpReader (`www.sharpreader.com`) is free and simple, as shown in Figure 13-9.

I like its clean, lean interface. This reader also uses the three-pane interface. You can drag an RSS or XML button onto the program to subscribe to a feed, but the program doesn't automatically accept a feed URL that you've copied to the Clipboard. SharpReader has a filter that you can use to search for feeds. For example, you can enter **RSS** into the filter to display only feeds whose titles contain the word "RSS."

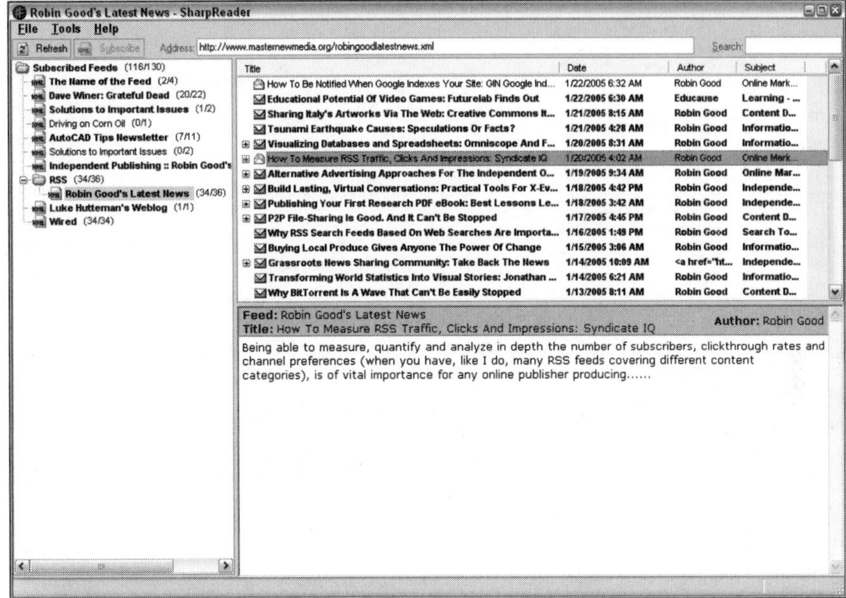

Figure 13-9: SharpReader is lean and clean.

Yahoo!

Yahoo's foray into RSS feeds is quite successfully implemented. The RSS feeds are at My Yahoo! (`my.yahoo.com`), the part of Yahoo! where you can customize the news that you see on this portal. Because so many people use My Yahoo! as their home page, Yahoo's support of RSS feeds is important to the popular acceptance of RSS feeds. As you can see in Figure 13-10, the RSS feeds appear at the top, center of the browser window.

As I explain in Chapter 2 in the section "Web-based readers," Yahoo! offers complete information on RSS for both readers and publishers. This support can help Yahoo! users learn more about RSS. Yahoo! has its own Subscribe button and encourages publishers to put this button on their site so that readers can instantly add feeds to their My Yahoo! list.

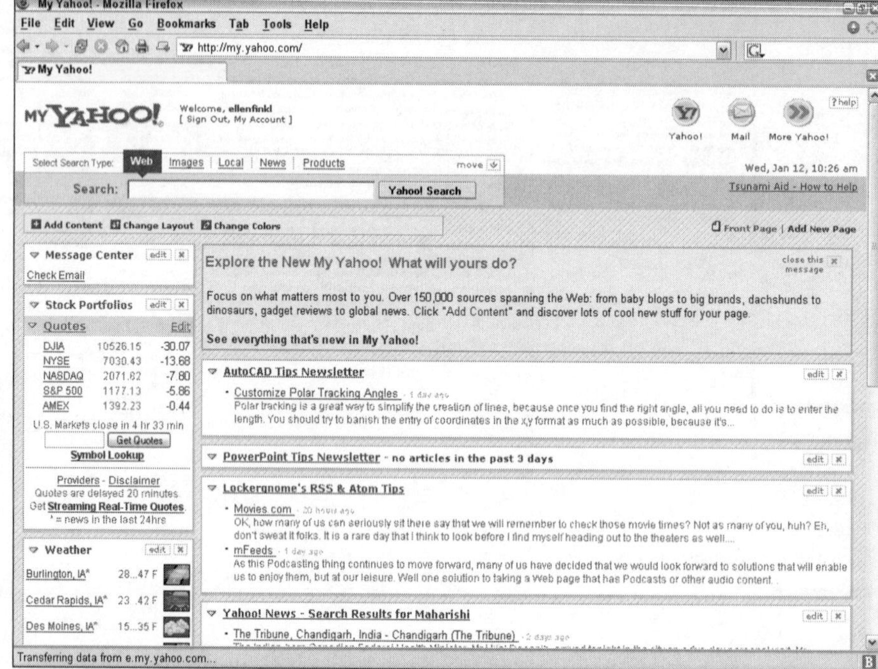

Figure 13-10: My Yahoo! has made RSS front and center to its widely-used portal.

More and Ever More

I expect more readers to appear and perhaps some to die off. The field is expanding and changing so rapidly that it's hard to tell how the dust will settle. For example, Microsoft has just introduced an online reader to its MSN portal (`my.msn.com`). In Chapter 2, I provide a thorough analysis of the various types of readers and the features they may include. Use that chapter as an overall guide when searching for the ideal reader.

Many readers let you export your feed list, usually in OPML format. If your reader allows this, you can easily change readers and import your OPML list into the new one. As a result, switching readers is not such a big deal, especially in the software category. A couple of Web-based readers also allow you to use OPML files, but most do not.

You can find a good list of readers at `www.rssjobs.com/rssreaders.jsp`. This list includes readers for Mac OS and Linux.

Chapter 14

Ten Ways to Market Your Web Site

In This Chapter

- Optimizing for search engines
- Registering your site
- Getting traffic statistics
- Placing ads
- Getting affiliated
- Getting links to your site
- Telling people about your site
- Creating an online community
- Publishing e-zines and blogs
- Writing articles

The more people that come to your Web site, the better.

After all, if no one sees your site, what's the point? Whether you're selling something or just have a blog, you want people to come. The more people come to your site, the more they will see your RSS feed — although your RSS feed is probably not the only reason that you want people to come to your site.

Now if you've been paying attention and reading all the chapters, by now you know that this book explains how an RSS feed can bring people to your site, including how to write in a way that gets people to your site in Chapter 5, and how to market your RSS feed in Chapter 11.

Here I give you ten other ways to market your site. The best way to market your site is to have useful, up-to-date content that is easy to find and use. A well-written and thought-out site practically markets itself. People find out about it and tell their friends — without you having to lift a finger! Nevertheless, you can also help the process along using the ten techniques I present in this chapter.

Optimizing for Search Engines

Many people come to a site after doing a search in a search engine. The top three search engines are Google, Yahoo!, and MSN. Therefore, if your site comes up near the top of a search listing, more people will come to your site. Search engine optimization (SEO) is all about getting as high a rank as possible on those search listings. You also want your site to appear useful in these listings.

Searches are based on *keywords.* A keyword is simply a word that is used in a search. For example, someone may do a search on the two words *PowerPoint* and *backgrounds.* The search engines take these two words and find sites that contain content with both these words. Because people almost always use two or three words when they search, you want to come up with some keyword combinations that you think are appropriate for your site.

Therefore, optimizing your site for search engines involves thinking about what keywords may bring people to your site. In other words, what is your site about? What would potential visitors want to see? Then, make sure that you have lots of useful content about your topic that uses words that you think people will search on.

The search engines search through Web sites automatically using spiders. A *spider* is a software application that automatically follows links on the Web and then sends the information it gathers back to a database. To determine rank, search engines apply formulas to the information they gather. Obviously, these formulas are quite technical. For example, search engines expect that content inside certain tags, such as `<h1>` and `<h2>` tags (first- and second-level headings), is important. Therefore, if you put words related to your topic in those tags, you help your ranking.

Similarly, the words that you use for the filename of your page and your page title — the text that appears on the title bar of your browser that you place between the `<title>` and `</title>` tags in your Web page — are important for your page's ranking. Another set of tags, called meta tags, also contain text that describe your Web page in general, and most search engines take this into account as well.

The first paragraph of your main content should also include your favored keywords. This usually happens naturally, because this is the place that you explain to your viewers what your site or page is about. Just be direct, clear, and succinct, and avoid chatting about irrelevant matters.

Search engine optimization (SEO) experts have lots of ideas about how to maximize your ranking. My advice is to keep your site simple and stick to the basics that I've described.

Reading more about SEO

SEO consultants make a living doing nothing but helping Web site owners improve the ranking of their site. If you want to learn more but aren't ready for a consultant, you can find plenty of material on the Web. Here are a few articles to start you out:

- **Search Engine Marketing Guide:** This is an excellent article that gives detailed information and instructions for optimizing your Web site, submitting it to search engines, and monitoring site traffic. Address: `www.insite.lycos.com/tutorial.asp#11`
- **Search engine optimization: Preparing your pages for the search engines:** This detailed, practical, and humorous article on SEO is an excellent overview of the entire SEO process. Address: `www.selfpromotion.com/search-engine-optimization.t?CF=Go2.site.registration`
- **Search Engine Marketing and Optimization:** This is a thorough analysis and tutorial of how to use keyword combinations to increase the relevance and ranking of your Web page, with links to many more resources. Address: `www.masternewmedia.org/2002/05/31/search_engine_marketing_and_optimization.htm`
- **Introduction to Search Engine Optimization:** This is a good portal on SEO, providing links to many articles, ranging from Web-site content and design to the nitty-gritty details of meta tags and keywords. Address: `websearch.about.com/od/keywordsandphrases`
- **Low-Budget Search Engine Marketing:** This article summarizes strategies for do-it-yourself Web-site marketing. Address: `www.searchenginewatch.com/searchday/article.php/2161191`
- Search Engine Forums.com has active forums on several Web–site–related topics, including SEO. Go to `www.searchengineforums.com/bin/forumdisplay.cgi?action=`.

Many of these articles lead you to more articles. Don't get lost — you could read for years! At some point, come back and start working on your site.

You should also delve into how specific search engines rank their search results. Each search engine uses complex algorithms that are highly secret. Nevertheless, the following articles provide some guidelines about how to set up your Web pages:

- **Google Information for Webmasters:** This isn't exactly an article, but it includes lots of great information that explains how Google searches the Web, minus the information that it considers proprietary. Address: `www.google.com/webmasters`
- **Yahoo! Search Help:** Here you can find a number of pages related to how Yahoo!'s search indexing and ranking works. Address: `help.yahoo.com/help/us/ysearch`

- **Site Owner Help:** This site presents topics related to indexing and ranking at MSN. Address: `beta.search.msn.com/docs/siteowner.aspx?FORM=WMDD2`

If you feel that you need professional help, you can hire a consultant. You can find a list at `www.seoconsultants.com`. SEO is a complex field and the details are beyond the scope of this book. For more information, see the sidebar, "Reading more about SEO."

Registering Your Site

The search engines may find your Web site eventually, but you can help them out by registering your site with major directories, such as DMOZ, Yahoo!, Google, AltaVista, and others. For the most part, you can register your site for free, although you may get better or faster results by paying a fee.

Some of the most important places to register your site are as follows:

- DMOZ, the Open Directory Project (see Figure 14-1), is a nonprofit directory that powers the search results of several of the top search engines. This directory is the granddaddy of all the directories, and most of the search engines use its results. Registration is free. Address: `www.dmoz.org/add.html`
- Overture maintains a submission site for Yahoo!, AltaVista, and others. The cost is $49 per year. Address: `www.content.overture.com/d/USm/ays/sm.jhtml`
- Yahoo! Search lets you submit URLs for free, although it offers upgrades for a fee. You must register with Yahoo! and log in first. Address: `login.yahoo.com/config/login?.src=srch&.done=http://submit.search.yahoo.com/free/request`
- Google is the most widely used search engine. You can submit a URL for free at `www.google.com/intl/en/addurl.html`.

Web-site marketers have lots of theories about the importance of registering your site and how to do it. For example, some people feel that using a service to submit all your sites may not be effective, because the search engines get such an overwhelming amount of duplicate submissions that they simply discount them. Others think that you should resubmit your site regularly or at least submit every new page that you create.

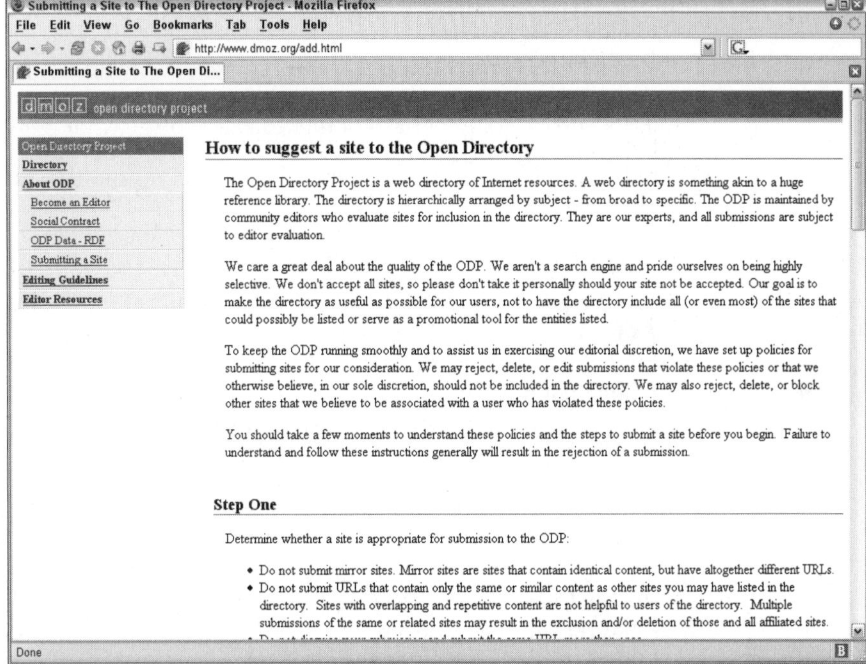

Figure 14-1: You register your Web site with DMOZ at this page.

For a thorough listing of the top search engines, with links for submitting your site, go to `www.101topranking.com/top_engines.htm`.

Lots of companies provide services to register your site for you, if you want to try them. Do a search for "search engine submission." Where else but in your favorite search engine?

Before signing on with a registration service, make sure that the service doesn't repeatedly register the same page, otherwise, known as spamming.

Getting Traffic Statistics

Traffic statistics (which you can gather in a few different ways, which I go into shortly) itemize how many people visit your site and give you general information about those visitors. You can use traffic statistics to analyze and improve your site. Analyzing traffic statistics is not a direct marketing technique, but it gives you important information for making your site a success.

Here are some typical statistics:

- **Number of hits (visits) per page, day, or month:** Obviously, the more, the merrier. You can see the results of a marketing campaign using these numbers and calculate a ratio of hits to sales to see what percentage of your visitors buy something.
- **Number of unique hits per page:** This statistic keeps track of the IP (computer) addresses of visitors and weeds out the same visitor coming back twice within a certain amount of hours.
- **Origin of visitors, that is, the URL they were at before they came to your site:** This shows which sites have links to yours and shows the search engines that people use to get to your site, including the search terms they used.
- **Entering page, that is, the page of your site where people enter:** This may not be your home page.
- **Exiting page, which is the page where people leave your site:** You may find ineffective pages by analyzing this statistic.
- **The browser, including the version that visitors use:** Use this information to make sure that your site looks good on the most common browsers that people use.
- **The resolution of visitors' computers:** Use this information to design your site to fit into the browser window for the most common resolutions, usually 800 × 600 or higher.

Traffic jam

If you want to find out more about traffic statistics, here are a few articles:

- **Understanding Traffic Statistics:** This article offers a detailed explanation of available Web statistics. The final section explains how to interpret traffic stats to help improve your site. Address: `www.help.thinkhost.com/web-development/server_space/understanding-traffic_176.html`
- **Web Site Access Logs: Guess (Literally) Who's Coming to Visit:** This site explains the uselessness of counters that display the number of visitors that have viewed a page and explains the value of traffic logs, which can reveal more detailed information. Address: `www.morebusiness.com/getting_started/website/d935705350.brc`
- **Log analyzers vs. Hosted statistics: An analysis:** This forum entry discusses Web-based versus software-based traffic analyzers. Address: `forum.webstat.com/viewtopic.php?t=36`

Some of these articles come from sites that are selling a product but they still offer useful information.

As you can see, a lot of data is available. All you need is time to analyze it, right? You can buy software to help you, and many Web hosts offer reports that are helpful. Whether you get your reports from your Web host or software, you'll get most of the information in the previous list. To read further about traffic statistics, see some of the articles in the sidebar, "Traffic jam."

One problem for RSS-feed publishers is that the statistics may not indicate how many people requested XML or RSS pages. Ask your Web host whether you can get this information.

If your Web host doesn't offer statistics (or only offers unformatted logs) you can use your own software. You can find many options for gathering and analyzing statistics, but here are a few that are free:

- **Analog:** This statistics software shows you the usage patterns on your Web server. It's fast, scalable, highly configurable, reports in 32 languages, and works on any operating system. Address: `www.analog.cx`
- **AWStats:** This log analyzer graphically displays the traffic information from raw traffic logs. Address: `awstats.sourceforge.net`
- **StatCounter:** This software provides a free invisible Web tracker, configurable hit counter, and real-time detailed site stats. You don't have to pay until you start to get over 9,000 page loads each day. Address: `www.statcounter.com`
- **WebSTAT:** The basic edition is free and tracks up to 20,000 page views per month. It includes ten reports and a free Web counter. Address: `www.webstat.com/?aref=1178`

Placing Ads

An obvious way to market your site is to place ads, either on search engine results or on other Web sites. You generally pay only when someone clicks on your ad, which is a link to your site. Today, placing ads is easier than ever.

To place ads in search engines, you choose certain keywords. People who use these keywords would probably be interested in what you have to offer. For example, if you are selling handmade South American crafts, you may want to attract people who are interested in handmade crafts, but don't care where they're from. So keywords could be *handmade* and *crafts.* Other keywords could be *gifts,* especially around holiday gift-giving time, *handicrafts,* and so on.

You then go to your chosen service and find out how much you have to pay to display an ad in response to those search terms. The cost depends on how many other people are paying for those same words. Your goal is to find the most appropriate keywords for the lowest cost per click.

The two most commonly used search engine ad-placement services are as follows:

- **Google AdWords:** This service places your ads to the right of Google searches, under the Sponsored Links heading. You pay a $5 activation fee, but no monthly minimum. Of course, you pay the stated amount each time someone clicks one of your ads. Address: https://adwords.google.com/select
- **Overture:** This service places ads for AltaVista, MSN, Yahoo!, and others. You pay a $20 monthly minimum, and the minimum cost per click is 10 cents. Address: www.content.overture.com/d

Of course, many other pay-per-click ad services are available that put your ads on other Web sites. Just do a search on "pay per click ads."

Finding the right keywords is both an art and a science. To help you do this, you can use Overture's free service at www.content.overture.com/d/USm/ays/index.jhtml. Scroll down to the bottom of the page and enter a couple of keywords in the How Many Searches Can Your Business Get? text box. Then click the Search button. A new window opens with a list of related searches that have been used recently and the number of searches for each combination. You can use the Get Suggestions For text box to try out other combinations of keywords.

Another excellent resource is Wordtracker, at www.wordtracker.com. You can use its free trial once and afterward, pay by the day, week, or month. This service helps you find keywords that people are looking for so that you can focus your Web site on those terms.

The 2ndSight Incorporated Web site offers a good set of articles that includes information about keyword discovery and evaluation. Go to www.2ndsightinc.com/sem and click the topics on the left-pane menu.

Getting Affiliated

You can bring potential buyers to your site by having an affiliate program. Do you have a product or service that other people may want to sell? Are you willing to pay a percentage of the sale to other sites that refer business to you? Then an affiliate program may work for you. Affiliate programs allow you to market your product or service by paying a commission to partners who drive traffic to your site.

The most well-known affiliate program is Amazon.com. Thousands of Web sites, including mine, sell products for Amazon, as shown in Figure 14-2. People click on links and go straight to the appropriate page on Amazon's Web site. Amazon pays a percentage of the sale to the referring Web site.

If you would like to offer an affiliate program, you need to be able to track each instance of someone coming to your site from one of your affiliates. In other words, if someone sees one of your products on another site, clicks on the link, and then purchases that product (or perhaps any product), you need a tool to let you know where the purchase originated, so that you can pay your affiliated site. After all, that site referred the sale to you and that's what affiliates get paid for.

For an affiliate site, you need to provide the following features:

- Special links and ads for affiliates to use on their Web sites.
- The ability to set cookies (small files saved to the clicker's computer which are necessary to keep track of who clicks on a link).
- A way to calculate commissions.
- Reports for affiliates so that they can keep track of how much they are earning.

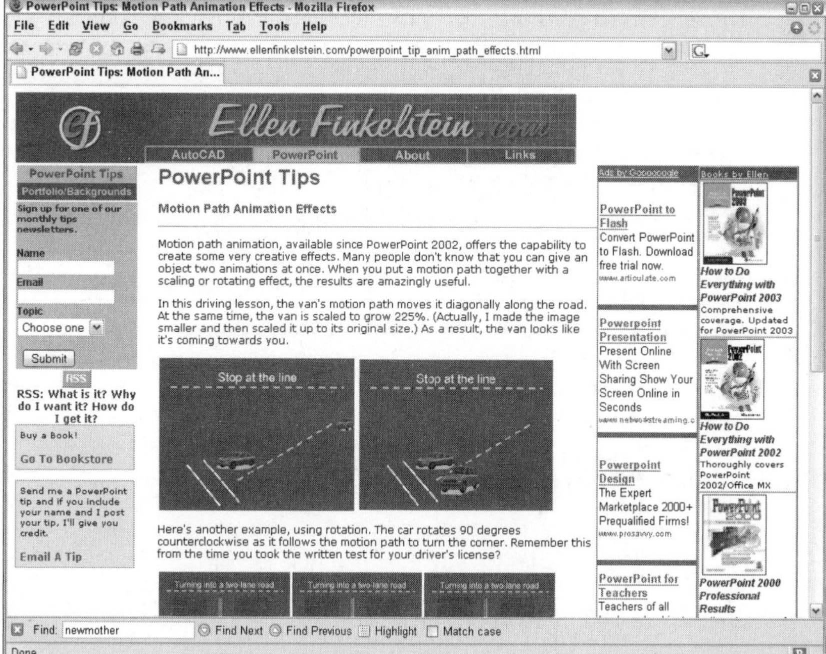

Figure 14-2: The book cover images are links to Amazon.com's Web site.

- Reports for you to see how much you are paying to your affiliates.
- Anti-fraud features. For example, you need to know if someone (perhaps a competitor) clicks the same ad over and over again to increase costs for the affiliate.

You can purchase affiliate software and run it on your Web site's server. One such software is Ultimate Affiliate Software (`www.groundbreak.com`). Alternatively, you can use a Web-based service such as Offers Quest (`offersquest.directtrack.com`).

Getting Links to Your Site

Many people come to your site from other sites that link to your site. Why would another site link to yours? Most informational sites have a page of links that they think their viewers would find valuable. People click these links and end up on your site. If you have a Web site, you've probably received requests to add links to other sites.

You can see the value of these sites in your traffic statistic reports. People don't need permission to link to your site, so you may get traffic from the most unexpected places. That's okay, because almost any link is a good link.

To get links to your site, start by setting up a links page, where you can put links to other useful sites. Then follow these steps:

1. **Link to other sites that you think your viewers will find useful.**
2. **Contact the owners or Webmasters of those sites, and let them know that you've linked to their site.**

   Mention that you linked to their site because you think their site is a useful resource for your visitors. Include the URL to your link page so that they can verify that you have linked to their site.
3. **Ask these Webmasters to link to your site.**

   Give them the URL so that all they have to do is copy and paste. You may want to provide a description of your site. You can even provide an image if you want. Explain what your site offers and why you think your site may be valuable to their visitors.

One strategy for getting links is to find out who is linking to your competitors and then request that these sites also link to you. Of course, you still follow the three steps that I just listed, linking first to these Web sites before you ask them to add a link to your site.

Why not use an RSS search feed to find links to your competitors? Use one of the services that provides RSS feeds on searches. I discuss search feeds in the section "Creating a new feed from a search" in Chapter 3. In Chapter 15, in the section "Feeds from searches," I list all the best sources. Then do a search for the home page URL of your competitors. You can find out which sites contain that URL, meaning that they link to your competitors.

Telling People about Your Site

If you like to write, you probably also like to talk. Your Web site may be just the conversation piece you need on your next date. Okay, maybe not. But talking to people about your Web site is a good way to spread the word. Remember that Google, which gets over 200 million hits a day, has never run a television ad and basically became popular by word of mouth. Of course, it also had a good product that was free of charge.

Other ways to let people know about your Web site is to place it on your e-mail signature (make it a link), stationery, brochures, and business card. When people e-mail you, invite them to visit your Web site in your reply. The more useful the content on your Web site, the easier it will be for your visitors to refer people there.

A common technique is to frequent discussion groups and forums on topics that relate to your site and mention your Web site. However, this technique can backfire if you do it in an obviously commercial way. Instead, frequent these discussion groups and provide answers to people's questions. In this way, you can establish yourself as being knowledgeable on a subject and can gently refer people to useful content on your Web site as a further resource. (Or you can put the answer on your site, if it's not already there, and then refer people.) You can often put your Web site beneath your name.

Press releases haven't gone out of style yet, and you can get some good publicity by sending out a well-worded page that explains why your Web site is useful. Gather a list of press resources and send out the press releases by mail, fax, or e-mail. Maybe someone will contact you for an interview!

A *Web ring* is a group of Web sites with similar content that are linked. Each site displays a banner with the name of the ring, which allows visitors to click to the next site in the ring. Before joining a Web ring, visit all the other sites in the ring to make sure that all content is appropriate and that the sites are properly maintained. To join or create a ring, visit `dir.webring.com/rw`.

Creating an Online Community

As a publisher of RSS feeds, you have probably noticed that people like to communicate with each other on the Internet. For example, throughout this book, I list forums and discussion groups that are related to the topic I am discussing. Web sites that offer this type of online community attract people who want to ask questions, provide answers, or just gab. Creating an online community has plusses and minuses, so you need to consider the concept carefully.

Some of the advantages of creating an online community are as follows:

- People come to your site for the information or sense of community, and they may stay to buy something.
- People who use a forum often become advocates of that site and recommend it to others.
- You can learn a great deal from the comments made in the forum, such as ideas for new products, improving service, your customers' preferences, and more.
- Your customers may find the answers they need in the forum, which may reduce calls to your support line.
- You get satisfaction from providing useful information to your Web-site visitors.

Be aware of the following disadvantages of creating an online community:

- Creating such a community usually involves using (or developing) software that goes on your server, so you need a Web host that gives you permission to use this software. In other words, it's not as easy as it sounds.
- You may need to monitor the forum carefully to remove spam or inappropriate postings. This can be time consuming, which is another way of saying that it's expensive.
- You may need to provide your own postings, especially when other visitors provide inaccurate or even harmful information.
- You may not get much out of the forum, especially if it doesn't fit in well with your Web site's goal.
- Visit other companies' forums to see how often they are used and whether they seem to be of real value to the forum's visitors. Investigate possible software to see whether you are comfortable with the technical details. To find suitable software, perform a search on "forum software."

Publishing E-Zines and Blogs

I discuss e-zines, e-newsletters, and blogs in several chapters of this book. In fact, blogs are one way of creating an online community, which I cover in the previous section. Many blogging services offer a way for readers to comment, turning the blog into something close to a forum. One difference is that you, the publisher, start the process and set the stage with an initial topic or discussion. Discussions are not threaded, and readers can't start new topics as they can in a typical forum.

E-zines are even more one-sided, but you can certainly offer readers the ability to reply to your e-mail. If you publish your e-mail on your Web site, you can include some of these replies.

How do RSS feeds fit into this picture? Many RSS feeds come from blogs, and they may (or may not) include readers' comments in the feed. Whatever discussion emerges from an RSS feed occurs on the originating Web site and may then spill over into the feed.

E-zines and blogs have links that bring interested people back to your Web site. These people have chosen to come and are therefore motivated to get some information. For this reason, e-zines and blogs are useful techniques for bringing people to your Web site. E-zines usually require people to sign up, so your readers have especially indicated their interest — they are even *more* motivated. In this way, e-zines are more like RSS feeds than blogs.

People who receive e-zines may also forward them to others, spreading the word about your Web site with no action required on your part. Of course, if you don't want your e-zine published without your permission, you may want to put a copyright notice on it.

Earlier in this chapter, in the section "Getting Links to Your Site," I mention the value of trading links with other sites. Why stop at trading links? A great way to get people to your site is to trade articles (or a mention in an e-zine) with other e-zines. For example, in one issue, you mention another site and then ask that site to mention you in its e-zine. Perhaps this site can even recommend that its readers sign up for your e-zine. This type of mention is effective, because it comes from a source that readers feel is trustworthy. You can often make this arrangement informally with colleagues in your field on the simple premise of helping each other out. Using (and helping) your personal contacts is always a good technique.

Another method, although not as effective, is to register your e-zine in e-zine directories. People don't often go to e-zine directories, but they may if they are looking for an e-zine on a hard-to-find topic or if they want to gather every available e-zine on a topic. `Nettop20.com` has a list of e-zine directories that you can look into; this site is a directory of directories. Go to `.ezines.nettop20.com`.

As any RSS-feed publisher knows, one problem with e-mail newsletters is that they may be considered spam. In fact, articles about how to successfully create an e-zine to avoid being considered spam are practically an advertisement for RSS technology.

Writing Articles

Many newsletters and magazines, both online and in print, accept articles from people (like you) who have expertise in their area. They usually provide a brief bio that can include your Web site's URL. These bios are excellent publicity, because readers see them in an environment where you are published as an expert in your field. Some of these newsletters and magazines may even pay your for your article, but many simply trade that bio with their link for an article. The fact that people want to write articles for free shows you how valuable they consider this link to be.

Of course, if you get really ambitious, you can write a book. After all, that's what I did!

Chapter 15

Ten Best RSS Resources

In This Chapter

- Using tutorials
- Researching technical specifications
- Finding the best directories
- Reading the best articles and feeds
- Finding sites with excellent RSS feeds
- Marketing with RSS
- Getting top-notch RSS-creation tools
- Choosing RSS-to-HTML tools
- Participating in discussion groups
- Investigating auxiliary RSS tools

Because RSS is based on Web technology, it only makes sense that the best RSS resources are on the Web. Lots of sites offer excellent information on creating and managing RSS feeds. These tutorials offer supplemental resources that you may find helpful. And yes, RSS feeds exist on the topic of RSS.

Although I've broken down the resources into types, the categories are not completely cut and dried. Some tutorials include technical specifications, and some essays include tutorials.

In this chapter, I find you the best RSS resources so that you can take your feeds to new heights of excellence. In true For Dummies fashion, I have broken this chapter into ten parts, but each part includes many resources, so you're really getting a lot more than ten for your money. (Don't tell my publisher!)

Many of these resources are discussed in earlier chapters in the book. However, I couldn't include every directory or every search-feed resource in those chapters, so here you can find longer lists, with less explanation to assist you with your own research. This list with active links is posted at www.wiley.com/legacy/compbooks/finkelstein/. Click the link for this book. There you can keep on clicking to your heart's content and avoid typing out those long URLs.

Working with Tutorials

In my humble opinion (IMHO), this book contains all you need to know about how to create RSS feeds, but putting humbleness aside, it's a fact that browsing through tutorials is a great way to reinforce and expand on all that you've discovered here. Several sites offer comprehensive tutorials on RSS. These sites were written by Web authors who are ahead of their time and were attracted to RSS early on. Each author has a slightly different perspective and includes different information and links, so why not look at them all?

- **GILS RSS Workshop (**rssgov.com/rssworkshop.html**):** This complete tutorial and resource is part of the Government Information Locator Service Web site. It starts by listing a number of example RSS feeds, including many from various state governments. The tutorial includes how to's, exercises, a comparison between the 0.91 and 1.0 RSS versions, and dozens of links to further RSS resources.
- **RSS – A Primer for Publishers & Content Providers (**www.eevl.ac.uk/rss_primer**):** This tutorial is also extremely thorough and wide ranging. It has a great introductory section and lots of good advice. You can find information on ways to create RSS feeds as well as a great technical section that includes lots of useful links.
- **RSS Tutorial for Content Publishers and Webmasters (**www.mnot.net/rss/tutorial/**):** This excellent overview of RSS explains how to do it — and how to do it well. The tutorial includes information on the various versions, tips for generating good feeds, and links to many RSS tools and resources.
- **Yahoo! RSS Syndication – Frequently Asked Questions for Publishers (**my.yahoo.com/s/publishers.html**):** Yahoo! has come up with a good overview of RSS and how to get started.
- **RSS Specifications: Everything You Need to Know about RSS (**www.rss-specifications.com/create-rss-feed.htm**):** In spite of the name, this site is more of a tutorial than a list of specifications. Topics include the history of RSS, XML basics, how to create feeds, and links to many RSS resources.

Understanding Technical Specifications

If you're more technically oriented, you may want to look at the following technical specifications for XML, RSS in its various versions, and Atom, all of which are published on the Web:

- **XML:** www.xml.com/pub/a/2002/12/18/dive-into-xml.html
- **RSS 0.91:** backend.userland.com/rss091
- **RSS 1.0:** web.resource.org/rss/1.0
- **RSS 2.0:** blogs.law.harvard.edu/tech/rss
- **Atom:** www.ietf.org/proceedings/04aug/I-D/draft-ietf-atompub-format-01.txt and www.atomenabled.org/developers/syndication/atom-format-spec.php

Using Directories

Directories are the place to find RSS feeds and to register your own. I've mentioned many of these in this book, but a handy summary is as follows:

- **Syndic8:** www.syndic8.com/suggest.php?Mode=data
- **Blogstreet:** www.blogstreet.com
- **Search4rss:** www.search4rss.com
- **Feedster:** www.feedster.com
- **CompleteRSS:** www.completerss.com
- **Moreover:** w.moreover.com/main_site/content/publishers.html
- **NewsIsFree:** www.newsisfree.com/contact.php?ctmode=suggest (See Figure 15-1.)
- **Daypop:** www.daypop.com/info/submit.htm
- **Blog Search Engine:** www.blogsearchengine.com/add_link.html
- **Boingboing:** boingboing.net/suggest.html
- **Phylum Chordata:** chordata.geckotribe.com
- **My Yahoo!:** my.yahoo.com. To register your feed, use My Yahoo! to sign up for your own feed. Then My Yahoo! will include the feed in its directory.

Figure 15-1: Here you see NewsIs Free's page for submitting your feed.

Reading Articles and Feeds

Many people have written articles or blog entries about RSS, but only a few are significant. Some are wide ranging, while others discuss a specific aspect of the technology. People are thinking and writing about how RSS fits in with e-commerce, the Internet publishing industry, and information access. You can find articles that range from the future of RSS to how to get the highest click-through rate to your site.

While articles are generally one-time events, the RSS feeds on the topic of RSS go on and on. If you want to keep up to date on this exciting technology, subscribe to some of these RSS feeds.

Articles

In the list, I describe a few articles that I think are valuable reading if you're interested in RSS, what it means, and where it's going.

- **Mediathink's White Paper.** You can download this article at `www.mediathink.com/rss/whitepaper.asp`. Mediathink attempts to analyze the effect and future of RSS and its impact on marketing. The comparative analysis of RSS aggregators is useful and thorough.

- **PC World's News on Demand.** You can find PC World's review at www.pcworld.com/resource/printable/article/0,aid,116018,00.asp. This concise article covers the basic concepts of RSS and reviews 19 RSS readers in a comprehensive table.
- **The Future of RSS – Is E-Mail Publishing Dead?** Robin Good's article on RSS is at www.llrx.com/features/rss.htm. He's definitely pro-RSS but dutifully provides both pros and cons, thereby giving a good overview of the technology.
- **Syndicated Content: It's More Than Just Some File Formats.** You can find this complete article at www.ariadne.ac.uk/issue35/miller. While the beginning of the article is mostly about the nuts and bolts of RSS, the end has a great section on best practices. It's good to look beyond trying to figure out why your feed won't validate and give some attention to the quality and organization of your entire feed. The list of eight guidelines to follow provided here can help ensure that your readers get top-quality RSS feeds — which will also keep them coming back.
- **Raising the Bar on RSS Feed Quality.** This article, at webservices.xml.com/pub/a/ws/2002/11/19/rssfeedquality.html, focuses on improving the quality of RSS feeds. The first page is quite technical, so don't forget to click to the second page, where you can find some excellent suggestions for writing effective feeds.
- **Advertisers Muscle into RSS.** Advertising in RSS feeds? Bloggers and other Web publishers resent the commercialization, but marketing executives want to make sure that they get a good return from their feeds. If this trend continues, RSS aggregators may start to filter ads. This short article explains one company's use of ads in RSS feeds for its customers. Go to www.wired.com/news/ebiz/0,1272,65745,00.html. "Overture Tests RSS Ads" is a similar article, which you can find at news.com.com/Overture+tests+RSS+ads/2100-1024_3-5457027.html.
- **Looking for the Perfect Feed: RSS 2.0 Templates.** If you're interested in exploring the possibilities of the RSS 2.0 format, this article by Mike Golding is the clearest I've seen. The article, shown in Figure 15-2, starts by showing a bare-bones 2.0 feed, using only the required tags, and then moves on to explain successively more complex versions that include namespaces and reference the Dublin Core and Syndication modules. Go to www.notestips.com/80256B3A007F2692/1/NAMO5P9UPQ. (I explain these RSS modules briefly in the sidebar "How RSS started" in Chapter 1.)
- **Syndic8.com has an entire page of links to articles and documents related to RSS.** Go to www.syndic8.com/documents.

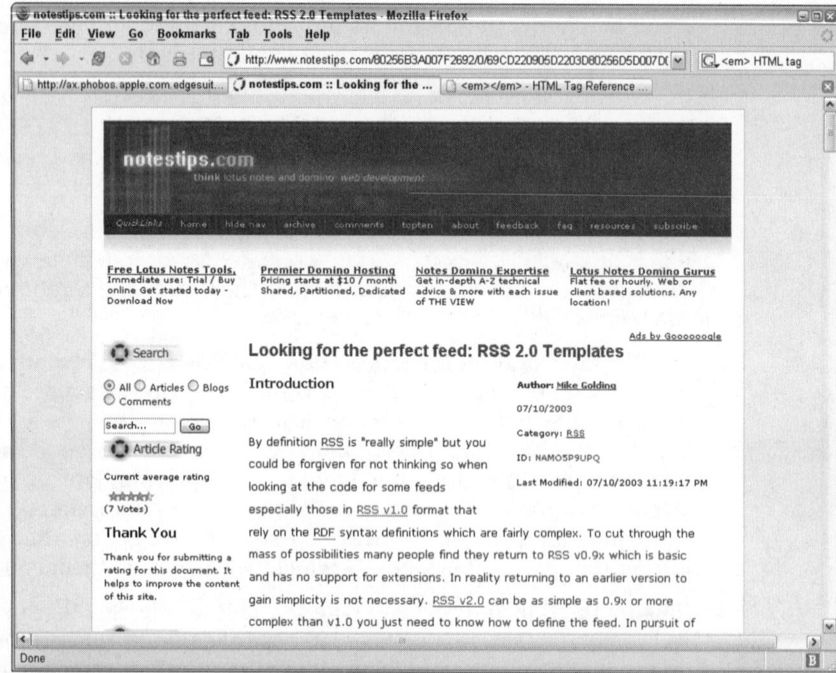

Figure 15-2: This article explains how flexible RSS 2.0 can be.

RSS feeds on RSS

Most of these feeds are also blogs, so you can find them on a Web-site page as well. While several RSS feeds on blogging exist, I've stuck to those that give a fair amount of attention to RSS. The following list describes places to go for the absolute latest on RSS — which would be about one second ago.

- **RSS & Atom Tips.** Lockergnome is Chris Pirillo's techie Web site, with news (and feeds) on several technical topics. The feed on RSS is at `www.lockergnome.com/rss/rss.php`. The Web page is at `http://channels.lockergnome.com/rss`. Almost everything related to RSS shows up here.
- **Robin Good's Independent Publishing News.** Robin Good's wide-ranging site offers a lot to chew on, and he's very excited about RSS's value for independent publishers. His RSS feed is at `www.masternewmedia.org/index-independent_publishing.rdf`. For his Web site, go to `www.masternewmedia.org/independent_publishing.htm`.
- **Derek Franklin's Digital Laboratory.** This feed, at `feeds.feedburner.com/derekfranklincomblogcontent`, is hosted by FeedBurner, as you can see by the URL. He calls it "A Daily Discovery of New Ideas Related to Multimedia, Marketing, Blogging, RSS, Search, and Creative Thinking." That title is enough for a full blog entry right there! The site is at `www.derekfranklin.com`.

- **Scripting News.** Dave Winer's own blog. (For more information on Dave Winer, see the sidebar "How RSS started" in Chapter 1.) The feed's URL is `www.scripting.com/rss.xml`. The Web site is at `www.scripting.com`. Dave is full of opinions on more than just RSS and sometimes gets fairly technical, but he's always interesting.

Finding Sites with RSS Feeds

Some Web sites have such complete and useful content that you want to keep up with them often. Some of these have RSS feeds to make that easy. Lots of sites have multiple RSS feeds, especially newspapers. The following is my own top site list. You can certainly find other sites that appeal to you.

- ***The Christian Science Monitor.*** *The Christian Science Monitor* offers a wide variety of feeds on many topics. You can find the list at `www.csmonitor.com/rss/index.html`. The *Monitor* has feeds on the various sections of the paper, from a number of columnists — even its copy editor has one on words and grammar, called "Verbal Energy." The bottom of the page has a great primer on RSS and an excellent list of RSS readers.
- **Amazon.com Syndicated Content.** Want to know the latest books, toys, or videos available from Amazon? This site has dozens of RSS feeds on every conceivable, purchasable object. Perhaps you're looking for pretend, play, and dress-up toys for your kids. Yes, Amazon has an RSS feed focused on that and only that. Interested in independently distributed DVDs? You can find a feed for that as well. Talk about fragmentation! You just get headlines, without descriptions, but follow the links to see more. To find the list, go to `www.amazon.com/exec/obidos/subst/xs/syndicate.html`.
- **Pickajob.** Pickajob is a job-search site, and it has an innovative feature that enables you to create a custom RSS feed based on the type of job you want. Feeds are broken down by state. Perhaps you want a job in human resources in Iowa. You just fill in the text boxes and find a feed that lists those jobs. What a great idea! Go to `www.pickajob.com/rss/default.asp`, which you can see in Figure 15-3.
- **League of Women Voters.** Are you interested in politics? Do you want to keep abreast of the latest issues of the day? The League of Women Voters has feeds on over 50 issues, both state and national. Go to `www.congress.org/congressorg/issuesaction/soapbox`.
- ***The New York Times.*** You can't get any more traditional than *The New York Times,* but this online version is up to date on the latest technology, too. The *Times* has feeds from 29 sections of the newspaper. Go to `www.nytimes.com/services/xml/rss/index.html`.

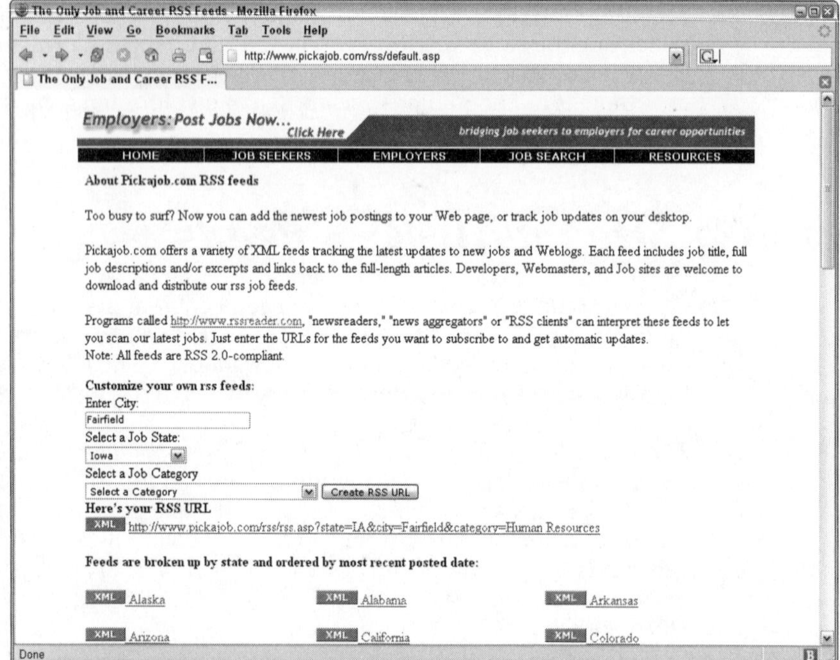

Figure 15-3: Pickajob offers custom RSS feeds based on the type of job you want.

- **National Public Radio.** If you want to know what's on public radio, try NPR's RSS feeds, including news feeds, feeds from specific NPR programs, and independent feeds from nine member stations. Visit `www.npr.org/rss`.
- **Moreover.com.** Moreover.com is an information company that provides free and custom feeds for its customers. It has over 330 free feeds in a wide variety of categories, such as world news, science, regional news, business, and sports. Some are quite specialized. For example, the lifestyle section includes feeds on natural health news and senior's news. Go to `w.moreover.com/categories/category_list_rss.html`.
- **Motley Fool.** Is money important to you (do ducks duck?). The Motley Fool, a well-known site that offers financial advice and information, also has an RSS feed containing its headlines. Visit `www.fool.com/About/headlines/headlines_rss.htm`.

The National Public Radio site includes a feed from its The Motley Fool Radio Show, so you can get your financial news that way.

- **National Weather Service.** Why not find out about your local weather via RSS? The National Weather Service (part of the National Oceanic and Atmospheric Administration) provides feeds for 1,800 locations in the

United States. Go to `weather.gov/data/current_obs` and choose your state. On the next page, choose your town to get your feed showing current weather conditions. Figure 15-4 shows some feeds for Iowa. At `weather.gov/alerts`, you also can get alerts of severe weather watches, warnings, and advisories, for your state or territory.

- **WebReference.com** and **Internet.com RSS** news feeds. WebReference.com and Internet.com offer RSS feeds on Internet news, e-commerce, Linux, and other techie topics. Go to `www.webreference.com/services/news`.
- **CBS MarketWatch.** CBS MarketWatch offers over a dozen investment-related feeds, including Mutual Funds, Stocks to Watch, and Market-Pulse. These are for personal, noncommercial use by individuals only. Go to `cbs.marketwatch.com/rss/default.asp?siteId=mktw&dist=mwanywhere`.
- **iTunes Music Store RSS Feed Generator.** Do you want to know about music-related new releases at the iTunes Music Store? Select the genres you like, and click the Generate button. You can also choose from new releases, just-added songs, most popular releases, or featured tunes. You get a feed customized for your taste in music. Go to `phobos.apple.com/WebObjects/MZSearch.woa/wa/MRSS/rssGenerator`.

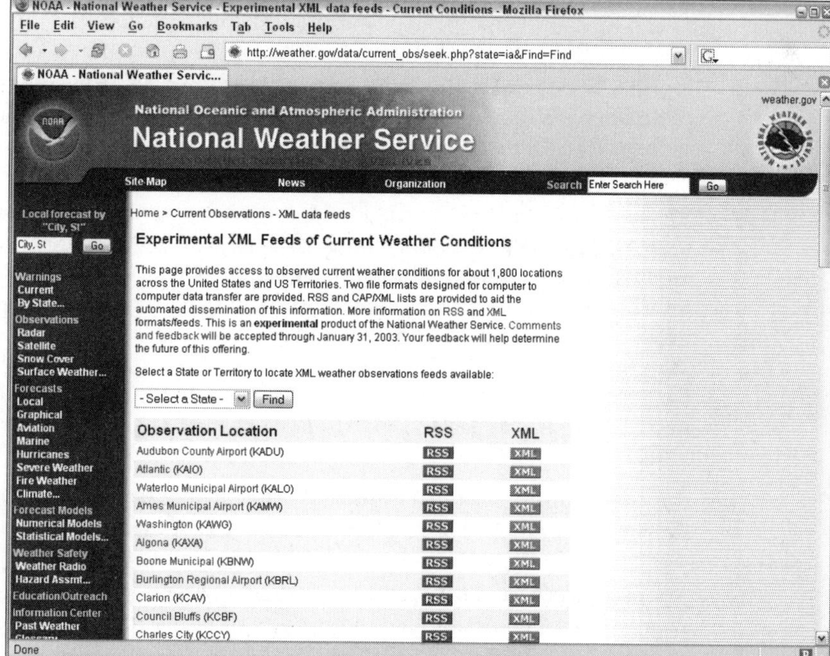

Figure 15-4: You can now get your local weather via an RSS feed.

Marketing with RSS

Are *opt-in* and *pull versus push* terms that you understand? If so, these articles are for you. E-mail marketers are especially interested in RSS because of the problems they're seeing with e-mail marketing. When people receive e-mail that they don't want — spam — they lose trust in the content of the e-mail. Opting in, which means that the reader subscribes, helps restore some trust. E-mail is pushed, meaning that the initiative comes from the publisher. RSS is an opt-in, pull medium, because readers subscribe and then decide when they want to read the content, hence people trust the content more.

While e-mail marketing is very established — some would say too established — the place that RSS holds in the scheme of e-commerce is still unclear. RSS is still in its childhood years, but people are already talking about the relationship between RSS and marketing.

Many people use RSS to drive traffic back to their site or to supplement their e-mail newsletters — that is, for marketing purposes. The many articles on the value of RSS for marketing can provide insight into how to make the most out of RSS.

Naturally, the articles that I mention in the following list are fairly current at the time of this writing (by the time you read this book, who knows what people will be writing?):

- **Email v RSS, Let Us Move On...** From Alex Barnett's blog comes a complete analysis of RSS versus e-mail, all neatly organized in a table, with plusses and minuses from the point of view of the marketer and the customer. Go to `http://weblogs.asp.net/alexbarn/archive/2004/05/22/139461.aspx`.
- **RSS: Marketing's Next Big Thing.** This two-part article by Tom Barnes analyzes RSS and its relationship to e-mail as well as to all types of Internet communication. He also discusses RSS as a marketing tool and provides some case studies and steps to get you started. Part 1 is at `www.MarketingProfs.com/ext/barnes10asp`. Part 2 is at `http://64.233.167.104/search?q=cache:7papvD88b9IJ:www.marketingprofs.com/4/barnes11.asp+Barnes+RSS+marketing+Part+2&hl=en&client=firefox-a`.
- **A Really Simple Content Solution?** This article by Rebecca Lieb summarizes what marketers are currently thinking about RSS. Go to `www.clickz.com/experts/brand/buzz/article.php/3302331`.
- **All About RSS.** Can It Save Email Marketing? This article analyzes some of RSS's pros and cons. You can find it at `www.webpronews.com/ebusiness/smallbusiness/wpn-2-20031021AllAboutRSSCanItSaveeMailMarketing.html`.

You may also find some of the articles in the section "Reading Articles and Feeds," earlier in this chapter, applicable to marketing.

Using Feed-Creation Tools

You can create RSS feeds in many ways, as I explain in Chapters 6, 7, and 8. In the following sections, I summarize some of the tools that you can use to create RSS feeds. I also include a list of sites that let you create feeds from Web searches.

Software tools

Software tools let you enter the RSS feed's content in text boxes, and the tools then form the feed for you. Generally, these tools can upload the feed to your Web site as well. You can't get too fancy with these tools, but they're probably the best way to publish a simple feed quickly, especially if you don't like digging into the code yourself. In Chapter 6, I cover some of these tools in detail.

Check out the following software tools:

- **NewzAlert's Composer.** This tool has a free trial period and costs $24.95. It is easy to use and now supports enclosures. See Chapter 6 to read more about how it works. Go to `www.castlesoftware.biz/NewzAlertComposer.htm`.
- **NotePage's FeedForAll.** FeedForAll has a lot of nice features. You can use the product during a free trial period, and it costs $39.95. Refer to Chapter 6 for more information about FeedForAll. Go to `www.feedforall.com`.
- **ListGarden.** ListGarden is a free, open source RSS feed generator. This program has many nice features but no technical support. It's a bit more difficult to use than Composer and FeedForAll. Go to `softwaregarden.com/products/listgarden`.

Building your feed online

Online tools don't require you to download and install a program. They create your feed on their server. Either you then download the feed or the tools host it. I cover several of these tools in Chapter 6.

- **UKOLN's RSS-xpress Channel Editor.** UKOLN creates RSS 1.0 feeds. It's simple, but it works. Go to `rssxpress.ukoln.ac.uk`.

- **WebReference's RSS Channel Editor.** This service is similar to UKOLN's. Fill in the blanks and you have a 0.91 RSS feed. Go to `www.webreference.com/cgi-bin/perl/rssedit.pl`.
- **WebDevTip's RSS Headliner.** This service also creates 0.91 RSS feeds. You enter the information in text boxes and then you can see the code in your browser. You select the code, copy it to the Clipboard, and paste it into a text editor. Go to `www.webdevtips.com/webdevtips/codegen/rss.shtml`.
- **Shared RSS Syndication Feeds.** This service is meant for people who want to create a feed but don't want to host it. Perhaps they don't have a Web site or don't want to get into the nitty-gritty of uploading and storing the file. You fill out text boxes, and the service hosts the feed. The service tells you the URL, which you can publicize any way you want. Go to `http://sharedrss.com`, which you can see in Figure 15-5.
- **IceRocket Free RSS Builder.** IceRocket Free RSS Builder hosts your feed for you. It has an online service that allows you to create and edit feeds. When you're done, it gives you the feed URL so that you can link to it from your site. This service is easy to use and nicely designed. Go to `http://rss.icerocket.com`, shown in Figure 15-6.
- **My RSS Creator.** This RSS creation service supports enclosures and submits your feed to RSS directories. After the 14-day free trial, you pay $19.95 per month. Go to `www.myrsscreator.com`.

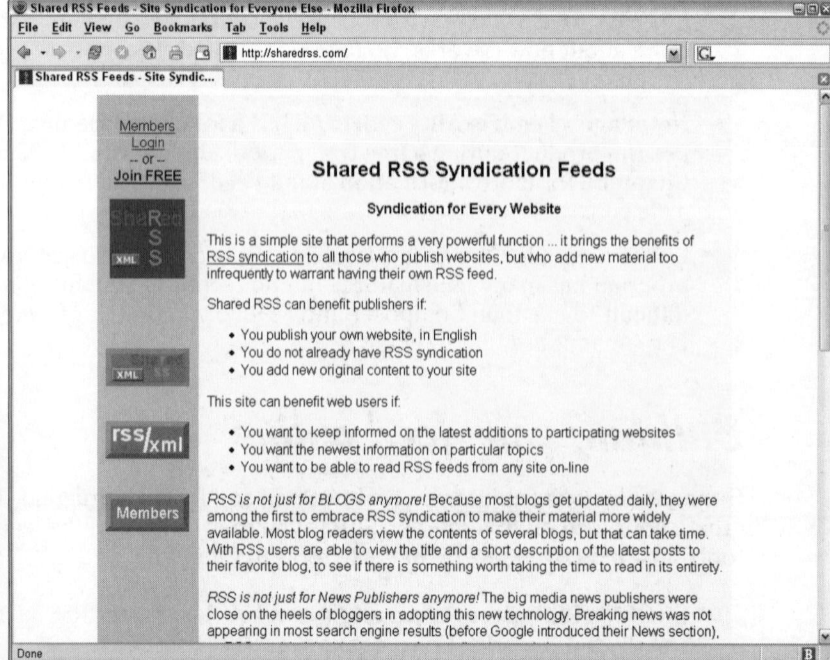

Figure 15-5: The Shared RSS Syndication Feeds Web site hosts your feed for you.

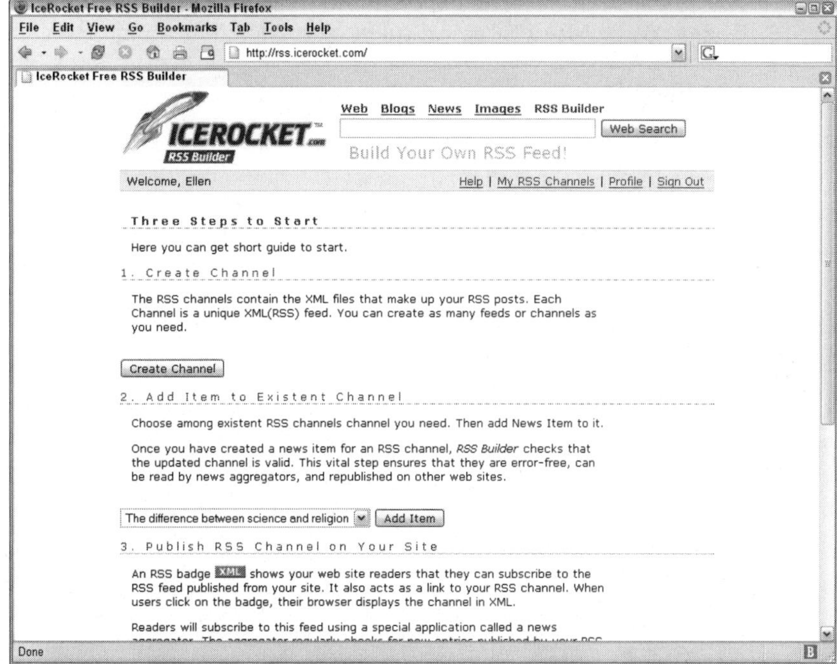

Figure 15-6: IceRocket Free RSS Builder is easy to use.

Ferreting out feeds from searches

Feeds from searches are cool. You enter a search keyword or keywords and get an RSS feed based on the results of the search. These are custom feeds, created just for you. This is the ultimate in personalized information.

Previously, customized e-mail notifications were available, such as those from Yahoo! and Google. But now, you can get the same information via an RSS feed. In my experience, if you want maximum results, you need to sign up for more than one feed, because each service gathers information from different sources or uses different methods to obtain its search results.

Of course, you can create a search for any topic that interests you. You can create an “ego” feed — do a search on your name or Web-site URL to receive notification of every mention of you or your site. (Along the way, you find out what other people who have the same name as you are doing.) You can create competitor feeds — this is the same concept, but you search for the name or Web-site URL of your competitor.

In some cases, the RSS feature is not obvious until you do a search using the Web site’s own search feature. Then, on the page that lists the search results, you see an RSS or XML button, allowing you to save the results as an RSS feed.

I discuss search-based feeds in Chapter 3 in the section "Creating a new feed from a search." Here's the list that I've collected, in alphabetical order:

- **BlogDigger:** `www.blogdigger.com`
- **Daypop:** `www.daypop.com`
- **Feedster:** `www.feedster.com`
- **Gogglealert:** `www.googlealert.com`
- **FindArticles.com:** `www.findarticles.com` (see Figure 15-7)
- **Justin Pfister.com:** `www.justinpfister.com/gnewsfeed.php`
- **Moreover:** `www.moreover.com`
- **Newsgator:** `www.newsgator.com`
- **NewsIsFree:** `www.newsisfree.com`
- **NewsTrove:** `www.newstrove.com`
- **NewsXS:** `www.newsxs.com`
- **PubSub:** `www.pubsub.com`

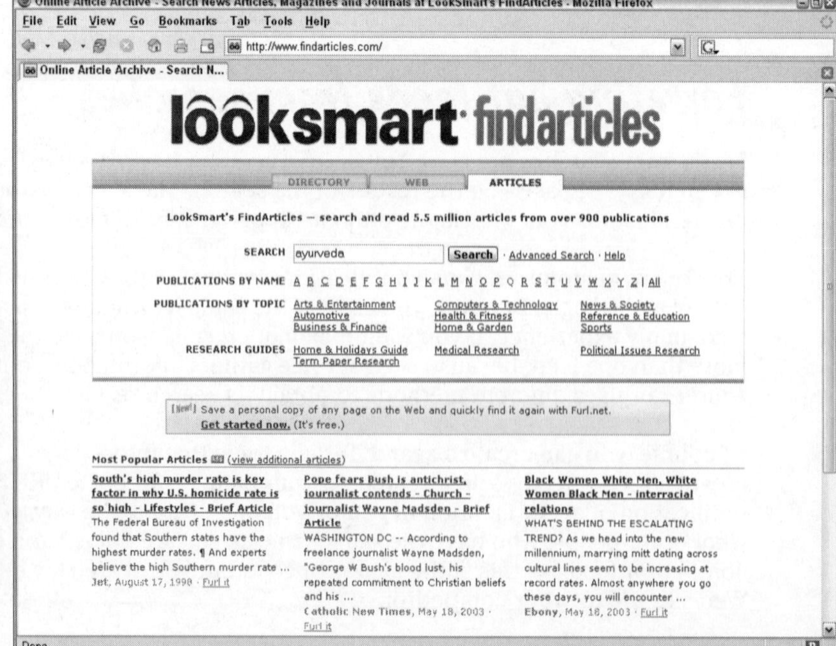

Figure 15-7: FindArticles.com searches through a huge resource of news. When you enter a search, you can get the results as an RSS feed.

- **RocketNews:** www.rocketnews.com/web/index.jsp (First do a search by entering a search term in the Search text box. Then click the XML button on the results page.)
- **Topix:** www.topix.net
- **Yahoo! News:** news.search.yahoo.com

Finding Podcasting Resources

Podcasting — the practice of enclosing MP3 or other multimedia files in an RSS feed — has generated a lot of excitement but little substance in the form of clear instructions. See Chapter 9 for clearer instructions than I've seen anywhere on the Web — although I must admit I'm biased.

Here are some podcasting tools and resources:

- **Bloglines.** As far as I know, this is the first online RSS reader to support enclosures. Address: www.bloglines.com
- **Vox Lite.** A little-known RSS reader, Vox Lite supports enclosures. Address: www.stevenwood.org/stories/2003/06/08/voxLite.htm
- **BlogMatrix Jager 1.6.** This is an RSS reader that supports enclosures. This program automatically downloads enclosures and adds them to your iTunes or Windows Media Player play list. Address: jaeger.blogmatrix.com
- **Doppler Radio.** This is another RSS reader that supports podcasts. Address: www.dopplerradio.net
- **Synclosure.** Synclosure is an RSS reader that supports enclosures. Address: www.raphb.ch/c/synclosure
- **NewsGator.** This RSS reader works in Microsoft Outlook and supports enclosures. Address: www.newsgator.com
- **iPodder:** iPodder helps you download audio files to your MP3 player or other device that supports Windows Media Player files. Address: www.ipodder.org
- **PodcastAlley:** This is a portal for all things podcast, as shown in Figure 15-8. Address: www.podcastalley.com
- **Random Thoughts from HowardGr:** This is an article on receiving podcasts if you don't have an iPod. Yes, there are a few of us out there. Address: www.howardgreenstein.com/blog/2003/10/05.html

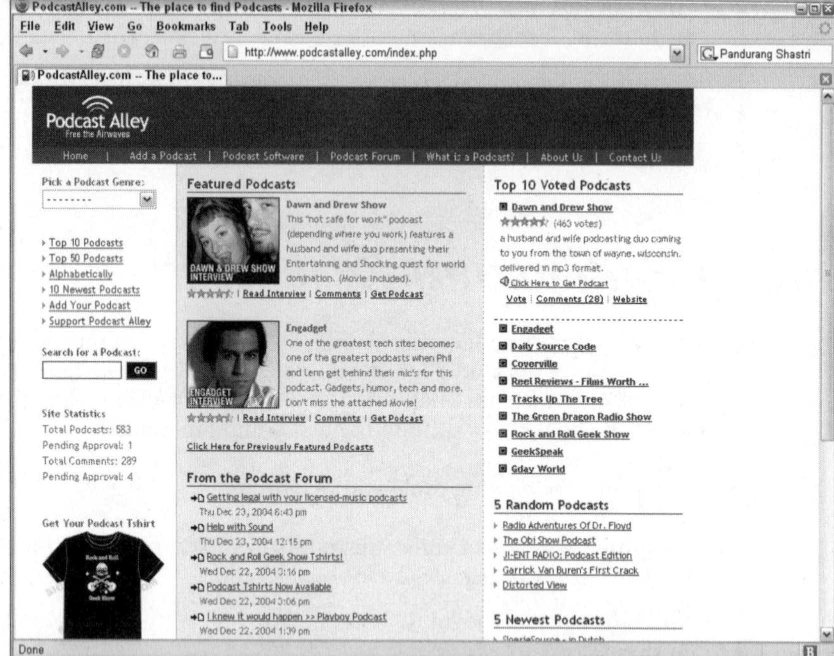

Figure 15-8: Podcast Alley is a portal for podcasting, with lots of resources, access to podcasts, and forums.

Using Discussion Groups

Some of the discussion groups are very technical, so don't bother with them if you aren't a programmer or if you aren't interested in the technical specifications of RSS. Others are for users, so these discussion groups are more general. I've included both types, as follows:

- **RSS-DEV.** This is an RSS 1.0 discussion group for developers. Address: `groups.yahoo.com/group/rss-dev`
- **RSS2-Support.** In spite of the hand-holding name, this is for developers. Address: `groups.yahoo.com/group/RSS2-Support`
- **Syndication.** This site offers a discussion of XML news, announcements, syndication, and resource discovery formats for developers. Address: `groups.yahoo.com/group/syndication`
- **RSS and Media.** Here you can find a discussion of metadata extensions to RSS for describing media enclosures. This is about podcasting for developers. Address: `groups.yahoo.com/group/rss-media`

- **Podcasters.** A Yahoo group for anyone interested in podcasting. Address: groups.yahoo.com/group/podcasters
- **RSS and Related Technologies.** This is a general forum for RSS topics on Webmaster World. It's quite active and useful for the nontechnical RSS publisher. You can ask questions and get answers, but you do need to register. Address: www.webmasterworld.com/forum98

Using Auxiliary RSS Tools

RSS is growing so rapidly that it's hard to keep track of it all. This is my everything-but-the-kitchen-sink section. In the following list, you can find tools relating to RSS that don't fit anywhere else:

- **Atom2RSS.** This Web-based service converts Atom feeds to RSS. Address: www.2rss.com/software.php?page=atom2rss
- **Webnote.** This is a tool for storing notes and images on your computer. The content is stored on the Web site's server. Read the tips to get instructions. Then save the note and go back to it at any time. You can share the URL with others by passing it on to them or by creating an RSS feed of the page. This tool ranks high on the cuteness scale — you can even choose the color of each note. You can see my first efforts in Figure 15-9. Address: www.aypwip.org/webnote
- **NewsAloud.** This is a tool that reads RSS feeds and other news sources out loud. Address: www.nextup.com/NewsAloud/index.html
- **WebNews.TV.** This service also ranks high on the cuteness scale. This tool reads feeds out loud, accompanied by funny, animated characters such as a penguin. It costs $19.95, but you can download a free trial. Address: www.webnews.tv
- **Great RSS Tools.** Here you find an editable list of a variety of RSS tools. You can add your favorites. Address: www.socialtext.net/rss-winterfest/index.cgi?great_rss_tools
- **The Atom Enabled Directory.** This is a directory of tools that are all related to Atom feeds. Address: www.atomenabled.org/everyone/atomenabled
- **Take-Off.** Take-Off is a tool that puts RSS feeds into a database and then displays them in a PowerPoint presentation. Address: www.take-off.as/datapoint/workshop/News.htm

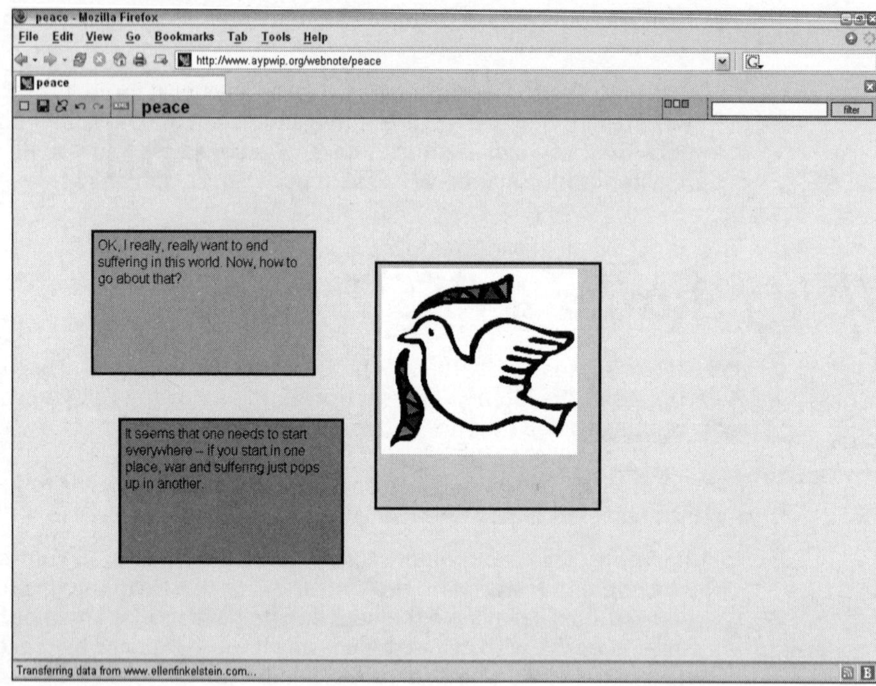

Figure 15-9: Webnote is a space for creating and collecting content. You can keep the content for yourself or easily share it with others.

Appendix

Setting Up a Web Site

In This Chapter

- Getting a URL
- Finding a Web host
- Choosing an HTML editor
- Creating the information architecture
- Adding content
- Selling from your site
- Uploading your site
- Testing your site

Throughout this book, I assume that you have a Web site and want to know how to create RSS feeds for the content on your site. Maybe that's a foolish assumption and you were so interested in RSS that you bought this book without knowing anything about creating your own Web site. So in this appendix, I breeze through the basics of setting up a Web site. Along the way, I point you to more resources, because this topic could (and does) take up whole books.

In fact, if you're interested in reading a whole book, check out *Creating Web Pages For Dummies,* by Bud E. Smith and Arthur Bebak (Wiley Publishing).

Getting a URL

The first step in getting on the Web is to register a domain — you know, something that starts with `http://www`. Almost any Web host provides a service to tell you whether the URL you want is available.

Think carefully about the URL you would like: The words in the URL are very important because they help people find you and help you market yourself more easily.

Here are some qualities of a good URL:

- It's easy to remember, which also means that it's not too long.
- People immediately know what the site is about.
- It improves your search-engine ranking, which means that it's related to keywords that you think people will search on to get to your site.

Consider two types of URLs — one type matches the name of your business (if you have one) and another type matches the content of your site. For example, if your business is Rainbow Resources and you do PowerPoint consulting, you could choose `www.rainbowresources.com` or `www.powerpointconsulting.com`, if they're available.

If the domain name you want is taken, you can check to see whether the current owner's license to use it will expire. Do a Web search for "expired domain names" to find sites that list these domains.

Perhaps you have had the experience of typing in a URL using .com and ended up at the wrong site because you needed to type .org or .edu. To avoid having people end up on your competitor's site, you could choose more than one extension. In fact, many businesses register more than one URL. In addition to registering both the name of the company and the type of business, they may register similar names, such as `powerpointconsultation`, and URLs with different extensions, such as `.com`, `.net`, .and `.biz`.

You may also want to register misspellings, both singular and plural forms of words (for example, `www.powerpointpresentation.com` and `www.powerpointpresentations.com`). In fact, you should at least check out these variations and see whether they exist. Just type the URLs into your browser's address text box. But beware: You may find a similarly named site whose content makes you uncomfortable — you certainly wouldn't want potential customers to end up there by mistake! If you plan to do any radio advertising, you may want to register similar sounding domains, such as presentations-forall.com and presentations4all.com. Take all these facts into account when you choose a name.

Most Web hosts let you check whether a name is available. Some offer similar alternatives, as well. One such site is `www.registerdomain.ws`. You can go there and try out as many URLs as you like.

When you've decided on one or more URLs, you can register them at a site that specializes in registering domains, but you may want to hold off till you decide on a hosting service. Most Web hosts register domains for you at a discount if you sign up for their service. Prices vary widely, from about $4 to $25 per year, so shop before you register.

If your chosen URL is available and you don't want to register it until you choose a Web host, hurry on to the next section in this chapter and choose a Web host. Your URL is not yours until you've registered it!

Finding a Web Host

After choosing a URL, you need a Web host. If you are very knowledgeable or willing to fiddle around, you could set up your own server, but most people pay for someone else to host their Web site so they can let them deal with the setup and maintenance of the server.

A good Web host is very important, because your Web site is in your host's hands, 24/7. However, choosing a Web host is difficult, if only because you have so many hosts to choose from. If you read the ads or go to their Web sites, they all sound pretty good. Furthermore, most hosts offer several packages at varying prices, so if your only concern is the amount of storage space you need, you can get that from practically any Web host.

Of course, you also need to decide how much you want to pay. If free is your only option, you don't have as many choices — maybe that's a blessing! Most services require that you pay, but often the cost is not very high. However, before you consider the cost, narrow your choices by getting information about the following features:

- **Support:** Is it 24/7, and how do you contact the host company's technical support service? Having a phone contact is better (and usually more expensive) than e-mail, because you can usually get an immediate answer to your question or problem. The worst support is a forum, unless the forum is very active. (Having all three options — phone, e-mail, and forums — is best.)
- **Size:** How much storage space do you have, how much bandwidth (the limit for uploading and downloading files per month) is available, and what is the maximum file size you can upload? If you want to podcast, remember that you will be dealing with large MP3 files! Also, if you exceed the limits, how much do they charge for anything over the minimum?
- **Traffic statistics:** What statistics about your site activity does the host provide? Does it offer software that displays the statistics in an easy-to-read format? Specifically, in regard to RSS feeds, what types of files do the statistics include? I've discovered that these reports may count only HTML files and ignore images and XML files.
- **Reliability:** This generally means *uptime,* when the host's servers are not down for some reason. If visitors try to open your Web page when the servers are down, they get an error message and often go somewhere else. You want the highest possible uptime number. An up time of 99.9% is reasonable.

- **Software support:** Some blogging and RSS-to-HTML conversion software requires that you upload PHP scripts to your server. PHP scripts are programs that run on a Web server and control what appears on your Web page. If you want to use these types of programs, you need permission to upload your own PHP scripts. You usually pay more for this. Other types of software support are CGI scripts, JSP, Perl, and so on. The Web host may have its own scripts, such as a form e-mailer, which e-mails you the results of an HTML form when a person completes the form and clicks a Submit button.
- **E-commerce support:** If you want to accept credit cards on your site, you need SSL (Secure Sockets Layer) support for a secure connection to protect data sent to and from the customer (and the bank). You may also want support for a database to store customer data. Discussion-group software often requires a database. You usually have to pay extra for these features.
- **E-mail accounts:** An e-mail address using your domain (`yourname@yoursite.com`) is not essential, but it looks good. Any e-mail sent to this address is generally forwarded to your regular e-mail account.

I've collected some resources that explain more thoroughly what to look for in a Web host. They are as follows:

- **The Site Wizard:** How to choose a Web host, by Christopher Heng, has two comprehensive lists, one for choosing a free host and one for choosing a commercial host. Address: `www.thesitewizard.com/archive/findhost.shtml`
- **What to look for in a Web host:** Issued by LockerGnome, this has an excellent list of some technical points that you should consider. Address: `www.channels.lockergnome.com/technobabble/archives/20041110_what_to_look_for_in_a_web_host.phtml`
- **What kind of hosting plan is the right one to buy?** This article has a discussion of Web host features and what they mean, including a calculator to help you figure out how much space and bandwidth you need. Address: `www.findmyhosting.com/webhosting-guide.htm#4`

When you complete this research you should have a useful list of the features you need. I recommend asking anyone you know who has a Web site which host they use. Find out whether their host meets their needs. Ask lots of questions. Your friend may have never used technical support or may not care whether the answer comes within 24 hours, so a general rave isn't helpful. You need details.

I've also noticed that people seem to be enthusiastic about any new venture that they've just started, so take recommendations from people who have used their Web host for only two days with a grain of salt.

In the next two sections, I briefly discuss two types of Web hosts: free and fee-based. The issues you face with each type are slightly different. Also, some Web hosts offer both options. In these sections, I also provide some resources for finding Web hosts.

You are not stuck with a Web host if you don't like the service. You can always switch your Web site to another host.

Using free space

Use free space only if your budget is very limited or if you're just doing RSS feeds to have fun, and not promote a business. Free space may also be a good place to start while you're testing the waters of Web site-dom. (Okay, that's probably a mixed metaphor, but you get the idea.)

You generally are required to put ads (provided by the Web host) on your free site. These ads may be in the form of a banner ad or the dreaded (to your viewers) pop-up or pop-under window ad.

On the other hand, you may find just what you want among the free Web hosts. Here are some sites that offer ratings and reviews of free Web hosts:

- **Free Web Hosting:** Address: `www.free-webhosts.com`
- **100 Best Free Webspace:** Address: `www.100-best-free-webspace.com`
- **FreeWebspace.net:** Address: `www.freewebspace.net`

Paying for power, flexibility, and service

For the most part, you can get more space, more service, and more features by paying something. That's because companies can use the money that they get from Web-site owners to provide better Web hosting. But there are so many options that you can get quite bewildered. If asking your friends doesn't work, here are some sites that rate and review Web hosts:

- **Find My Hosting.com:** Address: `www.findmyhosting.com`
- **Web Hosting Reviews:** Address: `www.web-hosting-reviews.org`
- **Upperhost Top 10 Independent Web Hosting Services:** Address: `www.upperhost.com`

If you find a Web host that seems to have the features you want, go directly to that host's site and sign up from there. Make sure that the fees are the same as they indicated on the reviewing site. (Some of the sites I just listed may get commissions, but they may also have arranged special deals. Check out the situation if you see any discrepancies in the costs.) Write up some questions and contact some of the Web-host companies. See how quickly you get an answer.

Take a look in your favorite search engine for the name of the host to see if you can find some independent comments and reviews. Then, finally, make your choice.

Choosing an HTML Editor

When you have your Web-site URL and your Web host, you need to create your Web site. Many Web hosts, especially those that cater to beginners, offer templates and wizards that can get you up and running within a couple of hours. (They may say within a few minutes, but don't believe that if you want your site to look the least bit good.)

While these tools may be a good place for a beginner to start, before too long, you'll be itching to customize your design, add new features, and more.

I can't overemphasize the importance of learning something about HTML. You may use a template/wizard, or a WYSIWYG (what you see is what you get) program that hides the HTML, but eventually you need to understand the innards of your Web page. If you don't, you'll get frustrated as you try to create just the look you want. A Web page is (usually) based on HTML, and you can't get around that. HTML Goodies (`www.htmlgoodies.com/primers/basics.html`) is a good HTML course for beginners.

If you're just starting out, find out a little about HTML and then start experimenting. Follow these steps to experiment with HTML right on your own computer:

1. **Type some HTML tags and some text in a plain-text editor such as Notepad.**

   For example, you could type the following:

   ```
   <html>
   <head>
   <title>My First HTML Page</title>
   </head>
   <body>
   <h1>Is It Really This Easy?</h1>
   Yes, it is!
   </body>
   </html>
   ```

2. **Save the file using an `.html` filename extension.**

   Many servers do not allow spaces in the file name, although on your own computer, you can use any name that's allowed by your operating system. For example, you could name the file `myfirstpage.html`. People often use an underscore (_) to create readable, spaceless filenames. So you could also name the page my_first_page.html.

3. **Open your browser and choose File➪Open or Open File.**

4. **Navigate to the file you just saved, and click the Open button.**

   You see your file displayed in your browser, as shown in Figure A-1.

Figure A-1: Sophisticated, isn't it?

If you're like me, the first time you see some code you typed in displayed in your browser, you'll be so excited that you just created a Web page that you'll jump up and down and start singing.

When you want to take the next step, you can go back to your file in Notepad, make some changes and resave it. Then, go back to your browser and click the Refresh button. You see the results of your changes. You don't have to close Notepad while you're trying this (but you must save each change), so you can quickly go back and forth between Notepad and your browser, making changes and seeing the results. Trust me, its lots of fun! This inputting, taking a look at the results, and saying "Cool!" is pretty much how you learn HTML.

The two heavyweights in WYSIWYG Web-page software are Macromedia Dreamweaver (`www.macromedia.com/software/dreamweaver`) and Microsoft FrontPage (`www.office.microsoft.com/en-us/FX010858021033.aspx`). The word on the street is that Dreamweaver is for professionals and FrontPage is for amateurs. This is a simplification, but there's some truth to it. However, if you're new to this, go for the easiest solution and upgrade later. (Shame-faced truth: I use FrontPage.)

Some other options for creating Web pages are as follows:

- **Adobe GoLive:** Address: `www.adobe.com/products/golive/main.html`
- **Mozilla Composer:** Address: `www.mozilla.org/products/mozilla1.x`
- **Netscape Composer:** Address: `wp.netscape.com/communicator/composer/v4.0/index.html`
- **Nvu (pronounced N-view):** Address: `www.nvu.com`

Getting down to HTML basics

Some people are control freaks and can never be satisfied with a WYSIWYG editor. They're always peeking under the hood to see the HTML code. Some Web-site programs appeal to split personalities and let you split the screen and see both the code and the graphics at the same time.

But some people just like typing that code. If you're like that, you may want a simple HTML editor that offers some features that tidy up and color-code your HTML, but don't otherwise interfere with your code. Here are some options for simple HTML editors:

- **Arachnophilia:** Address: `www.arachnoid.com/arachnophilia/index.html`
- **Bradbury Software's TopStyle:** Bradbury Software also created FeedDemon, a popular RSS reader. Address: `www.bradsoft.com/topstyle`
- **EditPlus Text Editor:** Address: `www.editplus.com`
- **Fookes Software NoteTab Pro:** Address: `www.notetab.com`
- **Macromedia HomeSite:** Comes with Dreamweaver, but you can buy it on its own. Address: `www.macromedia.com/software/homesite`

For the Mac, you can try Bare Bones Software's BBEdit (`www.barebones.com`) or PageSpinner (`www.optima-system.com/pagespinner`).

Creating the Information Architecture

Information architecture? Is that a house built of bits and bytes? Not exactly: It's one of the most important aspects of your Web site — the structure of your site. You need to lay out the pages so that visitors can easily find what they want. The organization should be simple and obvious to the visitor. Figure A-2 shows a simple information architecture diagram.

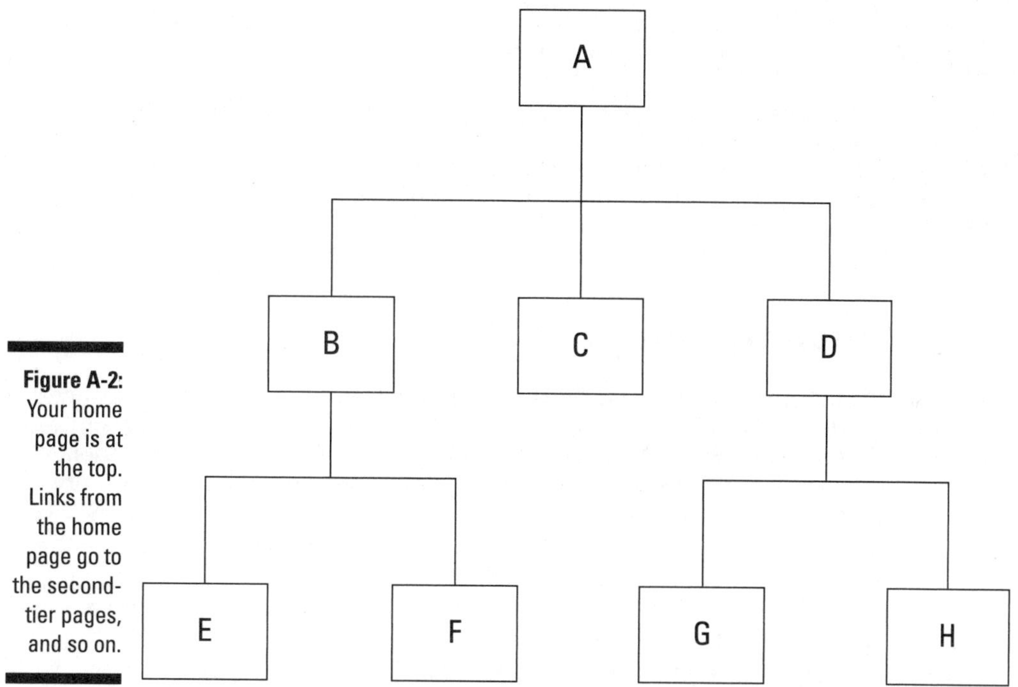

Figure A-2: Your home page is at the top. Links from the home page go to the second-tier pages, and so on.

You should lay out — probably physically on a large table — all the content that you want to put on your site. Then organize it in a logical fashion. You can then make a diagram like the one I show in Figure A-2. Lines between the boxes indicate the links that you need to create.

Planning your information architecture carefully helps to make sure that you don't leave anything out and allows for future expansion. Your site will be easier to navigate, and result in happier visitors.

Adding Content

When you know what you want to include and how you want to organize your content, you're ready to start creating your Web pages. You may want to begin by coming up with an overall design for your site. The design is what makes your site look good. Good design also makes the layout of a page appear clean and clear. Some people can do this successfully themselves; others, like yours truly, are fairly hopeless at making anything look good and should use a designer. A designer, who is an artist, can make your site look good — and make it seem easy. It isn't.

If you give your Web site to a designer to create, you need something to give that creative soul, so create the text first.

If you have no budget for a designer, call a local college's Media Arts or Digital Arts department and ask whether they have some students in their Web design program who are looking to create Web-site designs to add to their portfolio. You can often get a great design for free this way. Just make it clear that the site is yours, not the student's.

Tapping into text

If you already have the text you want in electronic form, you can copy and paste it into your Web-site–creation program. Or you can type from scratch. But hold on! Web-site text is not the same as text for printed documents. People don't like to read long paragraphs on their computer screen; moreover, they read more slowly on the computer.

Therefore, with Web-site text you should

- Be briefer.
- Break text into shorter paragraphs and bulleted or numbered lists
- Have a title on each page formatted in Heading 1 style. (In HTML, you create Heading 1 text using the `<h1>` tag.
- Use short titles.

Write your text with your viewers in mind. Give them the information they need to go to the next step, whether that's finding more details or buying a product.

Visualizing with images

All Web-site–creation software has a feature that allows you to insert images. Images are helpful for making your text clear, showing your product, and breaking up the content. If you have certain images that you want to add, insert them. If you're looking for an image to simply make the page look good, let your designer find it for you.

Be careful about including too many images. Images increase the size of your HTML page's file size and large files take longer to display in a browser.

Let there be links

A Web site is all about interconnectivity, and visitors need a way to get from one page to another. Use your Web-site software's linking feature to create links. You can attach links to text or images, and you often want to do both. Most Web sites have a navigation menu, made up of images that are linked to other pages. You — or your designer — can create lovely buttons for your menu if you want.

Be sure to put a link on every page that leads visitors back to your home page. A convention is to make the logo at the top of the page a link to the home page, but you should probably also include a more explicit link that says Home Page.

Checking it out

Before finalizing your Web site, ask a few people to try it out to see whether it works. Ask them to generally evaluate your site, and then ask them to perform some specific tasks that you want viewers to be able to accomplish, such as purchasing a product or getting support information. This process is called *usability testing,* and it's an important part of the process of creating a Web site. You can see where people get stuck or appear puzzled and then make corrections.

Selling from Your Site

If you want to offer products from your site, you need to find a way to collect payment, unless you're giving your products away. In this section I tell you ways to get the money.

Keeping things simple with PayPal

The simplest way to sell from a site is to sign up with PayPal (`www.paypal.com`). It's a little cumbersome for your visitors, but workable, and they can pay using a PayPal account, if they have one, or a credit card.

You can set up this feature in a few minutes, although PayPal needs to verify your checking account, which takes a couple of days. When people buy something, they are transferred to PayPal's site, where they can pay. When the payment is completed, PayPal e-mails you so that you can send your product to your customer. You pay only a small percentage of each sale, with no monthly feeds or initial setup cost. Use this method if you want to keep your site simple.

Pushing shopping carts

If you want to move one step up, you can use an outside (online) shopping cart. An outside shopping-cart company transfers your visitors to its site, where the visitors pay. As with PayPal, the shopping-cart company e-mails you to let you know that someone has purchased something from your site.

A *merchant account* is an account with a bank that lets you take credit card purchases from your Web site. You can go to a bank to get such an account. Many shopping-cart services have their own merchant accounts that you can use, but you usually pay extra for this service. Outside shopping carts generally charge you per month and may charge per purchase.

If you have a merchant account already (perhaps you already have an established business), you can buy shopping-cart software and put it on your site. This is more complex and may involve uploading the software to your Web host's server. As I discuss in the section "Finding a Web Host," earlier in this chapter, you may have to pay extra to do this. Finally, many Web hosts have their own shopping-cart software that you can use.

Shopping for shopping cart features

How do you choose a shopping cart? You start by understanding the concepts and features that are available. You need to consider the features you want, the capabilities of your system, the quality of the support, and the cost. Consider the following:

- **Cost:** Charges can be monthly, per transaction, or as a percentage of sale costs — or all of the above. Make sure you understand the costs.
- **East of use:** Before choosing, try to find out how easy the software is to use. Shopping carts can have many options.
- **Integration:** You want the purchasing process to be as seamless as possible when used with the rest of your site.
- **Purchasing features:** Can you offer discounts or coupons? Can you monitor inventory? Do you have a limit on the number of products? What types of payments can purchasers make — credit card, personal checks, COD, and so on?
- **Merchant account:** Is the merchant account included or do you need to obtain the account separately?
- **Shipping:** Can you offer more than one shipping option? Can you offer free shipping?
- **Reports:** You should be able to get reports that summarize your sales activity.

Taming the Beast's Shopping Carts & E-commerce Software Solutions Guide is an excellent article on shopping carts. Go to www.tamingthebeast.net/articles2/shopping-carts.htm.

Getting the shopping cart ratings

When you're ready to choose, look at some sites that rate shopping carts. Sample sites are as follows:

- **Top10 Reviews:** Shopping Cart Software Review compares 11 shopping carts. Address: www.shopping-cart-review.toptenreviews.com
- **The Merchant Account Adviser:** The Top Free Online Shopping Carts. Address: www.the-merchant-account-advisor.com/online-shopping-carts.html

When you choose a shopping cart, you receive instructions for using it. Follow the instructions and take advantage of technical support if you get stuck. Happy selling!

Uploading Your Site

You've created your site, and now you're ready to get it online. Have you tested it on your own computer first? You can test all the links locally and pretend that you're a visitor, trying out the site. If you think that everything is set to go, you can upload the files for the site.

Most Web-site–creation software comes with an FTP (File Transfer Protocol) feature so that you can upload the files for your site from within the software. In addition, most Web hosts have a mechanism for uploading your pages. For many people, either of these solutions is satisfactory.

Some people prefer to use their own FTP program, perhaps because their Web host's uploading feature is awkward, especially for multiple files. They may not like the FTP feature of their software. Regardless of the reason, you may want to investigate FTP software. Here are some of the more common options:

- **Cute FTP Home 6.0:** Free 30-day trial; $39.95 to buy. Address: www.globalscape.com/cuteftp/compare.asp
- **AceFTP 3.0:** Free. Address: software.visicommedia.com/en/products/aceftpfreeware
- **AceFTP Pro 3.61:** Free to try; $29.95 to buy. Address: software.visicommedia.com/en/products/aceftpfreeware
- **FileZilla:** Free. Address: filezilla.sourceforge.net

- **Core FTP Lite 1.3:** Free. Address: `www.coreftp.com`
- **BestFTP Explorer 2000 5.0:** Free to try; $15.00 to buy. Address: `www.ftpx.com`
- **WS_FTP Home 9.02:** Free to try; $34.95 to buy. Address: `www.ipswitch.com/Products/file-transfer.html`

FTP programs take a little getting used to if you're a beginner, but they're just a way to transfer files to another computer — in this case, your Web host's server.

If you've created subfolders on your computer — for example, many people put all their images in a separate folder called `Images` — you should create the same subfolders on your Web host's server. You can use your FTP software or your Web host's tools to do this.

Testing Your Site

After you upload your site, you should immediately check it out. After all, people can see it now, so it has to be good! The first time you go to your site, test all the links and read all the pages. For some reason, mistakes that you don't find on your hard drive just leap out at you after you've uploaded them. Check to see that all the images display — forgetting to upload images is a common mistake among beginners. Ask your friends or colleagues to check it out as well, in case you overlooked something.

If you find any errors, edit the pages in your software and upload them again. Recheck them until everything is perfect.

Good luck with your new venture!

Index

• B •

• F •

• G •

• H •

• I •

• J •

• K •

• L •

• Q •

• R •

• T •

• U •

• V •

• W •

Notes

Notes

Notes

Notes

Notes

Notes

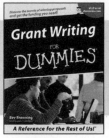

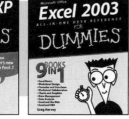

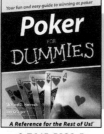

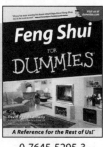

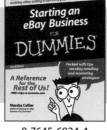

SPORTS, FITNESS, PARENTING, RELIGION & SPIRITUALITY

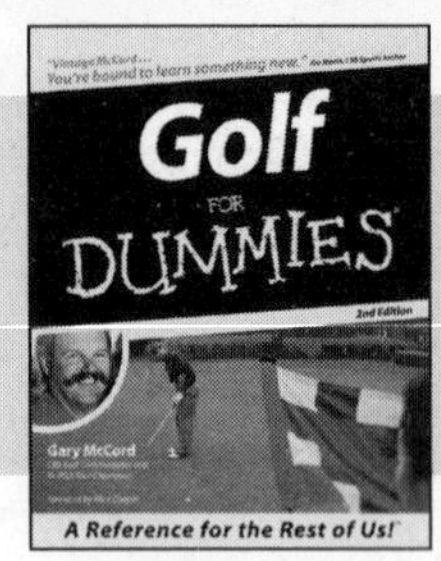

0-7645-5146-9 0-7645-5418-2

Also available:

- Adoption For Dummies 0-7645-5488-3
- Basketball For Dummies 0-7645-5248-1
- The Bible For Dummies 0-7645-5296-1
- Buddhism For Dummies 0-7645-5359-3
- Catholicism For Dummies 0-7645-5391-7
- Hockey For Dummies 0-7645-5228-7
- Judaism For Dummies 0-7645-5299-6
- Martial Arts For Dummies 0-7645-5358-5
- Pilates For Dummies 0-7645-5397-6
- Religion For Dummies 0-7645-5264-3
- Teaching Kids to Read For Dummies 0-7645-4043-2
- Weight Training For Dummies 0-7645-5168-X
- Yoga For Dummies 0-7645-5117-5

TRAVEL

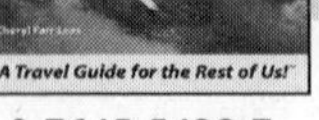

0-7645-5438-7 0-7645-5453-0

Also available:

- Alaska For Dummies 0-7645-1761-9
- Arizona For Dummies 0-7645-6938-4
- Cancún and the Yucatán For Dummies 0-7645-2437-2
- Cruise Vacations For Dummies 0-7645-6941-4
- Europe For Dummies 0-7645-5456-5
- Ireland For Dummies 0-7645-5455-7
- Las Vegas For Dummies 0-7645-5448-4
- London For Dummies 0-7645-4277-X
- New York City For Dummies 0-7645-6945-7
- Paris For Dummies 0-7645-5494-8
- RV Vacations For Dummies 0-7645-5443-3
- Walt Disney World & Orlando For Dummies 0-7645-6943-0

GRAPHICS, DESIGN & WEB DEVELOPMENT

0-7645-4345-8 0-7645-5589-8

Also available:

- Adobe Acrobat 6 PDF For Dummies 0-7645-3760-1
- Building a Web Site For Dummies 0-7645-7144-3
- Dreamweaver MX 2004 For Dummies 0-7645-4342-3
- FrontPage 2003 For Dummies 0-7645-3882-9
- HTML 4 For Dummies 0-7645-1995-6
- Illustrator CS For Dummies 0-7645-4084-X
- Macromedia Flash MX 2004 For Dummies 0-7645-4358-X
- Photoshop 7 All-in-One Desk Reference For Dummies 0-7645-1667-1
- Photoshop CS Timesaving Techniques For Dummies 0-7645-6782-9
- PHP 5 For Dummies 0-7645-4166-8
- PowerPoint 2003 For Dummies 0-7645-3908-6
- QuarkXPress 6 For Dummies 0-7645-2593-X

NETWORKING, SECURITY, PROGRAMMING & DATABASES

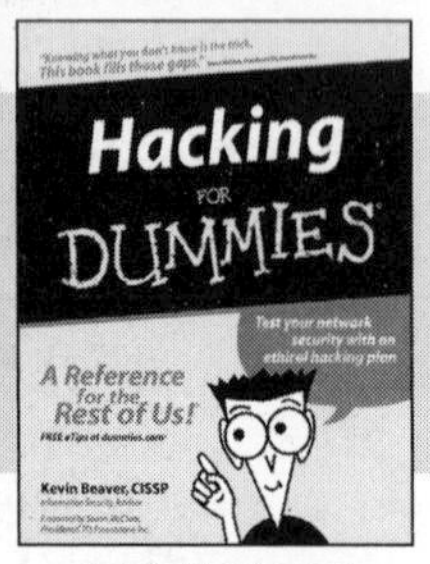

0-7645-6852-3 0-7645-5784-X

Also available:

- A+ Certification For Dummies 0-7645-4187-0
- Access 2003 All-in-One Desk Reference For Dummies 0-7645-3988-4
- Beginning Programming For Dummies 0-7645-4997-9
- C For Dummies 0-7645-7068-4
- Firewalls For Dummies 0-7645-4048-3
- Home Networking For Dummies 0-7645-42796
- Network Security For Dummies 0-7645-1679-5
- Networking For Dummies 0-7645-1677-9
- TCP/IP For Dummies 0-7645-1760-0
- VBA For Dummies 0-7645-3989-2
- Wireless All In-One Desk Reference For Dummies 0-7645-7496-5
- Wireless Home Networking For Dummies 0-7645-3910-8

HEALTH & SELF-HELP

0-7645-6820-5 *†

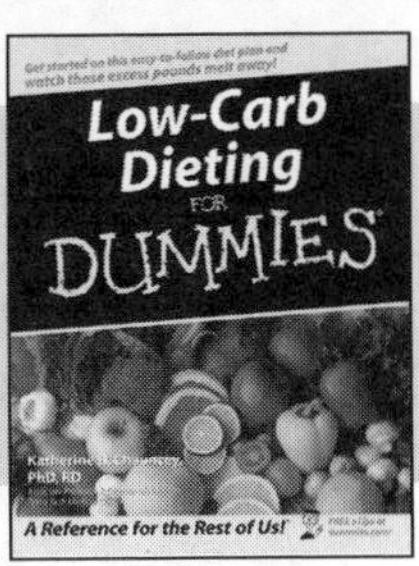

0-7645-2566-2

Also available:

- Alzheimer's For Dummies 0-7645-3899-3
- Asthma For Dummies 0-7645-4233-8
- Controlling Cholesterol For Dummies 0-7645-5440-9
- Depression For Dummies 0-7645-3900-0
- Dieting For Dummies 0-7645-4149-8
- Fertility For Dummies 0-7645-2549-2
- Fibromyalgia For Dummies 0-7645-5441-7
- Improving Your Memory For Dummies 0-7645-5435-2
- Pregnancy For Dummies † 0-7645-4483-7
- Quitting Smoking For Dummies 0-7645-2629-4
- Relationships For Dummies 0-7645-5384-4
- Thyroid For Dummies 0-7645-5385-2

EDUCATION, HISTORY, REFERENCE & TEST PREPARATION

0-7645-5194-9

0-7645-4186-2

Also available:

- Algebra For Dummies 0-7645-5325-9
- British History For Dummies 0-7645-7021-8
- Calculus For Dummies 0-7645-2498-4
- English Grammar For Dummies 0-7645-5322-4
- Forensics For Dummies 0-7645-5580-4
- The GMAT For Dummies 0-7645-5251-1
- Inglés Para Dummies 0-7645-5427-1
- Italian For Dummies 0-7645-5196-5
- Latin For Dummies 0-7645-5431-X
- Lewis & Clark For Dummies 0-7645-2545-X
- Research Papers For Dummies 0-7645-5426-3
- The SAT I For Dummies 0-7645-7193-1
- Science Fair Projects For Dummies 0-7645-5460-3
- U.S. History For Dummies 0-7645-5249-X

Get smart @ dummies.com®

- **Find a full list of Dummies titles**
- **Look into loads of FREE on-site articles**
- **Sign up for FREE eTips e-mailed to you weekly**
- **See what other products carry the Dummies name**
- **Shop directly from the Dummies bookstore**
- **Enter to win new prizes every month!**

*** Separate Canadian edition also available**
† Separate U.K. edition also available

Available wherever books are sold. For more information or to order direct: U.S. customers visit www.dummies.com or call 1-877-762-2974. U.K. customers visit www.wileyeurope.com or call 0800 243407. Canadian customers visit www.wiley.ca or call 1-800-567-4797.